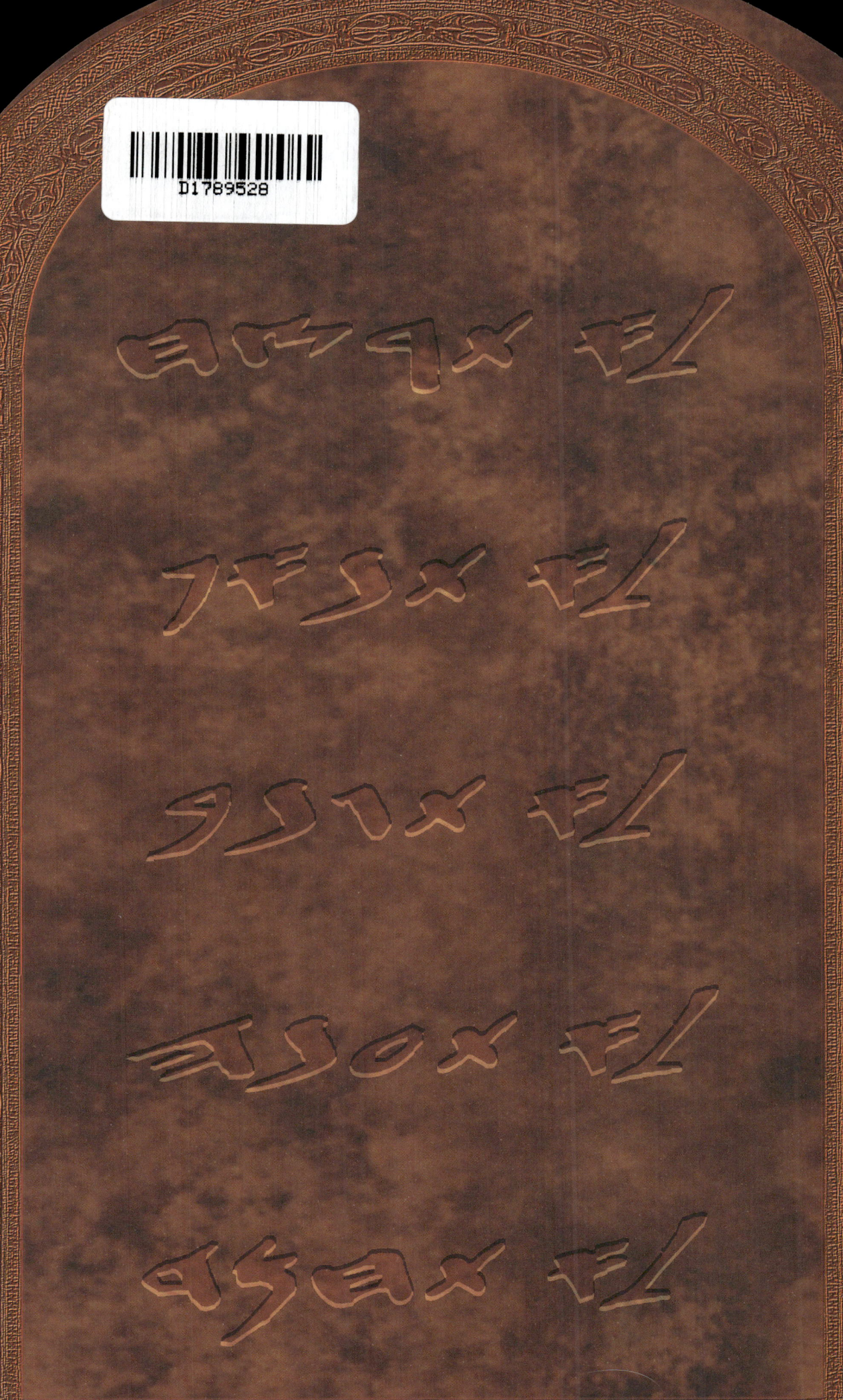

Name   שם

Date   תאריך

Place   מקום

פרטים מכפולת עמודים מאוירת בכלי המקדש, מעשה ידי אברהם בן אלישע קרסקס, מתוך "תנ"ך פרחי", קטלוניה, 1366-82, אוסף ששון, אנגליה

Details of a double page spread illustrated with Temple implements, made by Elisha Ben Abraham Crascas, from the "Farhi Bible", Catalonia, 1366-82, Sassoon Collection, England

© Copyright 2004 by Matan Arts Publishers Ltd.

No part of this publication may be reproduced in any manner whatsoever without permission in writing from the publisher.

Matan Arts Publishers Ltd.
P.O. Box 19, Kfar HaOranim 73134
Tel. 972-8-9764080, Fax. 972-8-9764081
mtn@matan-arts.co.il, www.matan-arts.co.il

ISBN 978-965-7309-00-1

Editor and production manager: David Arnon

Concept, art direction and design: Raymond Cintas

Assistant editor: Helli Duhani

Hebrew text editor: Eliyahu Shitrit, Jerusalem
English text: The Jewish Publication Society, USA

Pre-press, printing: Keter Press Ltd., Jerusalem
Post-printing: Hi-Tec Print Ltd., Holon
Binding: Tact Leather Man. Ltd. / Keter Press Ltd.

Printed in Israel

1st Edition - January 2004
11h Edition - October 2011

JPS Torah translation, copyright 1962, 1985, 1999 by
The Jewish Publication Society,
2100 Arch Street, Philadelphia, Pennsylvania 19103, USA

Used with permission from The Jewish Publication Society

9789657309001

שריד של כריכה פנימית עם עיטורים מיקרוגרפיים וצמחיים, מתוך כתב-יד של התנ"ך על קלף, מצרים, המאה ה-11, אוסף הספרייה הציבורית, סנט-פטרסבורג
Fragment of a carpet page with micrographic and floral decorations, from a manuscript of the Bible on vellum, Egypt, 11th century, collection of the Public Library, St. Petersburg

תורה
TORAH

	מבוא
9	Introduction

	בראשית ✡
17	GENESIS — Bereshit

	שמות ✡
65	EXODUS — Shemot

	ויקרא ✡
105	LEVITICUS — Vayikra

	במדבר ✡
133	NUMBERS — Bamidbar

	דברים ✡
175	DEUTERONOMY — Devarim

שריד מגילה עם קטע מספר שמות (ו:כה עד ז:יט) מתוך כתב-יד עברי עתיק מתקופת בית שני, 100 לפסה"נ בקירוב, נמצא במדבר יהודה, אוסף רשות העתיקות, ירושלים
Scroll fragment of Exodus (6:25-7:19), inscribed in Palaeo-Hebrew script dominant in the Second Temple period, ca. 100 BCE, found in Judean desert, collection of the Antiquities Authority, Jerusalem

EXODUS 6 — שמות ו

houses of the Levites by their families. 26 It is the same Aaron and Moses to whom the LORD said, "Bring forth the Israelites from the land of Egypt, troop by troop." 27 It was they who spoke to Pharaoh king of Egypt to free the Israelites from the Egyptians; these are the same Moses and Aaron. 28 For when the LORD spoke to Moses in the land of Egypt 29 and the LORD said to Moses, "I am the LORD: speak to Pharaoh king of Egypt

בעמוד ממול:
On the facing page:

שלמה המלך קורא בתורה, איור מתוך "סידור לונדון", כתב-יד עברי מאויר, צפון צרפת, 1280 בקירוב, אוסף הספרייה הבריטית, לונדון
King Solomon reading the Torah, illustration from "The London Miscellany", an illustrated Hebrew biblical and liturgical manuscript, north France, ca. 1280, collection of The British Library, London

8

Introduction · מבוא

The Jewish people is known among the peoples as the People of the Book, by virtue of the Book of Books, the *Tanakh* – the Hebrew Scriptures (the name is an acronym for its three main sections: *Torah*, *Nevi'im* [Prophets], and *Ketuvim* [Writings]) – and by virtue of its special relationship with the written word; nevertheless, artistic endeavor has been an inseparable part of Jewish culture since its very beginnings.

The Tent Tabernacle was resplendently decorated by the first of the Hebrew artists, Bezalel ben Uri, on Moses' instructions: "And Moses said to the Israelites: See, the Lord has singled out by name Bezalel, son of Uri son of Hur, of the tribe of Judah. He has endowed him with a divine spirit of skill, ability and knowledge in every kind of craft (Exodus 35:30-31). Likewise, the Temple – the place of the fixed abode of the Ark of the Covenant from the 10th century B.C.E. on – was decorated with impressive and diversified art and craft (see ivory pomegranate, p. 175).

The "Priests' Benediction" (Numbers 6:24-26), which was engraved on silver plates some 2650 years ago in the period of the Second Temple, is the earliest scriptural inscription that has reached us, and the earliest art work among those known to us that contains a scriptural text (see p. 133).

After the destruction of the Second Temple on the 9th of Av in the year 70 C.E., the artistic emphasis shifted gradually to decoration of synagogues that were established throughout Israel (until about the 6th

עם ישראל נודע בקרב העמים כעם הספר, בזכות ספר הספרים, התנ"ך, ובזכות יחסו המיוחד למלה הכתובה; אולם כבר מבראשית היה העיסוק האמנותי חלק בלתי נפרד מהתרבות היהודית המתהווה.

אוהל המשכן קושט לתפארה בידי ראשון האמנים העבריים, בצלאל בן-אורי, לבקשת משה רבנו: "ויאמר משה אל בני ישראל ראו קרא ה' בשם בצלאל בן-אורי בן-חור למטה יהודה; וימלא אותו רוח ה' בחכמה בתבונה ובדעת ובכל מלאכה" (שמות לה:30-31). בית המקדש – מקום משכנו הקבוע של ארון הברית החל במאה העשירית לפסה"נ – עוטר גם הוא במלאכת אמנות מרשימה ומגוונת [ראו רימון שנהב, עמ' 175].

"ברכת הכהנים" (במדבר ו:24-26), שנחרטה על גבי לוחות כסף לפני כ-2,650 שנה בתקופת בית המקדש השני, היא הכתובת המקראית הקדומה ביותר שהגיעה לידינו ויצירת האמנות הקדומה ביותר מבין אלה המוכרות לנו, הכוללת טקסט מקראי [ראו עמ' 133].

לאחר חורבן בית שני, ביום ט' באב בשנת 70 לסה"נ, הוסט הדגש האמנותי בהדרגה לעיטור בתי כנסת, שהוקמו ברחבי ישראל (עד המאה השישית לערך) ובתפוצות

"תנ״ך גוטנברג", הספר המודפס הראשון, גרמניה, 1455, אוסף ספריית פיירפונט מורגן, ניו-יורק
The Gutenberg Bible, the first printed book, Germany, 1455, collection of Pierpont Morgan Library, New York

century C.E.) and in the new Jewish dispersions abroad. The Torah scroll, kept in the Holy Ark, became the central pillar of the synagogues in Israel and in the diaspora. At this point a complex culture of artistic ornamentation for the Torah scrolls, such as embroidered coverings, silver and gold crowns, pointers, etc., began to develop.

When the Jews were exiled from Eretz-Israel, the artistic style became decentralized, and was much influenced by the cultures of the peoples among whom the Jews dwelt, but its essence was preserved over thousands of years in a way that arouses astonishment. It should also be mentioned that Jewish art, including the art of the illuminated manuscripts, came into being, established itself and flourished while taking into account the explicit prohibition in the Torah that "You shall not make for yourself a sculptured image, or any likeness…" (Exodus 20:4), and precepts that had been prescribed during the generations since.

The tradition of Tanakh ornamentation, which sets the scriptural text in decorated letters and surrounds them with colorful illuminations, probably began in the Graeco-Roman period, although no surviving texts from those remote times have reached us. The time that has passed, the many expulsions and wanderings and persecutions, as well as the censorship implemented by rulers in the lands of the diaspora, made it difficult to preserve the illuminated sacred writings.

The earliest illuminated manuscripts of the Tanakh extant today stem from the middle of the medieval period (see pp. 2-3, 6, 14, 15). These are most moving illuminations, which prefigure the impressive culture that later developed in the Jewish dispersions in Arab countries (see pp. 6, 14), in Spain and Portugal, (see pp. 2-3, 15, 75, 151, 163), in Ashkenaz [a name referring at first to a region including the Rhine and Alsace districts of Germany and France, and later to Western Europe in general] (see pp. 9, 37, 95, 139, 187), and even in isolated Yemen (see p. 12).

During the medieval times and the Renaissance period, Jews who could afford it would commission resplendent manuscripts, by means of which they sought to augment the atmosphere of prayer, the Sabbath and the holy days. The art of the Hebrew illuminated manuscripts reached the peak of its flourishing in the Renaissance period, which yielded magnificent works and techniques of illumination and micrography of unprecedented quality. In addition to the *Tanakh*, Jewish artists also illuminated Passover *Hagaddahs*, prayer books for holy days, inscriptions and various anthologies of sacred texts, as well as books of commentary and philosophy by Jewish scientists and scholars such as Nahmanides, Maimonides and others.

ישראל החדשות בנכר. ספר התורה, המוחזק בארון הקודש, היה לעמוד התווך של בתי הכנסת בישראל ובתפוצות. בתוך כך החלה מתפתחת תרבות מורכבת של עיטורים אמנותיים לספר התורה, בדמות כיסויים רקומים, כתרים מכסף וזהב, אצבעות לתורה ועוד.

כאשר גלו היהודים מארץ-ישראל בוזר הסגנון האמנותי והושפע רבות מתרבויות העמים שבקרבם ישבו, אך מהותו השתמרה באופן מעורר השתאות במשך אלפי שנים. עוד ראוי לציין שהאמנות היהודית, ובכלל זה אמנות כתבי-היד המאוירים, התהוותה, התבססה ופרחה תוך התחשבות באיסור המפורש בתורה, "לא תעשה לך פסל וכל תמונה" (שמות כ:ג), ובהלכות שנפסקו לאורך הדורות.

מסורת עיטור התנ"ך, המשבצת את הטקסט התנ"כי באותיות מקושטות ומקיפה אותו באיורים צבעוניים, ראשיתה כפי הנראה בתקופה היוונית-רומית, אם כי לידינו לא הגיעו כתבים ששרדו מימים רחוקים אלה. הזמן שחלף, גירושים ונדודים לרוב ופורענויות הצנזורה שהטילו שליטים בארצות הגלות, הקשו על השתמרותם של כתבי הקודש המאוירים.

המוקדמים מבין כתבי-היד המאוירים של התנ"ך המצויים בידינו כיום, מקורם באמצע ימי-הביניים [ראו עמ' 2-3, 6, 14, 15]. אלה איורים מרגשים ביותר, המבשרים את התרבות המרשימה שהתפתחה עם הזמן בגלויות ישראל שבארצות ערב [ראו עמ' 6, 14], בספרד ופורטוגל [ראו עמ' 2-3, 15, 75, 151, 163], באשכנז [ראו עמ' 9, 37, 95, 139, 187] ואף בתימן המבודדת [ראו עמ' 12].

בימי-הביניים ובתקופת הרנסנס, יהודים שידם היתה משגת נהגו להזמין כתבי-יד מפוארים, שבאמצעותם ביקשו להאדיר את אווירת התפילה, השבת והמועד. אמנות כתבי-היד העבריים המאוירים הגיעה לשיא פריחתה בתקופת הרנסנס, שהניבה יצירות מפוארות וטכניקות איור ומיקרוגרפיה באיכות חסרת תקדים. בנוסף לספרי התנ"ך אוירו אז גם הגדות לפסח, מחזורים, כתובות וקבצים שונים של כתבי קודש, וכן ספרי פרשנות ופילוסופיה מאת מדענים ומשכילים יהודים דוגמת הרמב"ן, הרמב"ם ואחרים.

גם הגויים, נוצרים ומוסלמים כאחד, נהגו לאייר ברוב פאר את כתבי הקודש היהודיים. בתקופות מסוימות, בעיקר באיטליה של תקופת הרנסנס, כאשר נדרשו לאיכויות

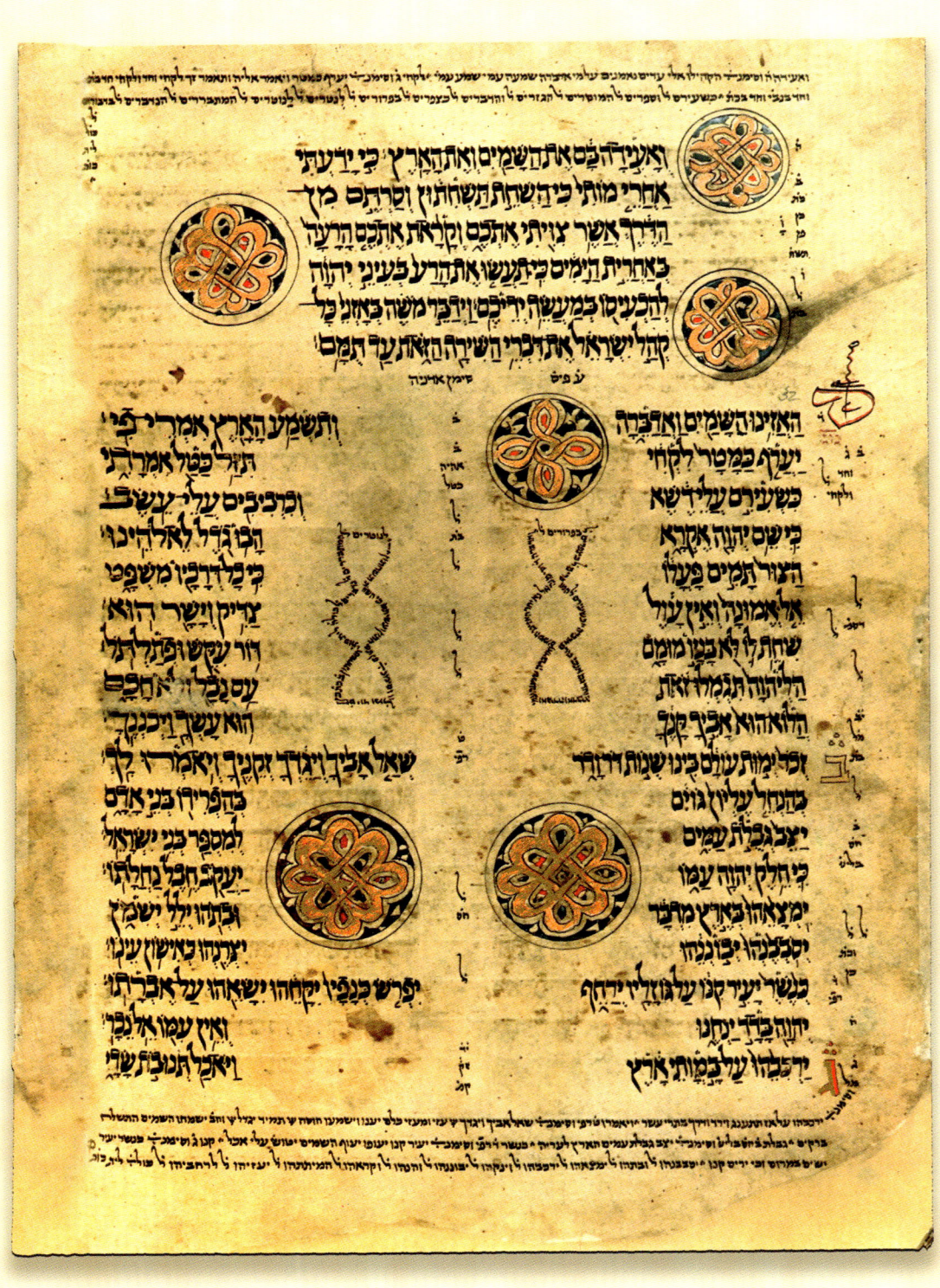

Verses from "Song of Moses" (Deuteronomy 32:1-13) in an illuminated Yemenite Pentateuch, San'a, 1469, collection of The British Museum, London

Gentiles too, both Christians and Muslims, used to illuminate the Jewish sacred texts. In certain periods, especially in Italy during the Renaissance, when the Jews sought qualities of writing and illumination that the Jewish artists could not achieve, they employed gentile artists; but among the Christians too there developed a magnificent independent tradition of illustration of the Bible, which contains both the *Tanakh* (which they call the "Old Testament") and the "New Testament". It is no accident that the first book ever printed, in 1455, was the Bible (see p. 10).

The *Tanakh*, in addition to its religious and historical importance, is a marvelous work of art that incorporates philosophy, laws, literature and poetry. And as numerous as are the facets of the *Tanakh*, equally numerous too are the facets of the commentaries and interpretations given it throughout the generations, which are traditionally divided into four principal domains, called for short by the acronym *PaRDeS*: *pshat* [the simple or literal meaning], *remez* [what the text hints at or alludes to], *drash* [what the text teaches] and *sod* [the secret, or esoteric meaning]. Such, too, are the facets of the works of visual art that accompany the scriptural text: some of them concentrate on the historical events, while in others we can find deep layers of interpretation, philosophical elucidations, and even utterances of a personal character.

The attitude of the prescribers of *halachah* [religious conduct] to the illumination of the sacred texts changed from time to time, and from place to place. There were some who not only permitted the illumination of sacred texts but also encouraged it. Rabbi Isaac of Majorca (1361-1444), for example, wrote on an illuminated book that "it will broaden and quicken the soul and strengthen its powers".

The flourishing of the art of the Hebrew illuminated manuscripts, which reached its peak in the Renaissance period, was quite short-lived. The worsening of the living conditions of the Jews on the Iberian peninsula heralded a turn in this field, as Jewish patrons commissioned fewer new works due to the political and economical uncertainty. The expulsion of the Jews from Spain (1492) and from Portugal (1496), as well as the heavier burden on the Jews and the persecutions they suffered in the lands of Ashkenaz, made it difficult to pursue the craft of writing and illuminating. Concurrently, people in the world began grappling with the assimilation of *the far-reaching ramifications of the invention of printing.*

The first printed Hebrew book was published in Rome in 1469 (about 14 years after the Gutenberg Bible, the first printed book.

עמודי שער מעוטרים מתוך "תנ״ך שלח", מצרים, 1106-07, אוסף בית הספרים הלאומי והאוניברסיטאי, ירושלים
Illuminated opening pages from the "Shelah Bible", Egypt, 1106-07, collection of The National and University Library, Jerusalem

כתבי-היד העבריים המאוירים שהשתמרו למעלה מאלף שנה, מספרים סיפור היסטורי ואמנותי מרתק. מחד-גיסא הקפידה אמנות יהודית זו לשמור על מצוות הדת ואיסוריה, ומאידך-גיסא הופרתה על-ידי אמנויות זרות בארצות הגלות, במזרח ובמערב כאחד. הפגשתם של הטקסטים הקדושים, ובראשם החומש, עם טיפוגרפיה מאירת עיניים ואיורים מרהיבים, היוו לדעת רבים שיא אמנותי של שילוב בין תכנים עמוקים לבין צורה עשירה ומגוונת, פרי פיתוחם של אמני ישראל לאורך הדורות.

בהוצאתו לאור של חומש זה ביקשנו לשוב ולהעלות משהו מן השילוב הנושן ההוא בין יפי התוכן המקראי לבין יפי הצורה היאה לו. מי יתן והעושר הצורני יימצא ראוי הן בעיני הבקיאים בעולמה של תורה והן בעיני הבקיאים בעולמה של האמנות, ואולי אף יהא מקרב בין שני העולמות, שאינם אלא אחד.

From this time on, artistic and financial attention was diverted to the domain of printing and distribution in numerous copies, which pushed the tradition of illuminated manuscripts to the side. The Hebrew illuminated manuscripts that have survived more than one thousand years tell a fascinating artistic and historical story. On the one hand, this Jewish art took care to observe the religious precepts and prohibitions; on the other hand it was fertilized by foreign arts in the lands of the diaspora, in both the East and the West. The bringing together of the sacred texts, principally the Pentateuch, with a clearly legible typography and with spectacular illuminations, was considered by many an artistic pinnacle of integration of profound content with rich and diversified form, as developed by Jewish artists throughout the generations.

In publishing this Pentateuch, we have sought to re-evoke something of that ancient integration of the scriptural content with the beauty of form that befits it. May this wealth of form be found worthy both by those who are versed in the world of Torah and those who are versed in the world of art, and perhaps it may even bring some rapprochement between these two worlds, which are essentially one.

כפולת עמודים מאירת בכלי המקדש, מעשה ידי אלישע בן אברהם קרסקס, מתוך "תנ"ך פרחי", קטלוניה, 1366-82, אוסף ששון, אנגליה
Double page spread illustrated with Temple implements, made by Elisha Ben Abraham Crascas, from the "Farhi Bible", Catalonia, 1366-82, Sassoon Collection, England

יד לתורה, גרמניה, 1904, אוסף מוזיאון ישראל, ירושלים
Torah pointer, Germany, 1904, collection of The Israel Museum, Jerusalem

בעמוד ממול: ספר תורה מעוטר, איראן, 1973, אוסף מוזיאון ישראל, ירושלים On the facing page:
Illuminated Torah scroll, Iran, 1973, collection of The Israel Museum, Jerusalem

פרטים משריד של כריכה פנימית עם עיטורים מיקרוגרפיים וצמחיים, מתוך כתב-יד של התנ"ך על קלף, מצרים, המאה ה-11, אוסף הספרייה הציבורית, סנט-פטרסבורג
Details of a fragment of a carpet page with micrographic and floral decorations, from a manuscript of the Bible on vellum, Egypt, 11th century, collection of the Public Library, St. Petersburg

GENESIS 1 בראשית א בראשית

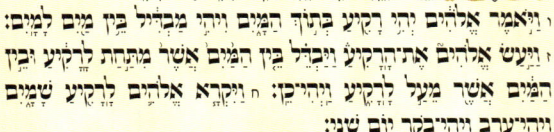

When God began to create heaven and earth 2 the earth being unformed and void, with darkness over the surface of the deep and a wind from God sweeping over the water 3 God said, "Let there be light"; and there was light. 4 God saw that the light was good, and God separated the light from the darkness. 5 God called the light Day, and the darkness He called Night. And there was evening and there was morning, a first day.

6 God said, "Let there be an expanse in the midst of the water, that it may separate water from water." 7 God made the expanse, and it separated the water which was below the expanse from the water which was above the expanse. And it was so. 8 God called the expanse Sky. And there was evening and there was morning, a second day.

9 God said, "Let the water below the sky be gathered into one area, that the dry land may appear." And it was so. 10 God called the dry land Earth, and the gathering of waters He called Seas. And God saw that this was good. 11 And God said, "Let the earth sprout vegetation: seed-bearing plants, fruit trees of every kind on earth that bear fruit with the seed in it." And it was so. 12 The earth brought forth vegetation: seed-bearing plants of every kind, and trees of every kind bearing fruit with the seed in it. And God saw that this was good. 13 And there was evening and there was morning, a third day.

14 God said, "Let there be lights in the expanse of the sky to separate day from night; they shall serve as signs for the set times – the days and the years; 15 and they serve as lights in the expanse of the sky to shine upon the earth." And it was so. 16 God made the two great lights, the greater light to dominate the day and the lesser light to dominate the night, and the stars. 17 And God set them in the expanse of the sky to shine upon the earth, 18 to dominate the day and the night, and to separate light from darkness. And God saw that this was good. 19 And there was evening and there was morning, a fourth day.

20 God said, "Let the waters bring forth swarms of living creatures, and birds that fly above the earth across the expanse of the sky." 21 God created the great sea monsters, and all the living creatures of every kind that creep, which the waters brought forth in swarms, and all the winged birds of every kind. And God saw that this was good. 22 God blessed them, saying, "Be fertile and increase, fill the waters in the seas, and let the birds increase on the earth." 23 And there was evening and there was morning, a fifth day.

24 God said, "Let the earth bring forth every kind of living creature: cattle, creeping things, and wild beasts of every kind." And it was so. 25 God made wild beasts of every kind and cattle of every kind, and all kinds of creeping things of the earth. And God saw that this was good. 26 And God said, "Let us make man in our image, after our likeness. They shall rule the fish of the sea, the birds of the sky, the cattle, the whole earth, and all the creeping things that creep on earth." 27 And God created man in His image, in the image of God He created him; male and female He created them. 28 God blessed them and God said to them, "Be fertile and increase, fill the earth and master it; and rule the fish of the sea, the birds of the sky, and all the living things that creep on earth." 29 God said, "See, I give you every seed-bearing plant that is upon all the earth, and every tree that has seed-bearing fruit; they shall be yours for food. 30 And to all the animals on land, to all the birds of the sky, and to everything that creeps on earth, in which there is the breath of life, [I give] all the green plants for food." And it was so. 31 And God saw all that He had made, and found it very good. And there was evening and there was morning, the sixth day.

2 1 The heaven and the earth were finished, and all their array. 2 On the seventh day God finished the work that He had been doing, and He ceaseda Or "rested." on the seventh day from all the work that He had done.

GENESIS 3 · בראשית ג

3 And God blessed the seventh day and declared it holy, because on it God ceased from all the work of creation that He had done. 4 Such is the story of heaven and earth when they were created. When the LORD God made earth and heaven - 5 when no shrub of the field was yet on earth and no grasses of the field had yet sprouted, because the LORD God had not sent rain upon the earth and there was no man to till the soil, 6 but a flow would well up from the ground and water the whole surface of the earth - 7 the LORD God formed man from the dust of the earth. He blew into his nostrils the breath of life, and man became a living being. 8 The LORD God planted a garden in Eden, in the east, and placed there the man whom He had formed. 9 And from the ground the LORD God caused to grow every tree that was pleasing to the sight and good for food, with the tree of life in the middle of the garden, and the tree of knowledge of good and bad. 10 A river issues from Eden to water the garden, and it then divides and becomes four branches. 11 The name of the first is Pishon, the one that winds through the whole land of Havilah, where the gold is. 12 The gold of that land is good; bdellium is there, and lapis lazuli. 13 The name of the second river is Gihon, the one that winds through the whole land of Cush. 14 The name of the third river is Tigris, the one that flows east of Asshur. And the fourth river is the Euphrates. 15 The LORD God took the man and placed him in the garden of Eden, to till it and tend it. 16 And the LORD God commanded the man, saying, "Of every tree of the garden you are free to eat; 17 but as for the tree of knowledge of good and bad, you must not eat of it; for as soon as you eat of it, you shall die." 18 The LORD God said, "It is not good for man to be alone; I will make a fitting helper for him." 19 And the LORD God formed out of the earth all the wild beasts and all the birds of the sky, and brought them to the man to see what he would call them; and whatever the man called each living creature, that would be its name. 20 And the man gave names to all the cattle and to the birds of the sky and to all the wild beasts; but for Adam no fitting helper was found. 21 So the LORD God cast a deep sleep upon the man; and, while he slept, He took one of his ribs and closed up the flesh at that spot. 22 And the LORD God fashioned the rib that He had taken from the man into a woman; and He brought her to the man. 23 Then the man said, "This one at last Is bone of my bones And flesh of my flesh. This one shall be called Woman, For from man was she taken." 24 Hence a man leaves his father and mother and clings to his wife, so that they become one flesh. 25 The two of them were naked, the man and his wife, yet they felt no shame. **3** 1 Now the serpent was the shrewdest of all the wild beasts that the LORD God had made. He said to the woman, "Did God really say: You shall not eat of any tree of the garden? 2 The woman replied to the serpent, "We may eat of the fruit of the other trees of the garden. 3 It is only about fruit of the tree in the middle of the garden that God said: You shall not eat of it or touch it, lest you die." 4 And the serpent said to the woman, "You are not going to die, 5 but God knows that as soon as you eat of it your eyes will be opened and you will be like divine beings who know good and bad." 6 When the woman saw that the tree was good for eating and a delight to the eyes, and that the tree was desirable as a source of wisdom, she took of its fruit and ate. She also gave some to her husband, and he ate. 7 Then the eyes of both of them were opened and they perceived that they were naked; and they sewed together fig leaves and made themselves loincloths. 8 They heard the sound of the LORD God moving about in the garden at the breezy time of day; and the man and his wife hid from the LORD God among the trees of the garden. 9 The LORD God called out to the man and said to him, "Where are you?" 10 He replied, "I heard the sound of You in the garden, and I was afraid because I was naked, so I hid." 11 Then He asked, "Who told you that you were naked? Did you eat of the tree from which I had forbidden you to eat?" 12 The man said, "The woman You put at my side - she gave me of the tree, and I ate." 13 And the LORD God said to the woman, "What is this you have done!" The woman replied, "The serpent duped me, and I ate." 14 Then the LORD God said to the serpent,

GENESIS 4 בראשית ד בראשית

"Because you did this, More cursed shall you be Than all cattle And all the wild beasts: On your belly shall you crawl And dirt shall you eat All the days of your life. 15 I will put enmity Between you and the woman, And between your offspring and hers; They shall strike at your head, And you shall strike at their heel." 16 And to the woman He said, "I will make most severe Your pangs in childbearing; In pain shall you bear children. Yet your urge shall be for your husband, And he shall rule over you." 17 To Adam He said, "Because you did as your wife said and ate of the tree about which I commanded you, 'You shall not eat of it,' Cursed be the ground because of you; By toil shall you eat of it All the days of your life: 18 Thorns and thistles shall it sprout for you. But your food shall be the grasses of the field; 19 By the sweat of your brow Shall you get bread to eat, Until you return to the ground - For from it you were taken. For dust you are, And to dust you shall return." 20 The man named his wife Eve, because she was the mother of all the living. 21 And the LORD God made garments of skins for Adam and his wife, and clothed them. 22 And the LORD God said, "Now that the man has become like one of us, knowing good and bad, what if he should stretch out his hand and take also from the tree of life and eat, and live forever!" 23 So the LORD God banished him from the garden of Eden, to till the soil from which he was taken. 24 He drove the man out, and stationed east of the garden of Eden the cherubim and the fiery ever-turning sword, to guard the way to the tree of life.

4 1 Now the man knew his wife Eve, and she conceived and bore Cain, saying, "I have gained a male child with the help of the LORD." 2 She bore his brother Abel. Abel became a keeper of sheep, and Cain became a tiller of the soil. 3 In the course of time, Cain brought an offering to the LORD from the fruit of the soil; 4 and Abel, for his part, brought the choicest of the firstlings of his flock. The LORD paid heed to Abel and his offering, 5 but to Cain and his offering He paid no heed. Cain was much distressed and his face fell. 6 And the LORD said to Cain, "Why are you distressed, And why is your face fallen? 7 Surely, if you do right, There is uplift. But if you do not do right Sin couches at the door; Its urge is toward you, Yet you can be its master." 8 Cain said to his brother Abel ... and when they were in the field, Cain set upon his brother Abel and killed him. 9 The LORD said to Cain, "Where is your brother Abel?" And he said, "I do not know. Am I my brother's keeper?" 10 Then He said, "What have you done? Hark, your brother's blood cries out to Me from the ground! 11 Therefore, you shall be more cursed than the ground, which opened its mouth to receive your brother's blood from your hand. 12 If you till the soil, it shall no longer yield its strength to you. You shall become a ceaseless wanderer on earth." 13 Cain said to the LORD, "My punishment is too great to bear! 14 Since You have banished me this day from the soil, and I must avoid Your presence and become a restless wanderer on earth - anyone who meets me may kill me!" 15 The LORD said to him, "I promise, if anyone kills Cain, sevenfold vengeance shall be taken on him." And the LORD put a mark on Cain, lest anyone who met him should kill him. 16 Cain left the presence of the LORD and settled in the land of Nod, east of Eden. 17 Cain knew his wife, and she conceived and bore Enoch. He then founded a city, and named the city after his son Enoch. 18 To Enoch was born Irad, and Irad begot Mehujael, and Mehujael begot Methusael, and Methusael begot Lamech. 19 Lamech took to himself two wives: the name of the one was Adah, and the name of the other was Zillah. 20 Adah bore Jabal; he was the ancestor of those who dwell in tents and amidst herds. 21 And the name of his brother was Jubal; he was the ancestor of all who play the lyre and the pipe. 22 As for Zillah, she bore Tubal-cain, who forged all implements of copper and iron. And the sister of Tubal-cain was Naamah. 23 And Lamech said to his wives, "Adah and Zillah, hear my voice; O wives of Lamech, give ear to my speech. I have slain a man for wounding me, And a lad for bruising me. 24 If Cain is avenged sevenfold, Then Lamech seventy-sevenfold." 25 Adam knew his wife again, and she bore a son and named him Seth, meaning, "God has provided me with another offspring in place of Abel," for Cain had killed him. 26 And to Seth, in turn, a son was born, and he named him Enosh. It was then that men began to invoke the LORD by name.

5 1 This is the record

GENESIS 6 · בראשית ו

of Adam's line. - When God created man, He made him in the likeness of God; 2 male and female He created them. And when they were created, He blessed them and called them Man. 3 When Adam had lived hundred and thirty years, he begot a son in his likeness after his image, and he named him Seth. 4 After the birth of Seth, Adam lived eight hundred years and begot sons and daughters. 5 All the days that Adam lived came to nine hundred and thirty years; then he died. 6 When Seth had lived hundred and five years, he begot Enosh. 7 After the birth of Enosh, Seth lived eight hundred and seven years and begot sons and daughters. 8 All the days of Seth came to nine hundred and twelve years; then he died. 9 When Enosh had lived ninety years, he begot Kenan. 10 After the birth of Kenan, Enosh lived eight hundred and fifteen years and begot sons and daughters. 11 All the days of Enosh came to nine hundred and five years; then he died. 12 When Kenan had lived seventy years, he begot Mahalalel. 13 After the birth of Mahalalel, Kenan lived eight hundred and forty years and begot sons and daughters. 14 All the days of Kenan came to nine hundred and ten years; then he died. 15 When Mahalalel had lived sixty and five years, he begot Jared. 16 After the birth of Jared, Mahalalel lived eight hundred and thirty years and begot sons and daughters. 17 All the days of Mahalalel came to eight hundred ninety and five years; then he died. 18 When Jared had lived hundred sixty and two years, he begot Enoch. 19 After the birth of Enoch, Jared lived eight hundred years and begot sons and daughters. 20 All the days of Jared came to nine hundred sixty and two years; then he died. 21 When Enoch had lived sixty and five years, he begot Methuselah. 22 After the birth of Methuselah, Enoch walked with God three hundred years; and he begot sons and daughters. 23 All the days of Enoch came to three hundred sixty and five years. 24 Enoch walked with God; then he was no more, for God took him. 25 When Methuselah had lived hundred eighty and seven years, he begot Lamech. 26 After the birth of Lamech, Methuselah lived seven hundred eighty and two years and begot sons and daughters. 27 All the days of Methuselah came to nine hundred sixty and nine years; then he died. 28 When Lamech had lived hundred eighty and two years, he begot a son. 29 And he named him Noah, saying, "This one will provide us relief from our work and from the toil of our hands, out of the very soil which the LORD placed under a curse." 30 After the birth of Noah, Lamech lived five hundred ninety and five years and begot sons and daughters. 31 All the days of Lamech came to seven hundred seventy and seven years; then he died. 32 When Noah had lived five hundred years, Noah begot Shem, Ham, and Japheth. ❊ 1 When men began to increase on earth and daughters were born to them, 2 the divine beings saw how beautiful the daughters of men were and took wives from among those that pleased them. 3 The LORD said, "My breath shall not abide in man forever, since he too is flesh; let the days allowed him be one hundred and twenty years." 4 It was then, and later too, that the Nephilim appeared on earth - when the divine beings cohabited with the daughters of men, who bore them offspring. They were the heroes of old, the men of renown. 5 The LORD saw how great was man's wickedness on earth, and how every plan devised by his mind was nothing but evil all the time. 6 And the LORD regretted that He had made man on earth, and His heart was saddened. 7 The LORD said, "I will blot out from the earth the men whom I created - men together with beasts, creeping things, and birds of the sky; for I regret that I made them."

GENESIS 7 בראשית ז נח

8 But Noah found favor with the LORD. 9 This is the line of Noah. Noah was a righteous man; he was blameless in his age; Noah walked with God. 10 Noah begot three sons: Shem, Ham, and Japheth. 11 The earth became corrupt before God; the earth was filled with lawlessness. 12 When God saw how corrupt the earth was, for all flesh had corrupted its ways on earth, 13 God said to Noah, "I have decided to put an end to all flesh, for the earth is filled with lawlessness because of them: I am about to destroy them with the earth. 14 Make yourself an ark of gopher wood; make it an ark with compartments, and cover it inside and out with pitch. 15 This is how you shall make it: the length of the ark shall be three hundred cubits, its width fifty cubits, and its height thirty cubits. 16 Make an opening for daylight in the ark, and terminate it within a cubit of the top. Put the entrance to the ark in its side; make it with bottom, second, and third decks. 17 For My part, I am about to bring the Flood - waters upon the earth - to destroy all flesh under the sky in which there is breath of life; everything on earth shall perish. 18 But I will establish My covenant with you, and you shall enter the ark, with your sons, your wife, and your sons' wives. 19 And of all that lives, of all flesh, you shall take two of each into the ark to keep alive with you; they shall be male and female. 20 From birds of every kind, cattle of every kind, every kind of creeping thing on earth, two of each shall come to you to stay alive. 21 For your part, take of everything that is eaten and store it away, to serve as food for you and for them." 22 Noah did so; just as God commanded him, so he did. **7** 1 Then the LORD said to Noah, "Go into the ark, with all your household, for you alone have I found righteous before Me in this generation. 2 Of every clean animal you shall take seven pairs, males and their mates; and of every animal that is not clean, two, a male and its mate; 3 of the birds of the sky also, seven pairs, male and female, to keep seed alive upon all the earth. 4 For in seven days' time I will make it rain upon the earth, forty days and forty nights, and I will blot out from the earth all existence that I created." 5 And Noah did just as the LORD commanded him. 6 Noah was six hundred years old when the Flood came, waters upon the earth. 7 Noah, with his sons, his wife, and his sons' wives, went into the ark because of the waters of the Flood. 8 Of the clean animals, of the animals that are not clean, of the birds, and of everything that creeps on the ground, 9 two of each, male and female, came to Noah into the ark, as God had commanded Noah. 10 And on the seventh day the waters of the Flood came upon the earth. 11 In the six hundredth year of Noah's life, in the second month, on the seventeenth day of the month, on that day all the fountains of the great deep burst apart. And the floodgates of the sky broke open. 12 The rain fell on the earth forty days and forty nights.) 13 That same day Noah and Noah's sons, Shem, Ham, and Japheth, went into the ark, with Noah's wife and the three wives of his sons 14 they and all beasts of every kind, all cattle of every kind, all creatures of every kind that creep on the earth, and all birds of every kind, every bird, every winged thing. 15 They came to Noah into the ark, two each of all flesh in which there was breath of life. 16 Thus they that entered comprised male and female of all flesh, as God had commanded him. And the LORD shut him in. 17 The Flood continued forty days on the earth, and the waters increased and raised the ark so that it rose above the earth. 18 The waters swelled and increased greatly upon the earth, and the ark drifted upon the waters. 19 When the waters had swelled much more upon the earth, all the highest mountains everywhere under the sky were covered. 20 Fifteen cubits higher did the waters swell, as the mountains were covered. 21 And all flesh that stirred on earth perished-birds, cattle, beasts,

GENESIS 8 בראשית ח

and all the things that swarmed upon the earth, and all mankind. 22 All in whose nostrils was the merest breath of life, all that was on dry land, died. 23 All existence on earth was blotted out—man, cattle, creeping things, and birds of the sky; they were blotted out from the earth. Only Noah was left, and those with him in the ark. 24 And when the waters had swelled on the earth one hundred and fifty days, 8 1 God remembered Noah and all the beasts and all the cattle that were with him in the ark, and God caused a wind to blow across the earth, and the waters subsided. 2 The fountains of the deep and the floodgates of the sky were stopped up, and the rain from the sky was held back; 3 the waters then receded steadily from the earth. At the end of one hundred and fifty days the waters diminished, 4 so that in the seventh month, on the seventeenth day of the month, the ark came to rest on the mountains of Ararat. 5 The waters went on diminishing until the tenth month; in the tenth month, on the first of the month, the tops of the mountains became visible. 6 At the end of forty days, Noah opened the window of the ark that he had made 7 and sent out the raven; it went to and fro until the waters had dried up from the earth. 8 Then he sent out the dove to see whether the waters had decreased from the surface of the ground. 9 But the dove could not find a resting place for its foot, and returned to him to the ark, for there was water over all the earth. So putting out his hand, he took it into the ark with him. 10 He waited another seven days, and again sent out the dove from the ark. 11 The dove came back to him toward evening, and there in its bill was a plucked-off olive leaf! Then Noah knew that the waters had decreased on the earth. 12 He waited still another seven days and sent the dove forth; and it did not return to him any more. 13 In the six hundred and first year, in the first month, on the first of the month, the waters began to dry from the earth; and when Noah removed the covering of the ark, he saw that the surface of the ground was drying. 14 And in the second month, on the twenty-seventh day of the month, the earth was dry.

15 God spoke to Noah, saying, 16 "Come out of the ark, together with your wife, your sons, and your sons' wives. 17 Bring out with you every living thing of all flesh that is with you: birds, animals, and everything that creeps on earth; and let them swarm on the earth and be fertile and increase on earth." 18 So Noah came out, together with his sons, his wife, and his sons' wives. 19 Every animal, every creeping thing, and every bird, everything that stirs on earth came out of the ark by families. 20 Then Noah built an altar to the LORD and, taking of every clean animal and of every clean bird, he offered burnt offerings on the altar. 21 The LORD smelled the pleasing odor, and the LORD said to Himself: "Never again will I doom the earth because of man, since the devisings of man's mind are evil from his youth; nor will I ever again destroy every living being, as I have done. 22 So long as the earth endures, Seedtime and harvest, Cold and heat, Summer and winter, Day and night Shall not cease." 9 1 God blessed Noah and his sons, and said to them, "Be fertile and increase, and fill the earth. 2 The fear and the dread of you shall be upon all the beasts of the earth and upon all the birds of the sky—everything with which the earth is astir—and upon all the fish of the sea; they are given into your hand. 3 Every creature that lives shall be yours to eat; as with the green grasses, I give you all these. 4 You must not, however, eat flesh with its life-blood in it. 5 But for your own life-blood I will require a reckoning: I will require it of every beast; of man, too, will I require a reckoning for human life, of every man for that of his fellow man! 6 Whoever sheds the blood of man, By man shall his blood be shed; For in His image Did God make man. 7 Be fertile, then, and increase; abound on the earth and increase on it."

8 And God said to Noah and to his sons with him, 9 "I now establish My covenant with you and your offspring to come, 10 and with every living thing that is with you—birds, cattle, and every wild beast as well—all that have come out of the ark, every living thing on earth. 11 I will maintain My covenant with you: never again shall all flesh be cut off by the waters of a flood, and never again shall there be a flood to destroy the earth." 12 God further said, "This is the sign

23

GENESIS 10 / בראשית י

that I set for the covenant between Me and you, and every living creature with you, for all ages to come. 13 I have set My bow in the clouds, and it shall serve as a sign of the covenant between Me and the earth. 14 When I bring clouds over the earth, and the bow appears in the clouds, 15 I will remember My covenant between Me and you and every living creature among all flesh, so that the waters shall never again become a flood to destroy all flesh. 16 When the bow is in the clouds, I will see it and remember the everlasting covenant between God and all living creatures, all flesh that is on earth. 17 That," God said to Noah, "shall be the sign of the covenant that I have established between Me and all flesh that is on earth."

18 The sons of Noah who came out of the ark were Shem, Ham, and Japheth— Ham being the father of Canaan. 19 These three were the sons of Noah, and from these the whole world branched out. 20 Noah, the tiller of the soil, was the first to plant a vineyard. 21 He drank of the wine and became drunk, and he uncovered himself within his tent. 22 Ham, the father of Canaan, saw his father's nakedness and told his two brothers outside. 23 But Shem and Japheth took a cloth, placed it against both their backs and, walking backward, they covered their father's nakedness; their faces were turned the other way, so that they did not see their father's nakedness. 24 When Noah woke up from his wine and learned what his youngest son had done to him, 25 he said, "Cursed be Canaan; The lowest of slaves Shall he be to his brothers." 26 And he said, "Blessed be the LORD, The God of Shem; Let Canaan be a slave to them. 27 May God enlarge Japheth, And let him dwell in the tents of Shem; And let Canaan be a slave to them." 28 Noah lived after the Flood 350 years. 29 And all the days of Noah came to 950 years; then he died.

10 1 These are the lines of Shem, Ham, and Japheth, the sons of Noah: sons were born to them after the Flood. 2 The descendants of Japheth: Gomer, Magog, Madai, Javan, Tubal, Meshech, and Tiras. 3 The descendants of Gomer: Ashkenaz, Riphath, and Togarmah. 4 The descendants of Javan: Elishah and Tarshish, the Kittim and the Dodanim. 5 From these the maritime nations branched out, by their lands - each with its language - their clans and their nations. 6 The descendants of Ham: Cush, Mizraim, Put, and Canaan. 7 The descendants of Cush: Seba, Havilah, Sabtah, Raamah, and Sabteca. The descendants of Raamah: Sheba and Dedan. 8 Cush also begot Nimrod, who was the first man of might on earth. 9 He was a mighty hunter by the grace of the LORD; hence the saying, "Like Nimrod a mighty hunter by the grace of the LORD." 10 The mainstays of his kingdom were Babylon, Erech, Accad, and Calneh in the land of Shinar. 11 From that land Asshur went forth and built Nineveh, Rehoboth-ir, Calah, 12 and Resen between Nineveh and Calah, that is the great city. 13 And Mizraim begot the Ludim, the Anamim, the Lehabim, the Naphtuhim, 14 the Pathrusim, the Casluhim, and the Caphtorim, whence the Philistines came forth.

15 Canaan begot Sidon, his first-born, and Heth; 16 and the Jebusites, the Amorites, the Girgashites, 17 the Hivites, the Arkites, the Sinites, 18 the Arvadites, the Zemarites, and the Hamathites. Afterward the clans of the Canaanites spread out. 19 The Canaanite territory extended from Sidon as far as Gerar, near Gaza, and as far as Sodom, Gomorrah, Admah, and Zeboiim, near Lasha. 20 These are the descendants of Ham, according to their clans and languages, by their lands and nations.

21 Sons were also born to Shem, ancestor of all the descendants of Eber and older brother of Japheth. 22 The descendants of Shem: Elam, Asshur, Arpachshad, Lud, and Aram. 23 The descendants of Aram: Uz, Hul, Gether, and Mash. 24 Arpachshad begot Shelah, and Shelah begot Eber. 25 Two sons were born to Eber: the name of the first was Peleg, for in his days the earth was divided; and the name of his brother was Joktan. 26 Joktan begot Almodad, Sheleph, Hazarmaveth, Jerah, 27 Hadoram, Uzal, Diklah, 28 Obal, Abimael, Sheba, 29 Ophir, Havilah, and Jobab; all these were the descendants of Joktan. 30 Their settlements extended from Mesha as far as Sephar, the hill country to the east. 31 These are the descendants of Shem according to their clans and languages, by their lands, according to their nations. 32 These are the groupings of Noah's descendants,

GENESIS 11 · בראשית יא

according to their origins, by their nations; and from these the nations branched out over the earth after the Flood.

11 1 Everyone on earth had the same language and the same words. 2 And as they migrated from the east, they came upon a valley in the land of Shinar and settled there. 3 They said to one another, "Come, let us make bricks and burn them hard." - Brick served them as stone, and bitumen served them as mortar. 4 And they said, "Come, let us build us a city, and a tower with its top in the sky, to make a name for ourselves; else we shall be scattered all over the world." 5 The LORD came down to look at the city and tower that man had built. 6 and the LORD said, "If, as one people with one language for all, this is how they have begun to act, then nothing that they may propose to do will be out of their reach. 7 Let us, then, go down and confound their speech there, so that they shall not understand one another's speech." 8 Thus the LORD scattered them from there over the face of the whole earth; and they stopped building the city. 9 That is why it was called Babel, because there the LORD confounded the speech of the whole earth; and from there the LORD scattered them over the face of the whole earth. 10 This is the line of Shem. Shem was 100 years old when he begot Arpachshad, two years after the Flood. 11 After the birth of Arpachshad, Shem lived 500 years and begot sons and daughters. 12 When Arpachshad had lived 35 years, he begot Shelah. 13 After the birth of Shelah, Arpachshad lived 403 years and begot sons and daughters.

14 When Shelah had lived 30 years, he begot Eber. 15 After the birth of Eber, Shelah lived 403 years and begot sons and daughters. 16 When Eber had lived 34 years, he begot Peleg. 17 After the birth of Peleg, Eber lived 430 years and begot sons and daughters. 18 When Peleg had lived 30 years, he begot Reu. 19 After the birth of Reu, Peleg lived 209 years and begot sons and daughters. 20 When Reu had lived 32 years, he begot Serug. 21 After the birth of Serug, Reu lived 207 years and begot sons and daughters. 22 When Serug had lived 30 years, he begot Nahor. 23 After the birth of Nahor, Serug lived 200 years and begot sons and daughters. 24 When Nahor had lived 29 years, he begot Terah. 25 After the birth of Terah, Nahor lived 119 years and begot sons and daughters.

26 When Terah had lived 70 years, he begot Abram, Nahor, and Haran. 27 Now this is the line of Terah: Terah begot Abram, Nahor, and Haran; and Haran begot Lot. 28 Haran died in the lifetime of his father Terah, in his native land, Ur of the Chaldeans. 29 Abram and Nahor took to themselves wives, the name of Abram's wife being Sarai and that of Nahor's wife Milcah, the daughter of Haran, the father of Milcah and Iscah. 30 Now Sarai was barren, she had no child. 31 Terah took his son Abram, his grandson Lot the son of Haran, and his daughter-in-law Sarai, the wife of his son Abram, and they set out together from Ur of the Chaldeans for the land of Canaan; but when they had come as far as Haran, they settled there. 32 The days of Terah came to two hundred and five years; and Terah died in Haran.

12 he LORD said to Abram, "Go forth from your native land and from your father's house to the land that I will show you. 2 I will make of you a great nation, And I will bless you; I will make your name great, And you shall be a blessing. 3 I will bless those who bless you And curse him that curses you; And all the families of the earth Shall bless themselves by you." 4 Abram went forth as the LORD had commanded him, and Lot went with him. Abram was seventy-five years old when he left Haran. 5 Abram took his wife Sarai and his brother's son Lot, and all the wealth that they had amassed,

GENESIS 13

and the persons that they had acquired in Haran; and they set out for the land of Canaan. When they arrived in the land of Canaan, 6 Abram passed through the land as far as the site of Shechem, at the terebinth of Moreh. The Canaanites were then in the land. 7 The LORD appeared to Abram and said, "I will assign this land to your offspring." And he built an altar there to the LORD who had appeared to him. 8 From there he moved on to the hill country east of Bethel and pitched his tent, with Bethel on the west and Ai on the east; and he built there an altar to the LORD and invoked the LORD by name. 9 Then Abram journeyed by stages toward the Negeb.

10 There was a famine in the land, and Abram went down to Egypt to sojourn there, for the famine was severe in the land. 11 As he was about to enter Egypt, he said to his wife Sarai, "I know what a beautiful woman you are. 12 If the Egyptians see you, and think, 'She is his wife,' they will kill me and let you live. 13 Please say that you are my sister, that it may go well with me because of you, and that I may remain alive thanks to you." 14 When Abram entered Egypt, the Egyptians saw how very beautiful the woman was. 15 Pharaoh's courtiers saw her and praised her to Pharaoh, and the woman was taken into Pharaoh's palace. 16 And because of her, it went well with Abram; he acquired sheep, oxen, asses, male and female slaves, she-asses, and camels. 17 But the LORD afflicted Pharaoh and his household with mighty plagues on account of Sarai, the wife of Abram. 18 Pharaoh sent for Abram and said, "What is this you have done to me! Why did you not tell me that she was your wife? 19 Why did you say, 'She is my sister,' so that I took her as my wife? Now, here is your wife; take her and begone!" 20 And Pharaoh put men in charge of him, and they sent him off with his wife and all that he possessed.

13 1 From Egypt, Abram went up into the Negeb, with his wife and all that he possessed, together with Lot. 2 Now Abram was very rich in cattle, silver, and gold. 3 And he proceeded by stages from the Negeb as far as Bethel, to the place where his tent had been formerly, between Bethel and Ai, 4 the site of the altar that he had built there at first; and there Abram invoked the LORD by name. 5 Lot, who went with Abram, also had flocks and herds and tents, 6 so that the land could not support their staying together; for their possessions were so great that they could not remain together. 7 And there was quarreling between the herdsmen of Abram's cattle and those of Lot's cattle. The Canaanites and Perizzites were then dwelling in the land. 8 Abram said to Lot, "Let there be no strife between you and me, between my herdsmen and yours, for we are kinsmen. 9 Is not the whole land before you? Let us separate: if you go north, I will go south; and if you go south, I will go north." 10 Lot looked about him and saw how well watered was the whole plain of the Jordan, all of it - this was before the LORD had destroyed Sodom and Gomorrah - all the way to Zoar, like the garden of the LORD, like the land of Egypt. 11 So Lot chose for himself the whole plain of the Jordan, and Lot journeyed eastward. Thus they parted from each other; 12 Abram remained in the land of Canaan, while Lot settled in the cities of the Plain, pitching his tents near Sodom. 13 Now the inhabitants of Sodom were very wicked sinners against the LORD. 14 And the LORD said to Abram, after Lot had parted from him, "Raise your eyes and look out from where you are, to the north and south, to the east and west, 15 for I give all the land that you see to you and your offspring forever. 16 I will make your offspring as the dust of the earth, so that if one can count the dust of the earth, then your offspring too can be counted. 17 Up, walk about the land, through its length and its breadth, for I give it to you." 18 And Abram moved his tent, and came to dwell at the terebinths of Mamre, which are in Hebron; and he built there an altar to the LORD.

14 1 Now, when King Amraphel of Shinar, King Arioch of Ellasar, King Chedorlaomer of Elam, and King Tidal of Goiim 2 made war on King Bera of Sodom, King Birsha of Gomorrah, King Shinab of Admah, King Shemeber of Zeboiim, and the king of Bela, which is Zoar, 3 all the latter joined forces at the Valley of Siddim, now the Dead Sea. 4 Twelve years they served Chedorlaomer, and in the thirteenth year they rebelled.

A page of the Book of Genesis, from the Bible illustrated by Gustave Doré, 1832-33, עמוד מספר בראשית, מתוך התנ״ך באיורו של גוסטב דורה

GENESIS 9 — son had done to him. 25 he said, "Cursed be Canaan; The lowest of slaves Shall he be to his brothers." 26 And he said, "Blessed

בראשית ט
כה וַיֹּאמֶר אָרוּר כְּנָעַן עֶבֶד עֲבָדִים יִהְיֶה לְאֶחָיו׃ כו וַיֹּאמֶר בָּרוּךְ יְהֹוָה אֱלֹהֵי שֵׁם

GENESIS 15 — בראשית טו לך לך

5 In the fourteenth year Chedorlaomer and the kings who were with him came and defeated the Rephaim at Ashteroth-karnaim, the Zuzim at Ham, the Emim at Shaveh-kiriathaim, 6 and the Horites in their hill country of Seir as far as El-paran, which is by the wilderness. 7 On their way back they came to En-mishpat, which is Kadesh, and subdued all the territory of the Amalekites, and also the Amorites who dwelt in Hazazon-tamar. 8 Then the king of Sodom, the king of Gomorrah, the king of Admah, the king of Zeboiim, and the king of Bela, which is Zoar, went forth and engaged them in battle in the Valley of Siddim: 9 King Chedorlaomer of Elam, King Tidal of Goiim, King Amraphel of Shinar, and King Arioch of Ellasar - four kings against those five. 10 Now the Valley of Siddim was dotted with bitumen pits; and the kings of Sodom and Gomorrah, in their flight, threw themselves into them, while the rest escaped to the hill country. 11 [The invaders] seized all the wealth of Sodom and Gomorrah and all their provisions, and went their way. 12 They also took Lot, the son of Abram's brother, and his possessions, and departed; for he had settled in Sodom. 13 A fugitive brought the news to Abram the Hebrew, who was dwelling at the terebinths of Mamre the Amorite, kinsman of Eshkol and Aner, these being Abram's allies. 14 When Abram heard that his kinsman had been taken captive, he mustered his retainers, born into his household, numbering three hundred and eighteen, and went in pursuit as far as Dan. 15 At night, he and his servants deployed against them and defeated them; and he pursued them as far as Hobah, which is north of Damascus. 16 He brought back all the possessions; he also brought back his kinsman Lot and his possessions, and the women and the rest of the people. 17 When he returned from defeating Chedorlaomer and the kings with him, the king of Sodom came out to meet him in the Valley of Shaveh, which is the Valley of the King. 18 And King Melchizedek of Salem brought out bread and wine; he was a priest of God Most High. 19 He blessed him, saying, "Blessed be Abram of God Most High, Creator of heaven and earth. 20 And blessed be God Most High, who has delivered your foes into your hand." And [Abram] gave him a tenth of everything. 21 Then the king of Sodom said to Abram, "Give me the persons, and take the possessions for yourself." 22 But Abram said to the king of Sodom, "I swear to the LORD, God Most High, Creator of heaven and earth: 23 I will not take so much as a thread or a sandal strap of what is yours; you shall not say, 'It is I who made Abram rich.' 24 For me, nothing but what my servants have used up; as for the share of the men who went with me - Aner, Eshkol, and Mamre - let them take their share."

15 1 Some time later, the word of the LORD came to Abram in a vision. He said, "Fear not, Abram, I am a shield to you; Your reward shall be very great." 2 But Abram said, "O Lord GOD, what can You give me, seeing that I shall die childless, and the one in charge of my household is Dammesek Eliezer!" 3 Abram said further, "Since You have granted me no offspring, my steward will be my heir." 4 The word of the LORD came to him in reply, "That one shall not be your heir; none but your very own issue shall be your heir." 5 He took him outside and said, "Look toward heaven and count the stars, if you are able to count them." And He added, "So shall your offspring be." 6 And because he put his trust in the LORD, He reckoned it to his merit. 7 Then He said to him, "I am the LORD who brought you out of Ur of the Chaldeans to assign this land to you as a possession." 8 And he said, "O Lord GOD, how shall I know that I am to possess it?" 9 He answered, "Bring Me a three-year-old heifer, a three-year-old she-goat, a three-year-old ram, a turtledove, and a young bird." 10 He brought Him all these and cut them in two, placing each half opposite the other; but he did not cut up the bird. 11 Birds of prey came down upon the carcasses, and Abram drove them away. 12 As the sun was about to set, a deep sleep fell upon Abram, and a great dark dread descended upon him. 13 And He said to Abram, "Know well that your offspring shall be strangers in a land not theirs, and they shall be enslaved and oppressed four hundred years; 14 but I will execute judgment on the nation they shall serve, and in the end they shall go free with great wealth. 15 As for you, You shall go to your fathers in peace; You shall be buried at a ripe old age. 16 And they shall return here in the fourth generation, for the iniquity of the Amorites is not yet complete." 17 When the sun set

GENESIS 16

and it was very dark, there appeared a smoking oven, and a flaming torch which passed between those pieces. 18 On that day the LORD made a covenant with Abram, saying, "To your offspring I assign this land, from the river of Egypt to the great river, the river Euphrates: 19 the Kenites, the Kenizzites, the Kadmonites, 20 the Hittites, the Perizzites, the Rephaim, 21 the Amorites, the Canaanites, the Girgashites, and the Jebusites."

16 1 Sarai, Abram's wife, had borne him no children. She had an Egyptian maidservant whose name was Hagar. 2 And Sarai said to Abram, "Look, the LORD has kept me from bearing. Consort with my maid; perhaps I shall have a son through her." And Abram heeded Sarai's request. 3 So Sarai, Abram's wife, took her maid, Hagar the Egyptian - after Abram had dwelt in the land of Canaan ten years - and gave her to her husband Abram as concubine. 4 He cohabited with Hagar and she conceived; and when she saw that she had conceived, her mistress was lowered in her esteem. 5 And Sarai said to Abram, "The wrong done me is your fault! I myself put my maid in your bosom; now that she sees that she is pregnant, I am lowered in her esteem. The LORD decide between you and me!" 6 Abram said to Sarai, "Your maid is in your hands. Deal with her as you think right." Then Sarai treated her harshly, and she ran away from her. 7 An angel of the LORD found her by a spring of water in the wilderness, the spring on the road to Shur. 8 and said, "Hagar, slave of Sarai, where have you come from, and where are you going?" And she said, "I am running away from my mistress Sarai." 9 And the angel of the LORD said to her, "Go back to your mistress, and submit to her harsh treatment." 10 And the angel of the LORD said to her, "I will greatly increase your offspring, And they shall be too many to count." 11 The angel of the LORD said to her further, "Behold, you are with child and shall bear a son; You shall call him Ishmael, for the LORD has paid heed to your suffering. 12 He shall be a wild ass of a man; his hand against everyone, and everyone's hand against him: he shall dwell alongside of all his kinsmen." 13 And she called the LORD who spoke to her, "You Are El-roi," by which she meant, "Have I not gone on seeing after He saw me!" 14 Therefore the well was called Beer-lahai-roi; it is between Kadesh and Bered. 15 Hagar bore a son to Abram, and Abram gave the son that Hagar bore him the name Ishmael. 16 Abram was eighty-six years old when Hagar bore Ishmael to Abram.

17 1 When Abram was ninety-nine years old, the LORD appeared to Abram and said to him, "I am El Shaddai. Walk in My ways and be blameless. 2 I will establish My covenant between Me and you, and I will make you exceedingly numerous." 3 Abram threw himself on his face; and God spoke to him further, 4 "As for Me, this is My covenant with you: You shall be the father of a multitude of nations. 5 And you shall no longer be called Abram, but your name shall be Abraham, for I make you the father of a multitude of nations. 6 I will make you exceedingly fertile, and make nations of you; and kings shall come forth from you. 7 I will maintain My covenant between Me and you, and your offspring to come, as an everlasting covenant throughout the ages, to be God to you and to your offspring to come. 8 I assign the land you sojourn in to you and your offspring to come, all the land of Canaan, as an everlasting holding. I will be their God." 9 God further said to Abraham, "As for you, you and your offspring to come throughout the ages shall keep My covenant. 10 Such shall be the covenant between Me and you and your offspring to follow which you shall keep: every male among you shall be circumcised. 11 You shall circumcise the flesh of your foreskin, and that shall be the sign of the covenant between Me and you. 12 And throughout the generations, every male among you shall be circumcised at the age of eight days. As for the homeborn slave and the one bought from an outsider who is not of your offspring, 13 they must be circumcised, homeborn, and purchased alike. Thus shall My covenant be marked in your flesh as an everlasting pact. 14 And if any male who is uncircumcised fails to circumcise the flesh of his foreskin, that person shall be cut off from his kin; he has broken My covenant." 15 And God said to Abraham, "As for your wife Sarai, you shall not call her Sarai, but her name shall be Sarah. 16 I will bless her; indeed, I will give you a son by her. I will bless her so that she shall give rise to nations: rulers of peoples shall issue from her." 17 Abraham threw himself on his face and laughed, as he said to himself, "Can a child be born to a

GENESIS 18

man a hundred years old, or can Sarah bear a child at ninety?" 18 And Abraham said to God, "O that Ishmael might live by Your favor!" 19 God said, "Nevertheless, Sarah your wife shall bear you a son, and you shall name him Isaac; and I will maintain My covenant with him as an everlasting covenant for his offspring to come. 20 As for Ishmael, I have heeded you. I hereby bless him. I will make him fertile and exceedingly numerous. He shall be the father of twelve chieftains, and I will make of him a great nation. 21 But My covenant I will maintain with Isaac, whom Sarah shall bear to you at this season next year." 22 And when He was done speaking with him, God was gone from Abraham. 23 Then Abraham took his son Ishmael, and all his homeborn slaves and all those he had bought, every male in Abraham's household, and he circumcised the flesh of their foreskins on that very day, as God had spoken to him. 24 Abraham was ninety-nine years old when he was circumcised the flesh of his foreskin. 25 and his son Ishmael was thirteen years old when he was circumcised in the flesh of his foreskin. 26 Thus Abraham and his son Ishmael were circumcised on that very day; 27 and all his household, his homeborn slaves and those that had been bought from outsiders, were circumcised with him.

18 The LORD appeared to him by the terebinths of Mamre; he was sitting at the entrance of the tent as the day grew hot. 2 Looking up, he saw three men standing near him. As soon as he saw them, he ran from the entrance of the tent to greet them and, bowing to the ground, 3 he said, "My lords, if it please you, do not go on past your servant. 4 Let a little water be brought; bathe your feet and recline under the tree. 5 And let me fetch a morsel of bread that you may refresh yourselves; then go on - seeing that you have come your servant's way." They replied, "Do as you have said." 6 Abraham hastened into the tent to Sarah, and said, "Quick, three seahs of choice flour! Knead and make cakes!" 7 Then Abraham ran to the herd, took a calf, tender and choice, and gave it to a servant-boy, who hastened to prepare it. 8 He took curds and milk and the calf that had been prepared and set these before them; and he waited on them under the tree as they ate. 9 They said to him, "Where is your wife Sarah?" And he replied, "There, in the tent." 10 Then one said, "I will return to you next year, and your wife Sarah shall have a son!" Sarah was listening at the entrance of the tent, which was behind him. 11 Now Abraham and Sarah were old, advanced in years; Sarah had stopped having the periods of women. 12 And Sarah laughed to herself, saying, "Now that I am withered, am I to have enjoyment - with my husband so old?" 13 Then the LORD said to Abraham, "Why did Sarah laugh, saying, 'Shall I in truth bear a child, old as I am?' 14 Is anything too wondrous for the LORD? I will return to you at the same season next year, and Sarah shall have a son." 15 Sarah lied, saying, "I did not laugh," for she was frightened. But He replied, "You did laugh." 16 The men set out from there and looked down toward Sodom, Abraham walking with them to see them off. 17 Now the LORD had said, "Shall I hide from Abraham what I am about to do, 18 since Abraham is to become a great and populous nation and all the nations of the earth are to bless themselves by him? 19 For I have singled him out, that he may instruct his children and his posterity to keep the way of the LORD by doing what is just and right, in order that the LORD may bring about for Abraham what He has promised him." 20 Then the LORD said, "The outrage of Sodom and Gomorrah is so great, and their sin so grave! 21 I will go down to see whether they have acted altogether according to the outcry that has reached Me; if not, I will take note." 22 The men went on from there to Sodom, while Abraham remained standing before the LORD. 23 Abraham came forward and said, "Will You sweep away the innocent along with the guilty? 24 What if there should be fifty innocent within the city; will You then wipe out the place and not forgive it for the sake of the innocent fifty who are in it? 25 Far be it from You to do such a thing, to bring death upon the innocent as well as the guilty, so that innocent and guilty fare alike. Far be it from You! Shall not the Judge of all the earth deal justly?" 26 And the LORD answered, "If I find within the city of Sodom fifty innocent ones, I will forgive the whole place for their sake." 27 Abraham spoke up, saying, "Here I venture to speak to my Lord, I who am but dust and ashes:

GENESIS 19 · בראשית יט · וירא

28 What if the fifty innocent should lack five? Will You destroy the whole city for want of the five?" And He answered, "I will not destroy if I find forty-five there." 29 But he spoke to Him again, and said, "What if forty should be found there?" And He answered, "I will not do it, for the sake of the forty." 30 "Let not my Lord be angry if I go on: What if thirty should be found there?" And He answered, "I will not do it if I find thirty there." 31 And he said, "I venture again to speak to my Lord: What if twenty should be found there?" And He answered, "I will not destroy, for the sake of the twenty." 32 And he said, "Let not my Lord be angry if I speak but this last time: What if ten should be found there?" And He answered, "I will not destroy, for the sake of the ten." 33 When the LORD had finished speaking to Abraham, He departed; and Abraham returned to his place.

19 1 The two angels arrived in Sodom in the evening, as Lot was sitting in the gate of Sodom. When Lot saw them, he rose to greet them and, bowing low with his face to the ground, 2 he said, "Please, my lords, turn aside to your servant's house to spend the night, and bathe your feet; then you may be on your way early." But they said, "No, we will spend the night in the square." 3 But he urged them strongly, so they turned his way and entered his house. He prepared a feast for them and baked unleavened bread, and they ate. 4 They had not yet lain down, when the townspeople, the men of Sodom, young and old - all the people to the last man - gathered about the house. 5 And they shouted to Lot and said to him, "Where are the men who came to you tonight? Bring them out to us, that we may be intimate with them." 6 So Lot went out to them to the entrance, shut the door behind him, 7 and said, "I beg you, my friends, do not commit such a wrong. 8 Look, I have two daughters who have not known a man. Let me bring them out to you, and you may do to them as you please; but do not do anything to these men, since they have come under the shelter of my roof." 9 But they said, "Stand back! The fellow," they said, "came here as an alien, and already he acts the ruler! Now we will deal worse with you than with them." And they pressed hard against the person of Lot, and moved forward to break the door. 10 But the men stretched out their hands and pulled Lot into the house with them, and shut the door. 11 And the people who were at the entrance of the house, young and old, they struck with blinding light, so that they were helpless to find the entrance. 12 Then the men said to Lot, "Whom else have you here? Sons-in-law, your sons and daughters, or anyone else that you have in the city - bring them out of the place. 13 For we are about to destroy this place; because the outcry against them before the LORD has become so great that the LORD has sent us to destroy it." 14 So Lot went out and spoke to his sons-in-law, who had married his daughters, and said, "Up, get out of this place, for the LORD is about to destroy the city." But he seemed to his sons-in-law as one who jests. 15 As dawn broke, the angels urged Lot on, saying, "Up, take your wife and your two remaining daughters, lest you be swept away because of the iniquity of the city." 16 Still he delayed. So the men seized his hand, and the hands of his wife and his two daughters - in the LORD's mercy on him - and brought him out and left him outside the city. 17 When they had brought them outside, one said, "Flee for your life! Do not look behind you, nor stop anywhere in the Plain; flee to the hills, lest you be swept away." 18 But Lot said to them, "Oh no, my lord! 19 You have been so gracious to your servant, and have already shown me so much kindness in order to save my life; but I cannot flee to the hills, lest the disaster overtake me and I die. 20 Look, that town there is near enough to flee to: it is such a little place! Let me flee there - it is such a little place - and let my life be saved." 21 He replied, "Very well, I will grant you this favor too, and I will not annihilate the town of which you have spoken. 22 Hurry, flee there, for I cannot do anything until you arrive there." Hence the town came to be called Zoar. 23 As the sun rose upon the earth and Lot entered Zoar, 24 the LORD rained upon Sodom and Gomorrah sulfurous fire from the LORD out of heaven. 25 He annihilated those cities and the entire Plain, and all the inhabitants of the cities and the vegetation of the ground. 26 Lot's wife looked back, and she thereupon turned into a pillar of salt.

GENESIS 20 בראשית כ • וירא

27 Next morning, Abraham hurried to the place where he had stood before the LORD, 28 and, looking down toward Sodom and Gomorrah and all the land of the Plain, he saw the smoke of the land rising like the smoke of a kiln. 29 Thus it was that, when God destroyed the cities of the Plain and annihilated the cities where Lot dwelt, God was mindful of Abraham and removed Lot from the midst of the upheaval. 30 Lot went up from Zoar and settled in the hill country with his two daughters, for he was afraid to dwell in Zoar; and he and his two daughters lived in a cave. 31 And the older one said to the younger, "Our father is old, and there is not a man on earth to consort with us in the way of all the world. 32 Come, let us make our father drink wine, and let us lie with him, that we may maintain life through our father." 33 That night they made their father drink wine, and the older one went in and lay with her father; he did not know when she lay down or when she rose. 34 The next day the older one said to the younger, "See, I lay with Father last night; let us make him drink wine tonight also, and you go and lie with him, that we may maintain life through our father." 35 That night also they made their father drink wine, and the younger one went and lay with him; he did not know when she lay down or when she rose. 36 Thus the two daughters of Lot came to be with child by their father. 37 The older one bore a son and named him Moab; he is the father of the Moabites of today. 38 And the younger also bore a son, and she called him Ben-ammi; he is the father of the Ammonites of today.

20 1 Abraham journeyed from there to the region of the Negeb and settled between Kadesh and Shur. While he was sojourning in Gerar, 2 Abraham said of Sarah his wife, "She is my sister." So King Abimelech of Gerar had Sarah brought to him. 3 But God came to Abimelech in a dream by night and said to him, "You are to die because of the woman that you have taken, for she is a married woman." 4 Now Abimelech had not approached her. He said, "O Lord, will You slay people even though innocent? 5 He himself said to me, 'She is my sister!' And she also said, 'He is my brother.' When I did this, my heart was blameless and my hands were clean." 6 And God said to him in the dream, "I knew that you did this with a blameless heart, and so I kept you from sinning against Me. That was why I did not let you touch her. 7 Therefore, restore the man's wife — since he is a prophet, he will intercede for you — to save your life. If you fail to restore her, know that you shall die, you and all that are yours." 8 Early next morning, Abimelech called his servants and told them all that had happened; and the men were greatly frightened. 9 Then Abimelech summoned Abraham and said to him, "What have you done to us? What wrong have I done that you should bring so great a guilt upon me and my kingdom? You have done to me things that ought not to be done. 10 What, then," Abimelech demanded of Abraham, "was your purpose in doing this thing?" 11 "I thought," said Abraham, "surely there is no fear of God in this place, and they will kill me because of my wife. 12 And besides, she is in truth my sister, my father's daughter though not my mother's; and she became my wife. 13 So when God made me wander from my father's house, I said to her, 'Let this be the kindness that you shall do me: whatever place we come to, say there of me: He is my brother.'" 14 Abimelech took sheep and oxen, and male and female slaves, and gave them to Abraham; and he restored his wife Sarah to him. 15 And Abimelech said, "Here, my land is before you; settle wherever you please." 16 And to Sarah he said, "I herewith give your brother a thousand pieces of silver; this will serve you as vindication before all who are with you, and you are cleared before everyone." 17 Abraham then prayed to God, and God healed Abimelech and his wife and his slave girls, so that they bore children; 18 for the LORD had closed fast every womb of the household of Abimelech because of Sarah, the wife of Abraham.

21 1 The LORD took note of Sarah as He had promised, and the LORD did for Sarah as He had spoken. 2 Sarah conceived and bore a son to Abraham in his old age, at the set time of which God had spoken. 3 Abraham gave his newborn son, whom Sarah had borne him, the name of Isaac. 4 And when his son Isaac was eight days old, Abraham circumcised him,

32

GENESIS 22 — בראשית כב וירא

as God had commanded him. 5 Now Abraham was a hundred years old when his son Isaac was born to him. 6 Sarah said, "God has brought me laughter; everyone who hears will laugh with me." 7 And she added, "Who would have said to Abraham that Sarah would suckle children! Yet I have borne a son in his old age." 8 The child grew up and was weaned, and Abraham held a great feast on the day that Isaac was weaned. 9 Sarah saw the son whom Hagar the Egyptian had borne to Abraham playing. 10 She said to Abraham, "Cast out that slave-woman and her son, for the son of that slave shall not share in the inheritance with my son Isaac." 11 The matter distressed Abraham greatly, for it concerned a son of his. 12 But God said to Abraham, "Do not be distressed over the boy or your slave; whatever Sarah tells you, do as she says, for it is through Isaac that offspring shall be continued for you. 13 As for the son of the slave-woman, I will make a nation of him, too, for he is your seed." 14 Early next morning Abraham took some bread and a skin of water, and gave them to Hagar. He placed them over her shoulder, together with the child, and sent her away. And she wandered about in the wilderness of Beer-sheba. 15 When the water was gone from the skin, she left the child under one of the bushes, 16 and went and sat down at a distance, a bowshot away; for she thought, "Let me not look on as the child dies." And sitting thus afar, she burst into tears. 17 God heard the cry of the boy, and an angel of God called to Hagar from heaven and said to her, "What troubles you, Hagar? Fear not, for God has heeded the cry of the boy where he is. 18 Come, lift up the boy and hold him by the hand, for I will make a great nation of him." 19 Then God opened her eyes and she saw a well of water. She went and filled the skin with water, and let the boy drink. 20 God was with the boy and he grew up; he dwelt in the wilderness and became a bowman. 21 He lived in the wilderness of Paran; and his mother got a wife for him from the land of Egypt.

22 At that time Abimelech and Phicol, chief of his troops, said to Abraham, "God is with you in everything that you do. 23 Therefore swear to me here by God that you will not deal falsely with me or with my kith and kin, but will deal with me and with the land in which you have sojourned as loyally as I have dealt with you." 24 And Abraham said, "I swear it." 25 Then Abraham reproached Abimelech for the well of water which the servants of Abimelech had seized. 26 But Abimelech said, "I do not know who did this; you did not tell me, nor have I heard of it until today." 27 Abraham took sheep and oxen and gave them to Abimelech, and the two of them made a pact. 28 Abraham then set seven ewes of the flock by themselves, 29 and Abimelech said to Abraham, "What mean these seven ewes which you have set apart?" 30 He replied, "You are to accept these seven ewes from me as proof that I dug this well." 31 Hence that place was called Beer-sheba, for there the two of them swore an oath. 32 When they had concluded the pact at Beer-sheba, Abimelech and Phicol, chief of his troops, departed and returned to the land of the Philistines. 33 [Abraham] planted a tamarisk at Beer-sheba, and invoked there the name of the LORD, the Everlasting God. 34 And Abraham resided in the land of the Philistines a long time.

22 1 Some time afterward, God put Abraham to the test. He said to him, "Abraham," and he answered, "Here I am." 2 And He said, "Take your son, your favored one, Isaac, whom you love, and go to the land of Moriah, and offer him there as a burnt offering on one of the heights that I will point out to you." 3 So early next morning, Abraham saddled his ass and took with him two of his servants, and his son Isaac. He split the wood for the burnt offering, and he set out for the place of which God had told him. 4 On the third day Abraham looked up and saw the place from afar. 5 Then Abraham said to his servants, "You stay here with the ass. The boy and I will go up there; we will worship and we will return to you." 6 Abraham took the wood for the burnt offering and put it on his son Isaac.

33

GENESIS 23   בראשית כג חיי שרה

He himself took the firestone and the knife; and the two walked off together. 7 Then Isaac said to his father Abraham, "Father!" And he answered, "Yes, my son." And he said, "Here are the firestone and the wood; but where is the sheep for the burnt offering?" 8 And Abraham said, "God will see to the sheep for His burnt offering, my son." And the two of them walked on together. 9 They arrived at the place of which God had told him. Abraham built an altar there; he laid out the wood; he bound his son Isaac; he laid him on the altar, on top of the wood. 10 And Abraham picked up the knife to slay his son. 11 Then an angel of the LORD called to him from heaven: "Abraham! Abraham!" And he answered, "Here I am." 12 And he said, "Do not raise your hand against the boy, or do anything to him. For now I know that you fear God, since you have not withheld your son, your favored one, from Me." 13 When Abraham looked up, his eye fell upon a ram, caught in the thicket by its horns. So Abraham went and took the ram and offered it up as a burnt offering in place of his son. 14 And Abraham named that site Adonai-yireh, whence the present saying, "On the mount of the LORD there is vision." 15 The angel of the LORD called to Abraham a second time from heaven, 16 and said, "By Myself I swear, the LORD declares: Because you have done this and have not withheld your son, your favored one, 17 I will bestow My blessing upon you and make your descendants as numerous as the stars of heaven and the sands on the seashore; and your descendants shall seize the gates of their foes. 18 All the nations of the earth shall bless themselves by your descendants, because you have obeyed My command." 19 Abraham then returned to his servants, and they departed together for Beer-sheba; and Abraham stayed in Beer-sheba.

20 Some time later, Abraham was told, "Milcah too has borne children to your brother Nahor: 21 Uz the first-born, and Buz his brother, and Kemuel the father of Aram; 22 and Chesed, Hazo, Pildash, Jidlaph, and Bethuel"— 23 Bethuel being the father of Rebekah. These eight Milcah bore to Nahor, Abraham's brother. 24 And his concubine, whose name was Reumah, also bore children: Tebah, Gaham, Tahash, and Maacah.

23

Sarah's lifetime—the span of Sarah's life—came to one hundred and twenty-seven years. 2 Sarah died in Kiriath-arba—now Hebron—in the land of Canaan; and Abraham proceeded to mourn for Sarah and to bewail her. 3 Then Abraham rose from beside his dead, and spoke to the Hittites, saying, 4 "I am a resident alien among you; sell me a burial site among you, that I may remove my dead for burial." 5 And the Hittites replied to Abraham, saying to him, 6 "Hear us, my lord: you are the elect of God among us. Bury your dead in the choicest of our burial places; none of us will withhold his burial place from you for burying your dead." 7 Thereupon Abraham bowed low to the people of the land, the Hittites, 8 and he said to them, "If it is your wish that I remove my dead for burial, you must agree to intercede for me with Ephron son of Zohar. 9 Let him sell me the cave of Machpelah that he owns, which is at the edge of his land. Let him sell it to me, at the full price, for a burial site in your midst." 10 Ephron was present among the Hittites; so Ephron the Hittite answered Abraham in the hearing of the Hittites, all who entered the gate of his town, saying, 11 "No, my lord, hear me: I give you the field and I give you the cave that is in it; I give it to you in the presence of my people. Bury your dead." 12 Then Abraham bowed low before the people of the land, 13 and spoke to Ephron in the hearing of the people of the land, saying, "If only you would hear me out! Let me pay the price of the land; accept it from me, that I may bury my dead there." 14 And Ephron replied to Abraham, saying to him, 15 "My lord, do hear me! A piece of land worth four hundred shekels of silver—what is that between you and me? Go and bury your dead." 16 Abraham accepted Ephron's terms. Abraham paid out to Ephron the money that he had named in the hearing of the Hittites—four hundred shekels of silver

34

GENESIS 24   בראשית כד חיי שרה

at the going merchants' rate. 17 So Ephron's land in Machpelah, near Mamre - the field with its cave and all the trees anywhere within the confines of that field - passed 18 to Abraham as his possession, in the presence of the Hittites, of all who entered the gate of his town. 19 And then Abraham buried his wife Sarah in the cave of the field of Machpelah, facing Mamre - now Hebron - in the land of Canaan. 20 Thus the field with its cave passed from the Hittites to Abraham, as a burial site.

24 1 Abraham was now old, advanced in years, and the LORD had blessed Abraham in all things. 2 And Abraham said to the senior servant of his household, who had charge of all that he owned, "Put your hand under my thigh 3 and I will make you swear by the LORD, the God of heaven and the God of the earth, that you will not take a wife for my son from the daughters of the Canaanites among whom I dwell, 4 but will go to the land of my birth and get a wife for my son Isaac." 5 And the servant said to him, "What if the woman does not consent to follow me to this land, shall I then take your son back to the land from which you came?" 6 Abraham answered him, "On no account must you take my son back there! 7 The LORD, the God of heaven, who took me from my father's house and from my native land, who promised me on oath, saying, 'I will assign this land to your offspring' - He will send His angel before you, and you will get a wife for my son from there. 8 And if the woman does not consent to follow you, you shall then be clear of this oath to me; but do not take my son back there." 9 So the servant put his hand under the thigh of his master Abraham and swore to him as bidden. 10 Then the servant took ten of his master's camels and set out, taking with him all the bounty of his master; and he made his way to Aram-naharaim, to the city of Nahor. 11 He made the camels kneel down by the well outside the city, at evening time, the time when women come out to draw water. 12 And he said, "O LORD, God of my master Abraham, grant me good fortune this day, and deal graciously with my master Abraham: 13 Here I stand by the spring as the daughters of the townsmen come out to draw water; 14 let the maiden to whom I say, 'Please, lower your jar that I may drink,' and who replies, 'Drink, and I will also water your camels' - let her be the one whom You have decreed for Your servant Isaac. Thereby shall I know that You have dealt graciously with my master." 15 He had scarcely finished speaking, when Rebekah, who was born to Bethuel, the son of Milcah the wife of Abraham's brother Nahor, came out with her jar on her shoulder. 16 The maiden was very beautiful, a virgin whom no man had known. She went down to the spring, filled her jar, and came up. 17 The servant ran toward her and said, "Please, let me sip a little water from your jar." 18 "Drink, my lord," she said, and she quickly lowered her jar upon her hand and let him drink. 19 When she had let him drink his fill, she said, "I will also draw for your camels, until they finish drinking." 20 Quickly emptying her jar into the trough, she ran back to the well to draw, and she drew for all his camels. 21 The man, meanwhile, stood gazing at her, silently wondering whether the LORD had made his errand successful or not. 22 When the camels had finished drinking, the man took a gold nose-ring weighing a half-shekel, and two gold bands for her arms, ten shekels in weight. 23 "Pray tell me," he said, "whose daughter are you? Is there room in your father's house for us to spend the night?" 24 She replied, "I am the daughter of Bethuel the son of Milcah, whom she bore to Nahor." 25 And she went on, "There is plenty of straw and feed at home, and also room to spend the night." 26 The man bowed low in homage to the LORD 27 and said, "Blessed be the LORD, the God of my master Abraham, who has not withheld His steadfast faithfulness from my master. For I have been guided on my errand by the LORD, to the house of my master's kinsmen." 28 The maiden ran and told all this to her mother's household. 29 Now Rebekah had a brother whose name was Laban. Laban ran out to the man at the spring 30 when he saw the nose-ring and the bands on his sister's arms, and when he heard his sister Rebekah say, "Thus the man spoke to me." He went up to the man, who was still standing beside the camels at the spring. 31 "Come in, O blessed of the LORD," he said,

עֹבֵ֣ר לַסֹּחֵֽר׃ יז וַיָּ֣קָם ׀ שְׂדֵ֣ה עֶפְר֗וֹן אֲשֶׁר֙ בַּמַּכְפֵּלָ֔ה אֲשֶׁ֖ר לִפְנֵ֣י מַמְרֵ֑א הַשָּׂדֶה֙ וְהַמְּעָרָ֣ה אֲשֶׁר־בּ֔וֹ וְכָל־הָעֵץ֙ אֲשֶׁ֣ר בַּשָּׂדֶ֔ה אֲשֶׁ֖ר בְּכָל־גְּבֻל֣וֹ סָבִֽיב׃ יח לְאַבְרָהָ֥ם לְמִקְנָ֖ה לְעֵינֵ֣י בְנֵי־חֵ֑ת בְּכֹ֖ל בָּאֵ֥י שַֽׁעַר־עִירֽוֹ׃ יט וְאַחֲרֵי־כֵן֩ קָבַ֨ר אַבְרָהָ֜ם אֶת־שָׂרָ֣ה אִשְׁתּ֗וֹ אֶל־מְעָרַ֞ת שְׂדֵ֧ה הַמַּכְפֵּלָ֛ה עַל־פְּנֵ֥י מַמְרֵ֖א הִ֣וא חֶבְר֑וֹן בְּאֶ֖רֶץ כְּנָֽעַן׃ כ וַיָּ֨קָם הַשָּׂדֶ֧ה וְהַמְּעָרָ֛ה אֲשֶׁר־בּ֖וֹ לְאַבְרָהָ֑ם לַאֲחֻזַּת־קָ֖בֶר מֵאֵ֥ת בְּנֵי־חֵֽת׃

כד א וְאַבְרָהָ֣ם זָקֵ֔ן בָּ֖א בַּיָּמִ֑ים וַֽיהוָ֛ה בֵּרַ֥ךְ אֶת־אַבְרָהָ֖ם בַּכֹּֽל׃ ב וַיֹּ֣אמֶר אַבְרָהָ֗ם אֶל־עַבְדּוֹ֙ זְקַ֣ן בֵּית֔וֹ הַמֹּשֵׁ֖ל בְּכָל־אֲשֶׁר־ל֑וֹ שִֽׂים־נָ֥א יָדְךָ֖ תַּ֥חַת יְרֵכִֽי׃ ג וְאַשְׁבִּ֣יעֲךָ֔ בַּֽיהוָה֙ אֱלֹהֵ֣י הַשָּׁמַ֔יִם וֵֽאלֹהֵ֖י הָאָ֑רֶץ אֲשֶׁ֨ר לֹֽא־תִקַּ֤ח אִשָּׁה֙ לִבְנִ֔י מִבְּנוֹת֙ הַֽכְּנַעֲנִ֔י אֲשֶׁ֥ר אָנֹכִ֖י יוֹשֵׁ֥ב בְּקִרְבּֽוֹ׃ ד כִּ֧י אֶל־אַרְצִ֛י וְאֶל־מוֹלַדְתִּ֖י תֵּלֵ֑ךְ וְלָקַחְתָּ֥ אִשָּׁ֖ה לִבְנִ֥י לְיִצְחָֽק׃ ה וַיֹּ֤אמֶר אֵלָיו֙ הָעֶ֔בֶד אוּלַי֙ לֹא־תֹאבֶ֣ה הָֽאִשָּׁ֔ה לָלֶ֥כֶת אַחֲרַ֖י אֶל־הָאָ֣רֶץ הַזֹּ֑את הֶֽהָשֵׁ֤ב אָשִׁיב֙ אֶת־בִּנְךָ֔ אֶל־הָאָ֖רֶץ אֲשֶׁר־יָצָ֥אתָ מִשָּֽׁם׃ ו וַיֹּ֥אמֶר אֵלָ֖יו אַבְרָהָ֑ם הִשָּׁ֣מֶר לְךָ֔ פֶּן־תָּשִׁ֥יב אֶת־בְּנִ֖י שָֽׁמָּה׃ ז יְהוָ֣ה ׀ אֱלֹהֵ֣י הַשָּׁמַ֗יִם אֲשֶׁ֤ר לְקָחַ֙נִי֙ מִבֵּ֣ית אָבִ֔י וּמֵאֶ֖רֶץ מֽוֹלַדְתִּ֑י וַאֲשֶׁ֨ר דִּבֶּר־לִ֜י וַאֲשֶׁ֤ר נִֽשְׁבַּֽע־לִי֙ לֵאמֹ֔ר לְזַ֨רְעֲךָ֔ אֶתֵּ֖ן אֶת־הָאָ֣רֶץ הַזֹּ֑את ה֗וּא יִשְׁלַ֤ח מַלְאָכוֹ֙ לְפָנֶ֔יךָ וְלָקַחְתָּ֥ אִשָּׁ֛ה לִבְנִ֖י מִשָּֽׁם׃ ח וְאִם־לֹ֨א תֹאבֶ֤ה הָֽאִשָּׁה֙ לָלֶ֣כֶת אַחֲרֶ֔יךָ וְנִקִּ֕יתָ מִשְּׁבֻעָתִ֖י זֹ֑את רַ֣ק אֶת־בְּנִ֔י לֹ֥א תָשֵׁ֖ב שָֽׁמָּה׃ ט וַיָּ֤שֶׂם הָעֶ֙בֶד֙ אֶת־יָד֔וֹ תַּ֛חַת יֶ֥רֶךְ אַבְרָהָ֖ם אֲדֹנָ֑יו וַיִּשָּׁ֣בַֽע ל֔וֹ עַל־הַדָּבָ֖ר הַזֶּֽה׃ י וַיִּקַּ֣ח הָ֠עֶבֶד עֲשָׂרָ֨ה גְמַלִּ֜ים מִגְּמַלֵּ֤י אֲדֹנָיו֙ וַיֵּ֔לֶךְ וְכָל־ט֥וּב אֲדֹנָ֖יו בְּיָד֑וֹ וַיָּ֗קָם וַיֵּ֛לֶךְ אֶל־אֲרַ֥ם נַֽהֲרַ֖יִם אֶל־עִ֥יר נָחֽוֹר׃ יא וַיַּבְרֵ֧ךְ הַגְּמַלִּ֛ים מִח֥וּץ לָעִ֖יר אֶל־בְּאֵ֣ר הַמָּ֑יִם לְעֵ֣ת עֶ֔רֶב לְעֵ֖ת צֵ֥את הַשֹּׁאֲבֹֽת׃ יב וַיֹּאמַ֓ר ׀ יְהוָ֗ה אֱלֹהֵי֙ אֲדֹנִ֣י אַבְרָהָ֔ם הַקְרֵה־נָ֥א לְפָנַ֖י הַיּ֑וֹם וַעֲשֵׂה־חֶ֕סֶד עִ֖ם אֲדֹנִ֥י אַבְרָהָֽם׃ יג הִנֵּ֛ה אָנֹכִ֥י נִצָּ֖ב עַל־עֵ֣ין הַמָּ֑יִם וּבְנוֹת֙ אַנְשֵׁ֣י הָעִ֔יר יֹצְאֹ֖ת לִשְׁאֹ֥ב מָֽיִם׃ יד וְהָיָ֣ה הַֽנַּעֲרָ֗ אֲשֶׁ֨ר אֹמַ֤ר אֵלֶ֙יהָ֙ הַטִּי־נָ֤א כַדֵּךְ֙ וְאֶשְׁתֶּ֔ה וְאָמְרָ֣ה שְׁתֵ֔ה וְגַם־גְּמַלֶּ֖יךָ אַשְׁקֶ֑ה אֹתָ֤הּ הֹכַ֙חְתָּ֙ לְעַבְדְּךָ֣ לְיִצְחָ֔ק וּבָ֣הּ אֵדַ֔ע כִּי־עָשִׂ֥יתָ חֶ֖סֶד עִם־אֲדֹנִֽי׃ טו וַֽיְהִי־ה֗וּא טֶרֶם֮ כִּלָּ֣ה לְדַבֵּר֒ וְהִנֵּ֧ה רִבְקָ֣ה יֹצֵ֗את אֲשֶׁ֤ר יֻלְּדָה֙ לִבְתוּאֵ֣ל בֶּן־מִלְכָּ֔ה אֵ֥שֶׁת נָח֖וֹר אֲחִ֣י אַבְרָהָ֑ם וְכַדָּ֖הּ עַל־שִׁכְמָֽהּ׃ טז וְהַֽנַּעֲרָ֗ טֹבַ֤ת מַרְאֶה֙ מְאֹ֔ד בְּתוּלָ֕ה וְאִ֖ישׁ לֹ֣א יְדָעָ֑הּ וַתֵּ֣רֶד הָעַ֔יְנָה וַתְּמַלֵּ֥א כַדָּ֖הּ וַתָּֽעַל׃ יז וַיָּ֥רָץ הָעֶ֖בֶד לִקְרָאתָ֑הּ וַיֹּ֕אמֶר הַגְמִיאִ֥ינִי נָ֛א מְעַט־מַ֖יִם מִכַּדֵּֽךְ׃ יח וַתֹּ֖אמֶר שְׁתֵ֣ה אֲדֹנִ֑י וַתְּמַהֵ֗ר וַתֹּ֧רֶד כַּדָּ֛הּ עַל־יָדָ֖הּ וַתַּשְׁקֵֽהוּ׃ יט וַתְּכַ֖ל לְהַשְׁקֹת֑וֹ וַתֹּ֗אמֶר גַּ֤ם לִגְמַלֶּ֙יךָ֙ אֶשְׁאָ֔ב עַ֥ד אִם־כִּלּ֖וּ לִשְׁתֹּֽת׃ כ וַתְּמַהֵ֗ר וַתְּעַ֤ר כַּדָּהּ֙ אֶל־הַשֹּׁ֔קֶת וַתָּ֥רָץ ע֛וֹד אֶֽל־הַבְּאֵ֖ר לִשְׁאֹ֑ב וַתִּשְׁאַ֖ב לְכָל־גְּמַלָּֽיו׃ כא וְהָאִ֥ישׁ מִשְׁתָּאֵ֖ה לָ֑הּ מַחֲרִ֕ישׁ לָדַ֗עַת הַֽהִצְלִ֧יחַ יְהוָ֛ה דַּרְכּ֖וֹ אִם־לֹֽא׃ כב וַיְהִ֗י כַּאֲשֶׁ֨ר כִּלּ֤וּ הַגְּמַלִּים֙ לִשְׁתּ֔וֹת וַיִּקַּ֤ח הָאִישׁ֙ נֶ֣זֶם זָהָ֔ב בֶּ֖קַע מִשְׁקָל֑וֹ וּשְׁנֵ֤י צְמִידִים֙ עַל־יָדֶ֔יהָ עֲשָׂרָ֥ה זָהָ֖ב מִשְׁקָלָֽם׃ כג וַיֹּ֙אמֶר֙ בַּת־מִ֣י אַ֔תְּ הַגִּ֥ידִי נָ֖א לִ֑י הֲיֵ֧שׁ בֵּית־אָבִ֛יךְ מָק֥וֹם לָ֖נוּ לָלִֽין׃ כד וַתֹּ֣אמֶר אֵלָ֔יו בַּת־בְּתוּאֵ֖ל אָנֹ֑כִי בֶּן־מִלְכָּ֕ה אֲשֶׁ֥ר יָלְדָ֖ה לְנָחֽוֹר׃ כה וַתֹּ֣אמֶר אֵלָ֔יו גַּם־תֶּ֥בֶן גַּם־מִסְפּ֖וֹא רַ֣ב עִמָּ֑נוּ גַּם־מָק֖וֹם לָלֽוּן׃ כו וַיִּקֹּ֣ד הָאִ֔ישׁ וַיִּשְׁתַּ֖חוּ לַֽיהוָֽה׃ כז וַיֹּ֗אמֶר בָּר֤וּךְ יְהוָה֙ אֱלֹהֵי֙ אֲדֹנִ֣י אַבְרָהָ֔ם אֲ֠שֶׁר לֹֽא־עָזַ֥ב חַסְדּ֛וֹ וַאֲמִתּ֖וֹ מֵעִ֣ם אֲדֹנִ֑י אָנֹכִ֗י בַּדֶּ֙רֶךְ֙ נָחַ֣נִי יְהוָ֔ה בֵּ֖ית אֲחֵ֥י אֲדֹנִֽי׃ כח וַתָּ֙רָץ֙ הַֽנַּעֲרָ֔ וַתַּגֵּ֖ד לְבֵ֣ית אִמָּ֑הּ כַּדְּבָרִ֖ים הָאֵֽלֶּה׃ כט וּלְרִבְקָ֥ה אָ֖ח וּשְׁמ֣וֹ לָבָ֑ן וַיָּ֨רָץ לָבָ֧ן אֶל־הָאִ֛ישׁ הַח֖וּצָה אֶל־הָעָֽיִן׃ ל וַיְהִ֣י ׀ כִּרְאֹ֣ת אֶת־הַנֶּ֗זֶם וְֽאֶת־הַצְּמִדִים֮ עַל־יְדֵ֣י אֲחֹתוֹ֒ וּכְשָׁמְע֗וֹ אֶת־דִּבְרֵ֞י רִבְקָ֤ה אֲחֹתוֹ֙ לֵאמֹ֔ר כֹּֽה־דִבֶּ֥ר אֵלַ֖י הָאִ֑ישׁ וַיָּבֹא֙ אֶל־הָאִ֔ישׁ וְהִנֵּ֛ה עֹמֵ֥ד עַל־הַגְּמַלִּ֖ים עַל־הָעָֽיִן׃ לא וַיֹּ֕אמֶר בּ֖וֹא בְּר֣וּךְ יְהוָ֑ה

※ 35 ※

GENESIS 24

"Why do you remain outside, when I have made ready the house and a place for the camels?" 32 So the man entered the house, and the camels were unloaded. The camels were given straw and feed, and water was brought to bathe his feet and the feet of the men with him. 33 But when food was set before him, he said, "I will not eat until I have told my tale." He said, "Speak, then." 34 "I am Abraham's servant," he began. 35 "The LORD has greatly blessed my master, and he has become rich: He has given him sheep and cattle, silver and gold, male and female slaves, camels and asses. 36 And Sarah, my master's wife, bore my master a son in her old age, and he has assigned to him everything he owns. 37 Now my master made me swear, saying, 'You shall not get a wife for my son from the daughters of the Canaanites in whose land I dwell; 38 but you shall go to my father's house, to my kindred, and get a wife for my son.' 39 And I said to my master, 'What if the woman does not follow me?' 40 He replied to me, 'The LORD, whose ways I have followed, will send His angel with you and make your errand successful; and you will get a wife for my son from my kindred, from my father's house. 41 Thus only shall you be freed from my adjuration: if, when you come to my kindred, they refuse you — only then shall you be freed from my adjuration.' 42 I came today to the spring, and I said: O LORD, God of my master Abraham, if You would indeed grant success to the errand on which I am engaged! 43 As I stand by the spring of water, let the young woman who comes out to draw and to whom I say, Please, let me drink a little water from your jar,' 44 and who answers, 'You may drink, and I will also draw for your camels' — let her be the wife whom the LORD has decreed for my master's son.' 45 I had scarcely finished praying in my heart, when Rebekah came out with her jar on her shoulder, and went down to the spring and drew. And I said to her, 'Please give me a drink.' 46 She quickly lowered her jar and said, 'Drink, and I will also water your camels.' So I drank, and she also watered the camels. 47 I inquired of her, 'Whose daughter are you?' And she said, 'The daughter of Bethuel, son of Nahor, whom Milcah bore to him.' And I put the ring on her nose and the bands on her arms. 48 Then I bowed low in homage to the LORD and blessed the LORD, the God of my master Abraham, who led me on the right way to get the daughter of my master's brother for his son. 49 And now, if you mean to treat my master with true kindness, tell me; and if not, tell me also, that I may turn right or left." 50 Then Laban and Bethuel answered, "The matter was decreed by the LORD; we cannot speak to you bad or good. 51 Here is Rebekah before you; take her and go, and let her be a wife to your master's son, as the LORD has spoken." 52 When Abraham's servant heard their words, he bowed low to the ground before the LORD. 53 The servant brought out objects of silver and gold, and garments, and gave them to Rebekah; and he gave presents to her brother and her mother. 54 Then he and the men with him ate and drank, and they spent the night. When they arose next morning, he said, "Give me leave to go to my master." 55 But her brother and her mother said, "Let the maiden remain with us some ten days; then you may go." 56 He said to them, "Do not delay me, now that the LORD has made my errand successful. Give me leave that I may go to my master." 57 And they said, "Let us call the girl and ask for her reply." 58 They called Rebekah and said to her, "Will you go with this man?" And she said, "I will." 59 So they sent off their sister Rebekah and her nurse along with Abraham's servant and his men. 60 And they blessed Rebekah and said to her, "O sister! May you grow into thousands of myriads; May your offspring seize the gates of their foes." 61 Then Rebekah and her maids arose, mounted the camels, and followed the man. So the servant took Rebekah and went his way. 62 Isaac had just come back from the vicinity of Beer-lahai-roi, for he was settled in the region of the Negeb. 63 And Isaac went out walking in the field toward evening and, looking up, he saw camels approaching. 64 Raising his eyes, Rebekah saw Isaac. She alighted from the camel 65 and said to the servant, "Who is that man walking in the field toward us?" And the servant said, "That is my master." So she took her veil and covered herself. 66 The servant told Isaac all the things that he had done. 67 Isaac then brought her into the tent of his mother Sarah, and he took Rebekah as his wife. Isaac loved her, and thus found comfort after his mother's death.

Opening page of the Book of Genesis, from an illustrated manuscript of the Bible, Avignon, France, ca. 1422, collection of Pierpont Morgan Library, New York

GENESIS 25 בראשית כה חיי שרה

25 1 Abraham took another wife, whose name was Keturah. 2 She bore him Zimran, Jokshan, Medan, Midian, Ishbak, and Shuah. 3 Jokshan begot Sheba and Dedan. The descendants of Dedan were the Asshurim, the Letushim, and the Leummim. 4 The descendants of Midian were Ephah, Epher, Enoch, Abida, and Eldaah. All these were descendants of Keturah. 5 Abraham willed all that he owned to Isaac; 6 but to Abraham's sons by concubines Abraham gave gifts while he was still living, and he sent them away from his son Isaac eastward, to the land of the East. 7 This was the total span of Abraham's life: one hundred and seventy-five years. 8 And Abraham breathed his last, dying at a good ripe age, old and contented; and he was gathered to his kin. 9 His sons Isaac and Ishmael buried him in the cave of Machpelah, in the field of Ephron son of Zohar the Hittite, facing Mamre, 10 the field that Abraham had bought from the Hittites; there Abraham was buried, and Sarah his wife. 11 After the death of Abraham, God blessed his son Isaac. And Isaac settled near Beer-lahai-roi.

12 This is the line of Ishmael, Abraham's son, whom Hagar the Egyptian, Sarah's slave, bore to Abraham. 13 These are the names of the sons of Ishmael, by their names, in the order of their birth: Nebaioth, the first-born of Ishmael, Kedar, Adbeel, Mibsam, 14 Mishma, Dumah, Massa, 15 Hadad, Tema, Jetur, Naphish, and Kedmah. 16 These are the sons of Ishmael and these are their names by their villages and by their encampments: twelve chieftains of as many tribes. 17 These were the years of the life of Ishmael: one hundred and thirty-seven years; then he breathed his last and died, and was gathered to his kin. 18 They dwelt from Havilah, by Shur, which is close to Egypt, all the way to Asshur; they camped alongside all their kinsmen.

19 This is the story of Isaac, son of Abraham. Abraham begot Isaac. 20 Isaac was forty years old when he took to wife Rebekah, daughter of Bethuel the Aramean of Paddan-aram, sister of Laban the Aramean. 21 Isaac pleaded with the LORD on behalf of his wife, because she was barren; and the LORD responded to his plea, and his wife Rebekah conceived. 22 But the children struggled in her womb, and she said, "If so, why do I exist?" She went to inquire of the LORD. 23 and the LORD answered her, "Two nations are in your womb, Two separate peoples shall issue from your body; One people shall be mightier than the other, And the older shall serve the younger." 24 When her time to give birth was at hand, there were twins in her womb. 25 The first one emerged red, like a hairy mantle all over; so they named him Esau. 26 Then his brother emerged, holding on to the heel of Esau; so they named him Jacob. Isaac was sixty years old when they were born. 27 When the boys grew up, Esau became a skillful hunter, a man of the outdoors; but Jacob was a mild man who stayed in camp. 28 Isaac favored Esau because he had a taste for game; but Rebekah favored Jacob. 29 Once when Jacob was cooking a stew, Esau came in from the open, famished. 30 And Esau said to Jacob, "Give me some of that red stuff to gulp down, for I am famished" – which is why he was named Edom. 31 Jacob said, "First sell me your birthright." 32 And Esau said, "I am at the point of death, so of what use is my birthright to me?" 33 But Jacob said, "Swear to me first." So he swore to him, and sold his birthright to Jacob. 34 Jacob then gave Esau bread and lentil stew; he ate and drank, and he rose and went away. Thus did Esau spurn the birthright.

26 1 There was a famine in the land – aside from the previous famine that had occurred in the days of Abraham – and Isaac went to Abimelech, king of the Philistines, in Gerar. 2 The LORD had appeared to him and said, "Do not go down to Egypt; stay in the land which I point out to you. 3 Reside in this land, and I will be with you and bless you; I will assign all these lands to you and to your heirs, fulfilling the oath that I swore to your father Abraham.

GENESIS 27 — בראשית כז תולדת

4 I will make your heirs as numerous as the stars of heaven, and assign to your heirs all these lands, so that all the nations of the earth shall bless themselves by your heirs 5 inasmuch as Abraham obeyed Me and kept My charge: My commandments, My laws, and My teachings." 6 So Isaac stayed in Gerar. 7 When the men of the place asked him about his wife, he said, "She is my sister," for he was afraid to say "my wife," thinking, "The men of the place might kill me on account of Rebekah, for she is beautiful." 8 When some time had passed, Abimelech king of the Philistines, looking out of the window, saw Isaac fondling his wife Rebekah. 9 Abimelech sent for Isaac and said, "So she is your wife! Why then did you say: 'She is my sister?'" Isaac said to him, "Because I thought I might lose my life on account of her." 10 Abimelech said, "What have you done to us! One of the people might have lain with your wife, and you would have brought guilt upon us." 11 Abimelech then charged all the people, saying, "Anyone who molests this man or his wife shall be put to death." 12 Isaac sowed in that land and reaped a hundredfold the same year. The LORD blessed him, 13 and the man grew richer and richer until he was very wealthy: 14 he acquired flocks and herds, and a large household, so that the Philistines envied him. 15 And the Philistines stopped up all the wells which his father's servants had dug in the days of his father Abraham, filling them with earth. 16 And Abimelech said to Isaac, "Go away from us, for you have become far too big for us." 17 So Isaac departed from there and encamped in the wadi of Gerar, where he settled. 18 Isaac dug anew the wells which had been dug in the days of his father Abraham and which the Philistines had stopped up after Abraham's death; and he gave them the same names that his father had given them. 19 But when Isaac's servants, digging in the wadi, found there a well of spring water, 20 the herdsmen of Gerar quarreled with Isaac's herdsmen, saying, "The water is ours." He named that well Esek, because they contended with him. 21 And when they dug another well, they disputed over that one also; so he named it Sitnah. 22 He moved from there and dug yet another well, and they did not quarrel over it; so he called it Rehoboth, saying, "Now at last the LORD has granted us ample space to increase in the land." 23 From there he went up to Beer-sheba. 24 That night the LORD appeared to him and said, "I am the God of your father Abraham. Fear not, for I am with you, and I will bless you and increase your offspring for the sake of My servant Abraham." 25 So he built an altar there and invoked the LORD by name. Isaac pitched his tent there and his servants started digging a well. 26 And Abimelech came to him from Gerar, with Ahuzzath his councilor and Phicol chief of his troops. 27 Isaac said to them, "Why have you come to me, seeing that you have been hostile to me and have driven me away from you?" 28 And they said, "We now see plainly that the LORD has been with you, and we thought: Let there be a sworn treaty between our two parties, between you and us. Let us make a pact with you 29 that you will not do us harm, just as we have not molested you but have always dealt kindly with you and sent you away in peace. From now on, be you blessed of the LORD!" 30 Then he made for them a feast, and they ate and drank. 31 Early in the morning, they exchanged oaths. Isaac then bade them farewell, and they departed from there in peace. 32 That same day Isaac's servants came and told him about the well they had dug, and said to him, "We have found water!" 33 He named it Shibah; therefore the name of the city is Beer-sheba to this day. 34 When Esau was forty years old, he took to wife Judith daughter of Beeri the Hittite, and Basemath daughter of Elon the Hittite; 35 and they were a source of bitterness to Isaac and Rebekah.

27 1 When Isaac was old and his eyes were too dim to see, he called his older son Esau and said to him, "My son." He answered, "Here I am." 2 And he said, "I am old now, and I do not know how soon I may die. 3 Take your gear, your quiver and bow, and go out into the open and hunt me some game. 4 Then prepare a dish for me such as I like, and bring it to me to eat, so that I may give you my innermost blessing before I die." 5 Rebekah had been listening as Isaac spoke to his son Esau. When Esau had gone out into the open to hunt game to bring home, 6 Rebekah

GENESIS 27 · בראשית כז תולדת

to her son Jacob, "I overheard your father speaking to your brother Esau, saying, 7 'Bring me some game and prepare a dish for me to eat, that I may bless you, with the LORD's approval, before I die.' 8 Now, my son, listen carefully as I instruct you. 9 Go to the flock and fetch me two choice kids, and I will make of them a dish for your father, such as he likes. 10 Then take it to your father to eat, in order that he may bless you before he dies." 11 Jacob answered his mother Rebekah, "But my brother Esau is a hairy man and I am smooth-skinned. 12 If my father touches me, I shall appear to him as a trickster and bring upon myself a curse, not a blessing." 13 But his mother said to him, "Your curse, my son, be upon me! Just do as I say and go fetch them for me." 14 He got them and brought them to his mother, and his mother prepared a dish such as his father liked. 15 Rebekah then took the best clothes of her older son Esau, which were there in the house, and had her younger son Jacob put them on; 16 and she covered his hands and the hairless part of his neck with the skins of the kids. 17 Then she put in the hands of her son Jacob the dish and the bread that she had prepared. 18 He went to his father and said, "Father." And he said, "Yes, which of my sons are you?" 19 Jacob said to his father, "I am Esau, your first-born; I have done as you told me. Pray sit up and eat of my game, that you may give me your innermost blessing." 20 Isaac said to his son, "How did you succeed so quickly, my son?" And he said, "Because the LORD your God granted me good fortune." 21 Isaac said to Jacob, "Come closer that I may feel you, my son—whether you are really my son Esau or not." 22 So Jacob drew close to his father Isaac, who felt him and wondered. "The voice is the voice of Jacob, yet the hands are the hands of Esau." 23 He did not recognize him, because his hands were hairy like those of his brother Esau; and so he blessed him. 24 He asked, "Are you really my son Esau?" And when he said, "I am," 25 he said, "Serve me and let me eat of my son's game that I may give you my innermost blessing." So he served him and he ate, and he brought him wine and he drank. 26 Then his father Isaac said to him, "Come close and kiss me, my son;" 27 and he went up and kissed him. And he smelled his clothes and he blessed him, saying, "Ah, the smell of my son is like the smell of the fields that the LORD has blessed. 28 May God give you of the dew of heaven and the fat of the earth, abundance of new grain and wine. 29 Let peoples serve you, and nations bow to you; be master over your brothers, and let your mother's sons bow to you. Cursed be they who curse you, blessed they who bless you." 30 No sooner had Jacob left the presence of his father Isaac - after Isaac had finished blessing Jacob - than his brother Esau came back from his hunt. 31 He too prepared a dish and brought it to his father. And he said to his father, "Let my father sit up and eat of his son's game, so that you may give me your innermost blessing." 32 His father Isaac said to him, "Who are you?" And he said, "I am your son, Esau, your first-born!" 33 Isaac was seized with very violent trembling. "Who was it then," he demanded, "that hunted game and brought it to me? Moreover, I ate of it before you came, and I blessed him; now he must remain blessed!" 34 When Esau heard his father's words, he burst into wild and bitter sobbing, and said to his father, "Bless me too, Father!" 35 But he answered, "Your brother came with guile and took away your blessing." 36 [Esau] said, "Was he, then, named Jacob that he might supplant me these two times? First he took away my birthright and now he has taken away my blessing!" And he added, "Have you not reserved a blessing for me?" 37 Isaac answered, saying to Esau, "But I have made him master over you: I have given him all his brothers for servants, and sustained him with grain and wine. What, then, can I still do for you, my son? 38 And Esau said to his father, "Have you but one blessing, Father? Bless me too, Father!" And Esau wept aloud. 39 And his father Isaac answered, saying to him, "See, your abode shall enjoy the fat of the earth and the dew of heaven above. 40 Yet by your sword you shall live, and you shall serve your brother; but when you grow restive, you shall break his yoke from your neck." 41 Now Esau harbored a grudge against Jacob because of the blessing which his father had given him, and Esau said to himself, "Let but the mourning period of my father come, and I will kill my brother Jacob." 42 When the words of her older son Esau were reported to Rebekah, she sent for her younger son Jacob and said to him, "Your brother

GENESIS 28 — בראשית כח תולדת

Esau is consoling himself by planning to kill you. 43 Now, my son, listen to me. Flee at once to Haran, to my brother Laban. 44 Stay with him a while, until your brother's fury subsides –45 until your brother's anger against you subsides – and he forgets what you have done to him. Then I will fetch you from there. Let me not lose you both in one day!" 46 Rebekah said to Isaac, "I am disgusted with my life because of the Hittite women. If Jacob marries a Hittite woman like these, from among the native women, what good will life be to me?" **28** 1 So Isaac sent for Jacob and blessed him. He instructed him, saying, "You shall not take a wife from among the Canaanite women. 2 Up, go to Paddan-aram, to the house of Bethuel, your mother's father, and take a wife from among the daughters of Laban, your mother's brother. 3 May El Shaddai bless you, make you fertile and numerous, so that you become an assembly of peoples. 4 May He grant the blessing of Abraham to you and your offspring, that you may possess the land where you are sojourning, which God assigned to Abraham." 5 Then Isaac sent Jacob off, and he went to Paddan-aram, to Laban the son of Bethuel the Aramean, the brother of Rebekah, mother of Jacob and Esau. 6 When Esau saw that Isaac had blessed Jacob and sent him off to Paddan-aram to take a wife from there, charging him, as he blessed him, "You shall not take a wife from among the Canaanite women," 7 and that Jacob had obeyed his father and mother and gone to Paddan-aram, 8 Esau realized that the Canaanite women displeased his father Isaac. 9 So Esau went to Ishmael and took to wife, in addition to the wives he had, Mahalath the daughter of Ishmael son of Abraham, sister of Nebaioth. 10 Jacob left Beer-sheba, and set out for Haran. 11 He came upon a certain place and stopped there for the night, for the sun had set. Taking one of the stones of that place, he put it under his head and lay down in that place. 12 He had a dream; a stairway was set on the ground and its top reached to the sky, and angels of God were going up and down on it. 13 And the LORD was standing beside him and He said, "I am the LORD, the God of your father Abraham and the God of Isaac: the ground on which you are lying I will assign to you and to your offspring. 14 Your descendants shall be as the dust of the earth; you shall spread out to the west and to the east, to the north and to the south. All the families of the earth shall bless themselves by you and your descendants. 15 Remember, I am with you: I will protect you wherever you go and will bring you back to this land. I will not leave you until I have done what I have promised you." 16 Jacob awoke from his sleep and said, "Surely the LORD is present in this place, and I did not know it!" 17 Shaken, he said, "How awesome is this place! This is none other than the abode of God, and that is the gateway to heaven." 18 Early in the morning, Jacob took the stone that he had put under his head and set it up as a pillar and poured oil on the top of it. 19 He named that site Bethel; but previously the name of the city had been Luz. 20 Jacob then made a vow, saying, "If God remains with me, if He protects me on this journey that I am making, and gives me bread to eat and clothing to wear, 21 and if I return safe to my father's house - the LORD shall be my God. 22 And this stone, which I have set up as a pillar, shall be God's abode: and of all that You give me, I will set aside a tithe for You." **29** 1 Jacob resumed his journey and came to the land of the Easterners. 2 There before his eyes was a well in the open. Three flocks of sheep were lying there beside it, for the flocks were watered from that well. The stone on the mouth of the well was large. 3 When all the flocks were gathered there, the stone would be rolled from the mouth of the well and the sheep watered; then the stone would be put back in its place on the mouth of the well. 4 Jacob said to them, "My friends, where are you from?" And they said, "We are from Haran." 5 He said to them, "Do you know Laban the son of Nahor?" And they said, "Yes, we do." 6 He continued, "Is he well?" They answered, "Yes, he is; and there is his daughter Rachel, coming with the flock." 7 He said, "It is still broad daylight, too early to round up the animals; water the flock and take them to pasture." 8 But they said, "We cannot, until all the flocks are rounded up; then the stone is rolled off the mouth of the well and we water the sheep." 9 While he was still speaking with them,

GENESIS 30 · בראשית ל ויצא

Rachel came with her father's flock; for she was a shepherdess. 10 And when Jacob saw Rachel, the daughter of his uncle Laban, and the flock of his uncle Laban, Jacob went up and rolled the stone off the mouth of the well, and watered the flock of his uncle Laban. 11 Then Jacob kissed Rachel, and broke into tears. 12 Jacob told Rachel that he was her father's kinsman, that he was Rebekah's son; and she ran and told her father. 13 On hearing the news of his sister's son Jacob, Laban ran to greet him; he embraced him and kissed him, and took him into his house. He told Laban all that had happened. 14 and Laban said to him, "You are truly my bone and flesh." When he had stayed with him a month's time, 15 Laban said to Jacob, "Just because you are a kinsman, should you serve me for nothing? Tell me, what shall your wages be?" 16 Now Laban had two daughters; the name of the older one was Leah, and the name of the younger was Rachel. 17 Leah had weak eyes; Rachel was shapely and beautiful. 18 Jacob loved Rachel; so he answered, "I will serve you seven years for your younger daughter Rachel." 19 Laban said, "Better that I give her to you than that I should give her to an outsider. Stay with me." 20 So Jacob served seven years for Rachel and they seemed to him but a few days because of his love for her. 21 Then Jacob said to Laban, "Give me my wife, for my time is fulfilled, that I may cohabit with her." 22 And Laban gathered all the people of the place and made a feast. 23 When evening came, he took his daughter Leah and brought her to him; and he cohabited with her. 24 Laban had given his maidservant Zilpah to his daughter Leah as her maid. 25 When morning came, there was Leah! So he said to Laban, "What is this you have done to me? I was in your service for Rachel! Why did you deceive me?" 26 Laban said, "It is not the practice in our place to marry off the younger before the older. 27 Wait until the bridal week of this one is over and we will give you that one too, provided you serve me another seven years." 28 Jacob did so: he waited out the bridal week of the one, and then he gave him his daughter Rachel as wife. 29 Laban had given his maidservant Bilhah to his daughter Rachel as her maid. 30 And Jacob cohabited with Rachel also; indeed, he loved Rachel more than Leah. And he served him another seven years. 31 The LORD saw that Leah was unloved and he opened her womb; but Rachel was barren. 32 Leah conceived and bore a son, and named him Reuben; for she declared, "It means: 'The LORD has seen my affliction'; it also means: 'Now my husband will love me.'" 33 She conceived again and bore a son, and declared, "This is because the LORD heard that I was unloved and has given me this one also"; so she named him Simeon. 34 Again she conceived and bore a son and declared, "This time my husband will become attached to me, for I have borne him three sons." Therefore he was named Levi. 35 She conceived again and bore a son, and declared, "This time I will praise the LORD." Therefore she named him Judah. Then she stopped bearing. **30** 1 When Rachel saw that she had borne Jacob no children, she became envious of her sister; and Rachel said to Jacob, "Give me children, or I shall die." 2 Jacob was incensed at Rachel, and said, "Can I take the place of God, who has denied you fruit of the womb?" 3 She said, "Here is my maid Bilhah. Consort with her, that she may bear on my knees and that through her I too may have children." 4 So she gave him her maid Bilhah as concubine, and Jacob cohabited with her. 5 Bilhah conceived and bore Jacob a son. 6 And Rachel said, "God has vindicated me; indeed, He has heeded my plea and given me a son." Therefore she named him Dan. 7 Rachel's maid Bilhah conceived again and bore Jacob a second son. 8 And Rachel said, "A fateful contest I waged with my sister; yes, and I have prevailed." So she named him Naphtali. 9 When Leah saw that she had stopped bearing, she took her maid Zilpah and gave her to Jacob as concubine. 10 And when Leah's maid Zilpah bore Jacob a son, 11 Leah said, "What luck!" So she named him Gad. 12 When Leah's maid Zilpah bore Jacob a second son, 13 Leah declared, "What fortune!" meaning, "Women will deem me fortunate." So she named him Asher. 14 Once, at the time of the wheat harvest, Reuben came upon some mandrakes in the field and brought them to his mother Leah. Rachel said to Leah, "Please give me some of your son's mandrakes." 15 But she said to her, "Was it not enough

GENESIS 31 בראשית לא ויצא

for you to take away my husband, that you would also take my son's mandrakes?" Rachel replied, "I promise, he shall lie with you tonight, in return for your son's mandrakes." 16 When Jacob came home from the field in the evening, Leah went out to meet him and said, "You are to sleep with me, for I have hired you with my son's mandrakes." And he lay with her that night. 17 God heeded Leah, and she conceived and bore him a fifth son. 18 And Leah said, "God has given me my reward for having given my maid to my husband." So she named him Issachar. 19 When Leah conceived again and bore Jacob a sixth son, 20 Leah said, "God has given me a choice gift: this time my husband will exalt me, for I have borne him six sons." So she named him Zebulun. 21 Last, she bore him a daughter, and named her Dina. 22 Now God remembered Rachel; God heeded her and opened her womb. 23 She conceived and bore a son, and said, "God has taken away my disgrace." 24 So she named him Joseph, which is to say, "May the LORD add another son for me." 25 After Rachel had borne Joseph, Jacob said to Laban, "Give me leave to go back to my own homeland. 26 Give me my wives and my children, for whom I have served you, that I may go; for well you know what services I have rendered you." 27 But Laban said to him, "If you will indulge me, I have learned by divination that the LORD has blessed me on your account." 28 And he continued, "Name the wages due from me, and I will pay you." 29 But he said, "You know well how I have served you and how your livestock has fared with me. 30 For the little you had before I came has grown to much, since the LORD has blessed you wherever I turned. And now, when shall I make provision for my own household?" 31 He said, "What shall I pay you?" And Jacob said, "Pay me nothing! If you will do this thing for me, I will again pasture and keep your flocks: 32 let me pass through your whole flock today, removing from there every speckled and spotted animal - every dark-colored sheep and every spotted and speckled goat. Such shall be my wages. 33 In the future when you go over my wages, let my honesty toward you testify for me: if there are among my goats any that are not speckled or spotted or any sheep that are not dark-colored, they got there by theft." 34 And Laban said, "Very well, let it be as you say." 35 But that same day he removed the streaked and spotted he-goats and all the speckled and spotted she-goats - every one that had white on it - and all the dark-colored sheep, and left them in the charge of his sons. 36 And he put a distance of three days' journey between himself and Jacob, while Jacob was pasturing the rest of Laban's flock. 37 Jacob then got fresh shoots of poplar, and of almond and plane, and peeled white stripes in them, laying bare the white of the shoots. 38 The rods that he had peeled he set up in front of the goats in the troughs, the water receptacles, that the goats came to drink from. Their mating occurred when they came to drink, 39 and since the goats mated by the rods, the goats brought forth streaked, speckled, and spotted young. 40 But Jacob dealt separately with the sheep: he made these animals face the streaked or wholly dark-colored animals in Laban's flock. And so he produced special flocks for himself, which he did not put with Laban's flocks. 41 Moreover, when the sturdier animals were mating, Jacob would place the rods in the troughs, in full view of the animals, so that they mated by the rods; 42 but with the feebler animals he would not place them there. Thus the feeble ones went to Laban and the sturdy to Jacob. 43 So the man grew exceedingly prosperous, and came to own large flocks, maidservants and menservants, camels and asses.

31 1 Now he heard the things that Laban's sons were saying: "Jacob has taken all that was our father's, and from that which was our father's he has built up all this wealth." 2 Jacob also saw that Laban's manner toward him was not as it had been in the past. 3 Then the LORD said to Jacob, "Return to the land of your fathers where you were born, and I will be with you." 4 Jacob had Rachel and Leah called to the field, where his flock was, 5 and said to them, "I see that your father's manner toward me is not as it has been in the past. But the God of my father has been with me. 6 As you know, I have served your father with all my might; 7 but your father has cheated me, changing my wages time and again. God, however, would not let him do me harm. 8 If he said thus, 'The speckled shall be your wages,' then all the flocks would drop speckled young; and if he said thus,

43

GENESIS 31

'The streaked shall be your wages.' then all the flocks would drop streaked young. 9 God has taken away your father's livestock and given it to me. 10 Once, at the mating time of the flocks. I had a dream in which I saw that the he-goats mating with the flock were streaked, speckled, and mottled. 11 And in the dream an angel of God said to me, Jacob! 'Here.' I answered. 12 And he said. 'Note well that all the he-goats which are mating with the flock are streaked, speckled, and mottled; for I have noted all that Laban has been doing to you. 13 I am the God of Beth-el, where you anointed a pillar and where you made a vow to Me. Now, arise and leave this land and return to your native land.'" 14 Then Rachel and Leah answered him, saying, 'Have we still a share in the inheritance of our father's house? 15 Surely, he regards us as outsiders, now that he has sold us and has used up our purchase price. 16 Truly, all the wealth that God has taken away from our father belongs to us and to our children. Now then, do just as God has told you.' 17 Thereupon Jacob put his children and wives on camels; 18 and he drove off all his livestock and all the wealth that he had amassed, the livestock in his possession that he had acquired in Paddan-aram, to go to his father Isaac in the land of Canaan. 19 Meanwhile Laban had gone to shear his sheep, and Rachel stole her father's household idols. 20 Jacob kept Laban the Aramean in the dark, not telling him that he was fleeing, 21 and fled with all that he had. Soon he was across the Euphrates and heading toward the hill country of Gilead. 22 On the third day, Laban was told that Jacob had fled. 23 So he took his kinsmen with him and pursued him a distance of seven days, catching up with him in the hill country of Gilead. 24 But God appeared to Laban the Aramean in a dream by night and said to him, 'Beware of attempting anything with Jacob, good or bad.' 25 Laban overtook Jacob. Jacob had pitched his tent on the Height, and Laban with his kinsmen encamped in the hill country of Gilead. 26 And Laban said to Jacob, 'What did you mean by keeping me in the dark and carrying off my daughters like captives of the sword? 27 Why did you flee in secrecy and mislead me and not tell me? I would have sent you off with festive music, with timbrel and lyre. 28 You did not even let me kiss my sons and daughters good-by! It was a foolish thing for you to do. 29 I have it in my power to do you harm; but the God of your father said to me last night, 'Beware of attempting anything with Jacob, good or bad.' 30 Very well, you had to leave because you were longing for your father's house; but why did you steal my gods?' 31 Jacob answered Laban, saying, 'I was afraid because I thought you would take your daughters from me by force. 32 But anyone with whom you find your gods shall not remain alive! In the presence of our kinsmen, point out what I have of yours and take it.' Jacob, of course, did not know that Rachel had stolen them. 33 So Laban went into Jacob's tent and Leah's tent and the tents of the two maidservants; but he did not find them. Leaving Leah's tent, he entered Rachel's tent. 34 Rachel, meanwhile, had taken the idols and placed them in the camel cushion and sat on them; and Laban rummaged through the tent without finding them. 35 For she said to her father, 'Let not my lord take it amiss that I cannot rise before you, for the period of women is upon me.' Thus he searched, but could not find the household idols. 36 Now Jacob became incensed and took up his grievance with Laban. Jacob spoke up and said to Laban, 'What is my crime, what is my guilt that you should pursue me? 37 You rummaged through all my things; what have you found of all your household objects? Set it here, before my kinsmen and yours, and let them decide between us two. 38 These twenty years I have spent in your service, your ewes and she-goats never miscarried, nor did I feast on rams from your flock. 39 That which was torn by beasts I never brought to you; I myself made good the loss; you exacted it of me, whether snatched by day or snatched by night. 40 Often, scorching heat ravaged me by day and frost by night; and sleep fled from my eyes. 41 Of the twenty years that I spent in your household. I served you fourteen years for your two daughters, and six years for your flocks; and you changed my wages time and again. 42 Had not the God of my father, the God of Abraham and the Fear of Isaac, been with me, you would have sent me away empty-handed. But God took notice of my plight and the toil of my hands, and He gave judgment last night.' 43 Then Laban spoke up and said to Jacob, 'The daughters are my daughters, the children are my children, and the flocks are my flocks;

GENESIS 32 — בראשית לב ויצא

all that you see is mine. Yet what can I do now about my daughters or the children they have borne? 44 Come, then, let us make a pact, you and I, that there may be a witness between you and me. 45 Thereupon Jacob took a stone and set it up as a pillar. 46 And Jacob said to his kinsmen, "Gather stones." So they took stones and made a mound; and they partook of a meal there by the mound. 47 Laban named it Yegar-sahadutha, but Jacob named it Gal-ed. 48 And Laban declared, "This mound is a witness between you and me this day." That is why it was named Gal-ed; 49 and [it was called] Mizpa, because he said, "May the LORD watch between you and me, when we are out of sight of each other. 50 If you ill-treat my daughters or take other wives besides my daughters — though no one else be about, remember, God Himself will be witness between you and me." 51 And Laban said to Jacob, "Here is this mound and here the pillar which I have set up between you and me; 52 this mound shall be witness and this pillar shall be witness that I am not to cross to you past this mound, and that you are not to cross to me past this mound and this pillar, with hostile intent. 53 May the God of Abraham and the god of Nahor" — their ancestral deities — "judge between us." And Jacob swore by the Fear of his father Isaac. 54 Jacob then offered up a sacrifice on the Height, and invited his kinsmen to partake of the meal. After the meal, they spent the night on the Height. 55 Early in the morning, Laban kissed his sons and daughters and bade them good-by; then Laban left on his journey homeward. **32** 1 Jacob went on his way, and angels of God encountered him. 2 When he saw them, Jacob said, "This is God's camp." So he named that place Mahanaim.

3 **J**acob sent messengers ahead to his brother Esau in the land of Seir, the country of Edom, 4 and instructed them as follows, "Thus shall you say, 'To my lord Esau, thus says your servant Jacob: I stayed with Laban and remained until now; 5 I have acquired cattle, asses, sheep, and male and female slaves; and I send this message to my lord in the hope of gaining your favor.'" 6 The messengers returned to Jacob, saying, "We came to your brother Esau; he himself is coming to meet you, and there are four hundred men with him." 7 Jacob was greatly frightened; in his anxiety, he divided the people and the flocks and herds and camels, into two camps, 8 thinking, "If Esau comes to the one camp and attacks it, the other camp may yet escape." 9 Then Jacob said, "O God of my father Abraham and God of my father Isaac, O LORD, who said to me, 'Return to your native land and I will deal bountifully with you'! 10 I am unworthy of all the kindness that You have so steadfastly shown Your servant: with my staff alone I crossed this Jordan, and now I have become two camps. 11 Deliver me, I pray, from the hand of my brother, from the hand of Esau; else, I fear, he may come and strike me down, mothers and children alike. 12 Yet You have said, 'I will deal bountifully with you and make your offspring as the sands of the sea, which are too numerous to count.'" 13 After spending the night there, he selected from what was at hand these presents for his brother Esau: 14 Two hundred she-goats and twenty he-goats; two hundred ewes and twenty rams; 15 thirty milch camels with their colts; 40 cows and ten bulls; twenty she-asses and ten he-asses. 16 These he put in the charge of his servants, drove by drove, and he told his servants, "Go on ahead, and keep a distance between droves." 17 He instructed the one in front as follows, "When my brother Esau meets you and asks you, 'Whose man are you? Where are you going? And whose [animals] are these ahead of you?' 18 you shall answer, 'Your servant Jacob's; they are a gift sent to my lord Esau; and [Jacob] himself is right behind us'." 19 He gave similar instructions to the second one, and the third, and all the others who followed the droves, namely, "Thus and so shall you say to Esau when you reach him. 20 And you shall add, 'And your servant Jacob himself is right behind us.'" For he reasoned, "If I propitiate him with presents in advance, and then face him, perhaps he will show me favor." 21 And so the gift went on ahead, while he remained in camp that night. 22 That same night he arose,

45

GENESIS 33 — בראשית לג · וישלח

and taking his two wives, his two maidservants, and his eleven children, he crossed the ford of the Jabbok. 23 After taking them across the stream, he sent across all his possessions. 24 Jacob was left alone. And a man wrestled with him until the break of dawn. 25 When he saw that he had not prevailed against him, he wrenched Jacob's hip at its socket, so that the socket of his hip was strained as he wrestled with him. 26 Then he said, "Let me go, for dawn is breaking." But he answered, "I will not let you go, unless you bless me." 27 Said the other, "What is your name?" He replied, "Jacob." 28 Said he, "Your name shall no longer be Jacob, but Israel, for you have striven with beings divine and human, and have prevailed." 29 Jacob asked, "Pray tell me your name." But he said, "You must not ask my name!" And he took leave of him there. 30 So Jacob named the place Peniel, meaning, "I have seen a divine being face to face, yet my life has been preserved." 31 The sun rose upon him as he passed Penuel, limping on his hip. 32 That is why the children of Israel to this day do not eat the thigh muscle that is on the socket of the hip, since Jacob's hip socket was wrenched at the thigh muscle. **33** 1 Looking up, Jacob saw Esau coming, accompanied by four hundred men. He divided the children among Leah, Rachel, and the two maids. 2 putting the maids and their children first, Leah and her children next, and Rachel and Joseph last. 3 He himself went on ahead and bowed low to the ground seven times until he was near his brother. 4 Esau ran to greet him. He embraced him and, falling on his neck, he kissed him; and they wept. 5 Looking about, he saw the women and the children. "Who," he asked, "are these with you?" He answered, "The children with whom God has favored your servant." 6 Then the maids, with their children, came forward and bowed low; 7 next Leah, with her children, came forward and bowed low; and last, Joseph and Rachel came forward and bowed low. 8 He asked, "What do you mean by all this company which I have met?" He answered, "To gain my lord's favor." 9 Esau said, "I have enough, my brother; let what you have remain yours." 10 But Jacob said, "No, I pray you; if you would do me this favor, accept from me this gift; for to see your face is like seeing the face of God, and you have received me favorably. 11 Please accept my present which has been brought to you, for God has favored me and I have plenty." And when he urged him, he accepted. 12 And [Esau] said, "Let us start on our journey, and I will proceed at your pace." 13 But he said to him, "My lord knows that the children are frail and that the flocks and herds, which are nursing, are a care to me; if they are driven hard a single day, all the flocks will die. 14 Let my lord go on ahead of his servant, while I travel slowly, at the pace of the cattle before me and at the pace of the children, until I come to my lord in Seir." 15 Then Esau said, "Let me assign to you some of the men who are with me." But he said, "Oh no, my lord is too kind to me!" 16 So Esau started back that day on his way to Seir. 17 But Jacob journeyed on to Succoth, and built a house for himself and made stalls for his cattle; that is why the place was called Succoth. 18 Jacob arrived safe in the city of Shechem which is in the land of Canaan - having come thus from Paddan-aram - and he encamped before the city. 19 The parcel of land where he pitched his tent he purchased from the children of Hamor, Shechem's father, for a hundred kesitahs. 20 He set up an altar there, and called it El-elohe-yisrael. **34** 1 Now Dinah, the daughter whom Leah had borne to Jacob, went out to visit the daughters of the land. 2 Shechem son of Hamor the Hivite, chief of the country, saw her, and took her and lay with her by force. 3 Being strongly drawn to Dinah daughter of Jacob, and in love with the maiden, he spoke to the maiden tenderly. 4 So Shechem said to his father Hamor, "Get me this girl as a wife." 5 Jacob heard that he had defiled his daughter Dinah; but since his sons were in the field with his cattle, Jacob kept silent until they came home. 6 Then Shechem's father Hamor came out to speak to him. 7 Meanwhile Jacob's sons, having heard the news, came in from the field. The men were distressed and very angry, because he had committed an outrage in Israel by lying with Jacob's daughter - a thing not to be done. 8 And Hamor spoke with them, saying, "My son Shechem longs for your daughter. Please give her to him in marriage. 9 Intermarry with us: give your daughters to us, and take our daughters for yourselves: 10 You will

A page of the Book of Genesis, from the Bible illustrated by Gustave Doré, 1832-33

GENESIS 22

and we will return to you." 6 Abraham took the wood for the burnt offering and put it on his son Isaac. He himself took the firestone and the knife; and the two walked off together. 7 Then Isaac said

GENESIS 35

dwell among us, and the land will be open before you; settle, move about, and acquire holdings in it." 11 Then Shechem said to her father and brothers, "Do me this favor, and I will pay whatever you tell me. 12 Ask of me a bride-price ever so high, as well as gifts, and I will pay what you tell me; only give me the maiden for a wife." 13 Jacob's sons answered Shechem and his father Hamor - speaking with guile because he had defiled their sister Dinah - 14 and said to them, "We cannot do this thing, to give our sister to a man who is uncircumcised, for that is a disgrace among us. 15 Only on this condition will we agree with you: that you will become like us in that every male among you is circumcised. 16 Then we will give our daughters to you and take your daughters to ourselves; and we will dwell among you and become as one kindred. 17 But if you will not listen to us and become circumcised, we will take our daughter and go." 18 Their words pleased Hamor and Hamor's son Shechem. 19 And the youth lost no time in doing the thing, for he wanted Jacob's daughter. Now he was the most respected in his father's house. 20 So Hamor and his son Shechem went to the public place of their town and spoke to their fellow townsmen, saying, 21 "These people are our friends; let them settle in the land and move about in it, for the land is large enough for them; we will take their daughters to wives and give our daughters to them. 22 But only on this condition will the men agree with us to dwell among us and be as one kindred: that all our males become circumcised as they are circumcised. 23 Their cattle and substance and all their beasts will be ours, if we only agree to their terms, so that they will settle among us." 24 All who went out of the gate of his town heeded Hamor and his son Shechem, and all males, all those who went out of the gate of his town, were circumcised. 25 On the third day, when they were in pain, Simeon and Levi, two of Jacob's sons, brothers of Dinah, took each his sword, came upon the city unmolested, and slew all the males. 26 They put Hamor and his son Shechem to the sword, took Dinah out of Shechem's house, and went away. 27 The other sons of Jacob came upon the slain and plundered the town, because their sister had been defiled. 28 They seized their flocks and herds and asses, all that was inside the town and outside; 29 all their wealth, all their children, and their wives, all that was in the houses, they took as captives and booty. 30 Jacob said to Simeon and Levi, "You have brought trouble on me, making me odious among the inhabitants of the land, the Canaanites and the Perizzites; my men are few in number, so that if they unite against me and attack me, I and my house will be destroyed." 31 But they answered, "Should our sister be treated like a whore?"

35 1 God said to Jacob, "Arise, go up to Bethel and remain there; and build an altar there to the God who appeared to you when you were fleeing from your brother Esau." 2 So Jacob said to his household and to all who were with him, "Rid yourselves of the alien gods in your midst, purify yourselves, and change your clothes. 3 Come, let us go up to Bethel, and I will build an altar there to the God who answered me when I was in distress and who has been with me wherever I have gone." 4 They gave to Jacob all the alien gods that they had, and the rings that were in their ears, and Jacob buried them under the terebinth that was near Shechem. 5 As they set out, a terror from God fell on the cities round about, so that they did not pursue the sons of Jacob. 6 Thus Jacob came to Luz - that is, Bethel - in the land of Canaan, he and all the people who were with him. 7 There he built an altar and named the site El-bethel, for it was there that God had revealed Himself to him when he was fleeing from his brother. 8 Deborah, Rebekah's nurse, died, and was buried under the oak below Bethel; so it was named Allon-bacuth.

9 God appeared again to Jacob on his arrival from Paddan-aram, and He blessed him. 10 God said to him, "You whose name is Jacob, you shall be called Jacob no more, but Israel shall be your name." Thus He named him Israel. 11 And God said to him, "I am El Shaddai. Be fertile and increase; a nation, yea an assembly of nations, shall descend from you. Kings shall issue from your loins. 12 The land that I assigned to Abraham and Isaac I assign to you; and to your offspring to come will I assign

48

GENESIS 36 · בראשית לו וישלח

the land." 13 God parted from him at the spot where He had spoken to him. 14 and Jacob set up a pillar at the site where He had spoken to him, a pillar of stone, and he offered a libation on it and poured oil upon it. 15 Jacob gave the site, where God had spoken to him, the name of Bethel. 16 They set out from Bethel; but when they were still some distance short of Ephrath, Rachel was in childbirth, and she had hard labor. 17 When her labor was at its hardest, the midwife said to her, "Have no fear, for it is another boy for you." 18 But as she breathed her last - for she was dying - she named him Ben-oni; but his father called him Benjamin. 19 Thus Rachel died. She was buried on the road to Ephrath - now Bethlehem. 20 Over her grave Jacob set up a pillar; it is the pillar at Rachel's grave to this day. 21 Israel journeyed on, and pitched his tent beyond Migdal-eder. 22 While Israel stayed in that land, Reuben went and lay with Bilhah, his father's concubine; and Israel

found out. Now the sons of Jacob were twelve in number. 23 The sons of Leah: Reuben - Jacob's first-born - Simeon, Levi, Judah, Issachar, and Zebulun. 24 The sons of Rachel: Joseph and Benjamin. 25 The sons of Bilhah, Rachel's maid: Dan and Naphtali. 26 And the sons of Zilpah, Leah's maid: Gad and Asher. These are the sons of Jacob who were born to him in Paddan-aram. 27 And Jacob came to his father Isaac at Mamre, at Kiriath-arba - now Hebron - where Abraham and Isaac had sojourned. 28 Isaac was a hundred and eighty years old 29 when he breathed his last and died. He was gathered to his kin in ripe old age; and he was buried by his sons Esau and Jacob.

36 1 This is the line of Esau - that is, Edom. 2 Esau took his wives from among the Canaanite women - Adah daughter of Elon the Hittite, and Oholibamah daughter of Anah daughter of Zibeon the Hivite - 3 and also Basemath daughter of Ishmael and sister of Nebaioth. 4 Adah bore to Esau Eliphaz; Basemath bore Reuel; 5 and Oholibamah bore Jeush, Jalam, and Korah. Those were the sons of Esau, who were born to him in the land of Canaan. 6 Esau took his wives, his sons and daughters, and all the members of his household, his cattle and all his livestock, and all the property that he had acquired in the land of Canaan, and went to another land because of his brother Jacob. 7 For their possessions were too many for them to dwell together, and the land where they sojourned could not support them because of their livestock. 8 So Esau settled in the hill country of Seir - Esau being Edom. 9 This, then, is the line of Esau, the ancestor of the Edomites, in the hill country of Seir. 10 These are the names of Esau's sons: Eliphaz, the son of Esau's wife Adah; Reuel, the son of Esau's wife Basemath. 11 The sons of Eliphaz were Teman, Omar, Zepho, Gatam, and Kenaz. 12 Timna was a concubine of Esau's son Eliphaz; she bore Amalek to Eliphaz. Those were the descendants of Esau's wife Adah. 13 And these were the sons of Reuel: Nahath, Zerah, Shammah, and Mizzah. Those were the descendants of Esau's wife Basemath. 14 And these were the sons of Esau's wife Oholibamah, daughter of Anah daughter of Zibeon: she bore to Esau Jeush, Jalam, and Korah. 15 These are the clans of the children of Esau. The descendants of Esau's first-born Eliphaz: the clans Teman, Omar, Zepho, Kenaz, 16 Korah, Gatam, and Amalek; these are the clans of Eliphaz in the land of Edom. Those are the descendants of Adah. 17 And these are the descendants of Esau's son Reuel: the clans Nahath, Zerah, Shammah, and Mizzah; these are the clans of Reuel in the land of Edom. Those are the descendants of Esau's wife Basemath. 18 And these are the descendants of Esau's wife Oholibamah: the clans Jeush, Jalam, and Korah; these are the clans of Esau's wife Oholibamah, the daughter of Anah. 19 Those were the sons of Esau - that is, Edom - and those are their clans. 20 These were the sons of Seir the Horite, who were settled in the land: Lotan, Shobal, Zibeon, Anah, 21 Dishon, Ezer, and Dishan. Those are the clans of the Horites, the descendants of Seir, in the land of Edom. 22 The sons of Lotan were Hori and Hemam; and Lotan's sister was Timna. 23 The sons of Shobal were these: Alvan, Manahath, Ebal, Shepho, and Onam. 24 The sons of Zibeon were: Aiah and Anah - that was the Anah who discovered the hot springs in the wilderness

GENESIS 37 — בראשית לז וישב

while pasturing the asses of his father Zibeon. 25 The children of Anah were these: Dishon and Anah's daughter Oholibamah. 26 The sons of Dishon were these: Hemdan, Eshban, Ithran, and Cheran. 27 The sons of Ezer were these: Bilhan, Zaavan, and Akan. 28 And the sons of Dishan were these: Uz and Aran. 29 These are the clans of the Horites: the clans Lotan, Shobal, Zibeon, Anah, 30 Dishon, Ezer, and Dishan. These are the clans of the Horites, clan by clan, in the land of Seir. 31 These are the kings who reigned in the land of Edom before any king reigned over the Israelites. 32 Bela son of Beor reigned in Edom, and the name of his city was Dinhabah. 33 When Bela died, Jobab son of Zerah, from Bozrah, succeeded him as king. 34 When Jobab died, Husham of the land of the Temanites succeeded him as king. 35 When Husham died, Hadad son of Bedad, who defeated the Midianites in the country of Moab, succeeded him as king; the name of his city was Avith. 36 When Hadad died, Samlah of Masrekah succeeded him as king. 37 When Samlah died, Saul of Rehoboth-on-the-river succeeded him as king. 38 When Saul died, Baal-hanan son of Achbor succeeded him as king. 39 And when Baal-hanan son of Achbor died, Hadar succeeded him as king; the name of his city was Pau, and his wife's name was Mehetabel daughter of Matred daughter of Me-zahab. 40 These are the names of the clans of Esau, each with its families and locality, name by name: the clans Timna, Alvah, Jetheth, 41 Oholibamah, Elah, Pinon, 42 Kenaz, Teman, Mibzar, 43 Magdiel, and Iram. Those are the clans of Edom — that is, of Esau, father of the Edomites — by their settlements in the land which they hold.

37 Now Jacob was settled in the land where his father had sojourned, the land of Canaan. 2 This, then, is the line of Jacob: At seventeen years of age, Joseph tended the flocks with his brothers, as a helper to the sons of his father's wives Bilhah and Zilpah. And Joseph brought bad reports of them to their father. 3 Now Israel loved Joseph best of all his sons, for he was the child of his old age; and he had made him an ornamented tunic. 4 And when his brothers saw that their father loved him more than any of his brothers, they hated him so that they could not speak a friendly word to him. 5 Once Joseph had a dream which he told to his brothers; and they hated him even more. 6 He said to them, "Hear this dream which I have dreamed: 7 There we were binding sheaves in the field, when suddenly my sheaf stood up and remained upright; then your sheaves gathered around and bowed low to my sheaf." 8 His brothers answered, "Do you mean to reign over us? Do you mean to rule over us?" And they hated him even more for his talk about his dreams. 9 He dreamed another dream and told it to his brothers, saying, "Look, I have had another dream: And this time, the sun, the moon, and eleven stars were bowing down to me." 10 And when he told it to his father and brothers, his father berated him. "What," he said to him, "is this dream you have dreamed? Are we to come, I and your mother and your brothers, and bow low to you to the ground?" 11 So his brothers were wrought up at him, and his father kept the matter in mind. 12 One time, when his brothers had gone to pasture their father's flock at Shechem, 13 Israel said to Joseph, "Your brothers are pasturing at Shechem. Come, I will send you to them." He answered, "I am ready." 14 And he said to him, "Go and see how your brothers are and how the flocks are faring, and bring me back word." So he sent him from the valley of Hebron. When he reached Shechem, 15 a man came upon him wandering in the fields. The man asked him, "What are you looking for?" 16 He answered, "I am looking for my brothers. Could you tell me where they are pasturing?" 17 The man said, "They have gone from here, for I heard them say: Let us go to Dothan." So Joseph followed his brothers and found them at Dothan. 18 They saw him from afar, and before he came close to them they conspired to kill him. 19 They said to one another, "Here comes that dreamer! 20 Come now, let us kill him and throw him into one of the pits; and we can say, 'A savage beast devoured him.' We shall see what comes of his dreams!" 21 But when Reuben heard it, he tried to save him from them. He said, "Let us not take his life." 22 And Reuben went on, "Shed no blood!

GENESIS 38 · בראשית לח · וישב

Cast him into that pit out in the wilderness, but do not touch him yourselves"—intending to save him from them and restore him to his father. 23 When Joseph came up to his brothers, they stripped Joseph of his tunic, the ornamented tunic that he was wearing, 24 and took him and cast him into the pit. The pit was empty; there was no water in it. 25 Then they sat down to a meal. Looking up, they saw a caravan of Ishmaelites coming from Gilead, their camels bearing gum, balm, and ladanum to be taken to Egypt. 26 Then Judah said to his brothers, "What do we gain by killing our brother and covering up his blood? 27 Come, let us sell him to the Ishmaelites, but let us not do away with him ourselves. After all, he is our brother, our own flesh." His brothers agreed. 28 When Midianite traders passed by, they pulled Joseph up out of the pit. They sold Joseph for twenty pieces of silver to the Ishmaelites, who brought Joseph to Egypt. 29 When Reuben returned to the pit and saw that Joseph was not in the pit, he rent his clothes. 30 Returning to his brothers, he said, "The boy is gone! Now, what am I to do?" 31 Then they took Joseph's tunic, slaughtered a kid, and dipped the tunic in the blood. 32 They had the ornamented tunic taken to their father, and they said, "We found this. Please examine it; is it your son's tunic or not?" 33 He recognized it, and said, "My son's tunic! A savage beast devoured him! Joseph was torn by a beast!" 34 Jacob rent his clothes, put sackcloth on his loins, and observed mourning for his son many days. 35 All his sons and daughters sought to comfort him; but he refused to be comforted, saying, "No, I will go down mourning to my son in Sheol." Thus his father bewailed him. 36 The Midianites, meanwhile, sold him in Egypt to Potiphar, a courtier of Pharaoh and his chief steward.

38 1 About that time Judah left his brothers and camped near a certain Adullamite whose name was Hirah. 2 There Judah saw the daughter of a certain Canaanite whose name was Shua, and he married her and cohabited with her. 3 She conceived and bore a son, and he named him Er. 4 She conceived again and bore a son, and named him Onan. 5 Once again she bore a son, and named him Shelah; he was at Chezib when she bore him. 6 Judah got a wife for Er his first-born; her name was Tamar. 7 But Er, Judah's first-born, was displeasing to the LORD, and the LORD took his life. 8 Then Judah said to Onan, "Join with your brother's wife and do your duty by her as a brother-in-law, and provide offspring for your brother." 9 But Onan, knowing that the seed would not count as his, let it go to waste whenever he joined with his brother's wife, so as not to provide offspring for his brother. 10 What he did was displeasing to the LORD, and He took his life also. 11 Then Judah said to his daughter-in-law Tamar, "Stay as a widow in your father's house until my son Shelah grows up" - for he thought, "He too might die like his brothers." So Tamar went to live in her father's house. 12 A long time afterward, Shua's daughter, the wife of Judah, died. When Judah's period of mourning was over, Judah went up to Timnah to his sheepshearers, together with his friend Hirah the Adullamite. 13 And Tamar was told, "Your father-in-law is coming up to Timnah for the sheepshearing." 14 So she took off her widow's garb, covered her face with a veil, and wrapping herself up, sat down at the entrance to Enaim, which is on the road to Timnah; for she saw that Shelah was grown up, yet she had not been given to him as wife. 15 When Judah saw her, he took her for a harlot, for she had covered her face. 16 So he turned aside to her by the road and said, "Here, let me sleep with you" - for he did not know that she was his daughter-in-law. "What," she asked, "will you pay for sleeping with me?" 17 He replied, "I will send a kid from my flock." But she said, "You must leave a pledge until you have sent it." 18 And he said, "What pledge shall I give you?" She replied, "Your seal and cord, and the staff which you carry." So he gave them to her and slept with her, and she conceived by him. 19 Then she went on her way. She took off her veil and again put on her widow's garb. 20 Judah sent the kid by his friend the Adullamite, to redeem the pledge from the woman; but he could not find her. 21 He inquired of the people of that town, "Where is the cult prostitute, the one at Enaim, by the road?" But they said, "There has been no prostitute here." 22 So he returned to Judah and said, "I could not find her; moreover, the townspeople said: There has been no prostitute here."

51

GENESIS 39　　　　　　　　　　　　　　　בראשית לט וישב

23 Judah said, "Let her keep them, lest we become a laughingstock. I did send her this kid, but you did not find her." 24 About three months later, Judah was told, "Your daughter-in-law Tamar has played the harlot; in fact, she is with child by harlotry." "Bring her out," said Judah, "and let her be burned." 25 As she was being brought out, she sent this message to her father-in-law, "I am with child by the man to whom these belong." And she added, "Examine these: whose seal and cord and staff are these?" 26 Judah recognized them, and said, "She is more in the right than I, inasmuch as I did not give her to my son Shelah." And he was not intimate with her again. 27 When the time came for her to give birth, there were twins in her womb! 28 While she was in labor, one of them put out his hand, and the midwife tied a crimson thread on that hand, to signify: This one came out first. 29 But just then he drew back his hand, and out came his brother; and she said, "What a breach you have made for yourself!" So he was named Perez. 30 Afterward his brother came out, on whose hand was the crimson thread; he was named Zerah.

39 1 When Joseph was taken down to Egypt, a certain Egyptian, Potiphar, a courtier of Pharaoh and his chief steward, bought him from the Ishmaelites who had brought him there. 2 The LORD was with Joseph, and he was a successful man; and he stayed in the house of his Egyptian master. 3 And when his master saw that the LORD was with him and that the LORD lent success to everything he undertook, 4 he took a liking to Joseph. He made him his personal attendant and put him in charge of his household, placing in his hands all that he owned. 5 And from the time that the Egyptian put him in charge of his household and of all that he owned, the LORD blessed his house for Joseph's sake, so that the blessing of the LORD was upon everything that he owned, in the house and outside. 6 He left all that he had in Joseph's hands and, with him there, he paid attention to nothing save the food that he ate. Now Joseph was well built and handsome. 7 After a time, his master's wife cast her eyes upon Joseph and said, "Lie with me." 8 But he refused. He said to his master's wife, "Look, with me here, my master gives no thought to anything in this house, and all that he owns he has placed in my hands. 9 He wields no more authority in this house than I, and he has withheld nothing from me except yourself, since you are his wife. How then could I do this most wicked thing, and sin before God?" 10 And much as she coaxed Joseph day after day, he did not yield to her request to lie beside her, to be with her. 11 One such day, he came into the house to do his work. None of the household being there inside, 12 she caught hold of him by his garment and said, "Lie with me!" But he left his garment in her hand and got away and fled outside. 13 When she saw that he had left it in her hand and had fled outside, 14 she called out to her servants and said to them, "Look, he had to bring us a Hebrew to dally with us! This one came to lie with me; but I screamed loud. 15 And when he heard me screaming at the top of my voice, he left his garment with me and got away and fled outside." 16 She kept his garment beside her, until his master came home. 17 Then she told him the same story, saying, "The Hebrew slave whom you brought into our house came to me to dally with me; 18 but when I screamed at the top of my voice, he left his garment with me and fled outside." 19 When his master heard the story that his wife told him, namely, "Thus and so your slave did to me," he was furious. 20 So Joseph's master had him put in prison, where the king's prisoners were confined. But even while he was there in prison, 21 the LORD was with Joseph: He extended kindness to him and disposed the chief jailer favorably toward him. 22 The chief jailer put in Joseph's charge all the prisoners who were in that prison, and he was the one to carry out everything that was done there. 23 The chief jailer did not supervise anything that was in Joseph's charge, because the LORD was with him, and whatever he did the LORD made successful.

40 1 Some time later, the cupbearer and the baker of the king of Egypt gave offense to their lord the king of Egypt. 2 Pharaoh was angry with his two courtiers, the chief cupbearer and the chief baker, 3 and put them in custody, in the house of the chief steward,

GENESIS 41  בראשית מא מקץ

in the same prison house where Joseph was confined. 4 The chief steward assigned Joseph to them, and he attended them. When they had been in custody for some time, 5 both of them - the cupbearer and the baker of the king of Egypt, who were confined in the prison -dreamed in the same night, each his own dream and each dream with its own meaning. 6 When Joseph came to them in the morning, he saw that they were distraught. 7 He asked Pharaoh's courtiers, who were with him in custody in his master's house, saying, "Why do you appear downcast today?" 8 And they said to him, "We had dreams, and there is no one to interpret them." So Joseph said, "Surely God can interpret! Tell me [your dreams]." 9 Then the chief cupbearer told his dream to Joseph. He said to him, "In my dream, there was a vine in front of me. 10 On the vine were three branches. It had barely budded, when out came its blossoms and its clusters ripened into grapes. 11 Pharaoh's cup was in my hand, and I took the grapes, pressed them into Pharaoh's cup, and placed the cup in Pharaoh's hand." 12 Joseph said to him, "This is its interpretation: The three branches are three days. 13 In three days Pharaoh will pardon you and restore you to your post; you will place Pharaoh's cup in his hand, as was your custom formerly when you were his cupbearer. 14 But think of me when all is well with you again, and do me the kindness of mentioning me to Pharaoh, so as to free me from this place. 15 For in truth, I was kidnapped from the land of the Hebrews; nor have I done anything here that they should have put me in the dungeon." 16 When the chief baker saw how favorably he had interpreted, he said to Joseph, "In my dream, similarly, there were three openwork baskets on my head. 17 In the uppermost basket were all kinds of food for Pharaoh that a baker prepares, and the birds were eating it out of the basket above my head." 18 Joseph answered, "This is its interpretation: The three baskets are three days. 19 In three days Pharaoh will lift off your head and impale you on a pole; and the birds will pick off your flesh." 20 On the third day - his birthday - Pharaoh made a banquet for all his officials, and he singled out his chief cupbearer and his chief baker from among his officials. 21 He restored the chief cupbearer to his cupbearing, and he placed the cup in Pharaoh's hand; 22 but the chief baker was impaled -just as Joseph had interpreted to them. 23 Yet the chief cupbearer did not think of Joseph; he forgot him.

41 After two years' time, Pharaoh dreamed that he was standing by the Nile. 2 when out of the Nile there came up seven cows, handsome and sturdy, and they grazed in the reed grass. 3 But presently, seven other cows came up from the Nile close behind them, ugly and gaunt, and stood beside the cows on the bank of the Nile; 4 the ugly gaunt cows ate up the seven handsome sturdy cows. And Pharaoh awoke. 5 He fell asleep and dreamed a second time: Seven ears of grain, solid and healthy, grew on a single stalk. 6 But close behind them sprouted seven ears, thin and scorched by the east wind. 7 And the thin ears swallowed up the seven solid and full ears. Then Pharaoh awoke: it was a dream! 8 Next morning, his spirit was agitated, and he sent for all the magicians of Egypt, and all its wise men; and Pharaoh told them his dreams, but none could interpret them for Pharaoh. 9 The chief cupbearer then spoke up and said to Pharaoh, "I must make mention today of my offenses. 10 Once Pharaoh was angry with his servants, and placed me in custody in the house of the chief steward, together with the chief baker. 11 We had dreams the same night, he and I, each of us a dream with a meaning of its own. 12 A Hebrew youth was there with us, a servant of the chief steward; and when we told him our dreams, he interpreted them for us, telling each of the meaning of his dream. 13 And as he interpreted for us, so it came to pass: I was restored to my post, and the other was impaled." 14 Thereupon Pharaoh sent for Joseph, and he was rushed from the dungeon. He had his hair cut and changed his clothes, and he appeared before Pharaoh. 15 And Pharaoh said

※ 53 ※

GENESIS 41 — בראשית מא

to Joseph, "I have had a dream, but no one can interpret it. Now I have heard it said of you that for you to hear a dream is to tell its meaning." 16 Joseph answered Pharaoh, saying, "Not I! God will see to Pharaoh's welfare." 17 Then Pharaoh said to Joseph, "In my dream, I was standing on the bank of the Nile. 18 when out of the Nile came up seven sturdy and well-formed cows and grazed in the reed grass. 19 Presently there followed them seven other cows, scrawny, ill-formed, and emaciated – never had I seen their likes for ugliness in all the land of Egypt! 20 And the seven lean and ugly cows ate up the first seven cows, the sturdy ones; 21 but when they had consumed them, one could not tell that they had consumed them, for they looked just as bad as before. And I awoke. 22 In my other dream, I saw seven ears of grain, full and healthy, growing on a single stalk; 23 but right behind them sprouted seven ears, shriveled, thin, and scorched by the east wind. 24 And the thin ears swallowed the seven healthy ears. I have told my magicians, but none has an explanation for me." 25 And Joseph said to Pharaoh, "Pharaoh's dreams are one and the same: God has told Pharaoh what He is about to do. 26 The seven healthy cows are seven years, and the seven healthy ears are seven years: it is the same dream. 27 The seven lean and ugly cows that followed are seven years, as are also the seven empty ears scorched by the east wind: they are seven years of famine. 28 It is just as I have told Pharaoh: God has revealed to Pharaoh what He is about to do. 29 Immediately ahead are seven years of great abundance in all the land of Egypt. 30 After them will come seven years of famine, and all the abundance in the land of Egypt will be forgotten. As the land is ravaged by famine, 31 no trace of the abundance will be left in the land because of the famine thereafter, for it will be very severe. 32 As for Pharaoh having had the same dream twice, it means that the matter has been determined by God, and that God will soon carry it out. 33 "Accordingly, let Pharaoh find a man of discernment and wisdom, and set him over the land of Egypt. 34 And let Pharaoh take steps to appoint overseers over the land, and organize the land of Egypt in the seven years of plenty. 35 Let all the food of these good years that are coming be gathered, and let the grain be collected under Pharaoh's authority as food to be stored in the cities. 36 Let that food be a reserve for the land for the seven years of famine which will come upon the land of Egypt, so that the land may not perish in the famine." 37 The plan pleased Pharaoh and all his courtiers. 38 And Pharaoh said to his courtiers, "Could we find another like him, a man in whom is the spirit of God?" 39 So Pharaoh said to Joseph, "Since God has made all this known to you, there is none so discerning and wise as you. 40 You shall be in charge of my court, and by your command shall all my people be directed; only with respect to the throne shall I be superior to you." 41 Pharaoh further said to Joseph, "See, I put you in charge of all the land of Egypt." 42 And removing his signet ring from his hand, Pharaoh put it on Joseph's hand; and he had him dressed in robes of fine linen, and put a gold chain about his neck. 43 He had him ride in the chariot of his second-in-command, and they cried before him, "Abrek!" Thus he placed him over all the land of Egypt. 44 Pharaoh said to Joseph, "I am Pharaoh; yet without you, no one shall lift up hand or foot in all the land of Egypt." 45 Pharaoh then gave Joseph the name Zaphenath-paneah; and he gave him for a wife Asenath daughter of Poti-phera, priest of On. Thus Joseph emerged in charge of the land of Egypt. 46 Joseph was thirty years old when he entered the service of Pharaoh king of Egypt. – Leaving Pharaoh's presence, Joseph traveled through all the land of Egypt. 47 During the seven years of plenty, the land produced in abundance. 48 And he gathered all the grain of the seven years that the land of Egypt was enjoying, and stored the grain in the cities; he put in each city the grain of the fields around it. 49 So Joseph collected produce in very large quantity, like the sands of the sea, until he ceased to measure it, for it could not be measured. 50 Before the years of famine came, Joseph became the father of two sons, whom Asenath daughter of Poti-phera, priest of On, bore to him. 51 Joseph named

— 54 —

GENESIS 42 — בראשית מב מקץ

the first-born Manasseh, meaning, "God has made me forget completely my hardship and my parental home." 52 And the second he named Ephraim, meaning, "God has made me fertile in the land of my affliction." 53 The seven years of abundance that the land of Egypt enjoyed came to an end, 54 and the seven years of famine set in, just as Joseph had foretold. There was famine in all lands, but throughout the land of Egypt there was bread. 55 And when all the land of Egypt felt the hunger, the people cried out to Pharaoh for bread; and Pharaoh said to all the Egyptians, "Go to Joseph; whatever he tells you, you shall do." – 56 Accordingly, when the famine became severe in the land of Egypt, Joseph laid open all that was within, and rationed out grain to the Egyptians. The famine, however, spread over the whole world. 57 So all the world came to Joseph in Egypt to procure rations, for the famine had become severe throughout the world. **42** 1 When Jacob saw that there were food rations to be had in Egypt, he said to his sons, "Why do you keep looking at one another? 2 Now I hear," he went on, "that there are rations to be had in Egypt. Go down and procure rations for us there, that we may live and not die." 3 So ten of Joseph's brothers went down to get grain rations in Egypt; 4 for Jacob did not send Joseph's brother Benjamin with his brothers, since he feared that he might meet with disaster. 5 Thus the sons of Israel were among those who came to procure rations, for the famine extended to the land of Canaan. 6 Now Joseph was the vizier of the land; it was he who dispensed rations to all the people of the land. And Joseph's brothers came and bowed low to him, with their faces to the ground. 7 When Joseph saw his brothers, he recognized them; but he acted like a stranger toward them and spoke harshly to them. He asked them, "Where do you come from?" And they said, "From the land of Canaan, to procure food." 8 For though Joseph recognized his brothers, they did not recognize him. 9 Recalling the dreams that he had dreamed about them, Joseph said to them, "You are spies, you have come to see the land in its nakedness." 10 But they said to him, "No, my lord! Truly, your servants have come to procure food. 11 We are all of us sons of the same man; we are honest men; your servants have never been spies!" 12 And he said to them, "No, you have come to see the land in its nakedness!" 13 And they replied, "We your servants are twelve brothers, sons of a certain man in the land of Canaan; the youngest, however, is now with our father, and one is no more." 14 But Joseph said to them, "It is just as I have told you: You are spies! 15 By this you shall be put to the test: unless your youngest brother comes here, by Pharaoh, you shall not depart from this place! 16 Let one of you go and bring your brother, while the rest of you remain confined, that your words may be put to the test whether there is truth in you. Else, by Pharaoh, you are nothing but spies!" 17 And he confined them in the guardhouse for three days. 18 On the third day Joseph said to them, "Do this and you shall live, for I am a God-fearing man. 19 If you are honest men, let one of you brothers be held in your place of detention, while the rest of you go and take home rations for your starving households; 20 but you must bring me your youngest brother, that your words may be verified and that you may not die." And they did accordingly. 21 They said to one another, "Alas, we are being punished on account of our brother, because we looked on at his anguish, yet paid no heed as he pleaded with us. That is why this distress has come upon us." 22 Then Reuben spoke up and said to them, "Did I not tell you, 'Do no wrong to the boy'? But you paid no heed. Now comes the reckoning for his blood." 23 They did not know that Joseph understood, for there was an interpreter between him and them. 24 He turned away from them and wept. But he came back to them and spoke to them; and he took Simeon from among them and had him bound before their eyes. 25 Then Joseph gave orders to fill their bags with grain, return each one's money to his sack, and give them provisions for the journey; and this was done for them. 26 So they loaded their asses with the rations and departed from there. 27 As one of them was opening his sack to give feed to his ass at the night encampment, he saw his money right there at the mouth of his bag. 28 And he said to his brothers, "My money has been returned! It is here in my bag!" Their hearts sank; and, trembling, they turned to one another, saying, "What is this that God has done to us?" 29 When they came to their father Jacob in the land of Canaan, they told him all that had befallen them, saying, 30 "The man who is lord of the land spoke harshly to us and accused us of spying on the land. 31 We said to him,

GENESIS 43 · בראשית מקץ

We are honest men; we have never been spies! 32 There were twelve of us brothers, sons by the same father; but one is no more, and the youngest is now with our father in the land of Canaan. 33 But the man who is lord of the land said to us, 'By this I shall know that you are honest men: leave one of your brothers with me, and take something for your starving households and be off. 34 And bring your youngest brother to me, that I may know that you are not spies but honest men. I will then restore your brother to you, and you shall be free to move about in the land.' 35 As they were emptying their sacks, there, in each one's sack, was his money-bag! When they and their father saw their money-bags, they were dismayed. 36 Their father Jacob said to them, "It is always me that you bereave: Joseph is no more and Simeon is no more, and now you would take away Benjamin. These things always happen to me!" 37 Then Reuben said to his father, "You may kill my two sons if I do not bring him back to you. Put him in my care, and I will return him to you." 38 But he said, "My son must not go down with you, for his brother is dead and he alone is left. If he meets with disaster on the journey you are taking, you will send my white head down to Sheol in grief." **43** 1 But the famine in the land was severe. 2 And when they had eaten up the rations which they had brought from Egypt, their father said to them, "Go again and procure some food for us." 3 But Judah said to him, "The man warned us, 'Do not let me see your faces unless your brother is with you.' 4 If you will let our brother go with us, we will go down and procure food for you; 5 but if you will not let him go, we will not go down, for the man said to us, 'Do not let me see your faces unless your brother is with you.'" 6 And Israel said, "Why did you serve me so ill as to tell the man that you had another brother?" 7 They replied, "But the man kept asking about us and our family, saying, 'Is your father still living? Have you another brother?' And we answered him accordingly. How were we to know that he would say, 'Bring your brother here'?" 8 Then Judah said to his father Israel, "Send the boy in my care, and let us be on our way, that we may live and not die - you and we and our children. 9 I myself will be surety for him; you may hold me responsible: if I do not bring him back to you and set him before you, I shall stand guilty before you forever. 10 For we could have been there and back twice if we had not dawdled." 11 Then their father Israel said to them, "If it must be so, do this: take some of the choice products of the land in your baggage, and carry them down as a gift for the man - some balm and some honey, gum, ladanum, pistachio nuts, and almonds. 12 And take with you double the money, carrying back with you the money that was replaced in the mouths of your bags; perhaps it was a mistake. 13 Take your brother too; and go back at once to the man. 14 And may El Shaddai dispose the man to mercy toward you, that he may release to you your other brother, as well as Benjamin. As for me, if I am to be bereaved, I shall be bereaved." 15 So the men took that gift, and they took with them double the money, as well as Benjamin. They made their way down to Egypt, where they presented themselves to Joseph. 16 When Joseph saw Benjamin with them, he said to his house steward, "Take the men into the house; slaughter and prepare an animal, for the men will dine with me at noon." 17 The man did as Joseph said, and he brought the men into Joseph's house. 18 But the men were frightened on being brought into Joseph's house. "It must be," they thought, "because of the money replaced in our bags the first time that we have been brought inside, as a pretext to attack us and seize us as slaves, with our pack animals." 19 So they went up to Joseph's house steward and spoke to him at the entrance of the house. 20 "If you please, my lord," they said, "we came down once before to procure food. 21 But when we arrived at the night encampment and opened our bags, there was each one's money in the mouth of his bag, our money in full. So we have brought it back with us. 22 And we have brought down with us other money to procure food. We do not know who put the money in our bags." 23 He replied, "All is well with you; do not be afraid. Your God, the God of your father, must have put treasure in your bags for you. I got your payment." And he brought out Simeon to them. 24 Then the man brought the men into Joseph's house; he gave them water to bathe their feet,

56

A page of the Book of Genesis, from the Bible illustrated by Gustave Doré, 1832-33

GENESIS 24

water from your jar." 18 "Drink, my lord," she said, and she quickly lowered her jar upon her hand and let him drink. 19 When she had

GENESIS 44 בראשית מד

and he provided feed for their asses. 25 They laid out their gifts to await Joseph's arrival at noon, for they had heard that they were to dine there. 26 When Joseph came home, they presented to him the gifts that they had brought with them into the house, bowing low before him to the ground. 27 He greeted them, and he said, "How is your aged father of whom you spoke? Is he still in good health?" 28 They replied, "It is well with your servant our father; he is still in good health." And they bowed and made obeisance. 29 Looking about, he saw his brother Benjamin, his mother's son, and asked, "Is this your youngest brother of whom you spoke to me?" And he went on, "May God be gracious to you, my boy." 30 With that, Joseph hurried out, for he was overcome with feeling toward his brother and was on the verge of tears; he went into a room and wept there. 31 Then he washed his face, reappeared, and - now in control of himself - gave the order, "Serve the meal." 32 They served him by himself, and them by themselves, and the Egyptians who ate with him by themselves; for the Egyptians could not dine with the Hebrews, since that would be abhorrent to the Egyptians. 33 As they were seated by his direction, from the oldest in the order of his seniority to the youngest in the order of his youth, the men looked at one another in astonishment. 34 Portions were served them from his table; but Benjamin's portion was several times that of anyone else. And they drank their fill with him. **44** 1 Then he instructed his house steward as follows, "Fill the men's bags with food, as much as they can carry, and put each one's money in the mouth of his bag. 2 Put my silver goblet in the mouth of the bag of the youngest one, together with his money for the rations." And he did as Joseph told him. 3 With the first light of morning, the men were sent off with their pack animals. 4 They had just left the city and had not gone far, when Joseph said to his steward, "Up, go after the men! And when you overtake them, say to them, 'Why did you repay good with evil? 5 It is the very one from which my master drinks and which he uses for divination. It was a wicked thing for you to do!' 6 He overtook them and spoke these words to them. 7 And they said to him, "Why does my lord say such things? Far be it from your servants to do anything of the kind! 8 Here we brought back to you from the land of Canaan the money that we found in the mouths of our bags. How then could we have stolen any silver or gold from your master's house? 9 Whichever of your servants it is found with shall die; the rest of us, moreover, shall become slaves to my lord." 10 He replied, "Although what you are proposing is right, only the one with whom it is found shall be my slave; but the rest of you shall go free." 11 So each one hastened to lower his bag to the ground, and each one opened his bag. 12 He searched, beginning with the oldest and ending with the youngest; and the goblet turned up in Benjamin's bag. 13 At this they rent their clothes. Each reloaded his pack animal, and they returned to the city. 14 When Judah and his brothers reentered the house of Joseph, who was still there, they threw themselves on the ground before him. 15 Joseph said to them, "What is this deed that you have done? Do you not know that a man like me practices divination?" 16 Judah replied, "What can we say to my lord? How can we plead, how can we prove our innocence? God has uncovered the crime of your servants. Here we are, then, slaves of my lord, the rest of us as much as he in whose possession the goblet was found." 17 But he replied, "Far be it from me to act thus! Only he in whose possession the goblet was found shall be my slave; the rest of you go back in peace to your father."

18 Then Judah went up to him and said, "Please, my lord, let your servant appeal to my lord, and do not be impatient with your servant, you who are the equal of Pharaoh. 19 My lord asked his servants, 'Have you a father or another brother?' 20 We told my lord, 'We have an old father, and there is a child of his old age, the youngest; his full brother is dead, so that he alone is left of his mother, and his father dotes on him.' 21 Then you said to your servants, 'Bring him down to me, that I may set eyes on him.' 22 We said to my lord, 'The boy cannot leave his father; if he were to leave him, his father would die.' 23 But you said to your servants, 'Unless your youngest brother comes down with you, do not let me see your faces.' 24 When we came back to your servant my father, we reported my lord's words to him. 25 Later our father said, 'Go back and procure some food for us.' 26 We answered, 'We cannot go down:

GENESIS 45 ויגש בראשית מה

only if our youngest brother is with us can we go down, for we may not show our faces to the man unless our youngest brother is with us.' 27 Your servant my father said to us, 'As you know, my wife bore me two sons. 28 But one is gone from me, and I said: Alas, he was torn by a beast! And I have not seen him since. 29 If you take this one from me, too, and he meets with disaster, you will send my white head down to Sheol in sorrow.' 30 Now, if I come to your servant my father and the boy is not with us - since his own life is so bound up with his - 31 when he sees that the boy is not with us, he will die, and your servants will send the white head of your servant our father down to Sheol in grief. 32 Now your servant has pledged himself for the boy to my father, saying, 'If I do not bring him back to you, I shall stand guilty before my father forever.' 33 Therefore, please let your servant remain as a slave to my lord instead of the boy, and let the boy go back with his brothers. 34 For how can I go back to my father unless the boy is with me? Let me not be witness to the woe that would overtake my father!" **45** 1 Joseph could no longer control himself before all his attendants, and he cried out, "Have everyone withdraw from me!" So there was no one else about when Joseph made himself known to his brothers. 2 His sobs were so loud that the Egyptians could hear, and so the news reached Pharaoh's palace. 3 Joseph said to his brothers, "I am Joseph. Is my father still well?" But his brothers could not answer him, so dumfounded were they on account of him. 4 Then Joseph said to his brothers, "Come forward to me." And when they came forward, he said, "I am your brother Joseph, whom you sold into Egypt. 5 Now, do not be distressed or reproach yourselves because you sold me hither; it was to save life that God sent me ahead of you. 6 It is now two years that there has been famine in the land, and there are yet five years to come in which there shall be no yield from tilling. 7 God has sent me ahead of you to ensure your survival on earth, and to save your lives in an extraordinary deliverance. 8 So, it was not you who sent me here, but God; and He has made me a father to Pharaoh, lord of all his household, and ruler over the whole land of Egypt. 9 Now, hurry back to my father and say to him: Thus says your son Joseph, 'God has made me lord of all Egypt: come down to me without delay. 10 You will dwell in the region of Goshen, where you will be near me - you and your children and your grandchildren, your flocks and herds, and all that is yours. 11 There I will provide for you - for there are yet five years of famine to come - that you and your household and all that is yours may not suffer want.' 12 You can see for yourselves, and my brother Benjamin for himself, that it is indeed I who am speaking to you. 13 And you must tell my father everything about my high station in Egypt and all that you have seen; and bring my father here with all speed." 14 With that he embraced his brother Benjamin around the neck and wept, and Benjamin wept on his neck. 15 He kissed all his brothers and wept upon them; only then were his brothers able to talk to him. 16 The news reached Pharaoh's palace: "Joseph's brothers have come." Pharaoh and his courtiers were pleased. 17 And Pharaoh said to Joseph, "Say to your brothers, Do as follows: load up your beasts and go at once to the land of Canaan. 18 Take your father and your households and come to me; I will give you the best of the land of Egypt and you shall live off the fat of the land. 19 And you are bidden [to add], 'Do as follows: take from the land of Egypt wagons for your children and your wives, and bring your father too. 20 And never mind your belongings, for the best of all the land of Egypt shall be yours.'" 21 The sons of Israel did so; Joseph gave them wagons as Pharaoh had commanded, and he supplied them with provisions for the journey. 22 To each of them, moreover, he gave a change of clothing; but to Benjamin he gave three hundred pieces of silver and several changes of clothing. 23 And to his father he sent the following: ten he-asses laden with the best things of Egypt, and ten she-asses laden with grain, bread, and provisions for his father on the journey. 24 As he sent his brothers off on their way, he told them, "Do not be quarrelsome on the way." 25 They went up from Egypt and came to their father Jacob in the land of Canaan. 26 And they told him, "Joseph is still alive; yes, he is ruler over the whole land of Egypt." His heart went numb, for he did not believe them. 27 But when they recounted all that Joseph had said to them, and when he saw the wagons that Joseph had sent to transport him, the spirit of their

GENESIS 46 ויגש בראשית מו

father Jacob revived. 28 "Enough!" said Israel. "My son Joseph is still alive! I must go and see him before I die." **46** 1 So Israel set out with all that was his, and he came to Beer-sheba, where he offered sacrifices to the God of his father Isaac. 2 God called to Israel in a vision by night: "Jacob! Jacob!" He answered, "Here." 3 And He said, "I am God, the God of your father. Fear not to go down to Egypt, for I will make you there into a great nation. 4 I Myself will go down with you to Egypt, and I Myself will also bring you back; and Joseph's hand shall close your eyes." 5 So Jacob set out from Beer-sheba. The sons of Israel put their father Jacob and their children and their wives in the wagons that Pharaoh had sent to transport him; 6 and they took along their livestock and the wealth that they had amassed in the land of Canaan. Thus Jacob and all his offspring with him came to Egypt: 7 he brought with him to Egypt his sons and grandsons, his daughters and granddaughters - all his offspring. 8 These are the names of the Israelites, Jacob and his descendants, who came to Egypt. Jacob's first-born Reuben; 9 Reuben's sons: Enoch, Pallu, Hezron, and Carmi. 10 Simeon's sons: Jemuel, Jamin, Ohad, Jachin, Zohar, and Saul the son of a Canaanite woman. 11 Levi's sons: Gershon, Kohath, and Merari. 12 Judah's sons: Er, Onan, Shelah, Perez, and Zerah - but Er and Onan had died in the land of Canaan; and Perez's sons were Hezron and Hamul. 13 Issachar's sons: Tola, Puvah, Iob, and Shimron. 14 Zebulun's sons: Sered, Elon, and Jahleel. 15 Those were the sons whom Leah bore to Jacob in Paddan-aram, in addition to his daughter Dinah. Persons in all, male and female: 33 persons. 16 Gad's sons: Ziphion, Haggi, Shuni, Ezbon, Eri, Arodi, and Areli. 17 Asher's sons: Imnah, Ishvah, Ishvi, and Beriah, and their sister Serah. Beriah's sons: Heber and Malchiel. 18 These were the descendants of Zilpah, whom Laban had given to his daughter Leah. These she bore to Jacob - 16 persons. 19 The sons of Jacob's wife Rachel were Joseph and Benjamin. 20 To Joseph were born in the land of Egypt Manasseh and Ephraim, whom Asenath daughter of Poti-phera priest of On bore to him. 21 Benjamin's sons: Bela, Becher, Ashbel, Gera, Naaman, Ehi, Rosh, Muppim, Huppim, and Ard. 22 These were the descendants of Rachel who were born to Jacob - 14 persons in all. 23 Dan's son: Hushim. 24 Naphtali's sons: Jahzeel, Guni, Jezer, and Shillem. 25 These were the descendants of Bilhah, whom Laban had given to his daughter Rachel. These she bore to Jacob - 7 persons in all. 26 All the persons belonging to Jacob who came to Egypt - his own issue, aside from the wives of Jacob's sons - all these persons numbered 66. 27 And Joseph's sons who were born to him in Egypt were two in number. Thus the total of Jacob's household who came to Egypt was seventy persons. 28 He had sent Judah ahead of him to Joseph, to point the way before him to Goshen. So when they came to the region of Goshen, 29 Joseph ordered his chariot and went to Goshen to meet his father Israel; he presented himself to him and, embracing him around the neck, he wept on his neck a good while. 30 Then Israel said to Joseph, "Now I can die, having seen for myself that you are still alive." 31 Then Joseph said to his brothers and to his father's household, "I will go up and tell the news to Pharaoh, and say to him, 'My brothers and my father's household, who were in the land of Canaan, have come to me. 32 The men are shepherds; they have always been breeders of livestock, and they have brought with them their flocks and herds and all that is theirs.' 33 So when Pharaoh summons you and asks, 'What is your occupation?' 34 you shall answer, 'Your servants have been breeders of livestock from the start until now, both we and our fathers' - so that you may stay in the region of Goshen. For all shepherds are abhorrent to Egyptians. **47** 1 Then Joseph came and reported to Pharaoh, saying, "My father and my brothers, with their flocks and herds and all that is theirs, have come from the land of Canaan and are now in the region of Goshen." 2 And selecting a few of his brothers, he presented them to Pharaoh. 3 Pharaoh said to his brothers, "What is your occupation?" They answered Pharaoh, "We your servants are shepherds, as were also our fathers. 4 We have come," they told Pharaoh, "to sojourn in this land, for there is no pasture for your servants' flocks, the famine being severe in the land of Canaan. Pray, then,

GENESIS 48 · בראשית מח ויחי

שְׁבִיעָנָא עֲבָדֶיךָ בְּאֶרֶץ גְּשֶׁן: ה וַיֹּאמֶר פַּרְעֹה אֶל־יוֹסֵף לֵאמֹר אָבִיךָ וְאַחֶיךָ בָּאוּ אֵלֶיךָ: ו אֶרֶץ מִצְרַיִם לְפָנֶיךָ הִוא בְּמֵיטַב הָאָרֶץ הוֹשֵׁב אֶת־אָבִיךָ וְאֶת־אַחֶיךָ יֵשְׁבוּ בְּאֶרֶץ גֹּשֶׁן וְאִם־יָדַעְתָּ וְיֶשׁ־בָּם אַנְשֵׁי־חַיִל וְשַׂמְתָּם שָׂרֵי מִקְנֶה עַל־אֲשֶׁר־לִי: ז וַיָּבֵא יוֹסֵף אֶת־יַעֲקֹב אָבִיו וַיַּעֲמִדֵהוּ לִפְנֵי פַרְעֹה וַיְבָרֶךְ יַעֲקֹב אֶת־פַּרְעֹה: ח וַיֹּאמֶר פַּרְעֹה אֶל־יַעֲקֹב כַּמָּה יְמֵי שְׁנֵי חַיֶּיךָ: ט וַיֹּאמֶר יַעֲקֹב אֶל־פַּרְעֹה יְמֵי שְׁנֵי מְגוּרַי שְׁלֹשִׁים וּמְאַת שָׁנָה מְעַט וְרָעִים הָיוּ יְמֵי שְׁנֵי חַיַּי וְלֹא הִשִּׂיגוּ אֶת־יְמֵי שְׁנֵי חַיֵּי אֲבֹתַי בִּימֵי מְגוּרֵיהֶם: י וַיְבָרֶךְ יַעֲקֹב אֶת־פַּרְעֹה וַיֵּצֵא מִלִּפְנֵי פַרְעֹה: יא וַיּוֹשֵׁב יוֹסֵף אֶת־אָבִיו וְאֶת־אֶחָיו וַיִּתֵּן לָהֶם אֲחֻזָּה בְּאֶרֶץ מִצְרַיִם בְּמֵיטַב הָאָרֶץ בְּאֶרֶץ רַעְמְסֵס כַּאֲשֶׁר צִוָּה פַרְעֹה: יב וַיְכַלְכֵּל יוֹסֵף אֶת־אָבִיו וְאֶת־אֶחָיו וְאֵת כָּל־בֵּית אָבִיו לֶחֶם לְפִי הַטָּף: יג וְלֶחֶם אֵין בְּכָל־הָאָרֶץ כִּי־כָבֵד הָרָעָב מְאֹד וַתֵּלַהּ אֶרֶץ מִצְרַיִם וְאֶרֶץ כְּנַעַן מִפְּנֵי הָרָעָב: יד וַיְלַקֵּט יוֹסֵף אֶת־כָּל־הַכֶּסֶף הַנִּמְצָא בְאֶרֶץ־מִצְרַיִם וּבְאֶרֶץ כְּנַעַן בַּשֶּׁבֶר אֲשֶׁר־הֵם שֹׁבְרִים וַיָּבֵא יוֹסֵף אֶת־הַכֶּסֶף בֵּיתָה פַרְעֹה: טו וַיִּתֹּם הַכֶּסֶף מֵאֶרֶץ מִצְרַיִם וּמֵאֶרֶץ כְּנַעַן וַיָּבֹאוּ כָל־מִצְרַיִם אֶל־יוֹסֵף לֵאמֹר הָבָה־לָּנוּ לֶחֶם וְלָמָּה נָמוּת נֶגְדֶּךָ כִּי אָפֵס כָּסֶף: טז וַיֹּאמֶר יוֹסֵף הָבוּ מִקְנֵיכֶם וְאֶתְּנָה לָכֶם בְּמִקְנֵיכֶם אִם־אָפֵס כָּסֶף: יז וַיָּבִיאוּ אֶת־מִקְנֵיהֶם אֶל־יוֹסֵף וַיִּתֵּן לָהֶם יוֹסֵף לֶחֶם בַּסּוּסִים וּבְמִקְנֵה הַצֹּאן וּבְמִקְנֵה הַבָּקָר וּבַחֲמֹרִים וַיְנַהֲלֵם בַּלֶּחֶם בְּכָל־מִקְנֵהֶם בַּשָּׁנָה הַהִוא: יח וַתִּתֹּם הַשָּׁנָה הַהִוא וַיָּבֹאוּ אֵלָיו בַּשָּׁנָה הַשֵּׁנִית וַיֹּאמְרוּ לוֹ לֹא־נְכַחֵד מֵאֲדֹנִי כִּי אִם־תַּם הַכֶּסֶף וּמִקְנֵה הַבְּהֵמָה אֶל־אֲדֹנִי לֹא נִשְׁאַר לִפְנֵי אֲדֹנִי בִּלְתִּי אִם־גְּוִיָּתֵנוּ וְאַדְמָתֵנוּ: יט לָמָּה נָמוּת לְעֵינֶיךָ גַּם־אֲנַחְנוּ גַּם אַדְמָתֵנוּ קְנֵה־אֹתָנוּ וְאֶת־אַדְמָתֵנוּ בַּלָּחֶם וְנִהְיֶה אֲנַחְנוּ וְאַדְמָתֵנוּ עֲבָדִים לְפַרְעֹה וְתֶן־זֶרַע וְנִחְיֶה וְלֹא נָמוּת וְהָאֲדָמָה לֹא תֵשָׁם: כ וַיִּקֶן יוֹסֵף אֶת־כָּל־אַדְמַת מִצְרַיִם לְפַרְעֹה כִּי־מָכְרוּ מִצְרַיִם אִישׁ שָׂדֵהוּ כִּי־חָזַק עֲלֵהֶם הָרָעָב וַתְּהִי הָאָרֶץ לְפַרְעֹה: כא וְאֶת־הָעָם הֶעֱבִיר אֹתוֹ לֶעָרִים מִקְצֵה גְבוּל־מִצְרַיִם וְעַד־קָצֵהוּ: כב רַק אַדְמַת הַכֹּהֲנִים לֹא קָנָה כִּי חֹק לַכֹּהֲנִים מֵאֵת פַּרְעֹה וְאָכְלוּ אֶת־חֻקָּם אֲשֶׁר נָתַן לָהֶם פַּרְעֹה עַל־כֵּן לֹא מָכְרוּ אֶת־אַדְמָתָם: כג וַיֹּאמֶר יוֹסֵף אֶל־הָעָם הֵן קָנִיתִי אֶתְכֶם הַיּוֹם וְאֶת־אַדְמַתְכֶם לְפַרְעֹה הֵא־לָכֶם זֶרַע וּזְרַעְתֶּם אֶת־הָאֲדָמָה: כד וְהָיָה בַּתְּבוּאֹת וּנְתַתֶּם חֲמִישִׁית לְפַרְעֹה וְאַרְבַּע הַיָּדֹת יִהְיֶה לָכֶם לְזֶרַע הַשָּׂדֶה וּלְאָכְלְכֶם וְלַאֲשֶׁר בְּבָתֵּיכֶם וְלֶאֱכֹל לְטַפְּכֶם: כה וַיֹּאמְרוּ הֶחֱיִתָנוּ נִמְצָא־חֵן בְּעֵינֵי אֲדֹנִי וְהָיִינוּ עֲבָדִים לְפַרְעֹה: כו וַיָּשֶׂם אֹתָהּ יוֹסֵף לְחֹק עַד־הַיּוֹם הַזֶּה עַל־אַדְמַת מִצְרַיִם לְפַרְעֹה לַחֹמֶשׁ רַק אַדְמַת הַכֹּהֲנִים לְבַדָּם לֹא הָיְתָה לְפַרְעֹה: כז וַיֵּשֶׁב יִשְׂרָאֵל בְּאֶרֶץ מִצְרַיִם בְּאֶרֶץ גֹּשֶׁן וַיֵּאָחֲזוּ בָהּ וַיִּפְרוּ וַיִּרְבּוּ מְאֹד:

כח וַיְחִי יַעֲקֹב בְּאֶרֶץ מִצְרַיִם שְׁבַע עֶשְׂרֵה שָׁנָה וַיְהִי יְמֵי־יַעֲקֹב שְׁנֵי חַיָּיו שֶׁבַע שָׁנִים וְאַרְבָּעִים וּמְאַת שָׁנָה: כט וַיִּקְרְבוּ יְמֵי־יִשְׂרָאֵל לָמוּת וַיִּקְרָא לִבְנוֹ לְיוֹסֵף וַיֹּאמֶר לוֹ אִם־נָא מָצָאתִי חֵן בְּעֵינֶיךָ שִׂים־נָא יָדְךָ תַּחַת יְרֵכִי וְעָשִׂיתָ עִמָּדִי חֶסֶד וֶאֱמֶת אַל־נָא תִקְבְּרֵנִי בְּמִצְרָיִם: ל וְשָׁכַבְתִּי עִם־אֲבֹתַי וּנְשָׂאתַנִי מִמִּצְרַיִם וּקְבַרְתַּנִי בִּקְבֻרָתָם וַיֹּאמַר אָנֹכִי אֶעֱשֶׂה כִדְבָרֶךָ: לא וַיֹּאמֶר הִשָּׁבְעָה לִי וַיִּשָּׁבַע לוֹ וַיִּשְׁתַּחוּ יִשְׂרָאֵל עַל־רֹאשׁ הַמִּטָּה:

מח א וַיְהִי אַחֲרֵי הַדְּבָרִים הָאֵלֶּה וַיֹּאמֶר לְיוֹסֵף הִנֵּה אָבִיךָ חֹלֶה וַיִּקַּח אֶת־שְׁנֵי בָנָיו עִמּוֹ אֶת־מְנַשֶּׁה וְאֶת־אֶפְרָיִם: ב וַיֻּגַּד לְיַעֲקֹב וַיֹּאמֶר

let your servants stay in the region of Goshen." 5 Then Pharaoh said to Joseph, "As regards your father and your brothers who have come to you, 6 the land of Egypt is open before you; settle your father and your brothers in the best part of the land; let them stay in the region of Goshen. And if you know any capable men among them, put them in charge of my livestock." 7 Joseph then brought his father Jacob and presented him to Pharaoh; and Jacob greeted Pharaoh. 8 Pharaoh asked Jacob, "How many are the years of your life?" 9 And Jacob answered Pharaoh, "The years of my sojourn [on earth] are one hundred and thirty. Few and hard have been the years of my life, nor do they come up to the life spans of my fathers during their sojourns." 10 Then Jacob bade Pharaoh farewell, and left Pharaoh's presence. 11 So Joseph settled his father and his brothers, giving them holdings in the choicest part of the land of Egypt, in the region of Rameses, as Pharaoh had commanded. 12 Joseph sustained his father, and his brothers, and all his father's household with bread, down to the little ones. 13 Now there was no bread in all the world, for the famine was very severe; both the land of Egypt and the land of Canaan languished because of the famine. 14 Joseph gathered in all the money that was to be found in the land of Egypt and in the land of Canaan, as payment for the rations that were being procured, and Joseph brought the money into Pharaoh's palace. 15 And when the money gave out in the land of Egypt and in the land of Canaan, all the Egyptians came to Joseph and said, "Give us bread, lest we die before your very eyes; for the money is gone!" 16 And Joseph said, "Bring your livestock, and I will sell to you against your livestock, if the money is gone." 17 So they brought their livestock to Joseph, and Joseph gave them bread in exchange for the horses, for the stocks of sheep and cattle, and the asses; thus he provided them with bread in exchange for all their livestock. 18 And when that year was ended, they came to him the next year and said to him, "We cannot hide from my lord that, with all the money and animal stocks consigned to my lord, nothing is left at my lord's disposal save our persons and our farmland. 19 Let us not perish before your eyes, both we and our land. Take us and our land in exchange for bread, and we with our land will be serfs to Pharaoh; provide the seed, that we may live and not die, and that the land may not become a waste." 20 So Joseph gained possession of all the farm land of Egypt for Pharaoh, every Egyptian having sold his field because the famine was too much for them; thus the land passed over to Pharaoh. 21 And he removed the population town by town, from one end of Egypt's border to the other. 22 Only the land of the priests he did not take over, for the priests had an allotment from Pharaoh, and they lived off the allotment which Pharaoh had made to them; therefore they did not sell their land. 23 Then Joseph said to the people, "Whereas I have this day acquired you and your land for Pharaoh, here is seed for you to sow the land. 24 And when harvest comes, you shall give one-fifth to Pharaoh, and four-fifths shall be yours as seed for the fields and as food for you and those in your households, and as nourishment for your children." 25 And they said, "You have saved our lives! We are grateful to my lord, and we shall be serfs to Pharaoh." 26 And Joseph made it into a land law in Egypt, which is still valid, that a fifth should be Pharaoh's; only the land of the priests did not become Pharaoh's. 27 Thus Israel settled in the country of Egypt, in the region of Goshen; they acquired holdings in it, and were fertile and increased greatly.

28 **J**acob lived seventeen years in the land of Egypt, so that the span of Jacob's life came to one hundred and forty-seven years. 29 And when the time approached for Israel to die, he summoned his son Joseph and said to him. "Do me this favor, place your hand under my thigh as a pledge of your steadfast loyalty: please do not bury me in Egypt. 30 When I lie down with my fathers, take me up from Egypt and bury me in their burial-place." He replied, "I will do as you have spoken." 31 And he said, "Swear to me." And he swore to him. Then Israel bowed at the head of the bed.

48 1 Some time afterward, Joseph was told, "Your father is ill." So he took with him his two sons, Manasseh and Ephraim. 2 When Jacob was told,

GENESIS 49

"Your son Joseph has come to see you." Israel summoned his strength and sat up in bed. 3 And Jacob said to Joseph, "El Shaddai appeared to me at Luz in the land of Canaan, and He blessed me, 4 and said to me, 'I will make you fertile and numerous, making of you a community of peoples; and I will assign this land to your offspring to come for an everlasting possession.' 5 Now, your two sons, who were born to you in the land of Egypt before I came to you in Egypt, shall be mine; Ephraim and Manasseh shall be mine no less than Reuben and Simeon. 6 But progeny born to you after them shall be yours; they shall be recorded instead of their brothers in their inheritance. 7 [I do this because], when I was returning from Paddan, Rachel died, to my sorrow, while I was journeying in the land of Canaan, when still some distance short of Ephrath; and I buried her there on the road to Ephrath" - now Bethlehem. 8 Noticing Joseph's sons, Israel asked, "Who are these?" 9 And Joseph said to his father, "They are my sons, whom God has given me here." "Bring them up to me," he said, "that I may bless them." 10 Now Israel's eyes were dim with age; he could not see. So [Joseph] brought them close to him, and he kissed them and embraced them. 11 And Israel said to Joseph, "I never expected to see you again, and here God has let me see your children as well." 12 Joseph then removed them from his knees, and bowed low with his face to the ground. 13 Joseph took the two of them, Ephraim with his right hand - to Israel's left - and Manasseh with his left hand - to Israel's right - and brought them close to him. 14 But Israel stretched out his right hand and laid it on Ephraim's head, though he was the younger, and his left hand on Manasseh's head - thus crossing his hands - although Manasseh was the first-born. 15 And he blessed Joseph, saying, "The God in whose ways my fathers Abraham and Isaac walked. The God who has been my shepherd from my birth to this day - 16 The Angel who has redeemed me from all harm - Bless the lads. In them may my name be recalled, And the names of my fathers Abraham and Isaac. And may they be teeming multitudes upon the earth." 17 When Joseph saw that his father was placing his right hand on Ephraim's head, he thought it wrong; so he took hold of his father's hand to move it from Ephraim's head to Manasseh's. 18 "Not so, Father," Joseph said to his father, "for the other is the first-born; place your right hand on his head." 19 But his father objected, saying, "I know, my son, I know. He too shall become a people, and he too shall be great. Yet his younger brother shall be greater than he, and his offspring shall be plentiful enough for nations." 20 So he blessed them that day, saying, "By you shall Israel invoke blessings, saying: God make you like Ephraim and Manasseh." Thus he put Ephraim before Manasseh. 21 Then Israel said to Joseph, "I am about to die; but God will be with you and bring you back to the land of your fathers. 22 And now, I assign to you one portion more than your brothers, which I wrested from the Amorites with my sword and bow."

49 1 And Jacob called his sons and said, "Come together that I may tell you what is to befall you in days to come. 2 Assemble and hearken, O sons of Jacob; Hearken to Israel your father: 3 Reuben, you are my first-born, My might and first fruit of my vigor, Exceeding in rank nd exceeding in honor. 4 Unstable as water, you shall excel no longer; For when you mounted your father's bed, You brought disgrace - my couch he mounted! 5 Simeon and Levi are a pair; Their weapons are tools of lawlessness. 6 Let not my person be included in their council, Let not my being be counted in their assembly. For when angry they slay men, And when pleased they maim oxen. 7 Cursed be their anger so fierce, And their wrath so relentless. I will divide them in Jacob, Scatter them in Israel. 8 You, O Judah, your brothers shall praise: Your hand shall be on the nape of your foes; Your father's sons shall bow low to you. 9 Judah is a lion's whelp; On prey, my son, have you grown. He crouches, lies down like a lion, Like the king of beasts - who dare rouse him? 10 The scepter shall not depart from Judah, Nor the ruler's staff from between his feet; So that tribute shall come to him And the homage of peoples be his. 11 He tethers his ass to a vine, His ass's foal to a choice vine; He washes his garment in wine, His robe in blood of grapes. 12 His eyes are darker than wine; His teeth are whiter than milk. 13 Zebulun shall dwell by the seashore; He shall be a haven for ships, And his flank shall rest on Sidon.

GENESIS 50

14 Issachar is a strong-boned ass, Crouching among the sheepfolds. 15 When he saw how good was security, And how pleasant was the country, He bent his shoulder to the burden, And became a toiling serf. 16 Dan shall govern his people, As one of the tribes of Israel. 17 Dan shall be a serpent by the road, A viper by the path, That bites the horse's heels So that his rider is thrown backward. 18 I wait for Your deliverance, O LORD! 19 Gad shall be raided by raiders, But he shall raid at their heels. 20 Asher's bread shall be rich, And he shall yield royal dainties. 21 Naphtali is a hind let loose, Which yields lovely fawns. 22 Joseph is a wild ass, A wild ass by a spring - Wild colts on a hillside. 23 Archers bitterly assailed him; They shot at him and harried him. 24 Yet his bow stayed taut, And his arms were made firm By the hands of the Mighty One of Jacob - There, the Shepherd, the Rock of Israel - 25 The God of your father helps you, And Shaddai who blesses you With blessings of heaven above, Blessings of the deep that couches below, Blessings of the breast and womb. 26 The blessings of your father Surpass the blessings of my ancestors, To the utmost bounds of the eternal hills. May they rest on the head of Joseph, On the brow of the elect of his brothers. 27 Benjamin is a ravenous wolf; In the morning he consumes the foe, And in the evening he divides the spoil." 28 All these were the tribes of Israel, twelve in number, and this is what their father said to them as he bade them farewell, addressing to each a parting word appropriate to him. 29 Then he instructed them, saying to them, "I am about to be gathered to my kin. Bury me with my fathers in the cave which is in the field of Ephron the Hittite, 30 the cave which is in the field of Machpelah, facing Mamre, in the land of Canaan, the field that Abraham bought from Ephron the Hittite for a burial site - 31 there Abraham and his wife Sarah were buried; there Isaac and his wife Rebekah were buried; and there I buried Leah - 32 the field and the cave in it, bought from the Hittites." 33 When Jacob finished his instructions to his sons, he drew his feet into the bed and, breathing his last, he was gathered to his people. 50 1 Joseph flung himself upon his father's face and wept over him and kissed him. 2 Then Joseph ordered the physicians in his service to embalm his father, and the physicians embalmed Israel. 3 It required forty days, for such is the full period of embalming. The Egyptians bewailed him seventy days; 4 and when the wailing period was over, Joseph spoke to Pharaoh's court, saying, "Do me this favor, and lay this appeal before Pharaoh: 5 My father made me swear, saying, 'I am about to die. Be sure to bury me in the grave which I made ready for myself in the land of Canaan.' Now, therefore, let me go up and bury my father; then I shall return." 6 And Pharaoh said, "Go up and bury your father, as he made you promise on oath." 7 So Joseph went up to bury his father; and with him went up all the officials of Pharaoh, the senior members of his court, and all of Egypt's dignitaries, 8 together with all of Joseph's household, his brothers, and his father's household; only their children, their flocks, and their herds were left in the region of Goshen. 9 Chariots, too, and horsemen went up with him; it was a very large troop. 10 When they came to Goren ha-Atad, which is beyond the Jordan, they held there a very great and solemn lamentation; and he observed a mourning period of seven days for his father. 11 And when the Canaanite inhabitants of the land saw the mourning at Goren ha-Atad, they said, "This is a solemn mourning on the part of the Egyptians." That is why it was named Abel-mizraim, which is beyond the Jordan. 12 Thus his sons did for him as he had instructed them. 13 His sons carried him to the land of Canaan, and buried him in the cave of the field of Machpelah, the field near Mamre, which Abraham had bought for a burial site from Ephron the Hittite. 14 After burying his father, Joseph returned to Egypt, he and his brothers and all who had gone up with him to bury his father. 15 When Joseph's brothers saw that their father was dead, they said, "What if Joseph still bears a grudge against us and pays us back for all the wrong that we did him!" 16 So they sent this message to Joseph, "Before his death your father left this instruction: 17 So shall you say to Joseph, Forgive, I urge you, the offense and guilt of your brothers who treated you so harshly. Therefore, please forgive the offense of the servants of the God of your father." And Joseph was in tears as they spoke to him. 18 His brothers went to him themselves,

GENESIS 50 — בראשית נ ויחי

flung themselves before him, and said, "We are prepared to be your slaves." 19 But Joseph said to them, "Have no fear! Am I a substitute for God? 20 Besides, although you intended me harm, God intended it for good, so as to bring about the present result - the survival of many people. 21 And so, fear not. I will sustain you and your children." Thus he reassured them, speaking kindly to them. 22 So Joseph and his father's household remained in Egypt. Joseph lived one hundred and ten years. 23 Joseph lived to see children of the third generation of Ephraim; the children of Machir son of Manasseh were likewise born upon Joseph's knees. 24 At length, Joseph said to his brothers, "I am about to die. God will surely take notice of you and bring you up from this land to the land that He promised on oath to Abraham, to Isaac, and to Jacob." 25 So Joseph made the sons of Israel swear, saying, "When God has taken notice of you, you shall carry up my bones from here." 26 Joseph died at the age of one hundred and ten years; and he was embalmed and placed in a coffin in Egypt.

On the facing page:
Seven-branched bronze candelabrum (menorah), 6th century (the Byzantine period), found in the synagogue at Ein-Gedi, collection of the Antiquities Authority, The Israel Museum, Jerusalem

Details of a fragment of a carpet page illustrated with Temple implements, from the "First Leningrad Bible", copied and illustrated by Solomon Ha-Levi Ben Bouya, Cairo, 929, collection of the Public Library, St. Petersburg

EXODUS 1 שמות א שמות

1 These are the names of the sons of Israel who came to Egypt with Jacob, each coming with his household: 2 Reuben, Simeon, Levi, and Judah; 3 Issachar, Zebulun, and Benjamin; 4 Dan and Naphtali, Gad and Asher. 5 The total number of persons that were of Jacob's issue came to seventy, Joseph being already in Egypt. 6 Joseph died, and all his brothers, and all that generation. 7 But the Israelites were fertile and prolific; they multiplied and increased very greatly, so that the land was filled with them. 8 A new king arose over Egypt who did not know Joseph. 9 And he said to his people, "Look, the Israelite people are much too numerous for us. 10 Let us deal shrewdly with them, so that they may not increase; otherwise in the event of war they may join our enemies in fighting against us and rise from the ground." 11 So they set taskmasters over them to oppress them with forced labor; and they built garrison cities for Pharaoh: Pithom and Raamses. 12 But the more they were oppressed, the more they increased and spread out, so that the [Egyptians] came to dread the Israelites. 13 The Egyptians ruthlessly imposed upon the Israelites 14 the various labors that they made them perform. Ruthlessly they made life bitter for them with harsh labor at mortar and bricks and with all sorts of tasks in the field. 15 The king of Egypt spoke to the Hebrew midwives, one of whom was named Shiphrah and the other Puah, 16 saying, "When you deliver the Hebrew women, look at the birthstool: if it is a boy, kill him; if it is a girl, let her live." 17 The midwives, fearing God, did not do as the king of Egypt had told them; they let the boys live. 18 So the king of Egypt summoned the midwives and said to them, "Why have you done this thing, letting the boys live?" 19 The midwives said to Pharaoh, "Because the Hebrew women are not like the Egyptian women: they are vigorous. Before the midwife can come to them, they have given birth." 20 And God dealt well with the midwives; and the people multiplied and increased greatly. 21 And because the midwives feared God, He established households for them. 22 Then Pharaoh charged all his people, saying, "Every boy that is born you shall throw into the Nile, but let every girl live."

2 1 A certain man of the house of Levi went and married a Levite woman. 2 The woman conceived and bore a son; and when she saw how beautiful he was, she hid him for three months. 3 When she could hide him no longer, she got a wicker basket for him and caulked it with bitumen and pitch. She put the child into it and placed it among the reeds by the bank of the Nile. 4 And his sister stationed herself at a distance, to learn what would befall him. 5 The daughter of Pharaoh came down to bathe in the Nile, while her maidens walked along the Nile. She spied the basket among the reeds and sent her slave girl to fetch it.

EXODUS 3 שמות ג

6 When she opened it, she saw that it was a child, a boy crying. She took pity on it and said, "This must be a Hebrew child." 7 Then his sister said to Pharaoh's daughter, "Shall I go and get you a Hebrew nurse to suckle the child for you?" 8 And Pharaoh's daughter answered, "Yes." So the girl went and called the child's mother. 9 And Pharaoh's daughter said to her, "Take this child and nurse it for me, and I will pay your wages." So the woman took the child and nursed it. 10 When the child grew up, she brought him to Pharaoh's daughter, who made him her son. She named him Moses, explaining, "I drew him out of the water." 11 Some time after that, when Moses had grown up, he went out to his kinsfolk and witnessed their labors. He saw an Egyptian beating a Hebrew, one of his kinsmen. 12 He turned this way and that and, seeing no one about, he struck down the Egyptian and hid him in the sand. 13 When he went out the next day, he found two Hebrews fighting; so he said to the offender, "Why do you strike your fellow?" 14 He retorted, "Who made you chief and ruler over us? Do you mean to kill me as you killed the Egyptian?" Moses was frightened, and thought: Then the matter is known! 15 When Pharaoh learned of the matter, he sought to kill Moses; but Moses fled from Pharaoh. He arrived in Midian, and sat down beside a well. 16 Now the priest of Midian had seven daughters. They came to draw water, and filled the troughs to water their father's flock; 17 but shepherds came and drove them off. Moses rose to their defense, and he watered their flock. 18 When they returned to their father Reuel, he said, "How is it that you have come back so soon today?" 19 They answered, "An Egyptian rescued us from the shepherds; he even drew water for us and watered the flock." 20 He said to his daughters, "Where is he then? Why did you leave the man? Ask him in to break bread." 21 Moses consented to stay with the man, and he gave Moses his daughter Zipporah as wife. 22 She bore a son whom she named Gershom, for he said, "I have been a stranger in a foreign land."

23 A long time after that, the king of Egypt died. The Israelites were groaning under the bondage and cried out; and their cry for help from the bondage rose up to God. 24 God heard their moaning, and God remembered His covenant with Abraham and Isaac and Jacob. 25 God looked upon the Israelites, and God took notice of them.

3 Now Moses, tending the flock of his father-in-law Jethro, the priest of Midian, drove the flock into the wilderness, and came to Horeb, the mountain of God. 2 An angel of the LORD appeared to him in a blazing fire out of a bush. He gazed, and there was a bush all aflame, yet the bush was not consumed. 3 Moses said, "I must turn aside to look at this marvelous sight; why doesn't the bush burn up?" 4 When the LORD saw that he had turned aside to look, God called to him out of the bush: "Moses! Moses!" He answered, "Here I am." 5 And He said, "Do not come closer. Remove your sandals from your feet, for the place on which you stand is holy ground. 6 I am," He said, "the God of your father, the God of Abraham, the God of Isaac, and the God of Jacob." And Moses hid his face, for he was afraid to look at God. 7 And the LORD continued, "I have marked well the plight of My people in Egypt and have heeded their outcry because of their taskmasters; yes, I am mindful of their sufferings. 8 I have come down to rescue them from the Egyptians and to bring them out of that land to a good and spacious land, a land flowing with milk and honey, the region of the Canaanites, the Hittites, the Amorites, the Perizzites, the Hivites, and the Jebusites. 9 Now the cry of the Israelites has reached Me; moreover, I have seen how the Egyptians oppress them. 10 Come, therefore, I will send you to Pharaoh, and you shall free My people, the Israelites, from Egypt." 11 But Moses said to God, "Who am I that I should go to Pharaoh and free the Israelites from Egypt?" 12 And He said, "I will be with you; that shall be your sign that it was I who sent you. And when you have freed the people from Egypt, you shall worship God at this mountain." 13 Moses said to God, "When I come to the Israelites

EXODUS 4 שמות ד

and say to them, 'The God of your fathers has sent me to you,' and they ask me, 'What is His name?' what shall I say to them?" 14 And God said to Moses, "Ehyeh-Asher-Ehyeh." He continued, "Thus shall you say to the Israelites, 'Ehyeh sent me to you.'" 15 And God said further to Moses, "Thus shall you speak to the Israelites: The LORD, the God of your fathers, the God of Abraham, the God of Isaac, and the God of Jacob, has sent me to you: This shall be My name forever, This My appellation for all eternity. 16 "Go and assemble the elders of Israel and say to them: the LORD, the God of your fathers, the God of Abraham, Isaac, and Jacob, has appeared to me and said, 'I have taken note of you and of what is being done to you in Egypt, 17 and I have declared: I will take you out of the misery of Egypt to the land of the Canaanites, the Hittites, the Amorites, the Perizzites, the Hivites, and the Jebusites, to a land flowing with milk and honey.' 18 They will listen to you; then you shall go with the elders of Israel to the king of Egypt and you shall say to him, 'The LORD, the God of the Hebrews, manifested Himself to us. Now therefore, let us go a distance of three days into the wilderness to sacrifice to the LORD our God.' 19 Yet I know that the king of Egypt will let you go only because of a greater might. 20 So I will stretch out My hand and smite Egypt with various wonders which I will work upon them; after that he shall let you go. 21 And I will dispose the Egyptians favorably toward this people, so that when you go, you will not go away empty-handed. 22 Each woman shall borrow from her neighbor and the lodger in her house objects of silver and gold, and clothing, and you shall put these on your sons and daughters, thus stripping the Egyptians." 4 1 But Moses spoke up and said, "What if they do not believe me and do not listen to me, but say: The LORD did not appear to you?" 2 The LORD said to him, "What is that in your hand?" And he replied, "A rod." 3 He said, "Cast it on the ground." He cast it on the ground and it became a snake; and Moses recoiled from it. 4 Then the LORD said to Moses, "Put out your hand and grasp it by the tail" - he put out his hand and seized it, and it became a rod in his hand - 5 "that they may believe that the LORD, the God of their fathers, the God of Abraham, the God of Isaac, and the God of Jacob, did appear to you." 6 The LORD said to him further, "Put your hand into your bosom." He put his hand into his bosom; and when he took it out, his hand was encrusted with snowy scales! 7 And He said, "Put your hand back into your bosom." - He put his hand back into his bosom; and when he took it out of his bosom, there it was again like the rest of his body. 8 "And if they do not believe you or pay heed to the first sign, they will believe the second. 9 And if they are not convinced by both these signs and still do not heed you, take some water from the Nile and pour it on the dry ground, and it - the water that you take from the Nile - will turn to blood on the dry ground." 10 But Moses said to the LORD, "Please, O Lord, I have never been a man of words, either in times past or now that You have spoken to Your servant; I am slow of speech and slow of tongue." 11 And the LORD said to him, "Who gives man speech? Who makes him dumb or deaf, seeing or blind? Is it not I, the LORD? 12 Now go, and I will be with you as you speak and will instruct you what to say." 13 But he said, "Please, O Lord, make someone else Your agent." 14 The LORD became angry with Moses, and He said, "There is your brother Aaron the Levite. He, I know, speaks readily. Even now he is setting out to meet you, and he will be happy to see you. 15 You shall speak to him and put the words in his mouth - I will be with you and with him as you speak, and tell both of you what to do - 16 and he shall speak for you to the people. Thus he shall serve as your spokesman, with you playing the role of God to him, 17 and take with you this rod, with which you shall perform the signs."

18 Moses went back to his father-in-law Jether and said to him, "Let me go back to my kinsmen in Egypt and see how they are faring." And Jethro said to Moses, "Go in peace." 19 The LORD said to Moses in Midian, "Go back to Egypt, for all the men who sought to kill you are dead." 20 So Moses took his wife and sons, mounted them on an ass, and went back to the land of Egypt; and Moses took the rod of God with him. 21 And the LORD said to Moses, "When you return to Egypt, see that

וְאָמַרְתִּ֣י לָהֶ֔ם אֱלֹהֵ֥י אֲבוֹתֵיכֶ֖ם שְׁלָחַ֣נִי אֲלֵיכֶ֑ם וְאָֽמְרוּ־לִ֣י מַה־שְּׁמ֔וֹ מָ֥ה אֹמַ֖ר אֲלֵהֶֽם׃ יד וַיֹּ֤אמֶר אֱלֹהִים֙ אֶל־מֹשֶׁ֔ה אֶֽהְיֶ֖ה אֲשֶׁ֣ר אֶֽהְיֶ֑ה וַיֹּ֗אמֶר כֹּ֤ה תֹאמַר֙ לִבְנֵ֣י יִשְׂרָאֵ֔ל אֶֽהְיֶ֖ה שְׁלָחַ֥נִי אֲלֵיכֶֽם׃ טו וַיֹּאמֶר֩ ע֨וֹד אֱלֹהִ֜ים אֶל־מֹשֶׁ֗ה כֹּֽה־תֹאמַר֮ אֶל־בְּנֵ֣י יִשְׂרָאֵל֒ יְהֹוָ֞ה אֱלֹהֵ֣י אֲבֹתֵיכֶ֗ם אֱלֹהֵ֨י אַבְרָהָ֜ם אֱלֹהֵ֥י יִצְחָ֛ק וֵֽאלֹהֵ֥י יַעֲקֹ֖ב שְׁלָחַ֣נִי אֲלֵיכֶ֑ם זֶה־שְּׁמִ֣י לְעֹלָ֔ם וְזֶ֥ה זִכְרִ֖י לְדֹ֥ר דֹּֽר׃ טז לֵ֣ךְ וְאָֽסַפְתָּ֞ אֶת־זִקְנֵ֣י יִשְׂרָאֵ֗ל וְאָמַרְתָּ֤ אֲלֵהֶם֙ יְהֹוָ֞ה אֱלֹהֵ֤י אֲבֹֽתֵיכֶם֙ נִרְאָ֣ה אֵלַ֔י אֱלֹהֵ֧י אַבְרָהָ֛ם יִצְחָ֥ק וְיַעֲקֹ֖ב לֵאמֹ֑ר פָּקֹ֤ד פָּקַ֙דְתִּי֙ אֶתְכֶ֔ם וְאֶת־הֶעָשׂ֥וּי לָכֶ֖ם בְּמִצְרָֽיִם׃ יז וָאֹמַ֗ר אַעֲלֶ֣ה אֶתְכֶם֮ מֵעֳנִ֣י מִצְרַיִם֒ אֶל־אֶ֤רֶץ הַֽכְּנַעֲנִי֙ וְהַ֣חִתִּ֔י וְהָֽאֱמֹרִי֙ וְהַפְּרִזִּ֔י וְהַחִוִּ֖י וְהַיְבוּסִ֑י אֶל־אֶ֛רֶץ זָבַ֥ת חָלָ֖ב וּדְבָֽשׁ׃ יח וְשָׁמְע֖וּ לְקֹלֶ֑ךָ וּבָאתָ֡ אַתָּה֩ וְזִקְנֵ֨י יִשְׂרָאֵ֜ל אֶל־מֶ֣לֶךְ מִצְרַ֗יִם וַאֲמַרְתֶּ֤ם אֵלָיו֙ יְהֹוָ֞ה אֱלֹהֵ֤י הָֽעִבְרִיִּים֙ נִקְרָ֣ה עָלֵ֔ינוּ וְעַתָּ֗ה נֵֽלְכָה־נָּ֞א דֶּ֣רֶךְ שְׁלֹ֤שֶׁת יָמִים֙ בַּמִּדְבָּ֔ר וְנִזְבְּחָ֖ה לַֽיהֹוָ֥ה אֱלֹהֵֽינוּ׃ יט וַאֲנִ֣י יָדַ֔עְתִּי כִּ֠י לֹֽא־יִתֵּ֥ן אֶתְכֶ֛ם מֶ֥לֶךְ מִצְרַ֖יִם לַהֲלֹ֑ךְ וְלֹ֖א בְּיָ֥ד חֲזָקָֽה׃ כ וְשָׁלַחְתִּ֤י אֶת־יָדִי֙ וְהִכֵּיתִ֣י אֶת־מִצְרַ֔יִם בְּכֹל֙ נִפְלְאֹתַ֔י אֲשֶׁ֥ר אֶֽעֱשֶׂ֖ה בְּקִרְבּ֑וֹ וְאַחֲרֵי־כֵ֖ן יְשַׁלַּ֥ח אֶתְכֶֽם׃ כא וְנָתַתִּ֛י אֶת־חֵ֥ן הָֽעָם־הַזֶּ֖ה בְּעֵינֵ֣י מִצְרָ֑יִם וְהָיָה֙ כִּ֣י תֵֽלֵכ֔וּן לֹ֥א תֵלְכ֖וּ רֵיקָֽם׃ כב וְשָׁאֲלָ֨ה אִשָּׁ֤ה מִשְּׁכֶנְתָּהּ֙ וּמִגָּרַ֣ת בֵּיתָ֔הּ כְּלֵי־כֶ֛סֶף וּכְלֵ֥י זָהָ֖ב וּשְׂמָלֹ֑ת וְשַׂמְתֶּ֗ם עַל־בְּנֵיכֶם֙ וְעַל־בְּנֹ֣תֵיכֶ֔ם וְנִצַּלְתֶּ֖ם אֶת־מִצְרָֽיִם׃ ד א וַיַּ֤עַן מֹשֶׁה֙ וַיֹּ֔אמֶר וְהֵן֙ לֹֽא־יַאֲמִ֣ינוּ לִ֔י וְלֹ֥א יִשְׁמְע֖וּ בְּקֹלִ֑י כִּ֣י יֹֽאמְר֔וּ לֹֽא־נִרְאָ֥ה אֵלֶ֖יךָ יְהֹוָֽה׃ ב וַיֹּ֧אמֶר אֵלָ֛יו יְהֹוָ֖ה מַזֶּ֣ה בְיָדֶ֑ךָ וַיֹּ֖אמֶר מַטֶּֽה׃ ג וַיֹּ֙אמֶר֙ הַשְׁלִיכֵ֣הוּ אַ֔רְצָה וַיַּשְׁלִיכֵ֥הוּ אַ֖רְצָה וַיְהִ֣י לְנָחָ֑שׁ וַיָּ֥נׇס מֹשֶׁ֖ה מִפָּנָֽיו׃ ד וַיֹּ֤אמֶר יְהֹוָה֙ אֶל־מֹשֶׁ֔ה שְׁלַח֙ יָֽדְךָ֔ וֶאֱחֹ֖ז בִּזְנָב֑וֹ וַיִּשְׁלַ֤ח יָדוֹ֙ וַיַּ֣חֲזֶק בּ֔וֹ וַיְהִ֥י לְמַטֶּ֖ה בְּכַפּֽוֹ׃ ה לְמַ֣עַן יַאֲמִ֔ינוּ כִּֽי־נִרְאָ֥ה אֵלֶ֛יךָ יְהֹוָ֖ה אֱלֹהֵ֣י אֲבֹתָ֑ם אֱלֹהֵ֧י אַבְרָהָ֛ם אֱלֹהֵ֥י יִצְחָ֖ק וֵאלֹהֵ֥י יַעֲקֹֽב׃ ו וַיֹּ֩אמֶר֩ יְהֹוָ֨ה ל֜וֹ ע֗וֹד הָֽבֵא־נָ֤א יָֽדְךָ֙ בְּחֵיקֶ֔ךָ וַיָּבֵ֥א יָד֖וֹ בְּחֵיק֑וֹ וַיּ֣וֹצִאָ֔הּ וְהִנֵּ֥ה יָד֖וֹ מְצֹרַ֥עַת כַּשָּֽׁלֶג׃ ז וַיֹּ֗אמֶר הָשֵׁ֤ב יָֽדְךָ֙ אֶל־חֵיקֶ֔ךָ וַיָּ֥שֶׁב יָד֖וֹ אֶל־חֵיק֑וֹ וַיּֽוֹצִאָהּ֙ מֵֽחֵיק֔וֹ וְהִנֵּה־שָׁ֖בָה כִּבְשָׂרֽוֹ׃ ח וְהָיָה֙ אִם־לֹ֣א יַאֲמִ֣ינוּ לָ֔ךְ וְלֹ֣א יִשְׁמְע֔וּ לְקֹ֖ל הָאֹ֣ת הָרִאשׁ֑וֹן וְהֶֽאֱמִ֔ינוּ לְקֹ֖ל הָאֹ֥ת הָאַחֲרֽוֹן׃ ט וְהָיָ֡ה אִם־לֹ֣א יַאֲמִ֡ינוּ גַּם֩ לִשְׁנֵ֨י הָאֹת֜וֹת הָאֵ֗לֶּה וְלֹ֤א יִשְׁמְעוּן֙ לְקֹלֶ֔ךָ וְלָקַחְתָּ֙ מִמֵּימֵ֣י הַיְאֹ֔ר וְשָׁפַכְתָּ֖ הַיַּבָּשָׁ֑ה וְהָי֤וּ הַמַּ֙יִם֙ אֲשֶׁ֣ר תִּקַּ֣ח מִן־הַיְאֹ֔ר וְהָי֥וּ לְדָ֖ם בַּיַּבָּֽשֶׁת׃ י וַיֹּ֨אמֶר מֹשֶׁ֣ה אֶל־יְהֹוָה֮ בִּ֣י אֲדֹנָי֒ לֹא֩ אִ֨ישׁ דְּבָרִ֜ים אָנֹ֗כִי גַּ֤ם מִתְּמוֹל֙ גַּ֣ם מִשִּׁלְשֹׁ֔ם גַּ֛ם מֵאָ֥ז דַּבֶּרְךָ֖ אֶל־עַבְדֶּ֑ךָ כִּ֧י כְבַד־פֶּ֛ה וּכְבַ֥ד לָשׁ֖וֹן אָנֹֽכִי׃ יא וַיֹּ֨אמֶר יְהֹוָ֜ה אֵלָ֗יו מִ֣י שָׂ֣ם פֶּה֮ לָֽאָדָם֒ א֚וֹ מִֽי־יָשׂ֣וּם אִלֵּ֔ם א֣וֹ חֵרֵ֔שׁ א֥וֹ פִקֵּ֖חַ א֣וֹ עִוֵּ֑ר הֲלֹ֥א אָנֹכִ֖י יְהֹוָֽה׃ יב וְעַתָּ֖ה לֵ֑ךְ וְאָנֹכִי֙ אֶֽהְיֶ֣ה עִם־פִּ֔יךָ וְהוֹרֵיתִ֖יךָ אֲשֶׁ֥ר תְּדַבֵּֽר׃ יג וַיֹּ֖אמֶר בִּ֣י אֲדֹנָ֑י שְֽׁלַֽח־נָ֖א בְּיַד־תִּשְׁלָֽח׃ יד וַיִּֽחַר־אַ֨ף יְהֹוָ֜ה בְּמֹשֶׁ֗ה וַיֹּ֙אמֶר֙ הֲלֹ֨א אַהֲרֹ֤ן אָחִ֙יךָ֙ הַלֵּוִ֔י יָדַ֕עְתִּי כִּֽי־דַבֵּ֥ר יְדַבֵּ֖ר ה֑וּא וְגַ֤ם הִנֵּה־הוּא֙ יֹצֵ֣א לִקְרָאתֶ֔ךָ וְרָאֲךָ֖ וְשָׂמַ֥ח בְּלִבּֽוֹ׃ טו וְדִבַּרְתָּ֣ אֵלָ֔יו וְשַׂמְתָּ֥ אֶת־הַדְּבָרִ֖ים בְּפִ֑יו וְאָנֹכִ֗י אֶֽהְיֶ֤ה עִם־פִּ֙יךָ֙ וְעִם־פִּ֔יהוּ וְהוֹרֵיתִ֣י אֶתְכֶ֔ם אֵ֖ת אֲשֶׁ֥ר תַּעֲשֽׂוּן׃ טז וְדִבֶּר־ה֥וּא לְךָ֖ אֶל־הָעָ֑ם וְהָ֤יָה הוּא֙ יִֽהְיֶה־לְּךָ֣ לְפֶ֔ה וְאַתָּ֖ה תִּֽהְיֶה־לּ֥וֹ לֵֽאלֹהִֽים׃ יז וְאֶת־הַמַּטֶּ֥ה הַזֶּ֖ה תִּקַּ֣ח בְּיָדֶ֑ךָ אֲשֶׁ֥ר תַּֽעֲשֶׂה־בּ֖וֹ אֶת־הָאֹתֹֽת׃

יח וַיֵּ֨לֶךְ מֹשֶׁ֜ה וַיָּ֣שׇׁב ׀ אֶל־יֶ֣תֶר חֹֽתְנ֗וֹ וַיֹּ֤אמֶר לוֹ֙ אֵ֣לְכָה נָּ֗א וְאָשׁ֙וּבָה֙ אֶל־אַחַ֣י אֲשֶׁר־בְּמִצְרַ֔יִם וְאֶרְאֶ֖ה הַעוֹדָ֣ם חַיִּ֑ים וַיֹּ֧אמֶר יִתְר֛וֹ לְמֹשֶׁ֖ה לֵ֥ךְ לְשָׁלֽוֹם׃ יט וַיֹּ֨אמֶר יְהֹוָ֤ה אֶל־מֹשֶׁה֙ בְּמִדְיָ֔ן לֵ֖ךְ שֻׁ֣ב מִצְרָ֑יִם כִּי־מֵ֙תוּ֙ כׇּל־הָ֣אֲנָשִׁ֔ים הַֽמְבַקְשִׁ֖ים אֶת־נַפְשֶֽׁךָ׃ כ וַיִּקַּ֨ח מֹשֶׁ֜ה אֶת־אִשְׁתּ֣וֹ וְאֶת־בָּנָ֗יו וַיַּרְכִּבֵם֙ עַֽל־הַחֲמֹ֔ר וַיָּ֖שׇׁב אַ֣רְצָה מִצְרָ֑יִם וַיִּקַּ֥ח מֹשֶׁ֛ה אֶת־מַטֵּ֥ה הָאֱלֹהִ֖ים בְּיָדֽוֹ׃ כא וַיֹּ֣אמֶר יְהֹוָה֮ אֶל־מֹשֶׁה֒ בְּלֶכְתְּךָ֙ לָשׁ֣וּב מִצְרַ֔יְמָה רְאֵ֗ה כׇּל־

EXODUS 5

you perform before Pharaoh all the marvels that I have put within your power. I, however, will stiffen his heart so that he will not let the people go. 22 Then you shall say to Pharaoh, 'Thus says the LORD: Israel is My first-born son. 23 I have said to you, "Let My son go, that he may worship Me," yet you refuse to let him go. Now I will slay your first-born son.'" 24 At a night encampment on the way, the LORD encountered him and sought to kill him. 25 So Zipporah took a flint and cut off her son's foreskin, and touched his legs with it, saying, "You are truly a bridegroom of blood to me!" 26 And when He let him alone, she added, "A bridegroom of blood because of the circumcision."

27 The LORD said to Aaron, "Go to meet Moses in the wilderness." He went and met him at the mountain of God, and he kissed him. 28 Moses told Aaron about all the things that the LORD had committed to him and all the signs about which He had instructed him. 29 Then Moses and Aaron went and assembled all the elders of the Israelites. 30 Aaron repeated all the words that the LORD had spoken to Moses, and he performed the signs in the sight of the people, 31 and the people were convinced. When they heard that the LORD had taken note of the Israelites and that He had seen their plight, they bowed low in homage.

5 Afterward Moses and Aaron went and said to Pharaoh, "Thus says the LORD, the God of Israel: Let My people go that they may celebrate a festival for Me in the wilderness." 2 But Pharaoh said, "Who is the LORD that I should heed Him and let Israel go? I do not know the LORD, nor will I let Israel go." 3 They answered, "The God of the Hebrews has manifested Himself to us. Let us go, we pray, a distance of three days into the wilderness to sacrifice to the LORD our God, lest He strike us with pestilence or sword." 4 But the king of Egypt said to them, "Moses and Aaron, why do you distract the people from their tasks? Get to your labors!" 5 And Pharaoh continued, "The people of the land are already so numerous, and you would have them cease from their labors!" 6 That same day Pharaoh charged the taskmasters and foremen of the people, saying, 7 "You shall no longer provide the people with straw for making bricks as heretofore; let them go and gather straw for themselves. 8 But impose upon them the same quota of bricks as they have been making heretofore; do not reduce it, for they are shirkers; that is why they cry, 'Let us go and sacrifice to our God!' 9 Let heavier work be laid upon the men; let them keep at it and not pay attention to deceitful promises."

10 So the taskmasters and foremen of the people went out and said to the people, "Thus says Pharaoh: I will not give you any straw. 11 You must go and get the straw yourselves wherever you can find it; but there shall be no decrease whatever in your work." 12 Then the people scattered throughout the land of Egypt to gather stubble for straw. 13 And the taskmasters pressed them, saying, "You must complete the same work assignment each day as when you had straw." 14 And the foremen of the Israelites, whom Pharaoh's taskmasters had set over them, were beaten. "Why," they were asked, "did you not complete the prescribed amount of bricks, either yesterday or today, as you did before?" 15 Then the foremen of the Israelites came to Pharaoh and cried: "Why do you deal thus with your servants? 16 No straw is issued to your servants, yet they demand of us: Make bricks! Thus your servants are being beaten, when the fault is with your own people." 17 He replied, "You are shirkers, shirkers! That is why you say, 'Let us go and sacrifice to the LORD.' 18 Be off now to your work! No straw shall be issued to you, but you must produce your quota of bricks!" 19 Now the foremen of the Israelites found themselves in trouble because of the order, "You must not reduce your daily quantity of bricks." 20 As they left Pharaoh's presence, they came upon Moses and Aaron standing in their path, 21 and they said to them, "May the LORD look upon you and punish you for making us loathsome to Pharaoh and his courtiers – putting a sword in their hands to slay us." 22 Then Moses returned to the LORD and said, "O Lord, why did You bring harm upon this people? Why did You send me? 23 Ever since I came to Pharaoh to speak in Your name, he has dealt worse with this people; and still You have not delivered Your people."

6 1 Then the LORD said to Moses, "You shall soon see what I will do to Pharaoh: he shall let them go because of a greater might; indeed, because of a greater might he shall drive them from his land."

EXODUS 7 — שמות ז וארא

God spoke to Moses and said to him. "I am the LORD. 3 I appeared to Abraham, Isaac, and Jacob as El Shaddai, but I did not make Myself known to them by My name 4 I also established My covenant with them, to give them the land of Canaan, the land in which they lived as sojourners. 5 I have now heard the moaning of the Israelites because the Egyptians are holding them in bondage, and I have remembered My covenant. 6 Say, therefore, to the Israelite people: I am the LORD. I will free you from the labors of the Egyptians and deliver you from their bondage. I will redeem you with an outstretched arm and through extraordinary chastisements. 7 And I will take you to be My people, and I will be your God. And you shall know that I, the LORD, am your God who freed you from the labors of the Egyptians. 8 I will bring you into the land which I swore to give to Abraham, Isaac, and Jacob, and I will give it to you for a possession. I the LORD." 9 But when Moses told this to the Israelites, they would not listen to Moses, their spirits crushed by cruel bondage.

10 The LORD spoke to Moses, saying, 11 "Go and tell Pharaoh king of Egypt to let the Israelites depart from his land." 12 But Moses appealed to the LORD, saying, "The Israelites would not listen to me; how then should Pharaoh heed me, a man of impeded speech!" 13 So the LORD spoke to both Moses and Aaron in regard to the Israelites and Pharaoh king of Egypt, instructing them to deliver the Israelites from the land of Egypt.

14 The following are the heads of their respective clans. The sons of Reuben, Israel's first-born: Enoch and Pallu, Hezron and Carmi; those are the families of Reuben. 15 The sons of Simeon: Jemuel, Jamin, Ohad, Jachin, Zohar, and Saul the son of a Canaanite woman; those are the families of Simeon. 16 These are the names of Levi's sons by their lineage: Gershon, Kohath, and Merari; and the span of Levi's life was 137 years. 17 The sons of Gershon: Libni and Shimei, by their families. 18 The sons of Kohath: Amram, Izhar, Hebron, and Uzziel; and the span of Kohath's life was 133 years. 19 The sons of Merari: Mahli and Mushi. These are the families of the Levites by their lineage. 20 Amram took to wife his father's sister Jochebed, and she bore him Aaron and Moses; and the span of Amram's life was 137 years. 21 The sons of Izhar: Korah, Nepheg, and Zichri. 22 The sons of Uzziel: Mishael, Elzaphan, and Sithri. 23 Aaron took to wife Elisheba, daughter of Amminadab and sister of Nahshon, and she bore him Nadab and Abihu, Eleazar and Ithamar. 24 The sons of Korah: Assir, Elkanah, and Abiasaph. These are the families of the Korahites. 25 And Aaron's son Eleazar took to wife one of Putiel's daughters, and she bore him Phinehas. Those are the heads of the fathers' houses of the Levites by their families. 26 It is the same Aaron and Moses to whom the LORD said, "Bring forth the Israelites from the land of Egypt, troop by troop." 27 It was they who spoke to Pharaoh king of Egypt to free the Israelites from the Egyptians; these are the same Moses and Aaron. 28 For when the LORD spoke to Moses in the land of Egypt

29 and the LORD said to Moses, "I am the LORD: speak to Pharaoh king of Egypt all that I will tell you." 30 Moses appealed to the LORD, saying, "See, I am of impeded speech; how then should Pharaoh heed me!"

7 1 The LORD replied to Moses, "See, I place you in the role of God to Pharaoh, with your brother Aaron as your prophet. 2 You shall repeat all that I command you, and your brother Aaron shall speak to Pharaoh to let the Israelites depart from his land. 3 But I will harden Pharaoh's heart, that I may multiply My signs and marvels in the land of Egypt. 4 When Pharaoh does not heed you, I will lay My hand upon Egypt and deliver My ranks, My people the Israelites, from the land of Egypt with extraordinary chastisements. 5 And the Egyptians shall know that I am the LORD, when I stretch out My hand over Egypt and bring out the Israelites from their midst.

EXODUS 8   שמות ח וארא

6 This Moses and Aaron did; as the LORD commanded them, so they did. 7 Moses was eighty years old and Aaron eighty-three, when they made their demand on Pharaoh. 8 The LORD said to Moses and Aaron, 9 "When Pharaoh speaks to you and says, 'Produce your marvel,' you shall say to Aaron, 'Take your rod and cast it down before Pharaoh.' It shall turn into a serpent." 10 So Moses and Aaron came before Pharaoh and did just as the LORD had commanded: Aaron cast down his rod in the presence of Pharaoh and his courtiers, and it turned into a serpent. 11 Then Pharaoh, for his part, summoned the wise men and the sorcerers; and the Egyptian magicians, in turn, did the same with their spells; 12 each cast down his rod, and they turned into serpents. But Aaron's rod swallowed their rods. 13 Yet Pharaoh's heart stiffened and he did not heed them, as the LORD had said.

14 And the LORD said to Moses, "Pharaoh is stubborn; he refuses to let the people go. 15 Go to Pharaoh in the morning, as he is coming out to the water, and station yourself before him at the edge of the Nile, taking with you the rod that turned into a snake. 16 And say to him, 'The LORD, the God of the Hebrews, sent me to you to say, "Let My people go that they may worship Me in the wilderness." But you have paid no heed until now. 17 Thus says the LORD, "By this you shall know that I am the LORD." See, I shall strike the water in the Nile with the rod that is in my hand, and it will be turned into blood; 18 and the fish in the Nile will die. The Nile will stink so that the Egyptians will find it impossible to drink the water of the Nile.'" 19 And the LORD said to Moses, "Say to Aaron: Take your rod and hold out your arm over the waters of Egypt – its rivers, its canals, its ponds, all its bodies of water – that they may turn to blood; there shall be blood throughout the land of Egypt, even in vessels of wood and stone." 20 Moses and Aaron did just as the LORD commanded: he lifted up the rod and struck the water in the Nile in the sight of Pharaoh and his courtiers, and all the water in the Nile was turned into blood 21 and the fish in the Nile died. The Nile stank so that the Egyptians could not drink water from the Nile; and there was blood throughout the land of Egypt. 22 But when the Egyptian magicians did the same with their spells, Pharaoh's heart stiffened and he did not heed them - as the LORD had spoken. 23 Pharaoh turned and went into his palace, paying no regard even to this. 24 And all the Egyptians had to dig round about the Nile for drinking water, because they could not drink the water of the Nile. 25 When seven days had passed after the LORD struck the Nile,

26 the LORD said to Moses, "Go to Pharaoh and say to him, 'Thus says the LORD: Let My people go that they may worship Me. 27 If you refuse to let them go, then I will plague your whole country with frogs. 28 The Nile shall swarm with frogs, and they shall come up and enter your palace, your bedchamber and your bed, the houses of your courtiers and your people, and your ovens and your kneading bowls. 29 The frogs shall come up on you and on your people and on all your courtiers.'"

8 1 And the LORD said to Moses, "Say to Aaron: Hold out your arm with the rod over the rivers, the canals, and the ponds, and bring up the frogs on the land of Egypt." 2 Aaron held out his arm over the waters of Egypt, and the frogs came up and covered the land of Egypt. 3 But the magicians did the same with their spells, and brought frogs upon the land of Egypt. 4 Then Pharaoh summoned Moses and Aaron and said, "Plead with the LORD to remove the frogs from me and my people, and I will let the people go to sacrifice to the LORD." 5 And Moses said to Pharaoh, "You may have this triumph over me: for what time shall I plead in behalf of you and your courtiers and your people, that the frogs be cut off from you and your houses, to remain only in the Nile?" 6 "For tomorrow," he replied. And [Moses] said, "As you say – that you may know that there is none like the LORD our God; 7 the frogs shall retreat from you and your courtiers and your people; they shall remain only in the Nile." 8 Then Moses and Aaron left Pharaoh's presence, and Moses cried out to the LORD in the matter of the frogs which He had inflicted upon Pharaoh. 9 And the LORD did as Moses asked; the frogs died out in the houses, the courtyards, and the fields. 10 And they piled them up in heaps,

EXODUS 9

till the land stank. 11 But when Pharaoh saw that there was relief, he became stubborn and would not heed them, as the LORD had spoken.

12 Then the LORD said to Moses, "Say to Aaron: Hold out your rod and strike the dust of the earth, and it shall turn to lice throughout the land of Egypt." 13 And they did so. Aaron held out his arm with the rod and struck the dust of the earth, and vermin came upon man and beast; all the dust of the earth turned to lice throughout the land of Egypt. 14 The magicians did the like with their spells to produce lice, but they could not. The vermin remained upon man and beast; 15 and the magicians said to Pharaoh, "This is the finger of God!" But Pharaoh's heart stiffened and he would not heed them, as the LORD had spoken. 16 And the LORD said to Moses, "Early in the morning present yourself to Pharaoh, as he is coming out to the water, and say to him, 'Thus says the LORD: Let My people go that they may worship Me. 17 For if you do not let My people go, I will let loose swarms of insects against you and your courtiers and your people and your houses; the houses of the Egyptians, and the very ground they stand on, shall be filled with swarms of insects. 18 But on that day I will set apart the region of Goshen, where My people dwell, so that no swarms of insects shall be there; that you may know that I the LORD am in the midst of the land. 19 And I will make a distinction between My people and your people. Tomorrow this sign shall come to pass.'" 20 And the LORD did so. Heavy swarms of insects invaded Pharaoh's palace and the houses of his courtiers; throughout the country of Egypt the land was ruined because of the swarms of insects. 21 Then Pharaoh summoned Moses and Aaron and said, "Go and sacrifice to your God within the land." 22 But Moses replied, "It would not be right to do this, for what we sacrifice to the LORD our God is untouchable to the Egyptians. If we sacrifice that which is untouchable to the Egyptians before their very eyes, will they not stone us! 23 So we must go a distance of three days into the wilderness and sacrifice to the LORD our God as He may command us." 24 Pharaoh said, "I will let you go to sacrifice to the LORD your God in the wilderness; but do not go very far. Plead, then, for me." 25 And Moses said, "When I leave your presence, I will plead with the LORD that the swarms of insects depart tomorrow from Pharaoh and his courtiers and his people; but let not Pharaoh again act deceitfully, not letting the people go to sacrifice to the LORD." 26 So Moses left Pharaoh's presence and pleaded with the LORD. 27 And the LORD did as Moses asked: He removed the swarms of insects from Pharaoh, from his courtiers, and from his people; not one remained. 28 But Pharaoh became stubborn this time also, and would not let the people go.

9 1 The LORD said to Moses, "Go to Pharaoh and say to him, 'Thus says the LORD, the God of the Hebrews: Let My people go to worship Me. 2 For if you refuse to let them go, and continue to hold them, 3 then the hand of the LORD will strike your livestock in the fields - the horses, the asses, the camels, the cattle, and the sheep - with a very severe pestilence. 4 But the LORD will make a distinction between the livestock of Israel and the livestock of the Egyptians, so that nothing shall die of all that belongs to the Israelites. 5 The LORD has fixed the time: tomorrow the LORD will do this thing in the land.'" 6 And the LORD did so the next day: all the livestock of the Egyptians died, but of the livestock of the Israelites not a beast died. 7 When Pharaoh inquired, he found that not a head of the livestock of Israel had died; yet Pharaoh remained stubborn, and he would not let the people go.

8 Then the LORD said to Moses and Aaron, "Each of you take handfuls of soot from the kiln, and let Moses throw it toward the sky in the sight of Pharaoh. 9 It shall become a fine dust all over the land of Egypt, and cause an inflammation breaking out in boils on man and beast throughout the land of Egypt." 10 So they took soot of the kiln and appeared before Pharaoh; Moses threw it toward the sky, and it caused an inflammation breaking out in boils on man and beast. 11 The magicians were unable to confront Moses because of the inflammation, for the inflammation afflicted the magicians as well as all the other Egyptians. 12 But the LORD stiffened the heart of Pharaoh, and he would not heed them, just as the LORD had told Moses.

13 The LORD said to Moses, "Early in the morning present yourself to Pharaoh and say to him, 'Thus says the LORD, the God

EXODUS 10

of the Hebrews: Let My people go to worship Me. 14 For this time I will send all My plagues upon your person, and your courtiers, and your people, in order that you may know that there is none like Me in all the world. 15 I could have stretched forth My hand and stricken you and your people with pestilence, and you would have been effaced from the earth. 16 Nevertheless I have spared you for this purpose: in order to show you My power, and in order that My fame may resound throughout the world. 17 Yet you continue to thwart My people, and do not let them go! 18 This time tomorrow I will rain down a very heavy hail, such as has not been in Egypt from the day it was founded until now. 19 Therefore, order your livestock and everything you have in the open brought under shelter; every man and beast that is found outside, not having been brought indoors, shall perish when the hail comes down upon them!" 20 Those among Pharaoh's courtiers who feared the LORD's word brought their slaves and livestock indoors to safety; 21 but those who paid no regard to the word of the LORD left their slaves and livestock in the open.

22 The LORD said to Moses, "Hold out your arm toward the sky that hail may fall on all the land of Egypt, upon man and beast and all the grasses of the field in the land of Egypt." 23 So Moses held out his rod toward the sky, and the LORD sent thunder and hail, and fire streamed down to the ground, as the LORD rained down hail upon the land of Egypt. 24 The hail was very heavy - fire flashing in the midst of the hail - such as had not fallen on the land of Egypt since it had become a nation. 25 Throughout the land of Egypt the hail struck down all that were in the open, both man and beast; the hail also struck down all the grasses of the field and shattered all the trees of the field. 26 Only in the region of Goshen, where the Israelites were, there was no hail. 27 Thereupon Pharaoh sent for Moses and Aaron and said to them, "I stand guilty this time. The LORD is in the right, and I and my people are in the wrong. 28 Plead with the LORD that there may be an end of God's thunder and of hail. I will let you go; you need stay no longer." 29 Moses said to him, "As I go out of the city, I shall spread out my hands to the LORD; the thunder will cease and the hail will fall no more, so that you may know that the earth is the LORD's. 30 But I know that you and your courtiers do not yet fear the LORD God." 31 Now the flax and barley were ruined, for the barley was in the ear and the flax was in bud; 32 but the wheat and the emmer were not hurt, for they ripen late.- 33 Leaving Pharaoh, Moses went outside the city and spread out his hands to the LORD; the thunder and the hail ceased, and no rain came pouring down upon the earth. 34 But when Pharaoh saw that the rain and the hail and the thunder had ceased, he became stubborn and reverted to his guilty ways, as did his courtiers. 35 So Pharaoh's heart stiffened and he would not let the Israelites go, just as the LORD had foretold through Moses.

10 Then the LORD said to Moses, "Go to Pharaoh. For I have hardened his heart and the hearts of his courtiers, in order that I may display these My signs among them, 2 and that you may recount in the hearing of your sons and of your sons' sons how I made a mockery of the Egyptians and how I displayed My signs among them - in order that you may know that I am the LORD." 3 So Moses and Aaron went to Pharaoh and said to him, "Thus says the LORD, the God of the Hebrews, How long will you refuse to humble yourself before Me? Let My people go that they may worship Me. 4 For if you refuse to let My people go, tomorrow I will bring locusts on your territory. 5 They shall cover the surface of the land, so that no one will be able to see the land. They shall devour the surviving remnant that was left to you after the hail; and they shall eat away all your trees that grow in the field. 6 Moreover, they shall fill your palaces and the houses of all your courtiers and of all the Egyptians - something that neither your fathers nor fathers' fathers have seen from the day they appeared on earth to this day." With that he turned and left Pharaoh's presence. 7 Pharaoh's courtiers said to him, "How long shall this one be a snare to us? Let the men go to worship the LORD their God! Are you not yet aware that Egypt is lost?" 8 So Moses and Aaron were brought back to Pharaoh and he said to them, "Go, worship the LORD your God!

73

EXODUS 11   שמות יא

Who are the ones to go?" 9 Moses replied, "We will all go, young and old: we will go with our sons and daughters, our flocks and herds; for we must observe the LORD's festival." 10 But he said to them, "The LORD be with you the same as I mean to let your children go with you! Clearly, you are bent on mischief. 11 No! You menfolk go and worship the LORD, since that is what you want." And they were expelled from Pharaoh's presence. 12 Then the LORD said to Moses, "Hold out your arm over the land of Egypt for the locusts, that they may come upon the land of Egypt and eat up all the grasses in the land, whatever the hail has left." 13 So Moses held out his rod over the land of Egypt, and the LORD drove an east wind over the land all that day and all night; and when morning came, the east wind had brought the locusts. 14 Locusts invaded all the land of Egypt and settled within all the territory of Egypt in a thick mass; never before had there been so many, nor will there ever be so many again. 15 They hid all the land from view, and the land was darkened; and they ate up all the grasses of the field and all the fruit of the trees which the hail had left, so that nothing green was left, of tree or grass of the field, in all the land of Egypt. 16 Pharaoh hurriedly summoned Moses and Aaron and said, "I stand guilty before the LORD your God and before you. 17 Forgive my offense just this once, and plead with the LORD your God that He but remove this death from me." 18 So he left Pharaoh's presence and pleaded with the LORD. 19 The LORD caused a shift to a very strong west wind, which lifted the locusts and hurled them into the Sea of Reeds; not a single locust remained in all the territory of Egypt. 20 But the LORD stiffened Pharaoh's heart, and he would not let the Israelites go.

21 Then the LORD said to Moses, "Hold out your arm toward the sky that there may be darkness upon the land of Egypt, a darkness that can be touched." 22 Moses held out his arm toward the sky and thick darkness descended upon all the land of Egypt for three days. 23 People could not see one another, and for three days no one could get up from where he was; but all the Israelites enjoyed light in their dwellings. 24 Pharaoh then summoned Moses and said, "Go, worship the LORD! Only your flocks and your herds shall be left behind; even your children may go with you." 25 But Moses said, "You yourself must provide us with sacrifices and burnt offerings to offer up to the LORD our God; 26 our own livestock, too, shall go along with us - not a hoof shall remain behind: for we must select from it for the worship of the LORD our God; and we shall not know with what we are to worship the LORD until we arrive there." 27 But the LORD stiffened Pharaoh's heart and he would not agree to let them go. 28 Pharaoh said to him, "Be gone from me! Take care not to see me again, for the moment you look upon my face you shall die." 29 And Moses replied, "You have spoken rightly. I shall not see your face again!"

11 1 And the LORD said to Moses, "I will bring but one more plague upon Pharaoh and upon Egypt; after that he shall let you go from here; indeed, when he lets you go, he will drive you out of here one and all. 2 Tell the people to borrow, each man from his neighbor and each woman from hers, objects of silver and gold." 3 The LORD disposed the Egyptians favorably toward the people. Moreover, Moses himself was much esteemed in the land of Egypt, among Pharaoh's courtiers and among the people. 4 Moses said, "Thus says the LORD: Toward midnight I will go forth among the Egyptians, 5 and every first-born in the land of Egypt shall die, from the first-born of Pharaoh who sits on his throne to the first-born of the slave girl who is behind the millstones; and all the first-born of the cattle. 6 And there shall be a loud cry in all the land of Egypt, such as has never been or will ever be again; 7 but not a dog shall snarl at any of the Israelites, at man or beast - in order that you may know that the LORD makes a distinction between Egypt and Israel. 8 Then all these courtiers of yours shall come down to me and bow low to me, saying, 'Depart, you and all the people who follow you!' After that I will depart." And he left Pharaoh's presence in hot anger. 9 Now the LORD had said to Moses, "Pharaoh will not heed you, in order that My marvels may be multiplied in the land of Egypt." Moses and Aaron had performed

כלי המקדש, איור מתוך כתב-יד עברי של התנ"ך, ספרד, ראשית המאה ה-14, אוסף ספריית אסטנזה, מודנה, איטליה
Temple implements, illustration from a Hebrew manuscript of the Bible, Spain, early 14th century,
collection of Biblioteca Estense, Modena, Italy

75

EXODUS 12

all these marvels before Pharaoh, but the LORD had stiffened the heart of Pharaoh so that he would not let the Israelites go from his land.

12 ₁ The LORD said to Moses and Aaron in the land of Egypt: ₂ This month shall mark for you the beginning of the months; it shall be the first of the months of the year for you. ₃ Speak to the whole community of Israel and say that on the tenth of this month each of them shall take a lamb to a family, a lamb to a household. ₄ But if the household is too small for a lamb, let him share one with a neighbor who dwells nearby, in proportion to the number of persons: you shall contribute for the lamb according to what each household will eat. ₅ Your lamb shall be without blemish, a yearling male; you may take it from the sheep or from the goats. ₆ You shall keep watch over it until the fourteenth day of this month; and all the assembled congregation of the Israelites shall slaughter it at twilight. ₇ They shall take some of the blood and put it on the two doorposts and the lintel of the houses in which they are to eat it. ₈ They shall eat the flesh that same night; they shall eat it roasted over the fire, with unleavened bread and with bitter herbs. ₉ Do not eat any of it raw, or cooked in any way with water, but roasted - head, legs, and entrails - over the fire. ₁₀ You shall not leave any of it over until morning; if any of it is left until morning, you shall burn it. ₁₁ This is how you shall eat it: your loins girded, your sandals on your feet, and your staff in your hand; and you shall eat it hurriedly: it is a passover offering to the LORD. ₁₂ For that night I will go through the land of Egypt and strike down every first-born in the land of Egypt, both man and beast; and I will mete out punishments to all the gods of Egypt, I the LORD. ₁₃ And the blood on the houses where you are staying shall be a sign for you; when I see the blood I will pass over you, so that no plague will destroy you when I strike the land of Egypt. ₁₄ This day shall be for you one of remembrance: you shall celebrate it as a festival to the LORD throughout the ages; you shall celebrate it as an institution for all time. ₁₅ Seven days you shall eat unleavened bread; on the very first day you shall remove leaven from your houses, for whoever eats leavened bread from the first day to the seventh day, that person shall be cut off from Israel. ₁₆ You shall celebrate a sacred occasion on the first day, and a sacred occasion on the seventh day; no work at all shall be done on them; only what every person is to eat, that alone may be prepared for you. ₁₇ You shall observe the [Feast of] Unleavened Bread, for on this very day I brought your ranks out of the land of Egypt; you shall observe this day throughout the ages as an institution for all time. ₁₈ In the first month, from the fourteenth day of the month at evening, you shall eat unleavened bread until the twenty-first day of the month at evening. ₁₉ No leaven shall be found in your houses for seven days. For whoever eats what is leavened, that person shall be cut off from the community of Israel, whether he is a stranger or a citizen of the country. ₂₀ You shall eat nothing leavened; in all your settlements you shall eat unleavened bread.

₂₁ Moses then summoned all the elders of Israel and said to them, "Go, pick out lambs for your families, and slaughter the passover offering. ₂₂ Take a bunch of hyssop, dip it in the blood that is in the basin, and apply some of the blood that is in the basin to the lintel and to the two doorposts. None of you shall go outside the door of his house until morning. ₂₃ For when the LORD goes through to smite the Egyptians, He will see the blood on the lintel and the two doorposts, and the LORD will pass over the door and not let the Destroyer enter and smite your home. ₂₄ "You shall observe this as an institution for all time, for you and for your descendants. ₂₅ And when you enter the land that the LORD will give you, as He has promised, you shall observe this rite. ₂₆ And when your children ask you, 'What do you mean by this rite?' ₂₇ you shall say, 'It is the passover sacrifice to the LORD, because He passed over the houses of the Israelites in Egypt when He smote the Egyptians, but saved our houses.'" The people then bowed low in homage. ₂₈ And the Israelites went and did so; just as the LORD had commanded Moses and Aaron, so they did.

₂₉ In the middle of the night the LORD struck down all the first-born in the land of Egypt, from the first-born of Pharaoh who sat on the throne to the first-born of the captive who was in the dungeon,

EXODUS 13

and all the first-born of the cattle. 30 And Pharaoh arose in the night, with all his courtiers and all the Egyptians - because there was a loud cry in Egypt; for there was no house where there was not someone dead. 31 He summoned Moses and Aaron in the night and said, "Up, depart from among my people, you and the Israelites with you! Go, worship the LORD as you said! 32 Take also your flocks and your herds, as you said, and begone! And may you bring a blessing upon me also!" 33 The Egyptians urged the people on, impatient to have them leave the country, for they said, "We shall all be dead." 34 So the people took their dough before it was leavened, their kneading bowls wrapped in their cloaks upon their shoulders. 35 The Israelites had done Moses' bidding and borrowed from the Egyptians objects of silver and gold, and clothing. 36 And the LORD had disposed the Egyptians favorably toward the people, and they let them have their request; thus they stripped the Egyptians.

37 The Israelites journeyed from Raamses to Succoth, about six hundred thousand men on foot, aside from children. 38 Moreover, a mixed multitude went up with them, and very much livestock, both flocks and herds. 39 And they baked unleavened cakes of the dough that they had taken out of Egypt, for it was not leavened, since they had been driven out of Egypt and could not delay; nor had they prepared any provisions for themselves. 40 The length of time that the Israelites lived in Egypt was four hundred and thirty years; 41 at the end of the four hundred and thirtieth year, to the very day, all the ranks of the LORD departed from the land of Egypt. 42 That was for the LORD a night of vigil to bring them out of the land of Egypt; that same night is the LORD's, one of vigil for all the children of Israel throughout the ages.

43 The LORD said to Moses and Aaron: This is the law of the passover offering: No foreigner shall eat of it. 44 But any slave a man has bought may eat of it once he has been circumcised. 45 No bound or hired laborer shall eat of it. 46 It shall be eaten in one house; you shall not take any of the flesh outside the house; nor shall you break a bone of it. 47 The whole community of Israel shall offer it. 48 If a stranger who dwells with you would offer the passover to the LORD, all his males must be circumcised; then he shall be admitted to offer it; he shall then be as a citizen of the country. But no uncircumcised person may eat of it. 49 There shall be one law for the citizen and for the stranger who dwells among you. 50 And all the Israelites did so; as the LORD had commanded Moses and Aaron, so they did. 51 That very day the LORD freed the Israelites from the land of Egypt, troop by troop.

13 1 The LORD spoke further to Moses, saying, 2 "Consecrate to Me every first-born: man and beast, the first issue of every womb among the Israelites is Mine." 3 And Moses said to the people, "Remember this day, on which you went free from Egypt, the house of bondage, how the LORD freed you from it with a mighty hand: no leavened bread shall be eaten. 4 You go free on this day, in the month of Abib. 5 So, when the LORD has brought you into the land of the Canaanites, the Hittites, the Amorites, the Hivites, and the Jebusites, which He swore to your fathers to give you, a land flowing with milk and honey, you shall observe in this month the following practice: 6 "Seven days you shall eat unleavened bread, and on the seventh day there shall be a festival of the LORD. 7 Throughout the seven days unleavened bread shall be eaten: no leavened bread shall be found with you, and no leaven shall be found in all your territory. 8 And you shall explain to your son on that day, 'It is because of what the LORD did for me when I went free from Egypt.' 9 "And this shall serve you as a sign on your hand and as a reminder on your forehead - in order that the Teaching of the LORD may be in your mouth - that with a mighty hand the LORD freed you from Egypt. 10 You shall keep this institution at its set time from year to year. 11 "And when the LORD has brought you into the land of the Canaanites, as He swore to you and to your fathers, and has given it to you, 12 you shall set apart for the LORD every first issue of the womb: every male firstling that your cattle drop shall be the LORD's. 13 But every firstling ass you shall redeem with a sheep; if you do not redeem it, you must break its neck. And you must redeem every first-born male among your children. 14 And when, in time to come, your son asks you, saying, 'What does this mean?' you shall say to him, 'It was with a mighty hand that the LORD brought us out from Egypt, the house of bondage. 15 When Pharaoh stubbornly refused to let us go, the LORD slew every first-born in the land of Egypt, the first-born of both man and beast. Therefore I sacrifice to the LORD

77

EXODUS 14 שמות יד בשלח

every first male issue of the womb, but redeem every first-born among my sons." 16 "And so it shall be as a sign upon your hand and as a symbol on your forehead that with a mighty hand the LORD freed us from Egypt."

17 Now when Pharaoh let the people go, God did not lead them by way of the land of the Phillistines, although it was nearer; for God said, "The people may have a change of heart when they see war, and return to Egypt." 18 So God led the people roundabout, by way of the wilderness at the Sea of Reeds. Now the Israelites went up armed out of the land of Egypt. 19 And Moses took with him the bones of Joseph, who had exacted an oath from the children of Israel, saying, "God will be sure to take notice of you: then you shall carry up my bones from here with you." 20 They set out from Succoth, and encamped at Etham, at the edge of the wilderness. 21 The LORD went before them in a pillar of cloud by day, to guide them along the way, and in a pillar of fire by night, to give them light, that they might travel day and night. 22 The pillar of cloud by day and the pillar of fire by night did not depart from before the people.

14 The LORD said to Moses: 2 Tell the Israelites to turn back and encamp before Pi-hahiroth, between Migdol and the sea, before Baal-zephon; you shall encamp facing it, by the sea. 3 Pharaoh will say of the Israelites, "They are astray in the land: the wilderness has closed in on them." 4 Then I will stiffen Pharaoh's heart and he will pursue them, that I may gain glory through Pharaoh and all his host; and the Egyptians shall know that I am the LORD. And they did so. 5 When the king of Egypt was told that the people had fled, Pharaoh and his courtiers had a change of heart about the people and said, "What is this we have done, releasing Israel from our service?" 6 He ordered his chariot and took his men with him; 7 he took six hundred of his picked chariots, and the rest of the chariots of Egypt, with officers in all of them. 8 The LORD stiffened the heart of Pharaoh king of Egypt, and he gave chase to the Israelites. As the Israelites were departing defiantly, 9 the Egyptians gave chase to them, and all the chariot horses of Pharaoh, his horsemen, and his warriors overtook them encamped by the sea, near Pi-hahiroth, before Baal-zephon. 10 As Pharaoh drew near, the Israelites caught sight of the Egyptians advancing upon them. Greatly frightened, the Israelites cried out to the LORD. 11 And they said to Moses, "Was it for want of graves in Egypt that you brought us to die in the wilderness? What have you done to us, taking us out of Egypt? 12 Is this not the very thing we told you in Egypt, saying, 'Let us be, and we will serve the Egyptians, for it is better for us to serve the Egyptians than to die in the wilderness'?" 13 But Moses said to the people, "Have no fear! Stand by, and witness the deliverance which the LORD will work for you today; for the Egyptians whom you see today you will never see again. 14 The LORD will battle for you; you hold your peace!"

15 Then the LORD said to Moses, "Why do you cry out to Me? Tell the Israelites to go forward. 16 And you lift up your rod and hold out your arm over the sea and split it, so that the Israelites may march into the sea on dry ground. 17 And I will stiffen the hearts of the Egyptians so that they go in after them; and I will gain glory through Pharaoh and all his warriors, his chariots and his horsemen. 18 Let the Egyptians know that I am the LORD, when I gain glory through Pharaoh, his chariots, and his horsemen." 19 The angel of God, who had been going ahead of the Israelite army, now moved and followed behind them; and the pillar of cloud shifted from in front of them and took up a place behind them. 20 It came between the army of the Egyptians and the army of Israel. Thus there was the cloud with the darkness, and it cast a spell upon the night, so that the one could not come near the other all through the night. 21 Then Moses held out his arm over the sea and the LORD drove back the sea with a strong east wind all that night, and turned the sea into dry ground. The waters were split, 22 and the Israelites went into the sea on dry ground, the waters forming a wall for them on their right and on their left. 23 The Egyptians came in pursuit after them into the sea, all of Pharaoh's horses, chariots, and horsemen. 24 At the morning watch, the LORD looked down upon the Egyptian army from a pillar of fire and cloud, and threw the Egyptian army into panic. 25 He locked the wheels

78

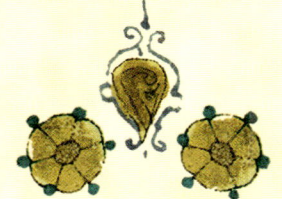

EXODUS 15   שמות טו בשלח

of their chariots so that they moved forward with difficulty. And the Egyptians said, "Let us flee from the Israelites, for the LORD is fighting for them against Egypt." 26 Then the LORD said to Moses, "Hold out your arm over the sea, that the waters may come back upon the Egyptians and upon their chariots and upon their horsemen." 27 Moses held out his arm over the sea, and at daybreak the sea returned to its normal state, and the Egyptians fled at its approach. But the LORD hurled the Egyptians into the sea. 28 The waters turned back and covered the chariots and the horsemen - Pharaoh's entire army that followed them into the sea; not one of them remained. 29 But the Israelites had marched through the sea on dry ground, the waters forming a wall for them on their right and on their left. 30 Thus the LORD delivered Israel that day from the Egyptians. Israel saw the Egyptians dead on the shore of the sea. 31 And when Israel saw the wondrous power which the LORD had wielded against the Egyptians, the people feared the LORD; they had faith in the LORD and His servant Moses.

15 1 Then Moses and the Israelites sang this song to the LORD. They said: I will sing to the LORD, for He has triumphed gloriously; Horse and driver He has hurled into the sea. 2 The LORD is my strength and might; He is become my deliverance. This is my God and I will enshrine Him; The God of my father, and I will exalt Him. 3 The LORD, the Warrior - LORD is His name! 4 Pharaoh's chariots and his army He has cast into the sea: And the pick of his officers Are drowned in the Sea of Reeds. 5 The deeps covered them; They went down into the depths like a stone. 6 Your right hand, O LORD, glorious in power, Your right hand, O LORD, shatters the foe! 7 In Your great triumph You break Your opponents; You send forth Your fury, it consumes them like straw. 8 At the blast of Your nostrils the waters piled up, The floods stood straight like a wall; The deeps froze in the heart of the sea. 9 The foe said, "I will pursue, I will overtake, I will divide the spoil; My desire shall have its fill of them. I will bare my sword - My hand shall subdue them." 10 You made Your wind blow, the sea covered them; They sank like lead in the majestic waters. 11 Who is like You, O LORD, among the celestials; Who is like You, majestic in holiness, Awesome in splendor, working wonders! 12 You put out Your right hand, The earth swallowed them. 13 In Your love You lead the people You redeemed; In Your strength You guide them to Your holy abode. 14 The peoples hear, they tremble; Agony grips the dwellers in Philistia. 15 Now are the clans of Edom dismayed; The tribes of Moab - trembling grips them; All the dwellers in Canaan are aghast. 16 Terror and dread descend upon them; Through the might of Your arm they are still as stone - Till Your people cross over, O LORD, Till Your people cross whom You have ransomed. 17 You will bring them and plant them in Your own mountain, The place You made to dwell in, O LORD, The sanctuary, O LORD, which Your hands established. 18 The LORD will reign for ever and ever! 19 For the horses of Pharaoh, with his chariots and horsemen, went into the sea; and the LORD turned back on them the waters of the sea: but the Israelites marched on dry ground in the midst of the sea.

20 Then Miriam the prophetess, Aaron's sister, took a timbrel in her hand, and all the women went out after her in dance with timbrels. 21 And Miriam chanted for them: Sing to the LORD, for He has triumphed gloriously; Horse and driver He has hurled into the sea. 22 Then Moses caused Israel to set out from the Sea of Reeds. They went on into the wilderness of Shur; they traveled three days in the wilderness and found no water. 23 They came to Marah, but they could not drink the water of Marah because it was bitter; that is why it was named Marah. 24 And the people grumbled against Moses, saying, "What shall we drink?" 25 So he cried out to the LORD, and the LORD showed him a piece of wood; he threw it into the water and the water became sweet. There He made for them a fixed rule, and there He put them to the test. 26 He said, "If you will heed the LORD your God diligently, doing what is upright in His sight, giving ear to His commandments and keeping all His laws, then I will not bring upon you any of the diseases that I brought upon the Egyptians, for I the LORD am your healer." 27 And they came to Elim, where there were twelve springs of water and seventy palm trees; and they encamped there beside the water. **16** 1 Setting out from Elim, the whole Israelite community came to the wilderness of Sin, which is between Elim and Sinai, on the fifteenth day of the second month after their departure from the land of Egypt. 2 The whole Israelite community grumbled against Moses

EXODUS 16 שמות טז בשלח

and Aaron, in the wilderness. 3 The Israelites said to them, "If only we had died by the hand of the LORD in the land of Egypt, when we sat by the fleshpots, when we ate our fill of bread! For you have brought us out into this wilderness to starve this whole congregation to death." 4 And the LORD said to Moses, "I will rain down bread for you from the sky, and the people shall go out and gather each day that day's portion — that I may thus test them, to see whether they will follow My instructions or not. 5 But on the sixth day, when they apportion what they have brought in, it shall prove to be double the amount they gather each day." 6 So Moses and Aaron said to all the Israelites, "By evening you shall know it was the LORD who brought you out from the land of Egypt; 7 and in the morning you shall behold the Presence of the LORD, because He has heard your grumblings against the LORD. For who are we that you should grumble against us?" 8 Since it is the LORD," Moses continued, "who will give you flesh to eat in the evening and bread in the morning to the full, because the LORD has heard the grumblings you utter against Him, what are we? Your grumbling is not against us, but against the LORD!" 9 Then Moses said to Aaron, "Say to the whole Israelite community: Advance toward the LORD, for He has heard your grumbling." 10 And as Aaron spoke to the whole Israelite community, they turned toward the wilderness, and there, in a cloud, appeared the Presence of the LORD.

11 The LORD spoke to Moses: 12 "I have heard the grumbling of the Israelites. Speak to them and say: By evening you shall eat flesh, and in the morning you shall have your fill of bread; and you shall know that I the LORD am your God." 13 In the evening quail appeared and covered the camp; in the morning there was a fall of dew about the camp. 14 When the fall of dew lifted, there, over the surface of the wilderness, lay a fine and flaky substance, as fine as frost on the ground. 15 When the Israelites saw it, they said to one another, "What is it?" — for they did not know what it was. And Moses said to them, "That is the bread which the LORD has given you to eat. 16 This is what the LORD has commanded: Gather as much of it as each of you requires to eat, an omer to a person for as many of you as there are; each of you shall fetch for those in his tent." 17 The Israelites did so, some gathering much, some little. 18 But when they measured it by the omer, he who had gathered much had no excess, and he who had gathered little had no deficiency: they had gathered as much as they needed to eat. 19 And Moses said to them, "Let no one leave any of it over until morning." 20 But they paid no attention to Moses: some of them left of it until morning, and it became infested with maggots and stank. And Moses was angry with them. 21 So they gathered it every morning, each as much as he needed to eat; for when the sun grew hot, it would melt. 22 On the sixth day they gathered double the amount of food, two omers for each; and when all the chieftains of the community came and told Moses, 23 he said to them, "This is what the LORD meant: Tomorrow is a day of rest, a holy sabbath of the LORD. Bake what you would bake and boil what you would boil; and all that is left put aside to be kept until morning." 24 So they put it aside until morning, as Moses had ordered; and it did not turn foul, and there were no maggots in it. 25 Then Moses said, "Eat it today, for today is a sabbath of the LORD; you will not find it today on the plain. 26 Six days you shall gather it; on the seventh day, the sabbath, there will be none." 27 Yet some of the people went out on the seventh day to gather, but they found nothing. 28 And the LORD said to Moses, "How long will you men refuse to obey My commandments and My teachings? 29 Mark that the LORD has given you the sabbath; therefore He gives you two days' food on the sixth day. Let everyone remain where he is: let no one leave his place on the seventh day." 30 So the people remained inactive on the seventh day. 31 The house of Israel named it manna; it was like coriander seed, white, and it tasted like wafers in honey. 32 Moses said, "This is what the LORD has commanded: Let one omer of it be kept throughout the ages, in order that they may see the bread that I fed you in the wilderness when I brought you out from the land of Egypt." 33 And Moses said to Aaron, "Take a jar, put one omer of manna in it, and place it before the LORD, to be kept throughout the ages." 34 As the LORD had commanded

EXODUS 17   שמות יז בשלח

Moses, Aaron placed it before the Pact, to be kept. 35 And the Israelites ate manna forty years, until they came to a settled land; they ate the manna until they came to the border of the land of Canaan. 36 The omer is a tenth of an ephah.

17 1 From the wilderness of Sin the whole Israelite community continued by stages as the LORD would command. They encamped at Rephidim, and there was no water for the people to drink. 2 The people quarreled with Moses. "Give us water to drink," they said; and Moses replied to them, "Why do you quarrel with me? Why do you try the LORD?" 3 But the people thirsted there for water; and the people grumbled against Moses and said, "Why did you bring us up from Egypt, to kill us and our children and livestock with thirst?" 4 Moses cried out to the LORD, saying, "What shall I do with this people? Before long they will be stoning me!" 5 Then the LORD said to Moses, "Pass before the people; take with you some of the elders of Israel, and take along the rod with which you struck the Nile, and set out. 6 I will be standing there before you on the rock at Horeb. Strike the rock and water will issue from it, and the people will drink." And Moses did so in the sight of the elders of Israel. 7 The place was named Massah and Meribah, because the Israelites quarreled and because they tried the LORD, saying, "Is the LORD present among us or not?"

8 Amalek came and fought with Israel at Rephidim. 9 Moses said to Joshua, "Pick some men for us, and go out and do battle with Amalek. Tomorrow I will station myself on the top of the hill, with the rod of God in my hand." 10 Joshua did as Moses told him and fought with Amalek, while Moses, Aaron, and Hur went up to the top of the hill. 11 Then, whenever Moses held up his hand, Israel prevailed; but whenever he let down his hand, Amalek prevailed. 12 But Moses' hands grew heavy; so they took a stone and put it under him and he sat on it, while Aaron and Hur, one on each side, supported his hands; thus his hands remained steady until the sun set. 13 And Joshua overwhelmed the people of Amalek with the sword.

14 Then the LORD said to Moses, "Inscribe this in a document as a reminder, and read it aloud to Joshua: I will utterly blot out the memory of Amalek from under heaven!" 15 And Moses built an altar and named it Adonai-nissi. 16 He said, "It means, 'Hand upon the throne of the LORD!' The LORD will be at war with Amalek throughout the ages."

18 Jethro priest of Midian, Moses' father-in-law, heard all that God had done for Moses and for Israel His people, how the LORD had brought Israel out from Egypt. 2 So Jethro, Moses' father-in-law, took Zipporah, Moses' wife, after she had been sent home, 3 and her two sons - of whom one was named Gershom, that is to say, "I have been a stranger in a foreign land"; 4 and the other was named Eliezer, meaning, "The God of my father was my help, and He delivered me from the sword of Pharaoh." 5 Jethro, Moses' father-in-law, brought Moses' sons and wife to him in the wilderness, where he was encamped at the mountain of God. 6 He sent word to Moses, "I, your father-in-law Jethro, am coming to you, with your wife and her two sons." 7 Moses went out to meet his father-in-law; he bowed low and kissed him; each asked after the other's welfare, and they went into the tent. 8 Moses then recounted to his father-in-law everything that the LORD had done to Pharaoh and to the Egyptians for Israel's sake, all the hardships that had befallen them on the way, and how the LORD had delivered them. 9 And Jethro rejoiced over all the kindness that the LORD had shown Israel who He delivered them from the Egyptians. 10 "Blessed be the LORD," Jethro said, "who delivered you from the Egyptians and from Pharaoh, and who delivered the people from under the hand of the Egyptians. 11 Now I know that the LORD is greater than all gods, yes, by the result of their very schemes against [the people]." 12 And Jethro, Moses' father-in-law, brought a burnt offering and sacrifices for God; and Aaron came with all the elders of Israel to partake of the meal before God with Moses' father-in-law. 13 Next day, Moses sat as magistrate among the people, while the people stood about Moses from morning until evening. 14 But when Moses' father-in-

81

EXODUS 19 שמות יט יתרו

saw how much he had to do for the people, he said, "What is this thing that you are doing to the people? Why do you act alone, while all the people stand about you from morning until evening?" 15 Moses replied to his father-in-law, "It is because the people come to me to inquire of God. 16 When they have a dispute, it comes before me, and I decide between one person and another, and I make known the laws and teachings of God." 17 But Moses' father-in-law said to him, "The thing you are doing is not right; 18 you will surely wear yourself out, and these people as well. For the task is too heavy for you; you cannot do it alone. 19 Now listen to me. I will give you counsel, and God be with you! You represent the people before God: you bring the disputes before God, 20 and enjoin upon them the laws and the teachings, and make known to them the way they are to go and the practices they are to follow. 21 You shall also seek out from among all the people capable men who fear God, trustworthy men who spurn ill-gotten gain. Set these over them as chiefs of thousands, hundreds, fifties, and tens, and 22 let them judge the people at all times. Have them bring every major dispute to you, but let them decide every minor dispute themselves. Make it easier for yourself by letting them share the burden with you. 23 If you do this - and God so commands you - you will be able to bear up; and all these people too will go home unwearied." 24 Moses heeded his father-in-law and did just as he had said. 25 Moses chose capable men out of all Israel, and appointed them heads over the people - chiefs of thousands, hundreds, fifties, and tens; 26 and they judged the people at all times: the difficult matters they would bring to Moses, and all the minor matters they would decide themselves. 27 Then Moses bade his father-in-law farewell, and he went his way to his own land.

19 1 On the third new moon after the Israelites had gone forth from the land of Egypt, on that very day, they entered the wilderness of Sinai. 2 Having journeyed from Rephidim, they entered the wilderness of Sinai and encamped in the wilderness. Israel encamped there in front of the mountain. 3 Moses went up to God. The LORD called to him from the mountain, saying, "Thus shall you say to the house of Jacob and declare to the children of Israel: 4 'You have seen what I did to the Egyptians, how I bore you on eagles' wings and brought you to Me. 5 Now then, if you will obey Me faithfully and keep My covenant, you shall be My treasured possession among all the peoples. Indeed, all the earth is Mine, 6 but you shall be to Me a kingdom of priests and a holy nation.' These are the words that you shall speak to the children of Israel." 7 Moses came and summoned the elders of the people and put before them all that the LORD had commanded him. 8 All the people answered as one, saying, "All that the LORD has spoken we will do!" And Moses brought back the people's words to the LORD. 9 And the LORD said to Moses, "I will come to you in a thick cloud, in order that the people may hear when I speak with you and so trust you ever after." Then Moses reported the people's words to the LORD. 10 and the LORD said to Moses, "Go to the people and warn them to stay pure today and tomorrow. Let them wash their clothes. 11 Let them be ready for the third day; for on the third day the LORD will come down, in the sight of all the people, on Mount Sinai. 12 You shall set bounds for the people round about, saying, 'Beware of going up the mountain or touching the border of it. Whoever touches the mountain shall be put to death: 13 no hand shall touch him, but he shall be either stoned or shot; beast or man, he shall not live.' When the ram's horn sounds a long blast, they may go up on the mountain." 14 Moses came down from the mountain to the people and warned the people to stay pure, and they washed their clothes. 15 And he said to the people, "Be ready for the third day: do not go near a woman." 16 On the third day, as morning dawned, there was thunder, and lightning, and a dense cloud upon the mountain, and a very loud blast of the horn; and all the people who were in the camp trembled. 17 Moses led the people out of the camp toward God, and they took their places at the foot of the mountain. 18 Now Mount Sinai was all in smoke, for the LORD had come down upon it in fire; the smoke rose like the smoke of a kiln, and the whole mountain trembled violently. 19 The blare of the horn grew louder and louder. As Moses spoke, God answered him in thunder.

EXODUS 20   שמות ב · יתרו

20 The LORD came down upon Mount Sinai, on the top of the mountain, and the LORD called Moses to the top of the mountain and Moses went up. 21 The LORD said to Moses, "Go down, warn the people not to break through to the LORD to gaze, lest many of them perish. 22 The priests also, who come near the LORD, must stay pure, lest the LORD break out against them." 23 But Moses said to the LORD, "The people cannot come up to Mount Sinai, for You warned us saying, 'Set bounds about the mountain and sanctify it.'" 24 So the LORD said to him, "Go down, and come back together with Aaron; but let not the priests or the people break through to come up to the LORD, lest He break out against them." 25 And Moses went down to the people and spoke to them. 20 1 God spoke all these words, saying: 2 I the LORD am your God who brought you out of the land of Egypt, the house of bondage; 3 You shall have no other gods besides Me. 4 You shall not make for yourself a sculptured image, or any likeness of what is in the heavens above, or on the earth below, or in the waters under the earth. 5 You shall not bow down to them or serve them. For I the LORD your God am an impassioned God, visiting the guilt of the parents upon the children, upon the third and upon the fourth generations of those who reject Me, 6 but showing kindness to the thousandth generation of those who love Me and keep My commandments. 7 You shall not swear falsely by the name of the LORD your God; for the LORD will not clear one who swears falsely by His name. 8 Remember the sabbath day and keep it holy. 9 Six days you shall labor and do all your work, 10 but the seventh day is a sabbath of the LORD your God: you shall not do any work - you, your son or daughter, your male or female slave, or your cattle, or the stranger who is within your settlements. 11 For in six days the LORD made heaven and earth and sea, and all that is in them, and He rested on the seventh day: therefore the LORD blessed the sabbath day and hallowed it. 12 Honor your father and your mother, that you may long endure on the land that the LORD your God is assigning to you. 13 You shall not murder. You shall not commit adultery. You shall not steal. You shall not bear false witness against your neighbor. 14 You shall not covet your neighbor's house: You shall not covet your neighbor's wife, or his male or female slave, or his ox or his ass, or anything that is your neighbor's. 15 All the people witnessed the thunder and lightning, the blare of the horn and the mountain smoking; and when the people saw it, they fell back and stood at a distance. 16 "You speak to us," they said to Moses, "and we will obey; but let not God speak to us, lest we die." 17 Moses answered the people, "Be not afraid; for God has come only in order to test you, and in order that the fear of Him may be ever with you, so that you do not go astray." 18 So the people remained at a distance, while Moses approached the thick cloud where God was. 19 The LORD said to Moses: Thus shall you say to the Israelites: You yourselves saw that I spoke to you from the very heavens; 20 With Me, therefore, you shall not make any gods of silver, nor shall you make for yourselves any gods of gold. 21 Make for Me an altar of earth and sacrifice on it your burnt offerings and your sacrifices of well-being, your sheep and your oxen: in every place where I cause My name to be mentioned I will come to you and bless you. 22 And if you make for Me an altar of stones, do not build it of hewn stones; for by wielding your tool upon them you have profaned them. 23 Do not ascend My altar by steps, that your nakedness may not be exposed upon it.

21 These are the rules that you shall set before them: 2 When you acquire a Hebrew slave, he shall serve six years; in the seventh year he shall go free, without payment. 3 If he came single, he shall leave single; if he had a wife, his wife shall leave with him. 4 If his master gave him a wife, and she has borne him children, the wife and her children shall belong to the master, and he shall leave alone. 5 But if the slave declares, "I love my master, and my wife

83

EXODUS 22 שמות בב משפטים

and children: I do not wish to go free." 6 his master shall take him before God. He shall be brought to the door or the doorpost, and his master shall pierce his ear with an awl: and he shall then remain his slave for life. 7 When a man sells his daughter as a slave, she shall not be freed as male slaves are. 8 If she proves to be displeasing to her master, who designated her for himself, he must let her be redeemed; he shall not have the right to sell her to outsiders, since he broke faith with her. 9 And if he designated her for his son, he shall deal with her as is the practice with free maidens. 10 If he marries another, he must not withhold from this one her food, her clothing, or her conjugal rights. 11 If he fails her in these three ways, she shall go free, without payment.

12 He who fatally strikes a man shall be put to death. 13 If he did not do it by design, but it came about by an act of God, I will assign you a place to which he can flee. 14 When a man schemes against another and kills him treacherously, you shall take him from My very altar to be put to death. 15 He who strikes his father or his mother shall be put to death. 16 He who kidnaps a man - whether he has sold him or is still holding him - shall be put to death.

17 He who insults his father or his mother shall be put to death. 18 When men quarrel and one strikes the other with stone or fist, and he does not die but has to take to his bed - 19 if then gets up and walks outdoors upon his staff, the assailant shall go unpunished, except that he must pay for his idleness and his cure.

20 When a man strikes his slave, male or female, with a rod, and he dies there and then, he must be avenged. 21 But if he survives a day or two, he is not to be avenged, since he is the other's property.

22 When men fight, and one of them pushes a pregnant woman and a miscarriage results, but no other damage ensues, the one responsible shall be fined according as the woman's husband may exact from him, the payment to be based on reckoning. 23 But if other damage ensues, the penalty shall be life for life, 24 eye for eye, tooth for tooth, hand for hand, foot for foot, 25 burn for burn, wound for wound, bruise for bruise.

26 When a man strikes the eye of his slave, male or female, and destroys it, he shall let him go free on account of his eye. 27 If he knocks out the tooth of his slave, male or female, he shall let him go free on account of his tooth. 28 When an ox gores a man or a woman to death, the ox shall be stoned and its flesh shall not be eaten, but the owner of the ox is not to be punished. 29 If, however, that ox has been in the habit of goring, and its owner, though warned, has failed to guard it, and it kills a man or a woman - the ox shall be stoned and its owner, too, shall be put to death. 30 If ransom is laid upon him, he must pay whatever is laid upon him to redeem his life. 31 So, too, if it gores a minor, male or female, [the owner] shall be dealt with according to the same rule. 32 But if the ox gores a slave, male or female, he shall pay thirty shekels of silver to the master, and the ox shall be stoned.

33 When a man opens a pit, or digs a pit and does not cover it, and an ox or an ass falls into it, 34 the one responsible for the pit must make restitution; he shall pay the price to the owner, but shall keep the dead animal. 35 When a man's ox injures his neighbor's ox and it dies, they shall sell the live ox and divide its price; they shall also divide the dead animal. 36 If, however, it is known that the ox was in the habit of goring, and its owner has failed to guard it, he must restore ox for ox, but shall keep the dead animal. 37 When a man steals an ox or a sheep, and slaughters it or sells it, he shall pay five oxen for the ox, and four sheep for the sheep. 22 1 If the thief is seized while tunneling, and he is beaten to death, there is no bloodguilt in his case. 2 If the sun has risen on him, there is bloodguilt in that case. - He must make restitution; if he lacks the means, he shall be sold for his theft. 3 But if what he stole - whether ox or ass or sheep - is found alive in his possession, he shall pay double.

4 When a man lets his livestock loose to graze in another's land, and so allows a field or a vineyard to be grazed bare, he must make restitution for the impairment of that field or vineyard. 5 When a fire is started and spreads to thorns, so that stacked, standing, or growing grain is consumed, he who started the fire must make restitution.

6 When a man gives money or goods to another for safekeeping, and they are stolen from the man's house - if the thief is caught, he shall pay double;

A page of the Book of Exodus, from the Bible illustrated by Gustave Doré, 1832-33 עמוד מספר שמות, מתוך התנ״ך באיורו של גוסטב דורה

EXODUS 2 שמות ב

5 The daughter of Pharaoh came down to bathe in the Nile, while her maidens walked along the Nile. She spied the basket among the reeds and sent her slave girl to fetch it.

EXODUS 23 שמות כג משפטים

7 if the thief is not caught, the owner of the house shall depose before God that he has not laid hands on the other's property. 8 In all charges of misappropriation — pertaining to an ox, an ass, a sheep, a garment, or any other loss, whereof one party alleges, "This is it" — the case of both parties shall come before God: he whom God declares guilty shall pay double to the other.

9 When a man gives to another an ass, an ox, a sheep or any other animal to guard, and it dies or is injured or is carried off, with no witness about, 10 an oath before the LORD shall decide between the two of them that the one has not laid hands on the property of the other: the owner must acquiesce, and no restitution shall be made. 11 But if [the animal] was stolen from him, he shall make restitution to its owner. 12 If it was torn by beasts, he shall bring it as evidence; he need not replace what has been torn by beasts.

13 When a man borrows [an animal] from another and it dies or is injured, its owner not being with it, he must make restitution. 14 If its owner was with it, no restitution need be made; but if it was hired, he is entitled to the hire.

15 If a man seduces a virgin for whom the bride-price has not been paid, and lies with her, he must make her his wife by payment of a bride-price. 16 If her father refuses to give her to him, he must still weigh out silver in accordance with the bride-price for virgins. 17 You shall not tolerate a sorceress. 18 Whoever lies with a beast shall be put to death.

19 Whoever sacrifices to a god other than the LORD alone shall be proscribed. 20 You shall not wrong a stranger or oppress him, for you were strangers in the land of Egypt. 21 You shall not ill-treat any widow or orphan. 22 If you do mistreat them, I will heed their outcry as soon as they cry out to Me, 23 and My anger shall blaze forth and I will put you to the sword, and your own wives shall become widows and your children orphans. 24 If you lend money to My people, to the poor among you, do not act toward them as a creditor; exact no interest from them. 25 If you take your neighbor's garment in pledge, you must return it to him before the sun sets; 26 it is his only clothing, the sole covering for his skin. In what else shall he sleep? Therefore, if he cries out to Me, I will pay heed, for I am compassionate.

27 You shall not revile God, nor put a curse upon a chieftain among your people. 28 You shall not put off the skimming of the first yield of your vats. You shall give Me the first-born among your sons. 29 You shall do the same with your cattle and your flocks: seven days it shall remain with its mother; on the eighth day you shall give it to Me. 30 You shall be holy people to Me; you must not eat flesh torn by beasts in the field: you shall cast it to the dogs. **23** 1 You must not carry false rumors; you shall not join hands with the guilty to act as a malicious witness; 2 You shall neither side with the mighty to do wrong — you shall not give perverse testimony in a dispute so as to pervert it in favor of the mighty — 3 nor shall you show deference to a poor man in his dispute. 4 When you encounter your enemy's ox or ass wandering, you must take it back to him. 5 When you see the ass of your enemy lying under its burden and would refrain from raising it, you must nevertheless raise it with him.

6 You shall not subvert the rights of your needy in their disputes. 7 Keep far from a false charge; do not bring death on those who are innocent and in the right, for I will not acquit the wrongdoer. 8 Do not take bribes, for bribes blind the clear-sighted and upset the pleas of those who are in the right. 9 You shall not oppress a stranger, for you know the feelings of the stranger, having yourselves been strangers in the land of Egypt. 10 Six years you shall sow your land and gather in its yield; 11 but in the seventh you shall let it rest and lie fallow. Let the needy among your people eat of it, and what they leave let the wild beasts eat. You shall do the same with your vineyards and your olive groves. 12 Six days you shall do your work, but on the seventh day you shall cease from labor, in order that your ox and your ass may rest, and that your bondman and the stranger may be refreshed. 13 Be on guard concerning all that I have told you. Make no mention of the names of other gods; they shall not be heard on your lips. 14 Three times a year you shall hold a festival for Me; 15 You shall observe the Feast of Unleavened Bread — eating unleavened bread for seven days as I have commanded you — at the set time in the month of Abib, for in it you went forth from Egypt; and none shall appear before Me empty-handed; 16 and the Feast of the Harvest, of the first fruits of your work, of what you sow in the field; and the Feast of Ingathering at the end of the year, when you gather in the results of your work from the field. 17 Three times a year all your males shall appear

EXODUS 24 שמות כד משפטים

before the Sovereign, the LORD. 18 You shall not offer the blood of My sacrifice with anything leavened; and the fat of My festal offering shall not be left lying until morning. 19 The choice first fruits of your soil you shall bring to the house of the LORD your God. You shall not boil a kid in its mother's milk. 20 I am sending an angel before you to guard you on the way and to bring you to the place that I have made ready. 21 Pay heed to him and obey him. Do not defy him, for he will not pardon your offenses, since My Name is in him; 22 but if you obey him and do all that I say, I will be an enemy to your enemies and a foe to your foes. 23 When My angel goes before you and brings you to the Amorites, the Hittites, the Perizzites, the Canaanites, the Hivites, and the Jebusites, and I annihilate them, 24 you shall not bow down to their gods in worship or follow their practices, but shall tear them down and smash their pillars to bits. 25 You shall serve the LORD your God, and He will bless your bread and your water. And I will remove sickness from your midst. 26 No woman in your land shall miscarry or be barren. I will let you enjoy the full count of your days. 27 I will send forth My terror before you, and I will throw into panic all the people among whom you come, and I will make all your enemies turn tail before you. 28 I will send a plague ahead of you, and it shall drive out before you the Hivites, the Canaanites, and the Hittites. 29 I will not drive them out before you in a single year, lest the land become desolate and the wild beasts multiply to your hurt. 30 I will drive them out before you little by little, until you have increased and possess the land. 31 I will set your borders from the Sea of Reeds to the Sea of Philistia, and from the wilderness to the Euphrates; for I will deliver the inhabitants of the land into your hands, and you will drive them out before you. 32 You shall make no covenant with them and their gods. 33 They shall not remain in your land, lest they cause you to sin against Me; for you will serve their gods - and it will prove a snare to you.

24 1 Then He said to Moses, "Come up to the LORD, with Aaron, Nadab and Abihu, and seventy elders of Israel, and bow low from afar. 2 Moses alone shall come near the LORD; but the others shall not come near, nor shall the people come up with him." 3 Moses went and repeated to the people all the commands of the LORD and all the rules; and all the people answered with one voice, saying, "All the things that the LORD has commanded we will do!" 4 Moses then wrote down all the commands of the LORD. Early in the morning, he set up an altar at the foot of the mountain, with twelve pillars for the twelve tribes of Israel. 5 He designated some young men among the Israelites, and they offered burnt offerings and sacrificed bulls as offerings of wellbeing to the LORD. 6 Moses took one part of the blood and put it in basins, and the other part of the blood he dashed against the altar. 7 Then he took the record of the covenant and read it aloud to the people. And they said, "All that the LORD has spoken we will faithfully do!" 8 Moses took the blood and dashed it on the people and said, "This is the blood of the covenant that the LORD now makes with you concerning all these commands." 9 Then Moses and Aaron, Nadab and Abihu, and seventy elders of Israel ascended; 10 and they saw the God of Israel: under His feet there was the likeness of a pavement of sapphire, like the very sky for purity. 11 Yet He did not raise His hand against the leaders of the Israelites; they beheld God, and they ate and drank.

12 The LORD said to Moses, "Come up to Me on the mountain and wait there, and I will give you the stone tablets with the teachings and commandments which I have inscribed to instruct them." 13 So Moses and his attendant Joshua arose, and Moses ascended the mountain of God. 14 To the elders he had said, "Wait here for us until we return to you. You have Aaron and Hur with you; let anyone who has a legal matter approach them." 15 When Moses had ascended the mountain, the cloud covered the mountain. 16 The Presence of the LORD abode on Mount Sinai, and the cloud hid it for six days. On the seventh day He called to Moses from the midst of the cloud. 17 Now the Presence of the LORD appeared in the sight of the Israelites as a consuming fire on the top of the mountain. 18 Moses went inside the cloud and ascended the mountain; and Moses remained on the mountain forty days and forty nights.

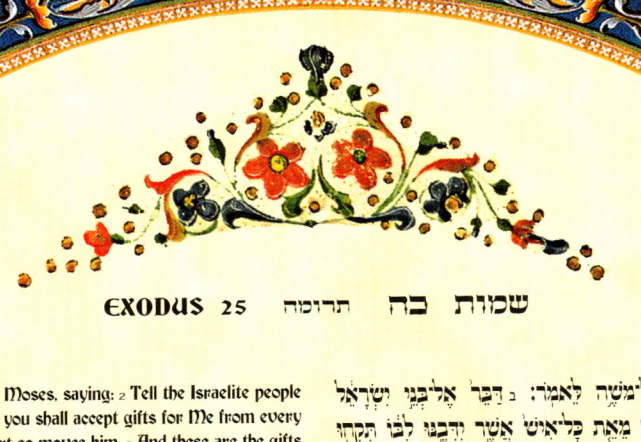

EXODUS 25 שמות כה תרומה

The LORD spoke to Moses, saying: ² Tell the Israelite people to bring Me gifts; you shall accept gifts for Me from every person whose heart so moves him. ³ And these are the gifts that you shall accept from them: gold, silver, and copper; ⁴ blue, purple, and crimson yarns, fine linen, goats' hair; ⁵ tanned ram skins, dolphin skins, and acacia wood; ⁶ oil for lighting, spices for the anointing oil and for the aromatic incense; ⁷ lapis lazuli and other stones for setting, for the ephod and for the breastpiece. ⁸ And let them make Me a sanctuary that I may dwell among them. ⁹ Exactly as I show you — the pattern of the Tabernacle and the pattern of all its furnishings — so shall you make it. ¹⁰ They shall make an ark of acacia wood, two and a half cubits long, a cubit and a half wide, and a cubit and a half high. ¹¹ Overlay it with pure gold — overlay it inside and out — and make upon it a gold molding round about. ¹² Cast four gold rings for it, to be attached to its four feet, two rings on one of its side walls and two on the other. ¹³ Make poles of acacia wood and overlay them with gold; ¹⁴ then insert the poles into the rings on the side walls of the ark, for carrying the ark. ¹⁵ The poles shall remain in the rings of the ark; they shall not be removed from it. ¹⁶ And deposit in the Ark [the tablets of] the Pact which I will give you. ¹⁷ You shall make a cover of pure gold, two and a half cubits long and a cubit and a half wide. ¹⁸ Make two cherubim of gold — make them of hammered work — at the two ends of the cover. ¹⁹ Make one cherub at one end and the other cherub at the other end; of one piece with the cover shall you make the cherubim at its two ends. ²⁰ The cherubim shall have their wings spread out above, shielding the cover with their wings. They shall confront each other, the faces of the cherubim being turned toward the cover. ²¹ Place the cover on top of the Ark, after depositing inside the Ark the Pact that I will give you. ²² There I will meet with you, and I will impart to you — from above the cover, from between the two cherubim that are on top of the Ark of the Pact — all that I will command you concerning the Israelite people.

²³ You shall make a table of acacia wood, two cubits long, one cubit wide, and a cubit and a half high. ²⁴ Overlay it with pure gold, and make a gold molding around it. ²⁵ Make a rim of a hand's breadth around it, and make a gold molding for its rim round about. ²⁶ Make four gold rings for it, and attach the rings to the four corners at its four legs. ²⁷ The rings shall be next to the rim, as holders for poles to carry the table. ²⁸ Make the poles of acacia wood, and overlay them with gold; by these the table shall be carried. ²⁹ Make its bowls, ladles, jars and jugs with which to offer libations; make them of pure gold. ³⁰ And on the table you shall set the bread of display, to be before Me always.

³¹ You shall make a lampstand of pure gold; the lampstand shall be made of hammered work; its base and its shaft, its cups, calyxes, and petals shall be of one piece. ³² Six branches shall issue from its sides; three branches from one side of the lampstand and three branches from the other side of the lampstand. ³³ On one branch there shall be three cups shaped like almond-blossoms, each with calyx and petals, and on the next branch there shall be three cups shaped like almond-blossoms, each with calyx and petals; so for all six branches issuing from the lampstand. ³⁴ And on the lampstand itself there shall be four cups shaped like almond-blossoms, each with calyx and petals; ³⁵ a calyx, of one piece with it, under a pair of branches; and a calyx, of one piece with it, under the second pair of branches, and a calyx, of one piece with it, under the last pair of branches; so for all six branches issuing from the lampstand. ³⁶ Their calyxes and their stems shall be of one piece with it, the whole of it a single hammered piece of pure gold. ³⁷ Make its seven lamps — the lamps shall be so mounted as to give the light on its front side — ³⁸ and its tongs and fire pans of pure gold. ³⁹ It shall be made, with all these furnishings, out of a talent of pure gold. ⁴⁰ Note well, and follow the patterns for them that are being shown you on the

EXODUS 26 שמות כו תרומה

❋mountain. 26 ¹ As for the Tabernacle, make it of ten strips of cloth; make these of fine twisted linen, of blue, purple, and crimson yarns, with a design of cherubim worked into them. ² The length of each cloth shall be twenty-eight cubits, and the width of each cloth shall be four cubits, all the cloths to have the same measurements. ³ Five of the cloths shall be joined to one another, and the other five cloths shall be joined to one another. ⁴ Make loops of blue wool on the edge of the outermost cloth of the one set; and do likewise on the edge of the outermost cloth of the other set; ⁵ make fifty loops on the one cloth, and fifty loops on the edge of the end cloth of the other set, the loops to be opposite one another. ⁶ And make fifty gold clasps, and couple the cloths to one another with the clasps, so that the Tabernacle becomes one whole.

⁷ You shall then make cloths of goats' hair for a tent over the Tabernacle; make the cloths eleven in number. ⁸ The length of each cloth shall be thirty cubits, and the width of each cloth shall be four cubits, the eleven cloths to have the same measurements. ⁹ Join five of the cloths by themselves, and the other six cloths by themselves; and fold over the sixth cloth at the front of the tent. ¹⁰ Make fifty loops on the edge of the outermost cloth of the one set, and fifty loops on the edge of the cloth of the other set. ¹¹ Make fifty copper clasps, and fit the clasps into the loops, and couple the tent together so that it becomes one whole. ¹² As for the overlapping excess of the cloths of the tent, the extra half-cloth shall overlap the back of the Tabernacle, ¹³ while the extra cubit at either end of each length of tent cloth shall hang down to the bottom of the two sides of the Tabernacle and cover it. ¹⁴ And make for the tent a covering of tanned ram skins, and a covering of dolphin skins above.

¹⁵ You shall make the planks for the Tabernacle of acacia wood, upright. ¹⁶ The length of each plank shall be ten cubits and the width of each plank a cubit and a half. ¹⁷ Each plank shall have two tenons, parallel to each other; do the same with all the planks of the Tabernacle. ¹⁸ Of the planks of the Tabernacle, make twenty planks on the south side: ¹⁹ making forty silver sockets under the twenty planks, two sockets under the one plank for its two tenons and two sockets under each following plank for its two tenons; ²⁰ and for the other side wall of the Tabernacle, on the north side, twenty planks, ²¹ with their forty silver sockets, two sockets under the one plank and two sockets under each following plank. ²² And for the rear of the Tabernacle, to the west, make six planks; ²³ and make two planks for the corners of the Tabernacle at the rear. ²⁴ They shall match at the bottom, and terminate alike at the top inside one ring; thus shall it be with both of them: they shall form the two corners. ²⁵ Thus there shall be eight planks with their sockets of silver: sixteen sockets, two sockets under the first plank, and two sockets under the other planks. ²⁶ You shall make bars of acacia wood: five for the planks of the one side wall of the Tabernacle, ²⁷ five bars for the planks of the other side wall of the Tabernacle, and five bars for the planks of the wall of the Tabernacle at the rear to the west. ²⁸ The center bar halfway up the planks shall run from end to end. ²⁹ Overlay the planks with gold, and make their rings of gold, as holders for the bars; and overlay the bars with gold. ³⁰ Then set up the Tabernacle according to the manner of it that you were shown on the mountain.

³¹ You shall make a curtain of blue, purple, and crimson yarns, and fine twisted linen; it shall have a design of cherubim worked into it. ³² Hang it upon four posts of acacia wood overlaid with gold and having hooks of gold, [set] in four sockets of silver. ³³ Hang the curtain under the clasps, and carry the Ark of the Pact there, behind the curtain,

EXODUS 27

so that the curtain shall serve you as a partition between the Holy and the Holy of Holies. 34 Place the cover upon the Ark of the Pact in the Holy of Holies. 35 Place the table outside the curtain, and the lampstand by the south wall of the Tabernacle opposite the table, which is to be placed by the north wall. 36 You shall make a screen for the entrance of the Tent, of blue, purple, and crimson yarns, and fine twisted linen, done in embroidery. 37 Make five posts of acacia wood for the screen and overlay them with gold - their hooks being of gold - and cast for them five sockets of copper. 27 1 You shall make the altar of acacia wood, five cubits long and five cubits wide - the altar is to be square - and three cubits high. 2 Make its horns on the four corners, the horns to be of one piece with it; and overlay it with copper. 3 Make the pails for removing its ashes, as well as its scrapers, basins, flesh hooks, and fire pans - make all its utensils of copper. 4 Make for it a grating of meshwork in copper; and on the mesh make four copper rings at its four corners. 5 Set the mesh below, under the ledge of the altar, so that it extends to the middle of the altar. 6 And make poles for the altar, poles of acacia wood, and overlay them with copper. 7 The poles shall be inserted into the rings, so that the poles remain on the two sides of the altar when it is carried. 8 Make it hollow, of boards. As you were shown on the mountain, so shall they be made.

9 You shall make the enclosure of the Tabernacle: On the south side, a hundred cubits of hangings of fine twisted linen for the length of the enclosure on that side - 10 with its twenty posts and their twenty sockets of copper, the hooks and bands of the posts to be of silver. 11 Again a hundred cubits of hangings for its length along the north side - with its twenty posts and their twenty sockets of copper, the hooks and bands of the posts to be of silver. 12 For the width of the enclosure, on the west side, fifty cubits of hangings, with their ten posts and their ten sockets. 13 For the width of the enclosure on the front, or east side, fifty cubits: 14 fifteen cubits of hangings on the one flank, with their three posts and their three sockets; 15 fifteen cubits of hangings on the other flank, with their three posts and their three sockets; 16 and for the gate of the enclosure, a screen of twenty cubits, of blue, purple, and crimson yarns, and fine twisted linen, done in embroidery, with their four posts and their four sockets. 17 All the posts round the enclosure shall be banded with silver and their hooks shall be of silver; their sockets shall be of copper. 18 The length of the enclosure shall be a hundred cubits, the width fifty throughout; and the height five cubits - [with hangings] of fine twisted linen. The sockets shall be of copper; 19 all the utensils of the Tabernacle, for all its service, as well as all its pegs and all the pegs of the court, shall be of copper.

20 You shall further instruct the Israelites to bring you clear oil of beaten olives for lighting, for kindling lamps regularly. 21 Aaron and his sons shall set them up in the Tent of Meeting, outside the curtain which is over [the Ark of] the Pact, [to burn] from evening to morning before the LORD. It shall be a due from the Israelites for all time, throughout the ages. 28 1 You shall bring forward your brother Aaron, with his sons, from among the Israelites, to serve Me as priests: Aaron, Nadab and Abihu, Eleazar and Ithamar, the sons of Aaron. 2 Make sacral vestments for your brother Aaron, for dignity and adornment. 3 Next you shall instruct all who are skillful, whom I have endowed with the gift of skill, to make Aaron's vestments, for consecrating him to serve Me as priest. 4 These are the vestments they are to make: a breastpiece, an ephod, a robe, a fringed tunic, a headdress, and a sash. They shall make those sacral vestments for your brother Aaron and his sons, for priestly service to Me; 5 they, therefore, shall receive the gold, the blue, purple, and crimson yarns, and the fine linen. 6 They shall make the ephod of gold, of blue, purple, and crimson yarns, and of fine twisted linen, worked into designs. 7 It shall have two shoulder-pieces attached: they shall be attached at its two ends. 8 And the decorated band that is upon it shall be made like it, of one piece with it: of gold, of blue, purple, and crimson yarns,

EXODUS 28 · שמות כח · תצוה

and of fine twisted linen. 9 Then take two lazuli stones and engrave on them the names of the sons of Israel: 10 six of their names on the one stone, and the names of the remaining six on the other stone, in the order of their birth. 11 On the two stones you shall make seal engravings - the work of a lapidary - of the names of the sons of Israel. Having bordered them with frames of gold, 12 attach the two stones to the shoulder-pieces of the ephod, as stones for remembrance of the Israelite people, whose names Aaron shall carry upon his two shoulder-pieces for remembrance before the LORD. 13 Then make frames of gold 14 and two chains of pure gold; braid these like corded work, and fasten the corded chains to the frames. 15 You shall make a breastpiece of decision, worked into a design; make it in the style of the ephod: make it of gold, of blue, purple, and crimson yarns, and of fine twisted linen. 16 It shall be square and doubled, a span in length and a span in width. 17 Set in it mounted stones, in four rows of stones. The first row shall be a row of carnelian, chrysolite, and emerald: 18 the second row: a turquoise, a sapphire, and an amethyst; 19 the third row: a jacinth, an agate, and a crystal; 20 and the fourth row: a beryl, a lapis lazuli, and a jasper. They shall be framed with gold in their mountings. 21 The stones shall correspond [in number] to the names of the sons of Israel: twelve, corresponding to their names. They shall be engraved like seals, each with its name, for the twelve tribes. 22 On the breastpiece make braided chains of corded work in pure gold. 23 Make two rings of gold on the breastpiece, and fasten the two rings at the two ends of the breastpiece, 24 attaching the two golden cords to the two rings at the ends of the breastpiece. 25 Then fasten the two ends of the cords to the two frames, which you shall attach to the shoulder-pieces of the ephod, at the front. 26 Make two rings of gold and attach them to the two ends of the breastpiece, at its inner edge, which faces the ephod. 27 And make two other rings of gold and fasten them on the front of the ephod, low on the two shoulder-pieces, close to its seam above the decorated band. 28 The breastpiece shall be held in place by a cord of blue from its rings to the rings of the ephod, so that the breastpiece rests on the decorated band and does not come loose from the ephod. 29 Aaron shall carry the names of the sons of Israel on the breastpiece of decision over his heart, when he enters the sanctuary, for remembrance before the LORD at all times. 30 Inside the breastpiece of decision you shall place the Urim and Thummim, so that they are over Aaron's heart when he comes before the LORD. Thus Aaron shall carry the instrument of decision for the Israelites over his heart before the LORD at all times. 31 You shall make the robe of the ephod of pure blue. 32 The opening for the head shall be in the middle of it; the opening shall have a binding of woven work round about - it shall be like the opening of a coat of mail - so that it does not tear. 33 On its hem make pomegranates of blue, purple, and crimson yarns, all around the hem, with bells of gold between them all around: 34 a golden bell and a pomegranate, a golden bell and a pomegranate, all around the hem of the robe. 35 Aaron shall wear it while officiating, so that the sound of it is heard when he comes into the sanctuary before the LORD and when he goes out - that he may not die. 36 You shall make a frontlet of pure gold and engrave on it the seal inscription: "Holy to the LORD." 37 Suspend it on a cord of blue, so that it may remain on the headdress; it shall remain on the front of the headdress. 38 It shall be on Aaron's forehead, that Aaron may take away any sin arising from the holy things that the Israelites consecrate, from any of their sacred donations; it shall be on his forehead at all times, to win acceptance for them before the LORD. 39 You shall make the fringed tunic of fine linen. You shall make the headdress of fine linen. You shall make the sash of embroidered work. 40 And for Aaron's sons also you shall make tunics, and make sashes for them, and make turbans for them, for dignity and adornment. 41 Put these on your brother Aaron and on his sons as well: anoint them, and ordain them and consecrate them to serve Me as priests. 42 You shall also make for them linen breeches to cover their nakedness; they shall extend from the hips to the thighs. 43 They shall

EXODUS 29 שמות כט תצוה

be worn by Aaron and his sons when they enter the Tent of Meeting or when they approach the altar to officiate in the sanctuary, so that they do not incur punishment and die. It shall be a law for all time for him and for his offspring to come. 29 ¹ This is what you shall do to them in consecrating them to serve Me as priests: Take a young bull of the herd and two rams without blemish; ² also unleavened bread, unleavened cakes with oil mixed in, and unleavened wafers spread with oil – make these of choice wheat flour. ³ Place these in one basket and present them in the basket, along with the bull and the two rams. ⁴ Lead Aaron and his sons up to the entrance of the Tent of Meeting, and wash them with water. ⁵ Then take the vestments, and clothe Aaron with the tunic, the robe of the ephod, the ephod, and the breastpiece, and gird him with the decorated band of the ephod. ⁶ Put the headdress on his head, and place the holy diadem upon the headdress. ⁷ Take the anointing oil and pour it on his head and anoint him. ⁸ Then bring his sons forward; clothe them with tunics ⁹ and wind turbans upon them. And gird both Aaron and his sons with sashes. And so they shall have priesthood as their right for all time. You shall then ordain Aaron and his sons. ¹⁰ Lead the bull up to the front of the Tent of Meeting, and let Aaron and his sons lay their hands upon the head of the bull. ¹¹ Slaughter the bull before the LORD, at the entrance of the Tent of Meeting, ¹² and take some of the bull's blood and put it on the horns of the altar with your finger; then pour out the rest of the blood at the base of the altar. ¹³ Take all the fat that covers the entrails, the protuberance on the liver, and the two kidneys with the fat on them, and turn these into smoke upon the altar. ¹⁴ The rest of the flesh of the bull, its hide, and its dung shall be put to the fire outside the camp: it is a sin offering. ¹⁵ Next take the one ram, and let Aaron and his sons lay their hands upon the ram's head. ¹⁶ Slaughter the ram, and take its blood and dash it against all sides of the altar. ¹⁷ Cut up the ram into sections, wash its entrails and legs, and put them with its quarters and its head. ¹⁸ Turn all of the ram into smoke upon the altar. It is a burnt offering to the LORD, a pleasing odor, an offering by fire to the LORD. ¹⁹ Then take the other ram, and let Aaron and his sons lay their hands upon the ram's head. ²⁰ Slaughter the ram, and take some of its blood and put it on the ridge of Aaron's right ear and on the ridges of his sons' right ears, and on the thumbs of their right hands, and on the big toes of their right feet; and dash the rest of the blood against every side of the altar round about. ²¹ Take some of the blood that is on the altar and some of the anointing oil and sprinkle upon Aaron and his sons and upon his sons and his sons' vestments. Thus shall he and his vestments be holy, as well as his sons and his sons' vestments. ²² You shall take from the ram the fat parts – the broad tail, the fat that covers the entrails, the protuberance on the liver, the two kidneys with the fat on them – and the right thigh; for this is a ram of ordination. ²³ Add one flat loaf of bread, one cake of oil bread, and one wafer, from the basket of unleavened bread that is before the LORD. ²⁴ Place all these on the palms of Aaron and his sons, and offer them as an elevation offering before the LORD. ²⁵ Take them from their hands and turn them into smoke upon the altar with the burnt offering, as a pleasing odor before the LORD: it is an offering by fire to the LORD. ²⁶ Then take the breast of Aaron's ram of ordination and offer it as an elevation offering before the LORD; it shall be your portion. ²⁷ You shall consecrate the breast that was offered as an elevation offering and the thigh that was offered as a gift offering from the ram of ordination – from that which was Aaron's and from that which was his sons' – ²⁸ and those parts shall be a due for all time from the Israelites to Aaron and his descendants. For they are a gift; and so shall they be a gift from the Israelites, their gift to the LORD out of their sacrifices of well-being. ²⁹ The sacral vestments of Aaron shall pass on to his sons after him, for them to be anointed and ordained in. ³⁰ He among his sons who becomes priest in his stead, who enters the Tent of Meeting to officiate within the sanctuary, shall wear them seven days. ³¹ You shall take the ram of ordination and boil its flesh in the sacred precinct; ³² and Aaron and his sons shall eat the flesh of the ram, and the bread that is in the basket, at the entrance of the Tent of Meeting. ³³ These things shall

EXODUS 30

be eaten only by those for whom expiation was made with them when they were ordained and consecrated; they may not be eaten by a layman, for they are holy. 34 And if any of the flesh of ordination, or any of the bread, is left until morning, you shall put what is left to the fire; it shall not be eaten, for it is holy. 35 Thus you shall do to Aaron and his sons, just as I have commanded you. You shall ordain them through seven days, 36 and each day you shall prepare a bull as a sin offering for expiation; you shall purge the altar by performing purification upon it, and you shall anoint it to consecrate it. 37 Seven days you shall perform purification for the altar to consecrate it, and the altar shall become most holy; whatever touches the altar shall become consecrated.

38 Now this is what you shall offer upon the altar: two yearling lambs each day, regularly. 39 You shall offer the one lamb in the morning, and you shall offer the other lamb at twilight. 40 There shall be a tenth of a measure of choice flour with a quarter of a hin of beaten oil mixed in, and a libation of a quarter hin of wine for one lamb; 41 and you shall offer the other lamb at twilight, repeating with it the meal offering of the morning with its libation — an offering by fire for a pleasing odor to the LORD. 42 A regular burnt offering throughout the generations, at the entrance of the Tent of Meeting before the LORD. For there I will meet with you, and there I will speak with you, 43 and there I will meet with the Israelites, and it shall be sanctified by My Presence. 44 I will sanctify the Tent of Meeting and the altar, and I will consecrate Aaron and his sons to serve Me as priests. 45 I will abide among the Israelites, and I will be their God. 46 And they shall know that I the LORD am their God, who brought them out from the land of Egypt that I might abide among them. I the LORD their God.

30 1 You shall make an altar for burning incense; make it of acacia wood. 2 It shall be a cubit long and a cubit wide — it shall be square — and two cubits high, its horns of one piece with it. 3 Overlay it with pure gold: its top, its sides round about, and its horns; and make a gold molding for it round about. 4 And make two gold rings for it under its molding; make them on its two side walls, on opposite sides. They shall serve as holders for poles with which to carry it. 5 Make the poles of acacia wood, and overlay them with gold. 6 Place it in front of the curtain that is over the Ark of the Pact — in front of the cover that is over the Pact — where I will meet with you. 7 On it Aaron shall burn aromatic incense: he shall burn it every morning when he tends the lamps, 8 and Aaron shall burn it at twilight when he lights the lamps — a regular incense offering before the LORD throughout the ages. 9 You shall not offer alien incense on it, or a burnt offering or a meal offering; neither shall you pour a libation on it. 10 Once a year Aaron shall perform purification upon its horns with blood of the sin offering of purification; purification shall be performed upon it once a year throughout the ages. It is most holy to the LORD.

11 The LORD spoke to Moses, saying: 12 When you take a census of the Israelite people according to their enrollment, each shall pay the LORD a ransom for himself on being enrolled, that no plague may come upon them through their being enrolled. 13 This is what everyone who is entered in the records shall pay: a half-shekel by the sanctuary weight — twenty gerahs to the shekel — a half-shekel as an offering to the LORD. 14 Everyone who is entered in the records, from the age of twenty years up, shall give the LORD's offering: 15 the rich shall not pay more and the poor shall not pay less than half a shekel when giving the LORD's offering as expiation for your persons. 16 You shall take the expiation money from the Israelites and assign it to the service of the Tent of Meeting; it shall serve the Israelites as a reminder before the LORD, as expiation for your persons.

17 The LORD spoke to Moses, saying: 18 Make a laver of copper and a stand of copper for it, for washing; and place it between the Tent of Meeting and the altar. Put water in it, 19 and let Aaron and his sons wash their hands and feet [in water drawn] from it. 20 When they enter the Tent of Meeting they shall wash with water, that they may not die; or when they approach the altar to serve, to turn into smoke an offering by fire to the LORD, 21 they shall wash their hands and feet, that they may not die. It shall be a law for all time for them

EXODUS 31 שמות לא כי תשא

- for him and his offspring - throughout the ages. 22 The LORD spoke to Moses, saying: 23 Next take choice spices: five hundred weight of solidified myrrh, half as much - two hundred and fifty - of fragrant cinnamon, two hundred and fifty of aromatic cane, 24 five hundred - by the sanctuary weight - of cassia, and a hin of olive oil. 25 Make of this a sacred anointing oil, a compound of ingredients expertly blended, to serve as sacred anointing oil. 26 With it anoint the Tent of Meeting, the Ark of the Pact, 27 the table and all its utensils, the lampstand and all its fittings, the altar of incense, 28 the altar of burnt offering and all its utensils, and the laver and its stand. 29 Thus you shall consecrate them so that they may be most holy: whatever touches them shall be consecrated. 30 You shall also anoint Aaron and his sons, consecrating them to serve Me as priests. 31 And speak to the Israelite people, as follows: This shall be an anointing oil sacred to Me throughout the ages. 32 It must not be rubbed on any person's body, and you must not make anything like it in the same proportions: it is sacred, to be held sacred by you. 33 Whoever compounds its like, or puts any of it on a layman, shall be cut off from his kin.

34 And the LORD said to Moses: Take the herbs stacte, onycha, and galbanum - these herbs together with pure frankincense; let there be an equal part of each. 35 Make them into incense, a compound expertly blended, refined, pure, sacred. 36 Beat some of it into powder, and put some before the Pact in the Tent of Meeting, where I will meet with you; it shall be most holy to you. 37 But when you make this incense, you must not make any in the same proportions for yourselves: it shall be held by you sacred to the LORD. Whoever makes any like it, to smell of it, shall be cut off from his kin.

31 1 The LORD spoke to Moses: 2 See, I have singled out by name Bezalel son of Uri son of Hur, of the tribe of Judah. 3 I have endowed him with a divine spirit of skill, ability, and knowledge in every kind of craft: 4 to make designs for work in gold, silver, and copper, 5 to cut stones for setting and to carve wood - to work in every kind of craft. 6 Moreover, I have assigned to him Oholiab son of Ahisamach, of the tribe of Dan; and I have also granted skill to all who are skillful, that they may make everything that I have commanded you: 7 the Tent of Meeting, the Ark for the Pact and the cover upon it, and all the furnishings of the Tent; 8 the table and its utensils, the pure lampstand and all its fittings, and the altar of incense; 9 the altar of burnt offering and all its utensils, and the laver and its stand; 10 the service vestments; the sacral vestments of Aaron the priest and the vestments of his sons, for their service as priests; 11 as well as the anointing oil and the aromatic incense for the sanctuary. Just as I have commanded you, they shall do.

12 And the LORD said to Moses: 13 Speak to the Israelite people and say: Nevertheless, you must keep My sabbaths, for this is a sign between Me and you throughout the ages, that you may know that I the LORD have consecrated you. 14 You shall keep the sabbath, for it is holy for you. He who profanes it shall be put to death: whoever does work on it, that person shall be cut off from among his kin. 15 Six days may work be done, but on the seventh day there shall be a sabbath of complete rest, holy to the LORD; whoever does work on the sabbath day shall be put to death. 16 The Israelite people shall keep the sabbath, observing the sabbath throughout the ages as a covenant for all time; 17 it shall be a sign for all time between Me and the people of Israel. For in six days the LORD made heaven and earth, and on the seventh day He ceased from work and was refreshed.

18 When He finished speaking with him on Mount Sinai, He gave Moses the two tablets of the Pact, stone tablets inscribed with the finger of God. 32 1 When the people saw that Moses was so long in coming down from the mountain, the people gathered against Aaron and said to him, "Come, make us a god who shall go before us, for that man Moses, who brought us from the land of Egypt - we do not know what has happened to him." 2 Aaron said to them, "Take off the gold rings that are on the ears of your wives, your sons, and your daughters, and bring them to me." 3 And all the people

עמוד שער לספר שמות, מתוך "חומש דה-קסטרו", כתב-יד מעוטר על קלף, גרמניה, 1344, אוסף מוזיאון ישראל, ירושלים

Opening page of the Book of Exodus, from the "De Castro Pentateuch", illuminated manuscript on vellum, Germany, 1344, collection of The Israel Museum, Jerusalem

EXODUS 32 שמות לב תשא

took off the gold rings that were in their ears and brought them to Aaron. 4 This he took from them and cast in a mold, and made it into a molten calf. And they exclaimed, "This is your god, O Israel, who brought you out of the land of Egypt!" 5 When Aaron saw this, he built an altar before it; and Aaron announced: "Tomorrow shall be a festival of the LORD!" 6 Early next day, the people offered up burnt offerings and brought sacrifices of well-being; they sat down to eat and drink, and then rose to dance.

7 The LORD spoke to Moses, "Hurry down, for your people, whom you brought out of the land of Egypt, have acted basely. 8 They have been quick to turn aside from the way that I enjoined upon them. They have made themselves a molten calf and bowed low to it and sacrificed to it, saying: 'This is your god, O Israel, who brought you out of the land of Egypt!'" 9 The LORD further said to Moses, "I see that this is a stiffnecked people. 10 Now, let Me be, that My anger may blaze forth against them and that I may destroy them, and make of you a great nation." 11 But Moses implored the LORD his God, saying, "Let not Your anger, O Lord, blaze forth against Your people, whom You delivered from the land of Egypt with great power and with a mighty hand. 12 Let not the Egyptians say, 'It was with evil intent that He delivered them, only to kill them off in the mountains and annihilate them from the face of the earth.' Turn from Your blazing anger, and renounce the plan to punish Your people. 13 Remember Your servants, Abraham, Isaac, and Israel, how You swore to them by Your Self and said to them: I will make your offspring as numerous as the stars of heaven, and I will give to your offspring this whole land of which I spoke, to possess forever." 14 And the LORD renounced the punishment He had planned to bring upon His people.

15 Thereupon Moses turned and went down from the mountain bearing the two tablets of the Pact, tablets inscribed on both their surfaces: they were inscribed on the one side and on the other. 16 The tablets were God's work, and the writing was God's writing, incised upon the tablets. 17 When Joshua heard the sound of the people in its boisterousness, he said to Moses, "There is a cry of war in the camp." 18 But he answered, "It is not the sound of the tune of triumph, Or the sound of the tune of defeat; It is the sound of song that I hear!" 19 As soon as Moses came near the camp and saw the calf and the dancing, he became enraged; and he hurled the tablets from his hands and shattered them at the foot of the mountain. 20 He took the calf that they had made and burned it; he ground it to powder and strewed it upon the water and so made the Israelites drink it. 21 Moses said to Aaron, "What did this people do to you that you have brought such great sin upon them?" 22 Aaron said, "Let not my lord be enraged. You know that this people is bent on evil. 23 They said to me, 'Make us a god to lead us; for that man Moses, who brought us from the land of Egypt - we do not know what has happened to him.' 24 So I said to them, 'Whoever has gold, take it off!' They gave it to me and I hurled it into the fire and out came this calf!" 25 Moses saw that the people were out of control - since Aaron had let them get out of control - so that they were a menace to any who might oppose them. 26 Moses stood up in the gate of the camp and said, "Whoever is for the LORD, come here!" And all the Levites rallied to him. 27 He said to them, "Thus says the LORD, the God of Israel: Each of you put sword on thigh, go back and forth from gate to gate throughout the camp, and slay brother, neighbor, and kin." 28 The Levites did as Moses had bidden; and some three thousand of the people fell that day. 29 And Moses said, "Dedicate yourselves to the LORD this day - for each of you has been against son and brother - that He may bestow a blessing upon you today." 30 The next day Moses said to the people, "You have been guilty of a great sin. Yet I will now go up to the LORD; perhaps I may win forgiveness for your sin." 31 Moses went back to the LORD and said, "Alas, this people is guilty of a great sin in making for themselves a god of gold. 32 Now, if You will forgive their sin [well and good]; but if not, erase me from the record which You have written." 33 But the LORD said to Moses, "He who has sinned against Me, him only will I erase from My record. 34 Go now, lead the people where I told you. See, My angel shall go before you. But when I make an accounting, I will bring them to account for their sins." 35 Then the LORD sent a plague upon the people, for what they did with the calf that

EXODUS 33 שמות לג תשא

❦ Aaron made. **33** ₁ Then the LORD said to Moses, "Set out from here, you and the people that you have brought up from the land of Egypt, to the land of which I swore to Abraham, Isaac, and Jacob, saying, 'To your offspring will I give it' - ₂ I will send an angel before you, and I will drive out the Canaanites, the Amorites, the Hittites, the Perizzites, the Hivites, and the Jebusites - ₃ a land flowing with milk and honey. But I will not go in your midst, since you are a stiffnecked people, lest I destroy you on the way." ₄ When the people heard this harsh word, they went into mourning, and none put on his finery. ₅ The LORD said to Moses, "Say to the Israelite people, 'You are a stiffnecked people. If I were to go in your midst for one moment, I would destroy you. Now, then, leave off your finery, and I will consider what to do to you.'" ₆ So the Israelites remained stripped of the finery from Mount Horeb on.
₇ Now Moses would take the Tent and pitch it outside the camp, at some distance from the camp. It was called the Tent of Meeting, and whoever sought the LORD would go out to the Tent of Meeting that was outside the camp. ₈ Whenever Moses went out to the Tent, all the people would rise and stand, each at the entrance of his tent, and gaze after Moses until he had entered the Tent. ₉ And when Moses entered the Tent, the pillar of cloud would descend and stand at the entrance of the Tent, while He spoke with Moses. ₁₀ When all the people saw the pillar of cloud poised at the entrance of the Tent, all the people would rise and bow low, each at the entrance of his tent. ₁₁ The LORD would speak to Moses face to face, as one man speaks to another. And he would then return to the camp; but his attendant, Joshua son of Nun, a youth, would not stir out of the Tent.
₁₂ Moses said to the LORD, "See, You say to me, 'Lead this people forward,' but You have not made known to me whom You will send with me. Further, You have said, 'I have singled you out by name, and you have, indeed, gained My favor.' ₁₃ Now, if I have truly gained Your favor, pray let me know Your ways, that I may know You and continue in Your favor. Consider, too, that this nation is Your people." ₁₄ And He said, "I will go in the lead and will lighten your burden." ₁₅ And he said to Him, "Unless You go in the lead, do not make us leave this place. ₁₆ For how shall it be known that Your people have gained Your favor unless You go with us, so that we may be distinguished, Your people and I, from every people on the face of the earth?"
₁₇ And the LORD said to Moses, "I will also do this thing that you have asked; for you have truly gained My favor and I have singled you out by name." ₁₈ He said, "Oh, let me behold Your Presence!" ₁₉ And He answered, "I will make all My goodness pass before you, and I will proclaim before you the name LORD, and the grace that I grant and the compassion that I show. ₂₀ But," He said, "you cannot see My face, for man may not see Me and live." ₂₁ And the LORD said, "See, there is a place near Me. Station yourself on the rock ₂₂ and, as My Presence passes by, I will put you in a cleft of the rock and shield you with My hand until I have passed by. ₂₃ Then I will take My hand away and you will see My back; but My face must not be seen."

❦ **34** ₁ The LORD said to Moses: "Carve two tablets of stone like the first, and I will inscribe upon the tablets the words that were on the first tablets, which you shattered. ₂ Be ready by morning, and in the morning come up to Mount Sinai and present yourself there to Me, on the top of the mountain. ₃ No one else shall come up with you, and no one shall be seen anywhere on the mountain; neither shall the flocks and the herds graze at the foot of this mountain." ₄ So Moses carved two tablets of stone, like the first, and early in the morning he went up on Mount Sinai, as the LORD had commanded him, taking the two stone tablets with him. ₅ The LORD came down in a cloud; He stood with him there, and proclaimed the name LORD. ₆ The LORD passed before him and proclaimed: "The LORD! the LORD! a God compassionate and gracious, slow to anger, abounding in kindness and faithfulness, ₇ extending kindness to the thousandth generation, forgiving iniquity, transgression, and sin; yet He does not remit all punishment, but visits the iniquity of parents upon children and children's children, upon the third and fourth generations." ₈ Moses hastened to bow low to the ground in homage, ₉ and said, "If I have gained Your favor, O Lord, pray, let the Lord go in our midst,

❦ 97 ❦

EXODUS 35   שמות לה ויקהל

even though this is a stiffnecked people. Pardon our iniquity and our sin, and take us for Your own!" 10 He said: I hereby make a covenant. Before all your people I will work such wonders as have not been wrought on all the earth or in any nation; and all the people who are with you shall see how awesome are the LORD's deeds which I will perform for you. 11 Mark well what I command you this day. I will drive out before you the Amorites, the Canaanites, the Hittites, the Perizzites, the Hivites, and the Jebusites. 12 Beware of making a covenant with the inhabitants of the land against which you are advancing, lest they be a snare in your midst. 13 No, you must tear down their altars, smash their pillars, and cut down their sacred posts: 14 for you must not worship any other god, because the LORD, whose name is Impassioned, is an impassioned God. 15 You must not make a covenant with the inhabitants of the land, for they will lust after their gods and sacrifice to their gods and invite you, and you will eat of their sacrifices. 16 And when you take wives from among their daughters for your sons, their daughters will lust after their gods and will cause your sons to lust after their gods. 17 You shall not make molten gods for yourselves. 18 You shall observe the Feast of Unleavened Bread - eating unleavened bread for seven days, as I have commanded you - at the set time of the month of Abib, for in the month of Abib you went forth from Egypt. 19 Every first issue of the womb is Mine, from all your livestock that drop a male as firstling, whether cattle or sheep. 20 But the firstling of an ass you shall redeem with a sheep; if you do not redeem it, you must break its neck. And you must redeem every first-born among your sons. None shall appear before Me empty-handed. 21 Six days you shall work, but on the seventh day you shall cease from labor; you shall cease from labor even at plowing time and harvest time. 22 You shall observe the Feast of Weeks, of the first fruits of the wheat harvest; and the Feast of Ingathering at the turn of the year. 23 Three times a year all your males shall appear before the Sovereign LORD, the God of Israel. 24 I will drive out nations from your path and enlarge your territory; no one will covet your land when you go up to appear before the LORD your God three times a year. 25 You shall not offer the blood of My sacrifice with anything leavened; and the sacrifice of the Feast of Passover shall not be left lying until morning. 26 The choice first fruits of your soil you shall bring to the house of the LORD your God. You shall not boil a kid in its mother's milk.

27 And the LORD said to Moses: Write down these commandments, for in accordance with these commandments I make a covenant with you and with Israel. 28 And he was there with the LORD forty days and forty nights; he ate no bread and drank no water; and he wrote down on the tablets the terms of the covenant, the Ten Commandments. 29 So Moses came down from Mount Sinai. And he was there with the LORD forty days and forty nights; he ate no bread and drank no water; and he wrote down on the tablets the terms of the covenant, the Ten Commandments. 29 So Moses came down from Mount Sinai. And as Moses came down from the mountain bearing the two tablets of the Pact, Moses was not aware that the skin of his face was radiant, since he had spoken with Him. 30 Aaron and all the Israelites saw that the skin of Moses' face was radiant; and they shrank from coming near him. 31 But Moses called to them, and Aaron and all the chieftains in the assembly returned to him, and Moses spoke to them. 32 Afterward all the Israelites came near, and he instructed them concerning all that the LORD had imparted to him on Mount Sinai. 33 And when Moses had finished speaking with them, he put a veil over his face. 34 Whenever Moses went in before the LORD to speak with Him, he would leave the veil off until he came out; and when he came out and told the Israelites what he had been commanded, 35 the Israelites would see how radiant the skin of Moses' face was. Moses would then put the veil back over his face until he went in to speak with Him.

35 Moses then convoked the whole Israelite community and said to them: These are the things that the LORD has commanded you to do: 2 On six days work may be done, but on the seventh day you shall have a sabbath of complete rest, holy to the LORD; whoever does any work on it shall be put to death. 3 You shall kindle no fire throughout your settlements on the sabbath day.

4 Moses said further to the whole community of Israelites: This is what the LORD has commanded: 5 Take from among you gifts to the LORD; everyone whose heart so moves him shall bring them - gifts for the LORD: gold, silver, and copper; 6 blue, purple, and crimson yarns, fine linen, and goats' hair; 7 tanned ram skins, dolphin skins, and acacia wood: 8 oil for

EXODUS 36 שמות לו ויקהל

lighting, spices for the anointing oil and for the aromatic incense; 9 lapis lazuli and other stones for setting, for the ephod and the breastpiece. 10 And let all among you who are skilled come and make all that the LORD has commanded; 11 the Tabernacle, its tent and its covering, its clasps and its planks, its bars, its posts, and its sockets; 12 the ark and its poles, the cover, and the curtain for the screen; 13 the table, and its poles and all its utensils; and the bread of display; 14 the lampstand for lighting, its furnishings and its lamps, and the oil for lighting; 15 the altar of incense and its poles; the anointing oil and the aromatic incense; and the entrance screen for the entrance of the Tabernacle; 16 the altar of burnt offering, its copper grating, its poles, and all its furnishings; the laver and its stand; 17 the hangings of the enclosure, its posts and its sockets, and the screen for the gate of the court; 18 the pegs for the Tabernacle, the pegs for the enclosure, and their cords; 19 the service vestments for officiating in the sanctuary, the sacral vestments of Aaron the priest and the vestments of his sons for priestly service. 20 So the whole community of the Israelites left Moses' presence. 21 And everyone who excelled in ability and everyone whose spirit moved him came, bringing to the LORD his offering for the work of the Tent of Meeting and for all its service and for the sacral vestments. 22 Men and women, all whose hearts moved them, all who would make an elevation offering of gold to the LORD, came bringing brooches, earrings, rings, and pendants - gold objects of all kinds. 23 And everyone who had in his possession blue, purple, and crimson yarns, fine linen, goats' hair, tanned ram skins, and dolphin skins, brought them; 24 everyone who would make gifts of silver or copper brought them as gifts for the LORD; and everyone who had in his possession acacia wood for any work of the service brought that. 25 And all the skilled women spun with their own hands, and brought what they had spun, in blue, purple, and crimson yarns, and in fine linen. 26 And all the women who excelled in that skill spun the goats' hair. 27 The chieftains brought lapis lazuli and other stones for setting, for the ephod and for the breastpiece; 28 and spices and oil for lighting, for the anointing oil, and for the aromatic incense. 29 Thus the Israelites, all the men and women whose hearts moved them to bring anything for the work that the LORD, through Moses, had commanded to be done, brought it as a freewill offering to the LORD.

30 And Moses said to the Israelites: See, the LORD has singled out by name Bezalel, son of Uri son of Hur, of the tribe of Judah. 31 He has endowed him with a divine spirit of skill, ability, and knowledge in every kind of craft 32 and has inspired him to make designs for work in gold, silver, and copper, 33 to cut stones for setting and to carve wood - to work in every kind of designer's craft - 34 and to give directions. He and Oholiab son of Ahisamach of the tribe of Dan 35 have been endowed with the skill to do any work - of the carver, the designer, the embroiderer in blue, purple, crimson yarns, and in fine linen, and of the weaver—as workers in all crafts and as makers of designs. 36 1 Let, then, Bezalel and Oholiab and all the skilled persons whom the LORD has endowed with skill and ability to perform expertly all the tasks connected with the service of the sanctuary carry out all that the LORD has commanded. 2 Moses then called Bezalel and Oholiab, and every skilled person whom the LORD had endowed with skill, everyone who excelled in ability, to undertake the task and carry it out. 3 They took over from Moses all the gifts that the Israelites had brought, to carry out the tasks connected with the service of the sanctuary. But when these continued to bring freewill offerings to him morning after morning, 4 all the artisans who were engaged in the tasks of the sanctuary came, each from the task upon which he was engaged, 5 and said to Moses, "The people are bringing more than is needed for the tasks entailed in the work that the LORD has commanded to be done." 6 Moses thereupon had this proclamation made throughout the camp: "Let no man or woman make further effort toward gifts for the sanctuary!"

EXODUS 37 שמות לז ויקהל

So the people stopped bringing; 7 their efforts had been more than enough for all the tasks to be done. 8 Then all the skilled among those engaged in the work made the Tabernacle of ten strips of cloth, which they made of fine twisted linen, blue, purple, and crimson yarns; into these they worked a design of cherubim. 9 The length of each cloth was twenty-eight cubits, and the width of each cloth was four cubits, all cloths having the same measurements. 10 They joined five of the cloths to one another, and they joined the other five cloths to one another. 11 They made loops of blue wool on the edge of the outermost cloth of the one set, and did the same on the edge of the outermost cloth of the other set: 12 they made fifty loops on the one cloth, and they made fifty loops on the end cloth of the other set, the loops being opposite one another. 13 And they made fifty gold clasps and coupled the units to one another with the clasps, so that the Tabernacle became one whole.

14 They made cloths of goats' hair for a tent over the Tabernacle; they made the cloths eleven in number. 15 The length of each cloth was thirty cubits, and the width of each cloth was four cubits, the eleven cloths having the same measurements. 16 They joined five of the cloths by themselves, and the other six cloths by themselves. 17 They made fifty loops on the edge of the outermost cloth of the one set, and they made fifty loops on the edge of the end cloth of the other set. 18 They made fifty copper clasps to couple the Tent together so that it might become one whole. 19 And they made a covering of tanned ram skins for the tent, and a covering of dolphin skins above.

20 They made the planks for the Tabernacle of acacia wood, upright. 21 The length of each plank was ten cubits, the width of each plank a cubit and a half. 22 Each plank had two tenons, parallel to each other; they did the same with all the planks of the Tabernacle. 23 Of the planks of the Tabernacle, they made twenty planks for the south side, 24 making forty silver sockets under the twenty planks, two sockets under one plank for its two tenons and two sockets under each following plank for its two tenons; 25 and for the other side wall of the Tabernacle, the north side, twenty planks, 26 with their forty silver sockets, two sockets under one plank and two sockets under each following plank. 27 And for the rear of the Tabernacle, to the west, they made six planks; 28 and they made two planks for the corners of the Tabernacle at the rear. 29 They matched at the bottom, but terminated as one at the top into one ring; they did so with both of them at the two corners. 30 Thus there were eight planks with their sockets of silver: sixteen sockets, two under each plank. 31 They made bars of acacia wood, five for the planks of the one side wall of the Tabernacle, 32 five bars for the planks of the other side wall of the Tabernacle, and five bars for the planks of the wall of the Tabernacle at the rear, to the west; 33 they made the center bar to run, halfway up the planks, from end to end. 34 They overlaid the planks with gold, and made their rings of gold, as holders for the bars; and they overlaid the bars with gold. 35 They made the curtain of blue, purple, and crimson yarns, and fine twisted linen, working into it a design of cherubim. 36 They made for it four posts of acacia wood and overlaid them with gold, with their hooks of gold; and they cast for them four silver sockets. 37 They made the screen for the entrance of the Tent, of blue, purple, and crimson yarns, and fine twisted linen, done in embroidery; 38 and five posts for it with their hooks. They overlaid their tops and their bands with gold; but the five sockets were of copper.

37 1 Bezalel made the ark of acacia wood, two and a half cubits long, a cubit and a half wide, and a cubit and a half high. 2 He overlaid it with pure gold, inside and out; and he made a gold molding for it round about. 3 He cast four gold rings for it, for its four

EXODUS 38 שמות לח ויקהל

feet; two rings on one of its side walls and two rings on the other. 4 He made poles of acacia wood, overlaid them with gold, 5 and inserted the poles into the rings on the side walls of the ark for carrying the ark. 6 He made a cover of pure gold, two and a half cubits long and a cubit and a half wide. 7 He made two cherubim of gold; he made them of hammered work, at the two ends of the cover; 8 one cherub at one end and the other cherub at the other end; he made the cherubim of one piece with the cover, at its two ends. 9 The cherubim had their wings spread out above, shielding the cover with their wings. They faced each other; the faces of the cherubim were turned toward the cover.

10 He made the table of acacia wood, two cubits long, one cubit wide, and a cubit and a half high; 11 he overlaid it with pure gold and made a gold molding around it. 12 He made a rim of a hand's breadth around it and made a gold molding for its rim round about. 13 He cast four gold rings for it and attached the rings to the four corners at its four legs. 14 The rings were next to the rim, as holders for the poles to carry the table. 15 He made the poles of acacia wood for carrying the table, and overlaid them with gold. 16 The utensils that were to be upon the table - its bowls, ladles, jugs, and jars with which to offer libations - he made of pure gold.

17 He made the lampstand of pure gold. He made the lampstand - its base and its shaft - of hammered work: its cups, calyxes, and petals were of one piece with it. 18 Six branches issued from its sides: three branches from one side of the lampstand, and three branches from the other side of the lampstand. 19 There were three cups shaped like almond-blossoms, each with calyx and petals, on one branch; and there were three cups shaped like almond-blossoms, each with calyx and petals, on the next branch; so for all six branches issuing from the lampstand. 20 On the lampstand itself there were four cups shaped like almond-blossoms, each with calyx and petals: 21 a calyx, of one piece with it, under a pair of branches; and a calyx, of one piece with it, under the second pair of branches; and a calyx, of one piece with it, under the last pair of branches; so for all six branches issuing from it. 22 Their calyxes and their stems were of one piece with it, the whole of it a single hammered piece of pure gold. 23 He made its seven lamps, its tongs, and its fire pans of pure gold. 24 He made it and all its furnishings out of a talent of pure gold.

25 He made the incense altar of acacia wood, a cubit long and a cubit wide - square - and two cubits high: its horns were of one piece with it. 26 He overlaid it with pure gold: its top, its sides round about, and its horns; and he made a gold molding for it round about. 27 He made two gold rings for it under its molding, on its two walls - on opposite sides - as holders for the poles with which to carry it. 28 He made the poles of acacia wood, and overlaid them with gold. 29 He prepared the sacred anointing oil and the pure aromatic incense, expertly blended.

38 1 He made the altar for burnt offering of acacia wood, five cubits long and five cubits wide - square - and three cubits high. 2 He made horns for it on its four corners, the horns being of one piece with it; and he overlaid it with copper. 3 He made all the utensils of the altar - the pails, the scrapers, the basins, the flesh hooks, and the fire pans; he made all these utensils of copper. 4 He made for the altar a grating of meshwork in copper, extending below, under its ledge, to its middle. 5 He cast four rings, at the four corners of the copper grating, as holders for the poles. 6 He made the poles of acacia wood and overlaid them with copper; 7 and he inserted the poles into the rings on the side walls of the altar, to carry it by them. He made it hollow, of boards. 8 He made the laver of copper and its stand of copper, from the mirrors of the women who performed tasks at the entrance of the Tent of Meeting.

9 He made the enclosure: On the south side, a hundred cubits of hangings of fine twisted linen for the enclosure 10 with their twenty posts and their twenty sockets of copper.

פְּנֻמֹתָיו וּשְׁתֵּי טַבָּעֹת עַל־צַלְעוֹ הָאֶחָת וּשְׁתֵּי טַבָּעֹת עַל־צַלְעוֹ הַשֵּׁנִית: ד וַיַּעַשׂ בַּדֵּי עֲצֵי שִׁטִּים וַיְצַף אֹתָם זָהָב: ה וַיָּבֵא אֶת־הַבַּדִּים בַּטַּבָּעֹת עַל צַלְעֹת הָאָרֹן לָשֵׂאת אֶת־הָאָרֹן: ו וַיַּעַשׂ כַּפֹּרֶת זָהָב טָהוֹר אַמָּתַיִם וָחֵצִי אָרְכָּהּ וְאַמָּה וָחֵצִי רָחְבָּהּ: ז וַיַּעַשׂ שְׁנֵי כְרֻבִים זָהָב מִקְשָׁה עָשָׂה אֹתָם מִשְּׁנֵי קְצוֹת הַכַּפֹּרֶת: ח כְּרוּב־אֶחָד מִקָּצָה מִזֶּה וּכְרוּב־אֶחָד מִקָּצָה מִזֶּה מִן־הַכַּפֹּרֶת עָשָׂה אֶת־הַכְּרֻבִים מִשְּׁנֵי קְצוֹותָיו (קְצוֹתָיו): ט וַיִּהְיוּ הַכְּרֻבִים פֹּרְשֵׂי כְנָפַיִם לְמַעְלָה סֹכְכִים בְּכַנְפֵיהֶם עַל־הַכַּפֹּרֶת וּפְנֵיהֶם אִישׁ אֶל־אָחִיו אֶל־הַכַּפֹּרֶת הָיוּ פְּנֵי הַכְּרֻבִים:

י וַיַּעַשׂ אֶת־הַשֻּׁלְחָן עֲצֵי שִׁטִּים אַמָּתַיִם אָרְכּוֹ וְאַמָּה רָחְבּוֹ וְאַמָּה וָחֵצִי קֹמָתוֹ: יא וַיְצַף אֹתוֹ זָהָב טָהוֹר וַיַּעַשׂ לוֹ זֵר זָהָב סָבִיב: יב וַיַּעַשׂ לוֹ מִסְגֶּרֶת טֹפַח סָבִיב וַיַּעַשׂ זֵר־זָהָב לְמִסְגַּרְתּוֹ סָבִיב: יג וַיִּצֹק לוֹ אַרְבַּע טַבְּעֹת זָהָב וַיִּתֵּן אֶת־הַטַּבָּעֹת עַל אַרְבַּע הַפֵּאֹת אֲשֶׁר לְאַרְבַּע רַגְלָיו: יד לְעֻמַּת הַמִּסְגֶּרֶת הָיוּ הַטַּבָּעֹת בָּתִּים לַבַּדִּים לָשֵׂאת אֶת־הַשֻּׁלְחָן: טו וַיַּעַשׂ אֶת־הַבַּדִּים עֲצֵי שִׁטִּים וַיְצַף אֹתָם זָהָב לָשֵׂאת אֶת־הַשֻּׁלְחָן: טז וַיַּעַשׂ אֶת־הַכֵּלִים אֲשֶׁר עַל־הַשֻּׁלְחָן אֶת־קְעָרֹתָיו וְאֶת־כַּפֹּתָיו וְאֵת מְנַקִּיֹּתָיו וְאֶת־הַקְּשָׂוֹת אֲשֶׁר יֻסַּךְ בָּהֵן זָהָב טָהוֹר:

יז וַיַּעַשׂ אֶת־הַמְּנֹרָה זָהָב טָהוֹר מִקְשָׁה עָשָׂה אֶת־הַמְּנֹרָה יְרֵכָהּ וְקָנָהּ גְּבִיעֶיהָ כַּפְתֹּרֶיהָ וּפְרָחֶיהָ מִמֶּנָּה הָיוּ: יח וְשִׁשָּׁה קָנִים יֹצְאִים מִצִּדֶּיהָ שְׁלֹשָׁה קְנֵי מְנֹרָה מִצִּדָּהּ הָאֶחָד וּשְׁלֹשָׁה קְנֵי מְנֹרָה מִצִּדָּהּ הַשֵּׁנִי: יט שְׁלֹשָׁה גְבִעִים מְשֻׁקָּדִים בַּקָּנֶה הָאֶחָד כַּפְתֹּר וָפֶרַח וּשְׁלֹשָׁה גְבִעִים מְשֻׁקָּדִים בְּקָנֶה אֶחָד כַּפְתֹּר וָפֶרַח כֵּן לְשֵׁשֶׁת הַקָּנִים הַיֹּצְאִים מִן־הַמְּנֹרָה: כ וּבַמְּנֹרָה אַרְבָּעָה גְבִעִים מְשֻׁקָּדִים כַּפְתֹּרֶיהָ וּפְרָחֶיהָ: כא וְכַפְתֹּר תַּחַת שְׁנֵי הַקָּנִים מִמֶּנָּה וְכַפְתֹּר תַּחַת שְׁנֵי הַקָּנִים מִמֶּנָּה וְכַפְתֹּר תַּחַת־שְׁנֵי הַקָּנִים מִמֶּנָּה לְשֵׁשֶׁת הַקָּנִים הַיֹּצְאִים מִמֶּנָּה: כב כַּפְתֹּרֵיהֶם וּקְנֹתָם מִמֶּנָּה הָיוּ כֻּלָּהּ מִקְשָׁה אַחַת זָהָב טָהוֹר: כג וַיַּעַשׂ אֶת־נֵרֹתֶיהָ שִׁבְעָה וּמַלְקָחֶיהָ וּמַחְתֹּתֶיהָ זָהָב טָהוֹר: כד כִּכָּר זָהָב טָהוֹר עָשָׂה אֹתָהּ וְאֵת כָּל־כֵּלֶיהָ:

כה וַיַּעַשׂ אֶת־מִזְבַּח הַקְּטֹרֶת עֲצֵי שִׁטִּים אַמָּה אָרְכּוֹ וְאַמָּה רָחְבּוֹ רָבוּעַ וְאַמָּתַיִם קֹמָתוֹ מִמֶּנּוּ הָיוּ קַרְנֹתָיו: כו וַיְצַף אֹתוֹ זָהָב טָהוֹר אֶת־גַּגּוֹ וְאֶת־קִירֹתָיו סָבִיב וְאֶת־קַרְנֹתָיו וַיַּעַשׂ לוֹ זֵר זָהָב סָבִיב: כז וּשְׁתֵּי טַבְּעֹת זָהָב עָשָׂה־לוֹ מִתַּחַת לְזֵרוֹ עַל שְׁתֵּי צַלְעֹתָיו עַל שְׁנֵי צִדָּיו לְבָתִּים לְבַדִּים לָשֵׂאת אֹתוֹ בָּהֶם: כח וַיַּעַשׂ אֶת־הַבַּדִּים עֲצֵי שִׁטִּים וַיְצַף אֹתָם זָהָב: כט וַיַּעַשׂ אֶת־שֶׁמֶן הַמִּשְׁחָה קֹדֶשׁ וְאֶת־קְטֹרֶת הַסַּמִּים טָהוֹר מַעֲשֵׂה רֹקֵחַ:

לח א וַיַּעַשׂ אֶת־מִזְבַּח הָעֹלָה עֲצֵי שִׁטִּים חָמֵשׁ אַמּוֹת אָרְכּוֹ וְחָמֵשׁ־אַמּוֹת רָחְבּוֹ רָבוּעַ וְשָׁלֹשׁ אַמּוֹת קֹמָתוֹ: ב וַיַּעַשׂ קַרְנֹתָיו עַל אַרְבַּע פִּנֹּתָיו מִמֶּנּוּ הָיוּ קַרְנֹתָיו וַיְצַף אֹתוֹ נְחֹשֶׁת: ג וַיַּעַשׂ אֶת־כָּל־כְּלֵי הַמִּזְבֵּחַ אֶת־הַסִּירֹת וְאֶת־הַיָּעִים וְאֶת־הַמִּזְרָקֹת אֶת־הַמִּזְלָגֹת וְאֶת־הַמַּחְתֹּת כָּל־כֵּלָיו עָשָׂה נְחֹשֶׁת: ד וַיַּעַשׂ לַמִּזְבֵּחַ מִכְבָּר מַעֲשֵׂה רֶשֶׁת נְחֹשֶׁת תַּחַת כַּרְכֻּבּוֹ מִלְּמַטָּה עַד־חֶצְיוֹ: ה וַיִּצֹק אַרְבַּע טַבָּעֹת בְּאַרְבַּע הַקְּצָוֹת לְמִכְבַּר הַנְּחֹשֶׁת בָּתִּים לַבַּדִּים: ו וַיַּעַשׂ אֶת־הַבַּדִּים עֲצֵי שִׁטִּים וַיְצַף אֹתָם נְחֹשֶׁת: ז וַיָּבֵא אֶת־הַבַּדִּים בַּטַּבָּעֹת עַל צַלְעֹת הַמִּזְבֵּחַ לָשֵׂאת אֹתוֹ בָּהֶם נְבוּב לֻחֹת עָשָׂה אֹתוֹ:

ח וַיַּעַשׂ אֵת הַכִּיּוֹר נְחֹשֶׁת וְאֵת כַּנּוֹ נְחֹשֶׁת בְּמַרְאֹת הַצֹּבְאֹת אֲשֶׁר צָבְאוּ פֶּתַח אֹהֶל מוֹעֵד:

ט וַיַּעַשׂ אֶת־הֶחָצֵר לִפְאַת נֶגֶב תֵּימָנָה קַלְעֵי הֶחָצֵר שֵׁשׁ מָשְׁזָר מֵאָה בָּאַמָּה: י עַמּוּדֵיהֶם עֶשְׂרִים וְאַדְנֵיהֶם עֶשְׂרִים נְחֹשֶׁת וָוֵי

EXODUS 39 שמות לט פקודי

the hooks and bands of the posts being silver. 11 On the north side, a hundred cubits - with their twenty posts and their twenty sockets of copper, the hooks and bands of the posts being silver. 12 On the west side, fifty cubits of hangings - with their ten posts and their ten sockets, the hooks and bands of the posts being silver. 13 And on the front side, to the east, fifty cubits: 14 fifteen cubits of hangings on the one flank, with their three posts and their three sockets, 15 and fifteen cubits of hangings on the other flank - on each side of the gate of the enclosure - with their three posts and their three sockets. 16 All the hangings around the enclosure were of fine twisted linen. 17 The sockets for the posts were of copper, the hooks and bands of the posts were of silver, the overlay of their tops was of silver; all the posts of the enclosure were banded with silver. · 18 The screen of the gate of the enclosure, done in embroidery, was of blue, purple, and crimson yarns, and fine twisted linen. It was twenty cubits long. Its height - or width - was five cubits, like that of the hangings of the enclosure. 19 The posts were four; their four sockets were of copper, their hooks of silver; and the overlay of their tops was of silver, as were also their bands. · 20 All the pegs of the Tabernacle and of the enclosure round about were of copper.

21 These are the records of the Tabernacle, the Tabernacle of the Pact, which were drawn up at Moses' bidding - the work of the Levites under the direction of Ithamar son of Aaron the priest. 22 Now Bezalel, son of Uri son of Hur, of the tribe of Judah, had made all that the LORD had commanded Moses: 23 at his side was Oholiab son of Ahisamach, of the tribe of Dan, carver and designer, and embroiderer in blue, purple, and crimson yarns and in fine linen. 24 All the gold that was used for the work, in all the work of the sanctuary - the elevation offering of gold - came to twenty and nine talents and seven hundred and thirty shekels by the sanctuary weight. 25 The silver of those of the community who were recorded came to hundred talents and thousand seven hundred and threescore and fifteen shekels by the sanctuary weight: 26 a half-shekel a head, half a shekel by the sanctuary weight, for each one who was entered in the records, from the age of twenty years up, six hundred thousand and three thousand and five hundred and fifty men. 27 The hundred talents of silver were for casting the sockets of the sanctuary and the sockets for the curtain, hundred sockets to the hundred talents, a talent a socket. 28 And of the thousand seven hundred and seventy five shekels he made hooks for the posts, overlay for their tops, and bands around them. 29 The copper from the elevation offering came to seventy talents and two thousand and four hundred shekels. 30 Of it he made the sockets for the entrance of the Tent of Meeting; the copper altar and its copper grating and all the utensils of the altar; 31 the sockets of the enclosure round about and the sockets of the gate of the enclosure; and all the pegs of the Tabernacle and all the pegs of the enclosure round about. 39 1 Of the blue, purple, and crimson yarns they also made the service vestments for officiating in the sanctuary; they made Aaron's sacral vestments - as the LORD had commanded Moses.

2 The ephod was made of gold, blue, purple, and crimson yarns, and fine twisted linen. 3 They hammered out sheets of gold and cut threads to be worked into designs among the blue, the purple, and the crimson yarns, and the fine linen. 4 They made for it attaching shoulder-pieces; they were attached at its two ends. 5 The decorated band that was upon it was made like it, of one piece with it; of gold, blue, purple, and crimson yarns, and fine twisted linen - as the LORD had commanded Moses.

6 They bordered the lazuli stones with frames of gold, engraved with seal engravings of the names of the sons of Israel. 7 They were set on the shoulder-pieces of the ephod, as stones of remembrance for the Israelites - as the LORD had commanded Moses.

8 The breastpiece was made in the style of the ephod: of gold, blue, purple, and crimson yarns, and fine twisted linen. 9 It was square; they made the breastpiece doubled - a span in length

EXODUS 40 · שמות מ פקודי

and a span in width, doubled. 10 They set in it four rows of stones. The first row was a row of carnelian, chrysolite, and emerald: 11 the second row: a turquoise, a sapphire, and an amethyst; 12 the third row: a jacinth, an agate, and a crystal; 13 and the fourth row: a beryl, a lapis lazuli, and a jasper. They were encircled in their mountings with frames of gold. 14 The stones corresponded [in number] to the names of the sons of Israel: twelve, corresponding to their names; engraved like seals, each with its name, for the twelve tribes. 15 On the breastpiece they made braided chains of corded work in pure gold. 16 They made two frames of gold and two rings of gold, and fastened the two rings at the two ends of the breastpiece, 17 attaching the two golden cords to the two rings at the ends of the breastpiece. 18 They then fastened the two ends of the cords to the two frames, attaching them to the shoulder-pieces of the ephod, at the front. 19 They made two rings of gold and attached them to the two ends of the breastpiece, at its inner edge, which faced the ephod. 20 They made two other rings of gold and fastened them on the front of the ephod, low on the two shoulder-pieces, close to its seam above the decorated band. 21 The breastpiece was held in place by a cord of blue from its rings to the rings of the ephod, so that the breastpiece rested on the decorated band and did not come loose from the ephod - as the LORD had commanded Moses.

22 The robe for the ephod was made of woven work, of pure blue. 23 The opening of the robe, in the middle of it, was like the opening of a coat of mail, with a binding around the opening, so that it would not tear. 24 On the hem of the robe they made pomegranates of blue, purple, and crimson yarns, twisted. 25 They also made bells of pure gold, and attached the bells between the pomegranates, all around the hem of the robe, between the pomegranates: 26 a bell and a pomegranate, a bell and a pomegranate, all around the hem of the robe for officiating in - as the LORD had commanded Moses. 27 They made the tunics of fine linen, of woven work, for Aaron and his sons: 28 and the headdress of fine linen, and the decorated turbans of fine linen, and the linen breeches of fine twisted linen; 29 and sashes of fine twisted linen, blue, purple, and crimson yarns, done in embroidery - as the LORD had commanded Moses. 30 They made the frontlet for the holy diadem of pure gold, and incised upon it the seal inscription: "Holy to the LORD." 31 They attached to it a cord of blue to fix it upon the headdress above - as the LORD had commanded Moses.

32 Thus was completed all the work of the Tabernacle of the Tent of Meeting. The Israelites did so; just as the LORD had commanded Moses, so they did.

33 Then they brought the Tabernacle to Moses, with the Tent and all its furnishings: its clasps, its planks, its bars, its posts, and its sockets; 34 the covering of tanned ram skins, the covering of dolphin skins, and the curtain for the screen: 35 the Ark of the Pact and its poles, and the cover: 36 the table and all its utensils, and the bread of display: 37 the pure lampstand, its lamps - lamps in due order - and all its fittings, and the oil for lighting: 38 the altar of gold, the oil for anointing, the aromatic incense, and the screen for the entrance of the Tent: 39 the copper altar with its copper grating, its poles and all its utensils, and the laver and its stand: 40 the hangings of the enclosure, its posts and its sockets, the screen for the gate of the enclosure, its cords and its pegs - all the furnishings for the service of the Tabernacle, the Tent of Meeting: 41 the service vestments for officiating in the sanctuary, the sacral vestments of Aaron the priest, and the vestments of his sons for priestly service. 42 Just as the LORD had commanded Moses, so the Israelites had done all the work. 43 And when Moses saw that they had performed all the tasks - as the LORD had commanded, so they had done - Moses blessed them.

40 1 And the LORD spoke to Moses, saying: 2 On the first day of the first month you shall thou set up the Tabernacle of the Tent of Meeting. 3 Place there the Ark of the Pact,

EXODUS 40 — שמות מ פקודי

and screen off the ark with the curtain. 4 Bring in the table and lay out its due setting; bring in the lampstand and light its lamps; 5 and place the gold altar of incense before the Ark of the Pact. Then put up the screen for the entrance of the Tabernacle. 6 You shall place the altar of burnt offering before the entrance of the Tabernacle of the Tent of Meeting. 7 Place the laver between the Tent of Meeting and the altar, and put water in it. 8 Set up the enclosure round about, and put in place the screen for the gate of the enclosure. 9 You shall take the anointing oil and anoint the Tabernacle and all that is in it to consecrate it and all its furnishings, so that it shall be holy. 10 Then anoint the altar of burnt offering and all its utensils to consecrate the altar, so that the altar shall be most holy. 11 And anoint the laver and its stand to consecrate it. 12 You shall bring Aaron and his sons forward to the entrance of the Tent of Meeting and wash them with the water. 13 Put the sacral vestments on Aaron, and anoint him and consecrate him, that he may serve Me as priest. 14 Then bring his sons forward, put tunics on them, 15 and anoint them as you have anointed their father, that they may serve Me as priests. This their anointing shall serve them for everlasting priesthood throughout the ages. 16 This Moses did; just as the LORD had commanded him, so he did. 17 In the first month of the second year, on the first of the month, the Tabernacle was set up. 18 Moses set up the Tabernacle, placing its sockets, setting up its planks, inserting its bars, and erecting its posts. 19 He spread the tent over the Tabernacle, placing the covering of the tent on top of it - just as the LORD had commanded Moses. 20 He took the Pact and placed it in the ark; he fixed the poles to the ark, placed the cover on top of the ark, 21 and brought the ark inside the Tabernacle. Then he put up the curtain for screening, and screened off the Ark of the Pact - just as the LORD had commanded Moses. 22 He placed the table in the Tent of Meeting, outside the curtain, on the north side of the Tabernacle. 23 Upon it he laid out the setting of bread before the LORD - as the LORD had commanded Moses. 24 He placed the lampstand in the Tent of Meeting opposite the table, on the south side of the Tabernacle. 25 And he lit the lamps before the LORD - as the LORD had commanded Moses. 26 He placed the altar of gold in the Tent of Meeting, before the curtain. 27 On it he burned aromatic incense - as the LORD had commanded Moses. 28 Then he put up the screen for the entrance of the Tabernacle. 29 At the entrance of the Tabernacle of the Tent of Meeting he placed the altar of burnt offering. On it he offered up the burnt offering and the meal offering - as the LORD had commanded Moses. 30 He placed the laver between the Tent of Meeting and the altar, and put water in it for washing. 31 From it Moses and Aaron and his sons would wash their hands and feet; 32 they washed when they entered the Tent of Meeting and when they approached the altar - as the LORD had commanded Moses. 33 And he set up the enclosure around the Tabernacle and the altar, and put up the screen for the gate of the enclosure. When Moses had finished the work, 34 the cloud covered the Tent of Meeting, and the Presence of the LORD filled the Tabernacle. 35 Moses could not enter the Tent of Meeting, because the cloud had settled upon it and the Presence of the LORD filled the Tabernacle. 36 When the cloud lifted from the Tabernacle, the Israelites would set out, on their various journeys; 37 but if the cloud did not lift, they would not set out until such time as it did lift. 38 For over the Tabernacle a cloud of the LORD rested by day, and fire would appear in it by night, in the view of all the house of Israel throughout their journeys.

חזק

On the facing page:
Oil lamp, ca. 1200 BCE, found in Eretz-Israel, collection of The Jewish Museum, New York
Details of a carpet page with micrographic and geometric decorations, from the "Second Leningrad Bible", copied by Samuel Ben Jacob, Cairo, 1008-10, collection of the Public Library, St. Petersburg

LEVITICUS
ויקרא

LEVITICUS 1 ויקרא א

1 The LORD called to Moses and spoke to him from the Tent of Meeting, saying: 2 Speak to the Israelite people, and say to them: When any of you presents an offering of cattle to the LORD, he shall choose his offering from the herd or from the flock. 3 If his offering is a burnt offering from the herd, he shall make his offering a male without blemish. He shall bring it to the entrance of the Tent of Meeting, for acceptance in his behalf before the LORD. 4 He shall lay his hand upon the head of the burnt offering, that it may be acceptable in his behalf, in expiation for him. 5 The bull shall be slaughtered before the LORD; and Aaron's sons, the priests, shall offer the blood, dashing the blood against all sides of the altar which is at the entrance of the Tent of Meeting. 6 The burnt offering shall be flayed and cut up into sections. 7 The sons of Aaron the priest shall put fire on the altar and lay out wood upon the fire; 8 and Aaron's sons, the priests, shall lay out the sections, with the head and the suet, on the wood that is on the fire upon the altar. 9 Its entrails and legs shall be washed with water, and the priest shall turn the whole into smoke on the altar as a burnt offering, an offering by fire of pleasing odor to the LORD. 10 If his offering for a burnt offering is from the flock, of sheep or of goats, he shall make his offering a male without blemish. 11 It shall be slaughtered before the LORD on the north side of the altar, and Aaron's sons, the priests, shall dash its blood against all sides of the altar. 12 When it has been cut up into sections, the priest shall lay them out, with the head and the suet, on the wood that is on the fire upon the altar. 13 The entrails and the legs shall be washed with water; the priest shall offer up and turn the whole into smoke on the altar. It is a burnt offering, an offering by fire of pleasing odor to the LORD. 14 If his offering to the LORD is a burnt offering of birds, he shall choose his offering from turtledoves or pigeons. 15 The priest shall bring it to the altar, pinch off its head, and turn it into smoke on the altar; and its blood shall be drained out against the side of the altar. 16 He shall remove its crop with its contents, and cast it into the place of the ashes, at the east side of the altar. 17 The priest shall tear it open by its wings, without severing it, and turn it into smoke on the altar, upon the wood that is on the fire. It is a burnt offering, an offering by fire, of pleasing odor to the LORD.

2 1 When a person presents an offering of meal to the LORD, his offering shall be of choice flour; he shall pour oil upon it, lay frankincense on it, 2 and present it to Aaron's sons, the priests. The priest shall scoop out of it a handful of its choice flour and oil, as well as all of its frankincense; and this token portion he shall turn into smoke on the altar, as an offering by fire, of pleasing odor to the LORD. 3 And the remainder of the meal offering shall be for Aaron and his sons, a most holy portion from the LORD's offerings by fire. 4 When you present an offering of meal baked in the oven, [it shall be of] choice flour: unleavened cakes with oil mixed in, or unleavened wafers spread with oil. 5 If your offering is a meal offering on a griddle, it shall be of choice flour with oil mixed in, unleavened. 6 Break it into bits and pour oil on it; it is a meal offering. 7 If your offering is a meal offering in a pan, it shall be made of choice flour in oil. 8 When you present to the LORD a meal offering that is made in any of these ways, it shall be brought to the priest who shall take it up to the altar. 9 The priest shall remove the token portion from the meal offering and turn it into smoke on the altar as an offering by fire, of pleasing odor to the LORD. 10 And the remainder of the meal offering shall be for Aaron and his sons, a most holy portion from the LORD's offerings by fire. 11 No meal offering that you offer to the LORD shall be made with leaven, for no leaven or honey may be turned into smoke as an offering by fire to the LORD. 12 You may bring them to the LORD as an offering of choice products; but they shall not be offered up on the altar for a pleasing odor. 13 You shall season your every offering of meal with salt; you shall not omit from your meal offering the salt of your covenant with God; with all your offerings you must offer salt. 14 If you bring a meal offering of first fruits to the LORD, you shall bring new ears parched with fire, grits of the fresh grain, as your meal offering of first fruits. 15 You shall add oil to it and lay frankincense on it; it is a meal offering. 16 And the priest shall turn a token portion of it into smoke: some of the grits and oil, with all of the frankincense, as an offering by fire to the LORD.

LEVITICUS 3 ויקרא ג

3 1 If his offering is a sacrifice of well-being - If he offers of the herd, whether a male or a female, he shall bring before the LORD one without blemish. 2 He shall lay his hand upon the head of his offering and slaughter it at the entrance of the Tent of Meeting; and Aaron's sons, the priests, shall dash the blood against all sides of the altar. 3 He shall then present from the sacrifice of well-being, as an offering by fire to the LORD, the fat that covers the entrails and all the fat that is about the entrails; 4 the two kidneys and the fat that is on them, that is at the loins; and the protuberance on the liver, which he shall remove with the kidneys. 5 Aaron's sons shall turn these into smoke on the altar, with the burnt offering which is upon the wood that is on the fire, as an offering by fire, of pleasing odor to the LORD.

6 And if his offering for a sacrifice of well-being to the LORD is from the flock, whether a male or a female, he shall offer one without blemish. 7 If he presents a sheep as his offering, he shall bring it before the LORD 8 and lay his hand upon the head of his offering. It shall be slaughtered before the Tent of Meeting, and Aaron's sons shall dash its blood against all sides of the altar. 9 He shall then present, as an offering by fire to the LORD, the fat from the sacrifice of well-being: the whole broad tail, which shall be removed close to the backbone; the fat that covers the entrails and all the fat that is about the entrails; 10 the two kidneys and the fat that is on them, that is at the loins; and the protuberance on the liver, which he shall remove with the kidneys. 11 The priest shall turn these into smoke on the altar as food, an offering by fire to the LORD.

12 And if his offering is a goat, he shall bring it before the LORD 13 and lay his hand upon its head. It shall be slaughtered before the Tent of Meeting, and Aaron's sons shall dash its blood against all sides of the altar. 14 He shall then present as his offering from it, as an offering by fire to the LORD, the fat that covers the entrails and all the fat that is about the entrails; 15 the two kidneys and the fat that is on them, that is at the loins; and the protuberance on the liver, which he shall remove with the kidneys. 16 The priest shall turn these into smoke on the altar as food, an offering by fire, of pleasing odor. All fat is the LORD's. 17 It is a law for all time throughout the ages, in all your settlements: you must not eat any fat or any blood.

4 1 The LORD spoke to Moses, saying: 2 Speak to the Israelite people thus: When a person unwittingly incurs guilt in regard to any of the LORD's commandments about things not to be done, and does one of them — 3 If it is the anointed priest who has incurred guilt, so that blame falls upon the people, he shall offer for the sin of which he is guilty a bull of the herd without blemish as a sin offering to the LORD. 4 He shall bring the bull to the entrance of the Tent of Meeting, before the LORD, and lay his hand upon the head of the bull. The bull shall be slaughtered before the LORD, 5 and the anointed priest shall take some of the bull's blood and bring it into the Tent of Meeting. 6 The priest shall dip his finger in the blood, and sprinkle of the blood seven times before the LORD, in front of the curtain of the Shrine. 7 The priest shall put some of the blood on the horns of the altar of aromatic incense, which is in the Tent of Meeting, before the LORD; and all the rest of the bull's blood he shall pour out at the base of the altar of burnt offering, which is at the entrance of the Tent of Meeting. 8 He shall remove all the fat from the bull of sin offering: the fat that covers the entrails and all the fat that is about the entrails; 9 the two kidneys and the fat that is on them, that is at the loins; and the protuberance on the liver, which he shall remove with the kidneys — 10 just as it is removed from the ox of the sacrifice of well-being. The priest shall turn them into smoke on the altar of burnt offering. 11 But the hide of the bull, and all its flesh, as well as its head and legs, its entrails and its dung — 12 all the rest of the bull - he shall carry to a clean place outside the camp, to the ash heap, and burn it up in a wood fire; it shall be burned on the ash heap. 13 If it is the whole community of Israel that has erred and the matter escapes the notice of the congregation, so that they do any of the things which by the LORD's commandments ought not to be done, and they realize their guilt — 14 when the sin through which they incurred guilt becomes known, the congregation shall offer a bull of the herd as a sin offering, and bring it before the Tent of Meeting. 15 The elders of the community shall lay their hands upon the head of the bull before the LORD, and the bull shall be slaughtered before the LORD. 16 The anointed priest shall bring some of the blood of the bull

LEVITICUS 5 ויקרא ה

into the Tent of Meeting, 17 and the priest shall dip his finger in the blood and sprinkle of it seven times before the LORD, in front of the curtain. 18 Some of the blood he shall put on the horns of the altar which is before the LORD in the Tent of Meeting, and all the rest of the blood he shall pour out at the base of the altar of burnt offering, which is at the entrance of the Tent of Meeting. 19 He shall remove all its fat from it and turn it into smoke on the altar. 20 He shall do with this bull just as is done with the [priest's] bull of sin offering: he shall do the same with it. Thus the priest shall make expiation for them, and they shall be forgiven. 21 He shall carry the bull outside the camp and burn it as he burned the first bull: it is the sin offering of the congregation.

22 In case it is a chieftain who incurs guilt by doing unwittingly any of the things which by the commandment of the LORD his God ought not to be done, and he realizes his guilt – 23 or the sin of which he is guilty is brought to his knowledge – he shall bring as his offering a male goat without blemish. 24 He shall lay his hand upon the goat's head, and it shall be slaughtered at the spot where the burnt offering is slaughtered before the LORD: it is a sin offering. 25 The priest shall take with his finger some of the blood of the sin offering and put it on the horns of the altar of burnt offering; and the rest of its blood he shall pour out at the base of the altar of burnt offering. 26 All its fat he shall turn into smoke on the altar, like the fat of the sacrifice of well-being. Thus the priest shall make expiation on his behalf for his sin, and he shall be forgiven. 27 If any person from among the populace unwittingly incurs guilt by doing any of the things which by the LORD's commandments ought not to be done, and he realizes his guilt – 28 or the sin of which he is guilty is brought to his knowledge – he shall bring a female goat without blemish as his offering for the sin of which he is guilty. 29 He shall lay his hand upon the head of the sin offering, and the sin offering shall be slaughtered at the place of the burnt offering. 30 The priest shall take with his finger some of its blood and put it on the horns of the altar of burnt offering; and all the rest of its blood he shall pour out at the base of the altar. 31 He shall remove all its fat, just as the fat is removed from the sacrifice of well-being; and the priest shall turn it into smoke on the altar, for a pleasing odor to the LORD. Thus the priest shall make expiation for him, and he shall be forgiven.

32 If the offering he brings as a sin offering is a sheep, he shall bring a female without blemish. 33 He shall lay his hand upon the head of the sin offering and it shall be slaughtered as a sin offering at the spot where the burnt offering is slaughtered. 34 The priest shall take with his finger some of the blood of the sin offering and put it on the horns of the altar of burnt offering, and all the rest of its blood he shall pour out at the base of the altar. 35 And all its fat he shall remove just as the fat of the sheep of the sacrifice of well-being is removed; and this the priest shall turn into smoke on the altar, over the LORD's offerings by fire. Thus the priest shall make expiation on his behalf for the sin of which he is guilty, and he shall be forgiven.

5 1 If a person incurs guilt – When he has heard a public imprecation and – although able to testify as one who has either seen or learned of the matter – he does not give information, so that he is subject to punishment; 2 Or when a person touches any unclean thing – be it the carcass of an unclean beast or the carcass of unclean cattle or the carcass of an unclean creeping thing – and the fact has escaped him, and then, being unclean, he realizes his guilt; 3 Or when he touches human uncleanness – any such uncleanness whereby one becomes unclean – and, though he has known it, the fact has escaped him, but later he realizes his guilt; 4 Or when a person utters an oath to bad or good purpose – whatever a man may utter in an oath – and, though he has known it, the fact has escaped him, but later he realizes his guilt in any of these matters – 5 when he realizes his guilt in any of these matters, he shall confess that wherein he has sinned. 6 And he shall bring as his penalty to the LORD, for the sin of which he is guilty, a female from the flock, sheep or goat, as a sin offering; and the priest shall make expiation on his behalf for his sin. 7 But if his means do not suffice for a sheep, he shall bring to the LORD, as his penalty for that of which he is guilty, two turtledoves or two pigeons, one for a sin offering and the other for a burnt offering. 8 He shall bring them to the priest, who shall offer first the one for the sin offering, pinching its head at the nape without severing it. 9 He shall sprinkle some of the blood of the sin offering on the side of the altar, and what remains of the blood shall be drained out at the base of the altar: it is a sin offering. 10 And the second he shall prepare as a burnt offering, according to regulation. Thus the priest shall make expiation on his behalf for the sin of which he is guilty, and he shall be forgiven. 11 And if his means do not suffice for two turtledoves or two pigeons, he shall bring as his offering for that of which he is guilty a tenth of an ephah of choice flour for a sin offering; he shall not add oil to it or lay frankincense on it, for it is a sin offering.

108

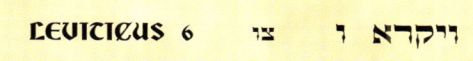

LEVITICUS 6

12 He shall bring it to the priest, and the priest shall scoop out of it a handful as a token portion and turn it into smoke on the altar, with the LORD's offerings by fire; it is a sin offering. 13 Thus the priest shall make expiation on his behalf for whichever of these sins he is guilty, and he shall be forgiven. It shall belong to the priest, like the meal offering. 14 And the LORD spoke to Moses, saying: 15 When a person commits a trespass, being unwittingly remiss about any of the LORD's sacred things, he shall bring as his penalty to the LORD a ram without blemish from the flock, convertible into payment in silver by the sanctuary weight, as a guilt offering. 16 He shall make restitution for that wherein he was remiss about the sacred things, and he shall add a fifth part to it and give it to the priest. The priest shall make expiation on his behalf with the ram of the guilt offering, and he shall be forgiven.

17 And when a person, without knowing it, sins in regard to any of the LORD's commandments about things not to be done, and then realizes his guilt, he shall be subject to punishment. 18 He shall bring to the priest a ram without blemish from the flock, or the equivalent, as a guilt offering. The priest shall make expiation on his behalf for the error that he committed unwittingly, and he shall be forgiven. 19 It is a guilt offering: he has incurred guilt before the LORD.

20 The LORD spoke to Moses, saying: 21 When a person sins and commits a trespass against the LORD by dealing deceitfully with his fellow in the matter of a deposit or a pledge, or through robbery, or by defrauding his fellow, 22 or by finding something lost and lying about it; if he swears falsely regarding any one of the various things that one may do and sin thereby – 23 when one has thus sinned and, realizing his guilt, would restore that which he got through robbery or fraud, or the deposit that was entrusted to him, or the lost thing that he found, 24 or anything else about which he swore falsely, he shall repay the principal amount and add a fifth part to it. He shall pay it to its owner when he realizes his guilt. 25 Then he shall bring to the priest, as his penalty to the LORD, a ram without blemish from the flock, or the equivalent, as a guilt offering. 26 The priest shall make expiation on his behalf before the LORD, and he shall be forgiven for whatever he may have done to draw blame thereby.

The LORD spoke to Moses, saying: 2 Command Aaron and his sons thus: This is the ritual of the burnt offering: The burnt offering itself shall remain where it is burned upon the altar all night until morning, while the fire on the altar is kept going on it. 3 The priest shall dress in linen raiment, with linen breeches next to his body; and he shall take up the ashes to which the fire has reduced the burnt offering on the altar and place them beside the altar. 4 He shall then take off his vestments and put on other vestments, and carry the ashes outside the camp to a clean place. 5 The fire on the altar shall be kept burning, not to go out: every morning the priest shall feed wood to it, lay out the burnt offering on it, and turn into smoke the fat parts of the offerings of well-being. 6 A perpetual fire shall be kept burning on the altar, not to go out. 7 And this is the ritual of the meal offering: Aaron's sons shall present it before the LORD, in front of the altar. 8 A handful of the choice flour and oil of the meal offering shall be taken from it, with all the frankincense that is on the meal offering, and this token portion shall be turned into smoke on the altar as a pleasing odor to the LORD. 9 What is left of it shall be eaten by Aaron and his sons; it shall be eaten as unleavened cakes, in the sacred precinct; they shall eat it in the enclosure of the Tent of Meeting. 10 It shall not be baked with leaven; I have given it as their portion from My offerings by fire; it is most holy, like the sin offering and the guilt offering. 11 Only the males among Aaron's descendants may eat of it, as their due for all time throughout the ages from the LORD's offerings by fire. Anything that touches these shall become holy.

12 The LORD spoke to Moses, saying: 13 This is the offering that Aaron and his sons shall offer to the LORD on the occasion of his anointment: a tenth of an ephah of choice flour as a regular meal offering, half of it in the morning and half of it in the evening, 14 shall be prepared with oil on a griddle. You shall bring it well soaked, and offer it as a meal offering of baked slices, of pleasing odor to the LORD. 15 And so shall the priest, anointed from among his sons to succeed him, prepare it: it is the LORD's – a law for all time – to be turned entirely into smoke. 16 So, too, every meal offering of a priest shall be a whole offering: it shall not be eaten.

17 The LORD spoke to Moses, saying: 18 Speak to Aaron and his sons thus:

LEVITICUS 7

This is the ritual of the sin offering: the sin offering shall be slaughtered before the LORD, at the spot where the burnt offering is slaughtered: it is most holy. 19 The priest who offers it as a sin offering shall eat of it; it shall be eaten in the sacred precinct, in the enclosure of the Tent of Meeting. 20 Anything that touches its flesh shall become holy; and if any of its blood is spattered upon a garment, you shall wash the bespattered part in the sacred precinct. 21 An earthen vessel in which it was boiled shall be broken; if it was boiled in a copper vessel, [the vessel] shall be scoured and rinsed with water. 22 Only the males in the priestly line may eat of it: it is most holy. 23 But no sin offering may be eaten from which any blood is brought into the Tent of Meeting for expiation in the sanctuary; any such shall be consumed in fire.

7 1 This is the ritual of the guilt offering: it is most holy. 2 The guilt offering shall be slaughtered at the spot where the burnt offering is slaughtered, and the blood shall be dashed on all sides of the altar. 3 All its fat shall be offered: the broad tail; the fat that covers the entrails; 4 the two kidneys and the fat that is on them at the loins; and the protuberance on the liver, which shall be removed with the kidneys. 5 The priest shall turn them into smoke on the altar as an offering by fire to the LORD; it is a guilt offering. 6 Only the males in the priestly line may eat of it; it shall be eaten in the sacred precinct: it is most holy. 7 The guilt offering is like the sin offering. The same rule applies to both: it shall belong to the priest who makes expiation thereby. 8 So, too, the priest who offers a man's burnt offering shall keep the skin of the burnt offering that he offered. 9 Further, any meal offering that is baked in an oven, and any that is prepared in a pan or on a griddle, shall belong to the priest who offers it. 10 But every other meal offering, with oil mixed in or dry, shall go to the sons of Aaron all alike. 11 This is the ritual of the sacrifice of well-being that one may offer to the LORD: 12 If he offers it for thanksgiving, he shall offer together with the sacrifice of thanksgiving unleavened cakes with oil mixed in, unleavened wafers spread with oil, and cakes of choice flour with oil mixed in, well soaked. 13 This offering, with cakes of leavened bread added, he shall offer along with his thanksgiving sacrifice of well-being. 14 Out of this he shall offer one of each kind as a gift to the LORD; it shall go to the priest who dashes the blood of the offering of well-being. 15 And the flesh of his thanksgiving sacrifice of well-being shall be eaten on the day that it is offered; none of it shall be set aside until morning. 16 If, however, the sacrifice he offers is a votive or a freewill offering, it shall be eaten on the day that he offers his sacrifice, and what is left of it shall be eaten on the morrow. 17 What is then left of the flesh of the sacrifice shall be consumed in fire on the third day. 18 If any of the flesh of his sacrifice of well-being is eaten on the third day, it shall not be acceptable; it shall not count for him who offered it. It is an offensive thing, and the person who eats of it shall bear his guilt. 19 Flesh that touches anything unclean shall not be eaten; it shall be consumed in fire. As for other flesh, only he who is clean may eat such flesh. 20 But the person who, in a state of uncleanness, eats flesh from the LORD's sacrifices of well-being, that person shall be cut off from his kin. 21 When a person touches anything unclean, be it human uncleanness or an unclean animal or any unclean creature, and eats flesh from the LORD's sacrifices of well-being, that person shall be cut off from his kin. 22 And the LORD spoke to Moses, saying: 23 Speak to the Israelite people thus: You shall eat no fat of ox or sheep or goat. 24 Fat from animals that died or were torn by beasts may be put to any use, but you must not eat it. 25 If anyone eats the fat of animals from which offerings by fire may be made to the LORD, the person who eats it shall be cut off from his kin. 26 And you must not consume any blood, either of bird or of animal, in any of your settlements. 27 Anyone who eats blood shall be cut off from his kin.

28 And the LORD spoke to Moses, saying: 29 Speak to the Israelite people thus: The offering to the LORD from a sacrifice of well-being must be presented by him who offers his sacrifice of well-being to the LORD. 30 His own hands shall present the LORD's offerings by fire. He shall present the fat with the breast, the breast to be elevated as an elevation offering before the LORD; 31 the priest shall turn the fat into smoke on the altar, and the breast shall go to Aaron and his sons. 32 And the right thigh from your sacrifices of well-being you shall present to the priest as a gift; 33 he from among Aaron's sons who offers the blood and the fat of the offering of well-being shall get the right thigh as his portion. 34 For I have taken the breast of elevation offering and the thigh of gift offering

LEVITICUS 8 ויקרא ח

from the Israelites, from their sacrifices of well-being, and given them to Aaron the priest and to his sons as their due from the Israelites for all time. 35 Those shall be the perquisites of Aaron and the perquisites of his sons from the LORD's offerings by fire, once they have been inducted to serve the LORD as priests; 36 these the LORD commanded to be given them, once they had been anointed, as a due from the Israelites for all time throughout the ages. 37 Such are the rituals of the burnt offering, the meal offering, the sin offering, the guilt offering, the offering of ordination, and the sacrifice of well-being, 38 with which the LORD charged Moses on Mount Sinai, when He commanded that the Israelites present their offerings to the LORD, in the wilderness of Sinai.

8 1 The LORD spoke to Moses, saying: 2 Take Aaron along with his sons, and the vestments, the anointing oil, the bull of sin offering, the two rams, and the basket of unleavened bread; 3 and assemble the whole community at the entrance of the Tent of Meeting. 4 Moses did as the LORD commanded him. And when the community was assembled at the entrance of the Tent of Meeting, 5 Moses said to the community, "This is what the LORD has commanded to be done." 6 Then Moses brought Aaron and his sons forward and washed them with water. 7 He put the tunic on him, girded him with the sash, clothed him with the robe, and put the ephod on him, girding him with the decorated band which he tied it to him. 8 He put the breastpiece on him, and put into the breastpiece the Urim and Thummim. 9 And he set the headdress on his head; and on the headdress, in front, he put the gold frontlet, the holy diadem - as the LORD had commanded Moses. 10 Moses took the anointing oil and anointed the Tabernacle and all that was in it, thus consecrating them. 11 He sprinkled some of it on the altar seven times, anointing the altar, all its utensils, and the laver with its stand, to consecrate them. 12 He poured some of the anointing oil upon Aaron's head and anointed him, to consecrate him. 13 Moses then brought Aaron's sons forward, clothed them in tunics, girded them with sashes, and wound turbans upon them, as the LORD had commanded Moses. 14 He led forward the bull of sin offering. Aaron and his sons laid their hands upon the head of the bull of sin offering, 15 and it was slaughtered. Moses took the blood and with his finger put some on each of the horns of the altar, cleansing the altar; then he poured out the blood at the base of the altar. Thus he consecrated it in order to make expiation upon it. 16 Moses then took all the fat that was about the entrails, and the protuberance of the liver, and the two kidneys and their fat, and turned them into smoke on the altar. 17 The rest of the bull, its hide, its flesh, and its dung, he put to the fire outside the camp - as the LORD had commanded Moses. 18 Then he brought forward the ram of burnt offering. Aaron and his sons laid their hands upon the ram's head, 19 and it was slaughtered. Moses dashed the blood against all sides of the altar. 20 The ram was cut up into sections and Moses turned the head, the sections, and the suet into smoke on the altar; 21 Moses washed the entrails and the legs with water and turned all of the ram into smoke. That was a burnt offering for a pleasing odor, an offering by fire to the LORD - as the LORD had commanded Moses. 22 He brought forward the second ram, the ram of ordination. Aaron and his sons laid their hands upon the ram's head, 23 and it was slaughtered. Moses took some of its blood and put it on the ridge of Aaron's right ear, and on the thumb of his right hand, and on the big toe of his right foot. 24 Moses then brought forward the sons of Aaron, and put some of the blood on the ridges of their right ears, and on the thumbs of their right hands, and on the big toes of their right feet; and the rest of the blood Moses dashed against every side of the altar. 25 He took the fat - the broad tail, all the fat about the entrails, the protuberance of the liver, and the two kidneys and their fat - and the right thigh. 26 From the basket of unleavened bread that was before the LORD, he took one cake of unleavened bread, one cake of oil bread, and one wafer, and placed them on the fat parts and on the right thigh. 27 He placed all these on the palms of Aaron and on the palms of his sons, and elevated them as an elevation offering before the LORD. 28 Then Moses took them from their hands and turned them into smoke on the altar with the burnt offering. This was an ordination offering for a pleasing odor; it was an offering by fire to the LORD. 29 Moses took the breast

LEVITICUS 9 · שמיני · ויקרא ט

and elevated it as an elevation offering before the LORD: it was Moses' portion of the ram of ordination - as the LORD had commanded Moses. 30 And Moses took some of the anointing oil and some of the blood that was on the altar, and sprinkled it upon Aaron and upon his vestments, and also upon his sons and upon their vestments. Thus he consecrated Aaron and his vestments, and also his sons and their vestments. 31 Moses said to Aaron and his sons: Boil the flesh at the entrance of the Tent of Meeting and eat it there with the bread that is in the basket of ordination - as I commanded: Aaron and his sons shall eat it; 32 and what is left over of the flesh and the bread you shall consume in fire. 33 You shall not go outside the entrance of the Tent of Meeting for seven days, until the day that your period of ordination is completed. For your ordination will require seven days. 34 Everything done today, the LORD has commanded to be done [seven days], to make expiation for you. 35 You shall remain at the entrance of the Tent of Meeting day and night for seven days, keeping the LORD's charge - that you may not die - for so I have been commanded. 36 And Aaron and his sons did all the things that the LORD had commanded through Moses.

9 On the eighth day Moses called Aaron and his sons, and the elders of Israel. 2 He said to Aaron: "Take a calf of the herd for a sin offering and a ram for a burnt offering, without blemish, and bring them before the LORD. 3 And speak to the Israelites, saying: Take a he-goat for a sin offering: a calf and a lamb, yearlings without blemish, for a burnt offering; 4 and an ox and a ram for an offering of well-being to sacrifice before the LORD; and a meal offering with oil mixed in. For today the LORD will appear to you." 5 They brought to the front of the Tent of Meeting the things that Moses had commanded, and the whole community came forward and stood before the LORD. 6 Moses said: "This is what the LORD has commanded that you do, that the Presence of the LORD may appear to you." 7 Then Moses said to Aaron: "Come forward to the altar and sacrifice your sin offering and your burnt offering, making expiation for yourself and for the people; and sacrifice the people's offering and make expiation for them, as the LORD has commanded." 8 Aaron came forward to the altar and slaughtered his calf of sin offering. 9 Aaron's sons brought the blood to him: he dipped his finger in the blood and put it on the horns of the altar; and he poured out the rest of the blood at the base of the altar. 10 The fat, the kidneys, and the protuberance of the liver from the sin offering he turned into smoke on the altar - as the LORD had commanded Moses. 11 and the flesh and the skin were consumed in fire outside the camp. 12 Then he slaughtered the burnt offering. Aaron's sons passed the blood to him, and he dashed it against all sides of the altar. 13 They passed the burnt offering to him in sections, as well as the head, and he turned it into smoke on the altar. 14 He washed the entrails and the legs, and turned them into smoke on the altar with the burnt offering. 15 Next he brought forward the people's offering. He took the goat for the people's sin offering, and slaughtered it, and presented it as a sin offering like the previous one. 16 He brought forward the burnt offering and sacrificed it according to regulation. 17 He then brought forward the meal offering, and taking a handful of it, he turned it into smoke on the altar - in addition to the burnt offering of the morning. 18 He slaughtered the ox and the ram, the people's sacrifice of well-being. Aaron's sons passed the blood to him - which he dashed against every side of the altar - 19 and the fat parts of the ox and the ram: the broad tail, the covering [fat], the kidneys, and the protuberances of the livers. 20 They laid these fat parts over the breasts, and Aaron turned the fat parts into smoke on the altar. 21 and elevated the breasts and the right thighs as an elevation offering before the LORD - as Moses had commanded. 22 Aaron lifted his hands toward the people and blessed them; and he stepped down after offering the sin offering, the burnt offering, and the offering of well-being. 23 Moses and Aaron then went inside the Tent of Meeting. When they came out, they blessed the people; and the Presence of the Lord appeared to all the people. 24 Fire came forth from before the LORD and consumed the burnt offering and the fat parts on the altar. And all the people saw, and shouted, and fell on their faces.

10 1 Now Aaron's sons Nadab and Abihu each took his fire pan, put fire in it, and laid incense on it; and they offered before the LORD alien fire, which He had not enjoined upon them. 2 And fire came forth from the LORD and consumed them; thus they died at the instance of the LORD. 3 Then Moses said

LEVITICUS 11 ויקרא יא שמיני

to Aaron, "This is what the LORD meant when He said: Through those near to Me I show Myself holy, And gain glory before all the people." And Aaron was silent. 4 Moses called Mishael and Elzaphan, sons of Uzziel the uncle of Aaron, and said to them, "Come forward and carry your kinsmen away from the front of the sanctuary to a place outside the camp. 5 They came forward and carried them out of the camp by their tunics, as Moses had ordered. 6 And Moses said to Aaron and to his sons Eleazar and Ithamar, "Do not bare your heads and do not rend your clothes, lest you die and anger strike the whole community. But your kinsmen, all the house of Israel, shall bewail the burning that the LORD has wrought. 7 And so do not go outside the entrance of the Tent of Meeting, lest you die, for the LORD's anointing oil is upon you." And they did as Moses had bidden.

8 And the LORD spoke to Aaron, saying: 9 Drink no wine or other intoxicant, you or your sons, when you enter the Tent of Meeting, that you may not die. This is a law for all time throughout the ages, 10 for you must distinguish between the sacred and the profane, and between the unclean and the clean; 11 and you must teach the Israelites all the laws which the LORD has imparted to them through Moses. 12 Moses spoke to Aaron and to his remaining sons, Eleazar and Ithamar: Take the meal offering that is left over from the LORD's offerings by fire and eat it unleavened beside the altar, for it is most holy. 13 You shall eat it in the sacred precinct, inasmuch as it is your due, and that of your children, from the LORD's offerings by fire; for so I have been commanded. 14 But the breast of elevation offering and the thigh of gift offering you, and your sons and daughters with you, may eat in any clean place, for they have been assigned as a due to you and your children from the Israelites' sacrifices of well-being. 15 Together with the fat of fire offering, they must present the thigh of gift offering and the breast of elevation offering, which are to be elevated as an elevation offering before the LORD, and which are to be your due and that of your children with you for all time – as the LORD has commanded. 16 Then Moses inquired about the goat of sin offering, and it had already been burned! He was angry with Eleazar and Ithamar, Aaron's remaining sons, and said, 17 "Why did you not eat the sin offering in the sacred area? For it is most holy, and He has given it to you to remove the guilt of the community and to make expiation for them before the LORD. 18 Since its blood was not brought inside the sanctuary, you should certainly have eaten it in the sanctuary, as I commanded." 19 And Aaron spoke to Moses, "See, this day they brought their sin offering and their burnt offering before the LORD, and such things have befallen me! Had I eaten sin offering today, would the LORD have approved?" 20 And when Moses heard this, he approved.

11 1 The LORD spoke to Moses and Aaron, saying to them: 2 Speak to the Israelite people thus: These are the creatures that you may eat from among all the land animals: 3 any animal that has true hoofs, with clefts through the hoofs, and that chews the cud – such you may eat. 4 The following, however, of those that either chew the cud or have true hoofs, you shall not eat: the camel – although it chews the cud, it has no true hoofs: it is unclean for you; 5 the daman – although it chews the cud, it has no true hoofs: it is unclean for you; 6 the hare – although it chews the cud, it has no true hoofs: it is unclean for you; 7 and the swine – although it has true hoofs, with the hoofs cleft through, it does not chew the cud: it is unclean for you. 8 You shall not eat of their flesh or touch their carcasses; they are unclean for you. 9 These you may eat of all that live in water, whether in the seas or in the streams, that has fins and scales – these you may eat. 10 But anything in the seas or in the streams that has no fins and scales, among all the swarming things of the water and among all the other living creatures that are in the water – they are an abomination for you 11 and an abomination for you they shall remain: you shall not eat of their flesh and you shall abominate their carcasses. 12 Everything in water that has no fins and scales shall be an abomination for you. 13 The following you shall abominate among the birds – they shall not be eaten, they are an abomination: the eagle, the vulture, and the black vulture; 14 the kite, falcons of every variety; 15 all varieties of raven; 16 the ostrich, the nighthawk, the sea gull; hawks of every variety; 17 the little owl,

LEVITICUS 12

the cormorant, and the great owl; 18 the white owl, the pelican, and the bustard; 19 the stork; herons of every variety; the hoopoe, and the bat. 20 All winged swarming things that walk on fours shall be an abomination for you. 21 But these you may eat among all the winged swarming things that walk on fours: all that have, above their feet, jointed legs to leap with on the ground – 22 of these you may eat the following: locusts of every variety; all varieties of bald locust; crickets of every variety; and all varieties of grasshopper. 23 But all other winged swarming things that have four legs shall be an abomination for you. 24 And the following shall make you unclean – whoever touches their carcasses shall be unclean until evening. 25 and whoever carries the carcasses of any of them shall wash his clothes and be unclean until evening – 26 every animal that has true hoofs but without clefts through the hoofs, or that does not chew the cud. They are unclean for you; whoever touches them shall be unclean. 27 Also all animals that walk on paws, among those that walk on fours, are unclean for you; whoever touches their carcasses shall be unclean until evening. 28 And anyone who carries their carcasses shall wash his clothes and remain unclean until evening. They are unclean for you.

29 The following shall be unclean for you from among the things that swarm on the earth: the mole, the mouse, and great lizards of every variety; 30 the gecko, the land crocodile, the lizard, the sand lizard, and the chameleon. 31 These are for you the unclean among all the swarming things: whoever touches them when they are dead shall be unclean until evening. 32 And anything on which one of them falls when dead shall be unclean: be it any article of wood, or a cloth, or a skin, or a sack – any such article that can be put to use shall be dipped in water, and it shall remain unclean until evening; then it shall be clean. 33 And if any of those falls into an earthen vessel, everything inside it shall be unclean and [the vessel] itself you shall break. 34 As to any food that may be eaten, it shall become unclean if it came in contact with water; as to any liquid that may be drunk, it shall become unclean if it was inside any vessel. 35 Everything on which the carcass of any of them falls shall be unclean: an oven or stove shall be smashed. They are unclean and unclean they shall remain for you. 36 However, a spring or cistern in which water is collected shall be clean, but whoever touches such a carcass in it shall be unclean. 37 If such a carcass falls upon seed grain that is to be sown, it is clean; 38 but if water is put on the seed and any part of a carcass falls upon it, it shall be unclean for you. 39 If an animal that you may eat has died, anyone who touches its carcass shall be unclean until evening; 40 anyone who eats of its carcass shall wash his clothes and remain unclean until evening; and anyone who carries its carcass shall wash his clothes and remain unclean until evening. 41 All the things that swarm upon the earth are an abomination; they shall not be eaten. 42 You shall not eat, among the things that swarm upon the earth, anything that crawls on its belly, or anything that walks on fours, or anything that has many legs; for they are an abomination. 43 You shall not draw abomination upon yourselves through anything that swarms; you shall not make yourselves unclean therewith and thus become unclean. 44 For I the LORD am your God: you shall sanctify yourselves and be holy, for I am holy. You shall not make yourselves unclean through any swarming thing that moves upon the earth. 45 For I the LORD am He who brought you up from the land of Egypt to be your God: you shall be holy, for I am holy. 46 These are the instructions concerning animals, birds, all living creatures that move in water, and all creatures that swarm on earth, 47 for distinguishing between the unclean and the clean, between the living things that may be eaten and the living things that may not be eaten.

12 1 The LORD spoke to Moses, saying: 2 Speak to the Israelite people thus: When a woman at childbirth bears a male, she shall be unclean seven days; she shall be unclean as at the time of her menstrual infirmity. 3 On the eighth day the flesh of his foreskin shall be circumcised. 4 She shall remain in a state of blood purification for thirty-three days: she shall not touch any consecrated thing, nor enter the sanctuary until her period of purification is completed. 5 If she bears a female, she shall be unclean two weeks as during her menstruation, and she shall remain in a state of blood purification for sixty-six days. 6 On the completion of her period of purification, for either son or daughter, she shall bring to the priest, at the entrance of the Tent of Meeting, a lamb in its first year for a burnt offering,

114

עמוד שער לספר ויקרא, מתוך "חומש דה-קסטרו", כתב-יד מעוטר על קלף, גרמניה, 1344, אוסף מוזיאון ישראל, ירושלים

Opening page of the Book of Leviticus, from the "De Castro Pentateuch", illuminated manuscript on vellum, Germany, 1344, collection of The Israel Museum, Jerusalem

LEVITICUS 13 ויקרא יג תזריע

and a pigeon or a turtledove for a sin offering. 7 He shall offer it before the LORD and make expiation on her behalf; she shall then be clean from her flow of blood. Such are the rituals concerning her who bears a child, male or female. 8 If, however, her means do not suffice for a sheep, she shall take two turtledoves or two pigeons, one for a burnt offering and the other for a sin offering. The priest shall make expiation on her behalf, and she shall be clean.

13 1 The LORD spoke to Moses and Aaron, saying: 2 When a person has on the skin of his body a swelling, a rash, or a discoloration, and it develops into a scaly affection on the skin of his body, it shall be reported to Aaron the priest or to one of his sons, the priests. 3 The priest shall examine the affection on the skin of his body: if hair in the affected patch has turned white and the affection appears to be deeper than the skin of his body, it is a leprous affection; when the priest sees it, he shall pronounce him unclean. 4 But if it is a white discoloration on the skin of his body which does not appear to be deeper than the skin and the hair in it has not turned white, the priest shall isolate the affected person for seven days. 5 On the seventh day the priest shall examine him, and if the affection has remained unchanged in color and the disease has not spread on the skin, the priest shall isolate him for another seven days. 6 On the seventh day the priest shall examine him again: if the affection has faded and has not spread on the skin, the priest shall pronounce him clean. It is a rash; he shall wash his clothes, and be shall be clean. 7 But if the rash should spread on the skin after he has presented himself to the priest and been pronounced clean, he shall present himself again to the priest. 8 And if the priest sees that the rash has spread on the skin, the priest shall pronounce him unclean; it is leprosy.

9 When a person has a scaly affection, it shall be reported to the priest. 10 If the priest finds on the skin a white swelling which has turned hair white, with a patch of undiscolored flesh in the swelling, 11 it is chronic leprosy on the skin of his body, and the priest shall pronounce him unclean; he need not isolate him, for he is unclean. 12 If the eruption spreads out over the skin so that it covers all the skin of the affected person from head to foot, wherever the priest can see – 13 if the priest sees that the eruption has covered the whole body - he shall pronounce the affected person clean; for he has turned all white. 14 But as soon as undiscolored flesh appears in it, he shall be unclean; 15 when the priest sees the undiscolored flesh, he shall pronounce him unclean. The undiscolored flesh is unclean; it is leprosy. 16 But if the undiscolored flesh again turns white, he shall come to the priest, 17 and the priest shall examine him: if the affection has turned white, the priest shall pronounce the affected person clean; he is clean.

18 When an inflammation appears on the skin of one's body and it heals, 19 and a white swelling or a white discoloration streaked with red develops where the inflammation was, he shall present himself to the priest. 20 If the priest finds that it appears lower than the rest of the skin and that the hair in it has turned white, the priest shall pronounce him unclean; it is a leprous affection that has broken out in the inflammation. 21 But if the priest finds that there is no white hair in it and it is not lower than the rest of the skin, and it is faded, the priest shall isolate him for seven days. 22 If it should spread in the skin, the priest shall pronounce him unclean; it is an affection. 23 But if the discoloration remains stationary, not having spread, it is the scar of the inflammation; the priest shall pronounce him clean.

24 When the skin of one's body sustains a burn by fire, and the patch from the burn is a discoloration, either white streaked with red, or white, 25 the priest shall examine it. If some hair has turned white in the discoloration, which itself appears to go deeper than the skin, it is leprosy that has broken out in the burn. The priest shall pronounce him unclean; it is a leprous affection. 26 But if the priest finds that there is no white hair in the discoloration, and that it is not lower than the rest of the skin, and it is faded, the priest shall isolate him for seven days. 27 On the seventh day the priest shall examine him: if it has spread in the skin, the priest shall pronounce him unclean; it is a leprous affection. 28 But if the discoloration has remained stationary, not having spread on the skin, and it is faded, it is the swelling from the burn. The priest shall pronounce him clean, for it is the scar of the burn.

29 If a man or a woman has an affection on the head or in the beard, 30 the priest shall examine the affection. If it appears to go deeper than the skin and there is thin yellow hair in it, the priest shall pronounce him unclean; it is a scall, a scaly eruption in the hair or beard. 31 But if the priest finds that the scall

LEVITICUS 14

affection does not appear to go deeper than the skin, yet there is no black hair in it, the priest shall isolate the person with the scall affection for seven days. 32 On the seventh day the priest shall examine the affection. If the scall has not spread and no yellow hair has appeared in it, and the scall does not appear to go deeper than the skin, 33 the person with the scall shall shave himself, but without shaving the scall; the priest shall isolate him for another seven days. 34 On the seventh day the priest shall examine the scall. If the scall has not spread on the skin, and does not appear to go deeper than the skin, the priest shall pronounce him clean; he shall wash his clothes, and he shall be clean. 35 If, however, the scall should spread on the skin after he has been pronounced clean, 36 the priest shall examine him. If the scall has spread on the skin, the priest need not look for yellow hair: he is unclean. 37 But if the scall has remained unchanged in color, and black hair has grown in it, the scall is healed; he is clean. The priest shall pronounce him clean. 38 If a man or a woman has the skin of the body streaked with white discolorations, 39 and the priest sees that the discolorations on the skin of the body are of a dull white, it is a tetter broken out on the skin; he is clean.

40 If a man loses the hair of his head and becomes bald, he is clean. 41 If he loses the hair on the front part of his head and becomes bald at the forehead, he is clean. 42 But if a white affection streaked with red appears on the bald part in the front or at the back of the head, it is a scaly eruption that is spreading over the bald part in the front or at the back of the head. 43 The priest shall examine him: if the swollen affection on the bald part in the front or at the back of his head is white streaked with red, like the leprosy of body skin in appearance, 44 the man is leprous; he is unclean. The priest shall pronounce him unclean; he has the affection on his head. 45 As for the person with a leprous affection, his clothes shall be rent, his head shall be left bare, and he shall cover over his upper lip; and he shall call out, "Unclean! Unclean!" 46 He shall be unclean as long as the disease is on him. Being unclean, he shall dwell apart; his dwelling shall be outside the camp.

47 When an eruptive affection occurs in a cloth of wool or linen fabric, 48 in the warp or in the woof of the linen or the wool, or in a skin or in anything made of skin; 49 if the affection in the cloth or the skin, in the warp or the woof, or in any article of skin, is streaky green or red, it is an eruptive affection. It shall be shown to the priest; 50 and the priest, after examining the affection, shall isolate the affected article for seven days. 51 On the seventh day he shall examine the affection: if the affection has spread in the cloth — whether in the warp or the woof, or in the skin, for whatever purpose the skin may be used — the affection is a malignant eruption; it is unclean. 52 The cloth — whether warp or woof in wool or linen, or any article of skin — in which the affection is found, shall be burned, for it is a malignant eruption; it shall be consumed in fire. 53 But if the priest sees that the affection in the cloth — whether in warp or in woof, or in any article of skin — has not spread, 54 the priest shall order the affected article washed, and he shall isolate it for another seven days. 55 And if, after the affected article has been washed, the priest sees that the affection has not changed color and that it has not spread, it is unclean. It shall be consumed in fire; it is a fret, whether on its inner side or on its outer side. 56 But if the priest sees that the affected part, after it has been washed, is faded, he shall tear it out from the cloth or skin, whether in the warp or in the woof; 57 and if it occurs again in the cloth — whether in warp or in woof — or in any article of skin, it is a wild growth; the affected article shall be consumed in fire. 58 If, however, the affection disappears from the cloth — warp or woof — or from any article of skin that has been washed, it shall be washed again, and it shall be clean. 59 Such is the procedure for eruptive affections of cloth, woolen or linen, in warp or in woof, or of any article of skin, for pronouncing it clean or unclean.

14 The LORD spoke to Moses, saying: 2 This shall be the ritual for a leper at the time that he is to be cleansed. When it has been reported to the priest, 3 the priest shall go outside the camp. If the priest sees that the leper has been healed of his scaly affection, 4 the priest shall order two live clean birds, cedar wood, crimson stuff, and hyssop to be brought for him who is to be cleansed. 5 The priest shall order one of the birds slaughtered over fresh water in an earthen vessel; 6 and he shall take the live bird,

LEVITICUS 14 ויקרא יד מצורע

along with the cedar wood, the crimson stuff, and the hyssop, and dip them together with the live bird in the blood of the bird that was slaughtered over the fresh water. 7 He shall then sprinkle it seven times on him who is to be cleansed of the eruption and cleanse him; and he shall set the live bird free in the open country. 8 The one to be cleansed shall wash his clothes, shave off all his hair, and bathe in water; then he shall be clean. After that he may enter the camp, but he must remain outside his tent seven days. 9 On the seventh day he shall shave off all his hair—of head, beard, and eyebrows. When he has shaved off all his hair, he shall wash his clothes and bathe his body in water; then he shall be clean. 10 On the eighth day he shall take two male lambs without blemish, one ewe lamb in its first year without blemish, three-tenths of a measure of choice flour with oil mixed in for a meal offering, and one log of oil. 11 These shall be presented before the LORD, with the man to be cleansed, at the entrance of the Tent of Meeting, by the priest who performs the cleansing. 12 The priest shall take one of the male lambs and offer it with the log of oil as a guilt offering, and he shall elevate them as an elevation offering before the LORD. 13 The lamb shall be slaughtered at the spot in the sacred area where the sin offering and the burnt offering are slaughtered. For the guilt offering, like the sin offering, goes to the priest; it is most holy. 14 The priest shall take some of the blood of the guilt offering, and the priest shall put it on the ridge of the right ear of him who is being cleansed, and on the thumb of his right hand, and on the big toe of his right foot. 15 The priest shall then take some of the log of oil and pour it into the palm of his own left hand. 16 And the priest shall dip his right finger in the oil that is in the palm of his left hand and sprinkle some of the oil with his finger seven times before the LORD. 17 Some of the oil left in his palm shall be put by the priest on the ridge of the right ear of the one being cleansed, on the thumb of his right hand, and on the big toe of his right foot - over the blood of the guilt offering. 18 The rest of the oil in his palm the priest shall put on the head of the one being cleansed. Thus the priest shall make expiation for him before the LORD. 19 The priest shall then offer the sin offering and make expiation for the one being cleansed of his uncleanness. Last, the burnt offering shall be slaughtered, 20 and the priest shall offer the burnt offering and the meal offering on the altar, and the priest shall make expiation for him. Then he shall be clean. 21 If, however, he is poor and his means are insufficient, he shall take one male lamb for a guilt offering, to be elevated in expiation for him, one-tenth of a measure of choice flour with oil mixed in for a meal offering, and a log of oil; 22 and two turtledoves or two pigeons, depending on his means, the one to be the sin offering and the other the burnt offering. 23 On the eighth day of his cleansing he shall bring them to the priest at the entrance of the Tent of Meeting, before the LORD. 24 The priest shall take the lamb of guilt offering and the log of oil, and elevate them as an elevation offering before the LORD. 25 When the lamb of guilt offering has been slaughtered, the priest shall take some of the blood of the guilt offering and put it on the ridge of the right ear of the one being cleansed, on the thumb of his right hand, and on the big toe of his right foot. 26 The priest shall then pour some of the oil into the palm of his own left hand, 27 and with the finger of his right hand the priest shall sprinkle some of the oil that is in the palm of his left hand seven times before the LORD. 28 Some of the oil in his palm shall be put by the priest on the ridge of the right ear of the one being cleansed, on the thumb of his right hand, and on the big toe of his right foot, over the same places as the blood of the guilt offering; 29 and what is left of the oil in his palm the priest shall put on the head of the one being cleansed, to make expiation for him before the LORD. 30 He shall then offer one of the turtledoves or pigeons, depending on his means - 31 whichever he can afford - the one as a sin offering and the other as a burnt offering, together with the meal offering. Thus the priest shall make expiation before the LORD for the one being cleansed. 32 Such is the ritual for him who has a scaly affection and whose means for his cleansing are limited.

33 The LORD spoke to Moses and Aaron, saying: 34 When you enter the land of Canaan that I give you as a possession, and I inflict an eruptive plague upon a house in the land you possess, 35 the owner of the house shall come and tell the priest, saying, "Something like a plague has appeared upon my house." 36 The priest shall order the house cleared before the priest enters to examine the plague, so that nothing in the house may become unclean; after that the priest shall enter to examine

LEVITICUS 15 ויקרא טו מצורע

the house. 37 If, when he examines the plague, the plague in the walls of the house is found to consist of greenish or reddish streaks that appear to go deep into the wall, 38 the priest shall come out of the house to the entrance of the house, and close up the house for seven days. 39 On the seventh day the priest shall return. If he sees that the plague has spread on the walls of the house, 40 the priest shall order the stones with the plague in them to be pulled out and cast outside the city into an unclean place. 41 The house shall be scraped inside all around, and the coating that is scraped off shall be dumped outside the city in an unclean place. 42 They shall take other stones and replace those stones with them, and take other coating and plaster the house. 43 If the plague again breaks out in the house, after the stones have been pulled out and after the house has been scraped and replastered, 44 the priest shall come to examine: if the plague has spread in the house, it is a malignant eruption in the house; it is unclean. 45 The house shall be torn down - its stones and timber and all the coating on the house - and taken to an unclean place outside the city. 46 Whoever enters the house while it is closed up shall be unclean until evening. 47 Whoever sleeps in the house must wash his clothes, and whoever eats in the house must wash his clothes. 48 If, however, the priest comes and sees that the plague has not spread in the house after the house was replastered, the priest shall pronounce the house clean, for the plague has healed. 49 To purge the house, he shall take two birds, cedar wood, crimson stuff, and hyssop. 50 He shall slaughter the one bird over fresh water in an earthen vessel. 51 He shall take the cedar wood, the hyssop, the crimson stuff, and the live bird, and dip them in the blood of the slaughtered bird and the fresh water, and sprinkle on the house seven times. 52 Having purged the house with the blood of the bird, the fresh water, the live bird, the cedar wood, the hyssop, and the crimson stuff, 53 he shall set the live bird free outside the city in the open country. Thus he shall make expiation for the house, and it shall be clean. 54 Such is the ritual for every eruptive affection - for scalls, 55 for an eruption on a cloth or a house, 56 for swellings, for rashes, or for discolorations - 57 to determine when they are unclean and when they are clean. Such is the ritual concerning eruptions.

15 1 The LORD spoke to Moses and Aaron, saying: 2 Speak to the Israelite people and say to them: When any man has a discharge issuing from his member, he is unclean. 3 The uncleanness from his discharge shall mean the following - whether his member runs with the discharge or is stopped up so that there is no discharge, his uncleanness means this: 4 Any bedding on which the one with the discharge lies shall be unclean, and every object on which he sits shall be unclean. 5 Anyone who touches his bedding shall wash his clothes, bathe in water, and remain unclean until evening. 6 Whoever sits on an object on which the one with the discharge has sat shall wash his clothes, bathe in water, and remain unclean until evening. 7 Whoever touches the body of the one with the discharge shall wash his clothes, bathe in water, and remain unclean until evening. 8 If one with a discharge spits on one who is clean, the latter shall wash his clothes, bathe in water, and remain unclean until evening. 9 Any means for riding that one with a discharge has mounted shall be unclean; 10 whoever touches anything that was under him shall be unclean until evening; and whoever carries such things shall wash his clothes, bathe in water, and remain unclean until evening. 11 If one with a discharge, without having rinsed his hands in water, touches another person, that person shall wash his clothes, bathe in water, and remain unclean until evening. 12 An earthen vessel that one with a discharge touches shall be broken; and any wooden implement shall be rinsed with water. 13 When one with a discharge becomes clean of his discharge, he shall count off seven days for his cleansing, wash his clothes, and bathe his body in fresh water; then he shall be clean. 14 On the eighth day he shall take two turtledoves or two pigeons and come before the LORD at the entrance of the Tent of Meeting and give them to the priest. 15 The priest shall offer them, the one as a sin offering and the other as a burnt offering. Thus the priest shall make expiation on his behalf, for his discharge, before the LORD. 16 When a man has an emission of semen, he shall bathe his whole body in water and remain unclean until evening. 17 All cloth or leather on which semen falls shall be washed in water and remain unclean until evening. 18 And if a man has carnal relations with a woman, they shall bathe in water and remain unclean until evening.

LEVITICUS 16 ויקרא טז אחרי מות

19 When a woman has a discharge, her discharge being blood from her body, she shall remain in her impurity seven days; whoever touches her shall be unclean until evening. 20 Anything that she lies on during her impurity shall be unclean; and anything that she sits on shall be unclean. 21 Anyone who touches her bedding shall wash his clothes, bathe in water, and remain unclean until evening; 22 and anyone who touches any object on which she has sat shall wash his clothes, bathe in water, and remain unclean until evening. 23 Be it the bedding or be it the object on which she has sat, on touching it he shall be unclean until evening. 24 And if a man lies with her, her impurity is communicated to him: he shall be unclean seven days, and any bedding on which he lies shall become unclean.

25 When a woman has had a discharge of blood for many days, not at the time of her impurity, or when she has a discharge beyond her period of impurity, she shall be unclean, as though at the time of her impurity, as long as her discharge lasts. 26 Any bedding on which she lies while her discharge lasts shall be for her like bedding during her impurity; and any object on which she sits shall become unclean, as it does during her impurity; 27 whoever touches them shall be unclean: he shall wash his clothes, bathe in water, and remain unclean until evening. 28 When she becomes clean of her discharge, she shall count off seven days, and after that she shall be clean. 29 On the eighth day she shall take two turtledoves or two pigeons, and bring them to the priest at the entrance of the Tent of Meeting. 30 The priest shall offer the one as a sin offering and the other as a burnt offering; and the priest shall make expiation on her behalf, for her unclean discharge, before the LORD. 31 You shall put the Israelites on guard against their uncleanness, lest they die through their uncleanness by defiling My Tabernacle which is among them. 32 Such is the ritual concerning him who has a discharge: concerning him who has an emission of semen and becomes unclean thereby, 33 and concerning her who is in menstrual infirmity, and concerning anyone, male or female, who has a discharge, and concerning a man who lies with an unclean woman.

16 The LORD spoke to Moses after the death of the two sons of Aaron who died when they drew too close to the presence of the LORD. 2 The LORD said to Moses: Tell your brother Aaron that he is not to come at will into the Shrine behind the curtain, in front of the cover that is upon the ark, lest he die; for I appear in the cloud over the cover. 3 Thus only shall Aaron enter the Shrine: with a bull of the herd for a sin offering and a ram for a burnt offering. 4 He shall be dressed in a sacral linen tunic, with linen breeches next to his flesh, and be girt with a linen sash, and he shall wear a linen turban. They are sacral vestments; he shall bathe his body in water and then put them on. 5 And from the Israelite community he shall take two he-goats for a sin offering and a ram for a burnt offering. 6 Aaron is to offer his own bull of sin offering, to make expiation for himself and for his household. 7 Aaron shall take the two he-goats and let them stand before the LORD at the entrance of the Tent of Meeting. 8 and he shall place lots upon the two goats, one marked for the LORD and the other marked for Azazel. 9 Aaron shall bring forward the goat designated by lot for the LORD, which he is to offer as a sin offering; 10 while the goat designated by lot for Azazel shall be left standing alive before the LORD, to make expiation with it and to send it off to the wilderness for Azazel. 11 Aaron shall then offer his bull of sin offering, to make expiation for himself and his household. He shall slaughter his bull of sin offering, 12 and he shall take a panful of glowing coals scooped from the altar before the LORD, and two handfuls of finely ground aromatic incense, and bring this behind the curtain. 13 He shall put the incense on the fire before the LORD, so that the cloud from the incense screens the cover that is over [the Ark of] the Pact, lest he die. 14 He shall take some of the blood of the bull and sprinkle it with his finger over the cover on the east side; and in front of the cover he shall sprinkle some of the blood with his finger seven times. 15 He shall then slaughter the people's goat of sin offering, bring its blood behind the curtain, and do with its blood as he has done with the blood of the bull: he shall sprinkle it over the cover and in front of the cover. 16 Thus he shall purge the Shrine of the uncleanness and transgression of the Israelites, whatever their sins; and he shall do the same for the Tent of Meeting, which abides with them in the midst of their uncleanness. 17 When he goes in to make expiation in the Shrine,

יט וְאִשָּׁה כִּי־תִהְיֶה זָבָה דָּם יִהְיֶה זֹבָהּ בִּבְשָׂרָהּ שִׁבְעַת יָמִים תִּהְיֶה בְנִדָּתָהּ וְכָל־הַנֹּגֵעַ בָּהּ יִטְמָא עַד־הָעָרֶב: כ וְכֹל אֲשֶׁר תִּשְׁכַּב עָלָיו בְּנִדָּתָהּ יִטְמָא וְכֹל אֲשֶׁר־תֵּשֵׁב עָלָיו יִטְמָא: כא וְכָל־הַנֹּגֵעַ בְּמִשְׁכָּבָהּ יְכַבֵּס בְּגָדָיו וְרָחַץ בַּמַּיִם וְטָמֵא עַד־הָעָרֶב: כב וְכָל־הַנֹּגֵעַ בְּכָל־כְּלִי אֲשֶׁר־תֵּשֵׁב עָלָיו יְכַבֵּס בְּגָדָיו וְרָחַץ בַּמַּיִם וְטָמֵא עַד־הָעָרֶב: כג וְאִם עַל־הַמִּשְׁכָּב הוּא אוֹ עַל־הַכְּלִי אֲשֶׁר־הִוא יֹשֶׁבֶת־עָלָיו בְּנָגְעוֹ־בוֹ יִטְמָא עַד־הָעָרֶב: כד וְאִם שָׁכֹב יִשְׁכַּב אִישׁ אֹתָהּ וּתְהִי נִדָּתָהּ עָלָיו וְטָמֵא שִׁבְעַת יָמִים וְכָל־הַמִּשְׁכָּב אֲשֶׁר־יִשְׁכַּב עָלָיו יִטְמָא:

כה וְאִשָּׁה כִּי־יָזוּב זוֹב דָּמָהּ יָמִים רַבִּים בְּלֹא עֶת־נִדָּתָהּ אוֹ כִי־תָזוּב עַל־נִדָּתָהּ כָּל־יְמֵי זוֹב טֻמְאָתָהּ כִּימֵי נִדָּתָהּ תִּהְיֶה טְמֵאָה הִוא: כו כָּל־הַמִּשְׁכָּב אֲשֶׁר־תִּשְׁכַּב עָלָיו כָּל־יְמֵי זוֹבָהּ כְּמִשְׁכַּב נִדָּתָהּ יִהְיֶה־לָּהּ וְכָל־הַכְּלִי אֲשֶׁר תֵּשֵׁב עָלָיו טָמֵא יִהְיֶה כְּטֻמְאַת נִדָּתָהּ: כז וְכָל־הַנּוֹגֵעַ בָּם יִטְמָא וְכִבֶּס בְּגָדָיו וְרָחַץ בַּמַּיִם וְטָמֵא עַד־הָעָרֶב: כח וְאִם־טָהֲרָה מִזּוֹבָהּ וְסָפְרָה לָּהּ שִׁבְעַת יָמִים וְאַחַר תִּטְהָר: כט וּבַיּוֹם הַשְּׁמִינִי תִּקַּח־לָהּ שְׁתֵּי תֹרִים אוֹ שְׁנֵי בְּנֵי יוֹנָה וְהֵבִיאָה אוֹתָם אֶל־הַכֹּהֵן אֶל־פֶּתַח אֹהֶל מוֹעֵד: ל וְעָשָׂה הַכֹּהֵן אֶת־הָאֶחָד חַטָּאת וְאֶת־הָאֶחָד עֹלָה וְכִפֶּר עָלֶיהָ הַכֹּהֵן לִפְנֵי יְהוָה מִזּוֹב טֻמְאָתָהּ: לא וְהִזַּרְתֶּם אֶת־בְּנֵי־יִשְׂרָאֵל מִטֻּמְאָתָם וְלֹא יָמֻתוּ בְּטֻמְאָתָם בְּטַמְּאָם אֶת־מִשְׁכָּנִי אֲשֶׁר בְּתוֹכָם: לב זֹאת תּוֹרַת הַזָּב וַאֲשֶׁר תֵּצֵא מִמֶּנּוּ שִׁכְבַת־זֶרַע לְטָמְאָה־בָהּ: לג וְהַדָּוָה בְּנִדָּתָהּ וְהַזָּב אֶת־זוֹבוֹ לַזָּכָר וְלַנְּקֵבָה וּלְאִישׁ אֲשֶׁר יִשְׁכַּב עִם־טְמֵאָה:

א וַיְדַבֵּר יְהוָה אֶל־מֹשֶׁה אַחֲרֵי מוֹת שְׁנֵי בְּנֵי אַהֲרֹן בְּקָרְבָתָם לִפְנֵי־יְהוָה וַיָּמֻתוּ: ב וַיֹּאמֶר יְהוָה אֶל־מֹשֶׁה דַּבֵּר אֶל־אַהֲרֹן אָחִיךָ וְאַל־יָבֹא בְכָל־עֵת אֶל־הַקֹּדֶשׁ מִבֵּית לַפָּרֹכֶת אֶל־פְּנֵי הַכַּפֹּרֶת אֲשֶׁר עַל־הָאָרֹן וְלֹא יָמוּת כִּי בֶּעָנָן אֵרָאֶה עַל־הַכַּפֹּרֶת: ג בְּזֹאת יָבֹא אַהֲרֹן אֶל־הַקֹּדֶשׁ בְּפַר בֶּן־בָּקָר לְחַטָּאת וְאַיִל לְעֹלָה: ד כְּתֹנֶת־בַּד קֹדֶשׁ יִלְבָּשׁ וּמִכְנְסֵי־בַד יִהְיוּ עַל־בְּשָׂרוֹ וּבְאַבְנֵט בַּד יַחְגֹּר וּבְמִצְנֶפֶת בַּד יִצְנֹף בִּגְדֵי־קֹדֶשׁ הֵם וְרָחַץ בַּמַּיִם אֶת־בְּשָׂרוֹ וּלְבֵשָׁם: ה וּמֵאֵת עֲדַת בְּנֵי יִשְׂרָאֵל יִקַּח שְׁנֵי־שְׂעִירֵי עִזִּים לְחַטָּאת וְאַיִל אֶחָד לְעֹלָה: ו וְהִקְרִיב אַהֲרֹן אֶת־פַּר הַחַטָּאת אֲשֶׁר־לוֹ וְכִפֶּר בַּעֲדוֹ וּבְעַד בֵּיתוֹ: ז וְלָקַח אֶת־שְׁנֵי הַשְּׂעִירִם וְהֶעֱמִיד אֹתָם לִפְנֵי יְהוָה פֶּתַח אֹהֶל מוֹעֵד: ח וְנָתַן אַהֲרֹן עַל־שְׁנֵי הַשְּׂעִירִם גֹּרָלוֹת גּוֹרָל אֶחָד לַיהוָה וְגוֹרָל אֶחָד לַעֲזָאזֵל: ט וְהִקְרִיב אַהֲרֹן אֶת־הַשָּׂעִיר אֲשֶׁר עָלָה עָלָיו הַגּוֹרָל לַיהוָה וְעָשָׂהוּ חַטָּאת: י וְהַשָּׂעִיר אֲשֶׁר עָלָה עָלָיו הַגּוֹרָל לַעֲזָאזֵל יָעֳמַד־חַי לִפְנֵי יְהוָה לְכַפֵּר עָלָיו לְשַׁלַּח אֹתוֹ לַעֲזָאזֵל הַמִּדְבָּרָה: יא וְהִקְרִיב אַהֲרֹן אֶת־פַּר הַחַטָּאת אֲשֶׁר־לוֹ וְכִפֶּר בַּעֲדוֹ וּבְעַד בֵּיתוֹ וְשָׁחַט אֶת־פַּר הַחַטָּאת אֲשֶׁר־לוֹ: יב וְלָקַח מְלֹא־הַמַּחְתָּה גַּחֲלֵי־אֵשׁ מֵעַל הַמִּזְבֵּחַ מִלִּפְנֵי יְהוָה וּמְלֹא חָפְנָיו קְטֹרֶת סַמִּים דַּקָּה וְהֵבִיא מִבֵּית לַפָּרֹכֶת: יג וְנָתַן אֶת־הַקְּטֹרֶת עַל־הָאֵשׁ לִפְנֵי יְהוָה וְכִסָּה עֲנַן הַקְּטֹרֶת אֶת־הַכַּפֹּרֶת אֲשֶׁר עַל־הָעֵדוּת וְלֹא יָמוּת: יד וְלָקַח מִדַּם הַפָּר וְהִזָּה בְאֶצְבָּעוֹ עַל־פְּנֵי הַכַּפֹּרֶת קֵדְמָה וְלִפְנֵי הַכַּפֹּרֶת יַזֶּה שֶׁבַע־פְּעָמִים מִן־הַדָּם בְּאֶצְבָּעוֹ: טו וְשָׁחַט אֶת־שְׂעִיר הַחַטָּאת אֲשֶׁר לָעָם וְהֵבִיא אֶת־דָּמוֹ אֶל־מִבֵּית לַפָּרֹכֶת וְעָשָׂה אֶת־דָּמוֹ כַּאֲשֶׁר עָשָׂה לְדַם הַפָּר וְהִזָּה אֹתוֹ עַל־הַכַּפֹּרֶת וְלִפְנֵי הַכַּפֹּרֶת: טז וְכִפֶּר עַל־הַקֹּדֶשׁ מִטֻּמְאֹת בְּנֵי יִשְׂרָאֵל וּמִפִּשְׁעֵיהֶם לְכָל־חַטֹּאתָם וְכֵן יַעֲשֶׂה לְאֹהֶל מוֹעֵד הַשֹּׁכֵן אִתָּם בְּתוֹךְ טֻמְאֹתָם: יז וְכָל־אָדָם לֹא־יִהְיֶה בְּאֹהֶל

LEVITICUS 17 ויקרא יז אחרי מות

nobody else shall be in the Tent of Meeting until he comes out. When he has made expiation for himself and his household, and for the whole congregation of Israel. 18 he shall go out to the altar that is before the LORD and purge it: he shall take some of the blood of the bull and of the goat and apply it to each of the horns of the altar, 19 and the rest of the blood he shall sprinkle on it with his finger seven times. Thus he shall cleanse it of the uncleanness of the Israelites and consecrate it. 20 When he has finished purging the Shrine, the Tent of Meeting, and the altar, the live goat shall be brought forward. 21 Aaron shall lay both his hands upon the head of the live goat and confess over it all the iniquities and transgressions of the Israelites, whatever their sins, putting them on the head of the goat; and it shall be sent off to the wilderness through a designated man. 22 Thus the goat shall carry on it all their iniquities to an inaccessible region; and the goat shall be set free in the wilderness. 23 And Aaron shall go into the Tent of Meeting, take off the linen vestments that he put on when he entered the Shrine, and leave them there. 24 He shall bathe his body in water in the holy precinct and put on his vestments; then he shall come out and offer his burnt offering and the burnt offering of the people, making expiation for himself and for the people. 25 The fat of the sin offering he shall turn into smoke on the altar. 26 He who set the Azazel-goat free shall wash his clothes and bathe his body in water; after that he may reenter the camp. 27 The bull of sin offering and the goat of sin offering whose blood was brought in to purge the Shrine shall be taken outside the camp; and their hides, flesh, and dung shall be consumed in fire. 28 He who burned them shall wash his clothes and bathe his body in water; after that he may re-enter the camp. 29 And this shall be to you a law for all time: In the seventh month, on the tenth day of the month, you shall practice self-denial; and you shall do no manner of work, neither the citizen nor the alien who resides among you. 30 For on this day atonement shall be made for you to cleanse you of all your sins; you shall be clean before the LORD. 31 It shall be a sabbath of complete rest for you, and you shall practice self-denial; it is a law for all time. 32 The priest who has been anointed and ordained to serve as priest in place of his father shall make expiation. He shall put on the linen vestments, the sacral vestments. 33 He shall purge the innermost Shrine; he shall purge the Tent of Meeting and the altar; and he shall make expiation for the priests and for all the people of the congregation. 34 This shall be to you a law for all time: to make atonement for the Israelites for all their sins once a year. And Moses did as the LORD had commanded him.

17 1 The LORD spoke to Moses, saying: 2 Speak to Aaron and his sons and to all the Israelite people and say to them: This is what the LORD has commanded: 3 if anyone of the house of Israel slaughters an ox or sheep or goat in the camp, or does so outside the camp, 4 and does not bring it to the entrance of the Tent of Meeting to present it as an offering to the LORD, before the LORD's Tabernacle, bloodguilt shall be imputed to that man: he has shed blood; that man shall be cut off from among his people. 5 This is in order that the Israelites may bring the sacrifices which they have been making in the open - that they may bring them before the LORD, to the priest, at the entrance of the Tent of Meeting, and offer them as sacrifices of well-being to the LORD; 6 that the priest may dash the blood against the altar of the LORD at the entrance of the Tent of Meeting, and turn the fat into smoke as a pleasing odor to the LORD; 7 that they may offer their sacrifices no more to the goat-demons after whom they stray. This shall be to them a law for all time, throughout the ages. 8 Say to them further: If anyone of the house of Israel or of the strangers who reside among them offers a burnt offering or a sacrifice, 9 and does not bring it to the entrance of the Tent of Meeting to offer it to the LORD, that person shall be cut off from his people. 10 And if anyone of the house of Israel or of the strangers who reside among them partakes of any blood, I will set My face against the person who partakes of the blood, and I will cut him off from among his kin. 11 For the life of the flesh is in the blood, and I have assigned it to you for making expiation for your lives upon the altar; it is the blood, as life, that effects expiation. 12 Therefore I say to the Israelite people: No person among you shall partake of blood, nor shall the stranger who resides among you partake of blood. 13 And if any Israelite or any stranger who resides among them hunts down an animal

LEVITICUS 18 ויקרא יח אחרי מות

of a bird that may be eaten, he shall pour out its blood and cover it with earth. 14 For the life of all flesh - its blood is its life. Therefore I say to the Israelite people: You shall not partake of the blood of any flesh, for the life of all flesh is its blood. Anyone who partakes of it shall be cut off. 15 Any person, whether citizen or stranger, who eats what has died or has been torn by beasts shall wash his clothes, bathe in water, and remain unclean until evening; then he shall be clean. 16 But if he does not wash [his clothes] and bathe his body, he shall bear his guilt.

18 1 The LORD spoke to Moses, saying: 2 Speak to the Israelite people and say to them: I the LORD am your God. 3 You shall not copy the practices of the land of Egypt where you dwelt, or of the land of Canaan to which I am taking you; nor shall you follow their laws. 4 My rules alone shall you observe, and faithfully follow My laws: I the LORD am your God. 5 You shall keep My laws and My rules, by the pursuit of which man shall live: I am the LORD.

6 None of you shall come near anyone of his own flesh to uncover nakedness: I am the LORD. 7 Your father's nakedness, that is, the nakedness of your mother, you shall not uncover; she is your mother - you shall not uncover her nakedness. 8 Do not uncover the nakedness of your father's wife; it is the nakedness of your father. 9 The nakedness of your sister - your father's daughter or your mother's, whether born into the household or outside - do not uncover their nakedness. 10 The nakedness of your son's daughter, or of your daughter's daughter - do not uncover their nakedness; for their nakedness is yours. 11 The nakedness of your father's wife's daughter, who has born into your father's household - she is your sister; do not uncover her nakedness. 12 Do not uncover the nakedness of your father's sister; she is your father's flesh. 13 Do not uncover the nakedness of your mother's sister; for she is your mother's flesh. 14 Do not uncover the nakedness of your father's brother: do not approach his wife; she is your aunt. 15 Do not uncover the nakedness of your daughter-in-law: she is your son's wife; you shall not uncover her nakedness. 16 Do not uncover the nakedness of your brother's wife; it is the nakedness of your brother.

17 Do not uncover the nakedness of a woman and her daughter; nor shall you marry her son's daughter or her daughter's daughter and uncover her nakedness: they are kindred; it is depravity. 18 Do not marry a woman as a rival to her sister and uncover her nakedness in the other's lifetime. 19 Do not come near a woman during her period of uncleanness to uncover her nakedness. 20 Do not have carnal relations with your neighbor's wife and defile yourself with her. 21 Do not allow any of your offspring to be offered up to Molech, and do not profane the name of your God: I am the LORD. 22 Do not lie with a male as one lies with a woman; it is an abhorrence. 23 Do not have carnal relations with any beast and defile yourself thereby; and let no woman lend herself to a beast to mate with it; it is perversion. 24 Do not defile yourselves in any of those ways, for it is by such that the nations that I am casting out before you defiled themselves. 25 Thus the land became defiled; and I called it to account for its iniquity, and the land spewed out its inhabitants. 26 But you must keep My laws and My rules, and you must not do any of those abhorrent things, neither the citizen nor the stranger who resides among you: 27 for all those abhorrent things were done by the people who were in the land before you, and the land became defiled. 28 So let not the land spew you out for defiling it, as it spewed out the nation that came before you. 29 All who do any of those abhorrent things - such persons shall be cut off from their people. 30 You shall keep My charge not to engage in any of the abhorrent practices that were carried on before you, and you shall not defile yourselves through them: I the LORD am your God.

19 he LORD spoke to Moses, saying: 2 Speak to the whole Israelite community and say to them: You shall be holy, for I, the LORD your God, am holy. 3 You shall each revere his mother and his father, and keep My sabbaths: I the LORD am your God. 4 Do not turn to idols or make molten gods for yourselves: I the LORD am your God. 5 When you sacrifice an offering of well-being to the LORD, sacrifice it so that it may be accepted on your behalf. 6 It shall be eaten on the day

מנורה עם לולב, אתרוג ושופר, מתוך פסיפס בבית הכנסת של חמת ליד טבריה, המאה הרביעית
Menorah with *Lulav*, *Etrog* and *Shofar* (ram's horn), from a mosaic in the synagogue of Hammath near Tiberias, 4th century

LEVITICUS 20

you sacrifice it, or on the day following; but what is left by the third day must be consumed in fire. 7 If it should be eaten on the third day, it is an offensive thing, it will not be acceptable. 8 And he who eats of it shall bear his guilt, for he has profaned what is sacred to the LORD; that person shall be cut off from his kin. 9 When you reap the harvest of your land, you shall not reap all the way to the edges of your field, or gather the gleanings of your harvest. 10 You shall not pick your vineyard bare, or gather the fallen fruit of your vineyard; you shall leave them for the poor and the stranger: I the LORD am your God. 11 You shall not steal; you shall not deal deceitfully or falsely with one another. 12 You shall not swear falsely by My name, profaning the name of your God: I am the LORD. 13 You shall not defraud your fellow. You shall not commit robbery. The wages of a laborer shall not remain with you until morning. 14 You shall not insult the deaf, or place a stumbling block before the blind. You shall fear your God: I am the LORD. 15 You shall not render an unfair decision: do not favor the poor or show deference to the rich; judge your kinsman fairly. 16 Do not deal basely with your countrymen. Do not profit by the blood of your fellow: I am the LORD. 17 You shall not hate your kinsfolk in your heart. Reprove your kinsman but incur no guilt because of him. 18 You shall not take vengeance or bear a grudge against your countrymen. Love your fellow as yourself: I am the LORD. 19 You shall observe My laws. You shall not let your cattle mate with a different kind; you shall not sow your field with two kinds of seed; you shall not put on cloth from a mixture of two kinds of material. 20 If a man has carnal relations with a woman who is a slave and has been designated for another man, but has not been redeemed or given her freedom, there shall be an indemnity; they shall not, however, be put to death, since she has not been freed. 21 But he must bring to the entrance of the Tent of Meeting, as his guilt offering to the LORD, a ram of guilt offering. 22 With the ram of guilt offering the priest shall make expiation for him before the LORD for the sin that he committed; and the sin that he committed will be forgiven him.

23 When you enter the land and plant any tree for food, you shall regard its fruit as forbidden. Three years it shall be forbidden for you, not to be eaten. 24 In the fourth year all its fruit shall be set aside for jubilation before the LORD; 25 and only in the fifth year may you use its fruit: that its yield to you may be increased: I the LORD am your God. 26 You shall not eat anything with its blood. You shall not practice divination or soothsaying. 27 You shall not round off the side-growth on your head, or destroy the side-growth of your beard. 28 You shall not make gashes in your flesh for the dead, or incise any marks on yourselves: I am the LORD. 29 Do not degrade your daughter and make her a harlot, and the land fall into harlotry and the land be filled with depravity. 30 You shall keep My sabbaths and venerate My sanctuary: I am the LORD. 31 Do not turn to ghosts and do not inquire of familiar spirits, to be defiled by them: I the LORD am your God. 32 You shall rise before the aged and show deference to the old; you shall fear your God: I am the LORD. 33 When a stranger resides with you in your land, you shall not wrong him. 34 The stranger who resides with you shall be to you as one of your citizens; you shall love him as yourself, for you were strangers in the land of Egypt: I the LORD am your God. 35 You shall not falsify measures of length, weight, or capacity. 36 You shall have an honest balance, honest weights, an honest ephah, and an honest hin. I the LORD am your God who freed you from the land of Egypt. 37 You shall faithfully observe all My laws and all My rules: I am the LORD.

20 1 And the LORD spoke to Moses: 2 Say further to the Israelite people: Anyone among the Israelites, or among the strangers residing in Israel, who gives any of his offspring to Molech, shall be put to death; the people of the land shall pelt him with stones. 3 And I will set My face against that man and will cut him off from among his people, because he gave of his offspring to Molech and so defiled My sanctuary and profaned My holy name. 4 And if the people of the land should shut their eyes to that man when he gives of his offspring to Molech, and should not put him to death, 5 I Myself will set My face against that man and his kin, and will cut off from among their people both him and all who follow him in going astray after Molech. 6 And if any person turns to ghosts and familiar spirits and goes astray after them, I will set My face against that person and cut him

124

LEVITICUS 21

off from among his people. 7 You shall sanctify yourselves and be holy, for I the LORD am your God. 8 You shall faithfully observe My laws: I the LORD make you holy. 9 If anyone insults his father or his mother, he shall be put to death; he has insulted his father and his mother - his bloodguilt is upon him. 10 If a man commits adultery with a married woman, committing adultery with another man's wife, the adulterer and the adulteress shall be put to death. 11 If a man lies with his father's wife, it is the nakedness of his father that he has uncovered; the two shall be put to death - their bloodguilt is upon them. 12 If a man lies with his daughter-in-law, both of them shall be put to death; they have committed incest - their bloodguilt is upon them. 13 If a man lies with a male as one lies with a woman, the two of them have done an abhorrent thing; they shall be put to death - their bloodguilt is upon them. 14 If a man marries a woman and her mother, it is depravity; both he and they shall be put to the fire, that there be no depravity among you. 15 If a man has carnal relations with a beast, he shall be put to death; and you shall kill the beast. 16 If a woman approaches any beast to mate with it, you shall kill the woman and the beast; they shall be put to death - their bloodguilt is upon them. 17 If a man marries his sister, the daughter of either his father or his mother, so that he sees her nakedness and she sees his nakedness, it is a disgrace; they shall be excommunicated in the sight of their kinsfolk. He has uncovered the nakedness of his sister; he shall bear his guilt. 18 If a man lies with a woman in her infirmity and uncovers her nakedness, he has laid bare her flow and she has exposed her blood flow; both of them shall be cut off from among their people. 19 You shall not uncover the nakedness of your mother's sister or of your father's sister, for that is laying bare one's own flesh; they shall bear their guilt. 20 If a man lies with his uncle's wife, it is his uncle's nakedness that he has uncovered. They shall bear their guilt; they shall die childless. 21 If a man marries the wife of his brother, it is indecency. It is the nakedness of his brother that he has uncovered; they shall remain childless. 22 You shall faithfully observe all My laws and all My regulations, lest the land to which I bring you to settle in spew you out. 23 You shall not follow the practices of the nation that I am driving out before you. For it is because they did all these things that I abhorred them 24 and said to you: You shall possess their land, for I will give it to you to possess, a land flowing with milk and honey. I the LORD am your God who has set you apart from other peoples. 25 So you shall set apart the clean beast from the unclean, the unclean bird from the clean. You shall not draw abomination upon yourselves through beast or bird or anything with which the ground is alive, which I have set apart for you to treat as unclean. 26 You shall be holy to Me, for I the LORD am holy, and I have set you apart from other peoples to be Mine. 27 A man or a woman who has a ghost or a familiar spirit shall be put to death; they shall be pelted with stones - their bloodguilt is upon them.

21 The LORD said to Moses: Speak to the priests, the sons of Aaron, and say to them: None shall defile himself for any [dead] person among his kin, 2 except for the relatives that are closest to him: his mother, his father, his son, his daughter, and his brother; 3 also for a virgin sister, close to him because she has not married, for her he may defile himself. 4 But he shall not defile himself as a kinsman by marriage, and so profane himself. 5 They shall not shave smooth any part of their heads, or cut the side-growth of their beards, or make gashes in their flesh. 6 They shall be holy to their God and not profane the name of their God; for they offer the LORD's offerings by fire, the food of their God, and so must be holy. 7 They shall not marry a woman defiled by harlotry, nor shall they marry one divorced from her husband. For they are holy to their God 8 and you must treat them as holy, since they offer the food of your God; they shall be holy to you, for I the LORD who sanctify you am holy. 9 When the daughter of a priest defiles herself through harlotry, it is her father whom she defiles; she shall be put to the fire. 10 The priest who is exalted above his fellows, on whose head the anointing oil has been poured and who has been ordained to wear the vestments, shall not bare his head or rend his vestments. 11 He shall not go in where there is any dead body; he shall not defile himself even for his father or mother. 12 He shall not go outside the sanctuary and profane the sanctuary of his God, for upon him is the distinction of the anointing oil of his God. Mine the LORD's. 13 He may

LEVITICUS 22 · ויקרא כב אמור

marry only a woman who is a virgin. 14 A widow, or a divorced woman, or one who is degraded by harlotry - such he may not marry. Only a virgin of his own kin may be take to wife. 15 that he may not profane his offspring among his kin, for I the LORD have sanctified him. 16 The LORD spoke further to Moses: 17 Speak to Aaron and say: No man of your offspring throughout the ages who has a defect shall be qualified to offer the food of his God. 18 No one at all who has a defect shall be qualified: no man who is blind, or lame, or has a limb too short or too long: 19 no man who has a broken leg or a broken arm: 20 or who is a hunchback, or a dwarf, or who has a growth in his eye, or who has a boil-scar, or scurvy, or crushed testes. 21 No man among the offspring of Aaron the priest who has a defect shall be qualified to offer the LORD's offering by fire: having a defect, he shall not be qualified to offer the food of his God. 22 He may eat of the food of his God, of the most holy as well as of the holy: 23 but he shall not enter behind the curtain or come near the altar, for he has a defect. He shall not profane these places sacred to Me, for I the LORD have sanctified them. 24 Thus Moses spoke to Aaron and his sons and to all the Israelites.

22 1 The LORD spoke to Moses, saying: 2 Instruct Aaron and his sons to be scrupulous about the sacred donations that the Israelite people consecrate to Me, lest they profane My holy name, Mine the LORD's. 3 Say to them: Throughout the ages, if any man among your offspring, while in a state of uncleanness, partakes of any sacred donation that the Israelite people may consecrate to the LORD, that person shall be cut off from before Me: I am the LORD. 4 No man of Aaron's offspring who has an eruption or a discharge shall eat of the sacred donations until he is clean. If one touches anything made unclean by a corpse, or if a man has an emission of semen, 5 or if a man touches any swarming thing by which he is made unclean or any human being by whom he is made unclean - whatever his uncleanness - 6 the person who touches such shall be unclean until evening and shall not eat of the sacred donations unless he has washed his body in water. 7 As soon as the sun sets, he shall be clean: and afterward he may eat of the sacred donations, for they are his food. 8 He shall not eat anything that died or was torn by beasts, thereby becoming unclean: I am the LORD. 9 They shall keep My charge, lest they incur guilt thereby and die for it, having committed profanation: I the LORD consecrate them. 10 No lay person shall eat of the sacred donations. No bound or hired laborer of a priest shall eat of the sacred donations: 11 but a person who is a priest's property by purchase may eat of them: and those that are born in his household may eat of his food. 12 If a priest's daughter marries a layman, she may not eat of the sacred gifts: 13 but if the priest's daughter is widowed or divorced and without offspring, and is back in her father's house as in her youth, she may eat of her father's food. No lay person may eat of it: 14 but if a man eats of a sacred donation unwittingly, he shall pay the priest for the sacred donation, adding one-fifth of its value. 15 But [the priests] must not allow the Israelites to profane the sacred donations that they set aside for the LORD, 16 or to incur guilt requiring a penalty payment, by eating such sacred donations: for it is I the LORD who make them sacred.

17 The LORD spoke to Moses, saying: 18 Speak to Aaron and his sons, and to all the Israelite people, and say to them: When any man of the house of Israel or of the strangers in Israel presents a burnt offering as his offering for any of the votive or any of the freewill offerings that they offer to the LORD, 19 it must, to be acceptable in your favor, be a male without blemish, from cattle or sheep or goats. 20 You shall not offer any that has a defect, for it will not be accepted in your favor. 21 And when a man offers, from the herd or the flock, a sacrifice of well-being to the LORD for an explicit vow or as a freewill offering, it must, to be acceptable, be without blemish: there must be no defect in it. 22 Anything blind, or injured, or maimed, or with a wen, boil-scar, or scurvy - such you shall not offer to the LORD: you shall not put any of them on the altar as offerings by fire to the LORD. 23 You may, however, present as a freewill offering an ox or a sheep with a limb extended or contracted: but it will not be accepted for a vow. 24 You shall not offer to the LORD anything [with its testes] bruised or crushed or torn or cut. You shall have no such practices in your own land. 25 nor shall you accept such [animals] from a foreigner for offering as food for your God, for they are mutilated, they have a defect; they shall not be accepted in your favor. 26 The LORD

LEVITICUS 23 אמור ויקרא כג

spoke to Moses, saying: 27 When an ox or a sheep or a goat is born, it shall stay seven days with its mother, and from the eighth day on it shall be acceptable as an offering by fire to the LORD. 28 However, no animal from the herd or from the flock shall be slaughtered on the same day with its young. 29 When you sacrifice a thanksgiving offering to the LORD, sacrifice it so that it may be acceptable in your favor. 30 It shall be eaten on the same day; you shall not leave any of it until morning: I am the LORD. 31 You shall faithfully observe My commandments: I am the LORD. 32 You shall not profane My holy name, that I may be sanctified in the midst of the Israelite people - I the LORD who sanctify you, 33 I who brought you out of the land of Egypt to be your God, I the LORD.

23 1 The LORD spoke to Moses, saying: 2 Speak to the Israelite people and say to them: These are My fixed times, the fixed times of the LORD, which you shall proclaim as sacred occasions. 3 On six days work may be done, but on the seventh day there shall be a sabbath of complete rest, a sacred occasion. You shall do no work; it shall be a sabbath of the LORD throughout your settlements. 4 These are the set times of the LORD, the sacred occasions, which you shall celebrate each at its appointed time: 5 In the first month, on the fourteenth day of the month, at twilight, there shall be a passover offering to the LORD, 6 and on the fifteenth day of that month the LORD's Feast of Unleavened Bread. You shall eat unleavened bread for seven days. 7 On the first day you shall celebrate a sacred occasion: you shall not work at your occupations. 8 Seven days you shall make offerings by fire to the LORD. The seventh day shall be a sacred occasion: you shall not work at your occupations.

9 The LORD spoke to Moses, saying: 10 Speak to the Israelite people and say to them: When you enter the land that I am giving to you and you reap its harvest, you shall bring the first sheaf of your harvest to the priest. 11 He shall elevate the sheaf before the LORD for acceptance in your behalf; the priest shall elevate it on the day after the sabbath. 12 On the day that you elevate the sheaf, you shall offer as a burnt offering to the LORD a lamb of the first year without blemish. 13 The meal offering with it shall be two-tenths of a measure of choice flour mixed in oil, an offering by fire of pleasing odor to the LORD; and the libation with it shall be of wine, a quarter of a hin. 14 Until that very day, until you have brought the offering of your God, you shall eat no bread or parched grain or fresh ears: it is a law for all time throughout the ages in all your settlements.

15 And from the day on which you bring the sheaf of elevation offering - the day after the sabbath - you shall count off seven weeks. They must be complete. 16 You must count until the day after the seventh week - fifty days; then you shall bring an offering of new grain to the LORD. 17 You shall bring from your settlements two loaves of bread as an elevation offering; each shall be made of two-tenths of a measure of choice flour, baked after leavening, as first fruits to the LORD. 18 With the bread you shall present, as burnt offerings to the LORD, seven yearling lambs without blemish, one bull of the herd, and two rams, with their meal offerings and libations, an offering by fire of pleasing odor to the LORD. 19 You shall also offer one he-goat as a sin offering and two yearling lambs as a sacrifice of well-being. 20 The priest shall elevate these - the two lambs - together with the bread of first fruits as an elevation offering before the LORD; they shall be holy to the LORD, for the priest. 21 On that same day you shall hold a celebration; it shall be a sacred occasion for you; you shall not work at your occupations. This is a law for all time in all your settlements, throughout the ages. 22 And when you reap the harvest of your land, you shall not reap all the way to the edges of your field, or gather the gleanings of your harvest; you shall leave them for the poor and the stranger: I the LORD am your God.

23 The LORD spoke to Moses, saying: 24 Speak to the Israelite people thus: In the seventh month, on the first day of the month, you shall observe complete rest, a sacred occasion commemorated with loud blasts. 25 You shall not work at your occupations; and you shall bring an offering by fire to the LORD. 26 The LORD spoke to Moses, saying: 27 Mark, the tenth day of this seventh month is the Day of Atonement. It shall be a sacred occasion for you: you shall practice self-denial, and you shall bring an offering by fire to the LORD; 28 you shall do no work throughout that day.

LEVITICUS 24 ויקרא כד אמור

For it is a Day of Atonement, on which expiation is made on your behalf before the LORD your God. 29 Indeed, any person who does not practice self-denial throughout that day shall be cut off from his kin; 30 and whoever does any work throughout that day, I will cause that person to perish from among his people. 31 Do no work whatever; it is a law for all time, throughout the ages in all your settlements. 32 It shall be a sabbath of complete rest for you, and you shall practice self-denial; on the ninth day of the month at evening, from evening to evening, you shall observe this your sabbath.

33 The LORD spoke to Moses, saying: 34 Say to the Israelite people: On the fifteenth day of this seventh month there shall be the Feast of Booths to the LORD, [to last] seven days. 35 The first day shall be a sacred occasion: you shall not work at your occupations. 36 Seven days you shall bring offerings by fire to the LORD. On the eighth day you shall observe a sacred occasion and bring an offering by fire to the LORD; it is a solemn gathering: you shall not work at your occupations. 37 Those are the set times of the LORD that you shall celebrate as sacred occasions, bringing offerings by fire to the LORD - burnt offerings, meal offerings, sacrifices, and libations, on each day what is proper to it - 38 apart from the sabbaths of the LORD, and apart from your gifts and from all your votive offerings and from all your freewill offerings that you give to the LORD. 39 Mark, on the fifteenth day of the seventh month, when you have gathered in the yield of your land, you shall observe the festival of the LORD [to last] seven days: a complete rest on the first day, and a complete rest on the eighth day. 40 On the first day you shall take the product of hadar trees, branches of palm trees, boughs of leafy trees, and willows of the brook, and you shall rejoice before the LORD your God seven days. 41 You shall observe it as a festival of the LORD for seven days in the year: you shall observe it in the seventh month as a law for all time, throughout the ages. 42 You shall live in booths seven days; all citizens in Israel shall live in booths, 43 in order that future generations may know that I made the Israelite people live in booths when I brought them out of the land of Egypt, I the LORD your God. 44 So Moses declared to the Israelites the set times of the LORD.

24 1 The LORD spoke to Moses, saying: 2 Command the Israelite people to bring you clear oil of beaten olives for lighting, for kindling lamps regularly. 3 Aaron shall set them up in the Tent of Meeting outside the curtain of the Pact [to burn] from evening to morning before the LORD regularly; it is a law for all time throughout the ages. 4 He shall set up the lamps on the pure lampstand before the LORD [to burn] regularly.

5 You shall take choice flour and bake of it twelve loaves, two-tenths of a measure for each loaf. 6 Place them on the pure table before the LORD in two rows, six to a row. 7 With each row you shall place pure frankincense, which is to be a token offering for the bread, as an offering by fire to the LORD. 8 He shall arrange them before the LORD regularly every sabbath day - it is a commitment for all time on the part of the Israelites. 9 They shall belong to Aaron and his sons, who shall eat them in the sacred precinct; for they are his as most holy things from the LORD's offerings by fire, a due for all time. 10 There came out among the Israelites one whose mother was Israelite and whose father was Egyptian. And a fight broke out in the camp between that half-Israelite and a certain Israelite. 11 The son of the Israelite woman pronounced the Name in blasphemy, and he was brought to Moses - now his mother's name was Shelomith daughter of Dibri of the tribe of Dan - 12 and he was placed in custody, until the decision of the LORD should be made clear to them.

13 And the LORD spoke to Moses, saying: 14 Take the blasphemer outside the camp; let all who were within hearing lay their hands upon his head, and let the whole community stone him. 15 And to the Israelite people speak thus: Anyone who blasphemes his God shall bear his guilt; 16 if he also pronounces the name LORD, he shall be put to death. The whole community shall stone him; stranger or citizen, if he has thus pronounced the Name, be shall be put to death. 17 If anyone kills any human being, he shall be put to death. 18 One who kills a beast shall make restitution for it: life for life. 19 If anyone maims his fellow,

128

LEVITICUS 25 ויקרא כה בהר סיני

as he has done so shall it be done to him: 20 fracture for fracture, eye for eye, tooth for tooth. The injury he inflicted on another shall be inflicted on him. 21 One who kills a beast shall make restitution for it; but one who kills a human being shall be put to death. 22 You shall have one standard for stranger and citizen alike: for I the LORD am your God. 23 Moses spoke thus to the Israelites. And they took the blasphemer outside the camp and pelted him with stones. The Israelites did as the LORD had commanded Moses.

25 he LORD spoke to Moses on Mount Sinai: 2 Speak to the Israelite people and say to them: When you enter the land that I assign to you, the land shall observe a sabbath of the LORD. 3 Six years you may sow your field and six years you may prune your vineyard and gather in the yield. 4 But in the seventh year the land shall have a sabbath of complete rest, a sabbath of the LORD; you shall not sow your field or prune your vineyard. 5 You shall not reap the aftergrowth of your harvest or gather the grapes of your untrimmed vines: it shall be a year of complete rest for the land. 6 But you may eat whatever the land during its sabbath will produce - you, your male and female slaves, the hired and bound laborers who live with you, 7 and your cattle and the beasts in your land may eat all its yield. 8 You shall count off seven weeks of years - seven times seven years - so that the period of seven weeks of years gives you a total of forty-nine years. 9 Then you shall sound the horn loud; in the seventh month, on the tenth day of the month - the Day of Atonement - you shall have the horn sounded throughout your land 10 and you shall hallow the fiftieth year. You shall proclaim release throughout the land for all its inhabitants. It shall be a jubilee for you: each of you shall return to his holding and each of you shall return to his family. 11 That fiftieth year shall be a jubilee for you: you shall not sow, neither shall you reap the aftergrowth or harvest the untrimmed vines, 12 for it is a jubilee. It shall be holy to you: you may only eat the growth direct from the field. 13 In this year of jubilee, each of you shall return to his holding. 14 When you sell property to your neighbor, or buy any from your neighbor, you shall not wrong one another. 15 In buying from your neighbor, you shall deduct only for the number of years since the jubilee: and in selling to you, he shall charge you only for the remaining crop years: 16 the more such years, the higher the price you pay; the fewer such years, the lower the price: for what he is selling you is a number of harvests. 17 Do not wrong one another, but fear your God: for I the LORD am your God. 18 You shall observe My laws and faithfully keep My rules, that you may live upon the land in security. 19 The land shall yield its fruit and you shall eat your fill, and you shall live upon it in security. 20 And should you ask, "What are we to eat in the seventh year, if we may neither sow nor gather in our crops?" 21 I will ordain My blessing for you in the sixth year, so that it shall yield a crop sufficient for three years. 22 When you sow in the eighth year, you will still be eating old grain of that crop; you will be eating the old until the ninth year, until its crops come in. 23 But the land must not be sold beyond reclaim, for the land is Mine; you are but strangers resident with Me. 24 Throughout the land that you hold, you must provide for the redemption of the land. 25 If your kinsman is in straits and has to sell part of his holding, his nearest redeemer shall come and redeem what his kinsman has sold. 26 If a man has no one to redeem for him, but prospers and acquires enough to redeem with, 27 he shall compute the years since its sale, refund the difference to the man to whom he sold it, and return to his holding. 28 If he lacks sufficient means to recover it, what he sold shall remain with the purchaser until the jubilee; in the jubilee year it shall be released, and he shall return to his holding. 29 If a man sells a dwelling house in a walled city, it may be redeemed until a year has elapsed after its sale; the redemption period shall be a year. 30 If it is not redeemed before a full year has elapsed, the house in the walled city shall pass to the purchaser beyond reclaim throughout the ages: it shall not be released in the jubilee. 31 But houses in villages that have no encircling walls shall be classed as open country:

LEVITICUS 26 ויקרא בהר סיני

they may be redeemed, and they shall be released through the jubilee. 32 As for the cities of the Levites, the houses in the cities they hold - the Levites shall forever have the right of redemption. 33 Such property as may be redeemed from the Levites - houses sold in a city they hold - shall be released through the jubilee; for the houses in the cities of the Levites are their holding among the Israelites. 34 But the unenclosed land about their cities cannot be sold, for that is their holding for all time.

35 If your kinsman, being in straits, comes under your authority, and you hold him as though a resident alien, let him live by your side; 36 do not exact from him advance or accrued interest, but fear your God. Let him live by your side as your kinsman. 37 Do not lend him your money at advance interest, or give him your food at accrued interest. 38 I the LORD am your God, who brought you out of the land of Egypt, to give you the land of Canaan, to be your God.

39 If your kinsman under you continues in straits and must give himself over to you, do not subject him to the treatment of a slave. 40 He shall remain with you as a hired or bound laborer; he shall serve with you only until the jubilee year. 41 Then he and his children with him shall be free of your authority; he shall go back to his family and return to his ancestral holding. - 42 For they are My servants, whom I freed from the land of Egypt; they may not give themselves over into servitude. - 43 You shall not rule over him ruthlessly; you shall fear your God. 44 Such male and female slaves as you may have - it is from the nations round about you that you may acquire male and female slaves. 45 You may also buy them from among the children of aliens resident among you, or from their families that are among you, whom they begot in your land. These shall become your property; 46 you may keep them as a possession for your children after you, for them to inherit as property for all time. Such you may treat as slaves. But as for your Israelite kinsmen, no one shall rule ruthlessly over the other. 47 If a resident alien among you has prospered, and your kinsman being in straits, comes under his authority and gives himself over to the resident alien among you, or to an offshoot of an alien's family, 48 he shall have the right of redemption even after he has given himself over. One of his kinsmen shall redeem him, 49 or his uncle or his uncle's son shall redeem him, or anyone of his family who is of his own flesh shall redeem him; or, if he prospers, he may redeem himself. 50 He shall compute with his purchaser the total from the year he gave himself over to him until the jubilee year; the price of his sale shall be applied to the number of years, as though it were for a term as a hired laborer under the other's authority. 51 If many years remain, he shall pay back for his redemption in proportion to his purchase price; 52 and if few years remain until the jubilee year, he shall so compute: he shall make payment for his redemption according to the years involved. 53 He shall be under his authority as a laborer hired by the year: he shall not rule ruthlessly over him in your sight. 54 If he has not been redeemed in any of those ways, he and his children with him shall go free in the jubilee year. 55 For it is to Me that the Israelites are servants: they are My servants, whom I freed from the land of Egypt, I the LORD your God. **26** 1 You shall not make idols for yourselves, or set up for yourselves carved images or pillars, or place figured stones in your land to worship upon, for I the LORD am your God. 2 You shall keep My sabbaths and venerate My sanctuary, Mine, the LORD's.

3 **I**f you follow My laws and faithfully observe My commandments, 4 I will grant your rains in their season, so that the earth shall yield its produce and the trees of the field their fruit. 5 Your threshing shall overtake the vintage, and your vintage shall overtake the sowing; you shall eat your fill of bread and dwell securely in your land. 6 I will grant peace in the land, and you shall lie down untroubled by anyone; I will give the land respite from vicious beasts, and no sword shall cross your land. 7 You shall give chase to your enemies, and they shall fall before you by the sword. 8 Five of you shall give chase to a hundred, and a hundred of you shall give chase to ten thousand; your enemies shall fall before you by the sword. 9 I will look with favor upon you, and make you fertile and multiply you; and I will maintain My covenant with you. 10 You shall eat old grain long stored, and you shall have to clear out the old to make room for the new. 11 I will establish My abode in your midst, and I will not spurn you. 12 I will be ever present in your midst; I will be your God, and you shall be My people. 13 I the LORD am your God who brought you out from the land of the Egyptians to be their slaves no more, who broke the bars of your yoke and made you walk erect.

— 130 —

LEVITICUS 27 · ויקרא בז בחקתי

14 But if you do not obey Me and do not observe all these commandments, 15 if you reject My laws and spurn My rules, so that you do not observe all My commandments and you break My covenant, 16 I in turn will do this to you: I will wreak misery upon you — consumption and fever, which cause the eyes to pine and the body to languish; you shall sow your seed to no purpose, for your enemies shall eat it. 17 I will set My face against you: you shall be routed by your enemies, and your foes shall dominate you. You shall flee though none pursues. 18 And if, for all that, you do not obey Me, I will go on to discipline you sevenfold for your sins, 19 and I will break your proud glory. I will make your skies like iron and your earth like copper, 20 so that your strength shall be spent to no purpose. Your land shall not yield its produce, nor shall the trees of the land yield their fruit. 21 And if you remain hostile toward Me and refuse to obey Me, I will go on smiting you sevenfold for your sins. 22 I will loose wild beasts against you, and they shall bereave you of your children and wipe out your cattle. They shall decimate you, and your roads shall be deserted. 23 And if these things fail to discipline you for Me, and you remain hostile to Me, 24 I too will remain hostile to you: I in turn will smite you sevenfold for your sins. 25 I will bring a sword against you to wreak vengeance for the covenant; and if you withdraw into your cities, I will send pestilence among you, and you shall be delivered into enemy hands. 26 When I break your staff of bread, ten women shall bake your bread in a single oven; they shall dole out your bread by weight, and though you eat, you shall not be satisfied. 27 But if, despite this, you disobey Me and remain hostile to Me, 28 I will act against you in wrathful hostility; I, for My part, will discipline you sevenfold for your sins. 29 You shall eat the flesh of your sons and the flesh of your daughters. 30 I will destroy your cult places and cut down your incense stands, and I will heap your carcasses upon your lifeless fetishes. I will spurn you. 31 I will lay your cities in ruin and make your sanctuaries desolate, and I will not savor your pleasing odors. 32 I will make the land desolate, so that your enemies who settle in it shall be appalled by it. 33 And I will scatter among the nations, and I will unsheath the sword against you. Your land shall become a desolation and your cities a ruin. 34 Then shall the land make up for its sabbath years throughout the time that it is desolate and you are in the land of your enemies; then shall the land rest and make up for its sabbath years. 35 Throughout the time that it is desolate, it shall observe the rest that it did not observe in your sabbath years while you were dwelling upon it. 36 As for those of you who survive, I will cast a faintness into their hearts in the land of their enemies. The sound of a driven leaf shall put them to flight. Fleeing as though from the sword, they shall fall though none pursues. 37 With no one pursuing, they shall stumble over one another as before the sword. You shall not be able to stand your ground before your enemies. 38 but shall perish among the nations; and the land of your enemies shall consume you. 39 Those of you who survive shall be heartsick over their iniquity in the land of their enemies; more, they shall be heartsick over the iniquities of their fathers. 40 and they shall confess their iniquity and the iniquity of their fathers, in that they trespassed against Me, yea, were hostile to Me. 41 When I, in turn, have been hostile to them and have removed them into the land of their enemies, then at last shall their obdurate heart humble itself, and they shall atone for their iniquity. 42 Then will I remember My covenant with Jacob; I will remember also My covenant with Isaac, and also My covenant with Abraham; and I will remember the land. 43 For the land shall be forsaken of them, making up for its sabbath years by being desolate of them, while they atone for their iniquity; for the abundant reason that they rejected My rules and spurned My laws. 44 Yet, even then, when they are in the land of their enemies, I will not reject them or spurn them so as to destroy them, annulling My covenant with them: for I the LORD am their God. 45 I will remember in their favor the covenant with the ancients, whom I freed from the land of Egypt in the sight of the nations to be their God; I, the LORD. 46 These are the laws, rules, and instructions that the LORD established, through Moses on Mount Sinai, between Himself and the Israelite people.

27 The LORD spoke to Moses, saying: 2 Speak to the Israelite people and say

LEVITICUS 27 ויקרא כז בחקתי

to them: When anyone explicitly vows to the LORD the equivalent for a human being, 3 the following scale shall apply: If it is a male from twenty to sixty years of age, the equivalent is fifty shekels of silver by the sanctuary weight; 4 if it is a female, the equivalent is thirty shekels. 5 If the age is from five years to twenty years, the equivalent is twenty shekels for a male and ten shekels for a female. 6 If the age is from one month to five years, the equivalent for a male is five shekels of silver, and the equivalent for a female is three shekels of silver. 7 If the age is sixty years or over, the equivalent is fifteen shekels in the case of a male and ten shekels for a female. 8 But if one cannot afford the equivalent, he shall be presented before the priest, and the priest shall assess him; the priest shall assess him according to what the vower can afford. 9 If [the vow concerns] any animal that may be brought as an offering to the LORD, any such that may be given to the LORD shall be holy. 10 One may not exchange or substitute another for it, either good for bad, or bad for good; if one does substitute one animal for another, the thing vowed and its substitute shall both be holy. 11 If [the vow concerns] any unclean animal that may not be brought as an offering to the LORD, the animal shall be presented before the priest, 12 and the priest shall assess it. Whether high or low, whatever assessment is set by the priest shall stand; 13 and if he wishes to redeem it, he must add one-fifth to its assessment. 14 If anyone consecrates his house to the LORD, the priest shall assess it. Whether high or low, as the priest assesses it, so it shall stand; 15 and if he who has consecrated his house wishes to redeem it, he must add one-fifth to the sum at which it was assessed, and it shall be his. 16 If anyone consecrates to the LORD any land that he holds, its assessment shall be in accordance with its seed requirement: fifty shekels of silver to a homer of barley seed. 17 If he consecrates his land as of the jubilee year, its assessment stands. 18 But if he consecrates his land after the jubilee, the priest shall compute the price according to the years that are left until the jubilee year, and its assessment shall be so reduced; 19 and if he who consecrated the land wishes to redeem it, he must add one-fifth to the sum at which it was assessed, and it shall pass to him. 20 But if he does not redeem the land, and the land is sold to another, it shall no longer be redeemable: 21 when it is released in the jubilee, the land shall be holy to the LORD, as land proscribed; it becomes the priest's holding. 22 If he consecrates to the LORD land that he purchased, which is not land of his holding, 23 the priest shall compute for him the proportionate assessment up to the jubilee year, and he shall pay the assessment as of that day, a sacred donation to the LORD. 24 In the jubilee year the land shall revert to him from whom it was bought, whose holding the land is. 25 All assessments shall be by the sanctuary weight, the shekel being twenty gerahs. 26 A firstling of animals, however, which – as a firstling – is the LORD's, cannot be consecrated by anybody; whether ox or sheep, it is the LORD's. 27 But if it is of unclean animals, it may be ransomed as its assessment, with one-fifth added; if it is not redeemed, it shall be sold at its assessment. 28 But of all that anyone owns, be it man or beast or land of his holding, nothing that he has proscribed for the LORD may be sold or redeemed; every proscribed thing is totally consecrated to the LORD. 29 No human being who has been proscribed can be ransomed: he shall be put to death. 30 All tithes from the land, whether seed from the ground or fruit from the tree, are the LORD's; they are holy to the LORD. 31 If anyone wishes to redeem any of his tithes, he must add one-fifth to them. 32 All tithes of the herd or flock – of all that passes under the shepherd's staff, every tenth one – shall be holy to the LORD. 33 He must not look out for good as against bad, or make substitution for it. If he does make substitution for it, then it and its substitute shall both be holy; it cannot be redeemed. 34 These are the commandments that the LORD gave Moses for the Israelite people on Mount Sinai.

On the facing page:
Torah Ark curtain, Germany, 1728, collection of The Israel Museum, Jerusalem
"Priestly Benediction" (earliest biblical inscription, Numbers 6:24-25, found at Ketef Hinnom), silver plaque, mid-7th century BCE, collection of The Israel Museum, Jerusalem

NUMBERS
במדבר

NUMBERS 1   במדבר א

¹ On the first day of the second month, in the second year following the exodus from the land of Egypt, the LORD spoke to Moses in the wilderness of Sinai, in the Tent of Meeting, saying: ² Take a census of the whole Israelite community by the clans of its ancestral houses, listing the names, every male, head by head. ³ You and Aaron shall record them by their groups, from the age of twenty years up, all those in Israel who are able to bear arms. ⁴ Associated with you shall be a man from each tribe, each one the head of his ancestral house. ⁵ These are the names of the men who shall assist you: From Reuben, Elizur son of Shedeur. ⁶ From Simeon, Shelumiel son of Zurishaddai. ⁷ From Judah, Nahshon son of Amminadab. ⁸ From Issachar, Nethanel son of Zuar. ⁹ From Zebulun, Eliab son of Helon. ¹⁰ From the sons of Joseph: from Ephraim, Elishama son of Ammihud; from Manasseh, Gamaliel son of Pedahzur. ¹¹ From Benjamin, Abidan son of Gideoni. ¹² From Dan, Ahiezer son of Ammishaddai. ¹³ From Asher, Pagiel son of Ochran. ¹⁴ From Gad, Eliasaph son of Deuel. ¹⁵ From Naphtali, Ahira son of Enan. ¹⁶ Those are the elected of the assembly, the chieftains of their ancestral tribes: they are the heads of the contingents of Israel. ¹⁷ So Moses and Aaron took those men, who were designated by name, ¹⁸ and on the first day of the second month they convoked the whole community, who were registered by the clans of their ancestral houses - the names of those aged twenty years and over being listed head by head. ¹⁹ As the LORD had commanded Moses, so he recorded them in the wilderness of Sinai.   ²⁰ They totaled as follows: The descendants of Reuben, Israel's first-born, the registration of the clans of their ancestral house, as listed by name, head by head, all males aged twenty years and over, all who were able to bear arms - ²¹ those enrolled from the tribe of Reuben: 46,500.

²² Of the descendants of Simeon, the registration of the clans of their ancestral house, their enrollment as listed by name, head by head, all males aged twenty years and over, all who were able to bear arms - ²³ those enrolled from the tribe of Simeon: 59,300.

²⁴ Of the descendants of Gad, the registration of the clans of their ancestral house, as listed by name, aged twenty years and over, all who were able to bear arms - ²⁵ those enrolled from the tribe of Gad: 45,650.

²⁶ Of the descendants of Judah, the registration of the clans of their ancestral house, as listed by name, aged twenty years and over, all who were able to bear arms - ²⁷ those enrolled from the tribe of Judah: 74,600.

²⁸ Of the descendants of Issachar, the registration of the clans of their ancestral house, as listed by name, aged twenty years and over, all who were able to bear arms - ²⁹ those enrolled from the tribe of Issachar: 54,400.

³⁰ Of the descendants of Zebulun, the registration of the clans of their ancestral house, as listed by name, aged twenty years and over, all who were able to bear arms - ³¹ those enrolled from the tribe of Zebulun: 57,400.

³² Of the descendants of Joseph: Of the descendants of Ephraim, the registration of the clans of their ancestral house, as listed by name, aged twenty years and over, all who were able to bear arms - ³³ those enrolled from the tribe of Ephraim: 40,500.

³⁴ Of the descendants of Manasseh, the registration of the clans of their ancestral house, as listed by name, aged twenty years and over, all who were able to bear arms - ³⁵ those enrolled from the tribe of Manasseh: 32,200.

³⁶ Of the descendants of Benjamin, the registration of the clans of their ancestral house, as listed by name, aged twenty years and over, all who were able to bear arms - ³⁷ those enrolled from the tribe of Benjamin: 35,400.

³⁸ Of the descendants of Dan, the registration of the clans of their

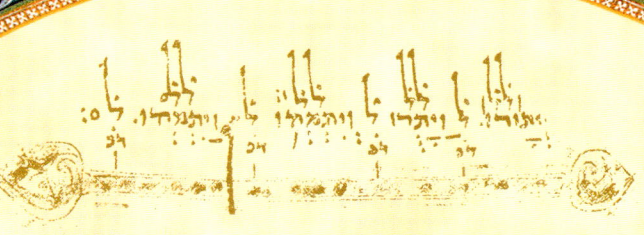

NUMBERS 2 במדבר ב

ancestral house, as listed by name, aged twenty years and over, all who were able to bear arms – 39 those enrolled from the tribe of Dan: 62,700. 40 Of the descendants of Asher, the registration of the clans of their ancestral house, as listed by name, aged twenty years and over, all who were able to bear arms – 41 those enrolled from the tribe of Asher: 41,500. 42 [Of] the descendants of Naphtali, the registration of the clans of their ancestral house as listed by name, aged twenty years and over, all who were able to bear arms – 43 those enrolled from the tribe of Naphtali: 53,400. 44 These are the enrollments recorded by Moses and Aaron and by the chieftains of Israel, who were twelve in number, one man to each ancestral house. 45 All the Israelites, aged twenty years and over, enrolled by ancestral houses, all those in Israel who were able to bear arms – 46 all who were enrolled came to 603,550. 47 The Levites, however, were not recorded among them by their ancestral tribe.

48 For the LORD had spoken to Moses, saying: 49 Do not on any account enroll the tribe of Levi or take a census of them with the Israelites. 50 You shall put the Levites in charge of the Tabernacle of the Pact, all its furnishings, and everything that pertains to it: they shall carry the Tabernacle and all its furnishings, and they shall tend it; and they shall camp around the Tabernacle. 51 When the Tabernacle is to set out, the Levites shall take it down, and when the Tabernacle is to be pitched, the Levites shall set it up: any outsider who encroaches shall be put to death. 52 The Israelites shall encamp troop by troop, each man with his division and each under his standard. 53 The Levites, however, shall camp around the Tabernacle of the Pact, that wrath may not strike the Israelite community; the Levites shall stand guard around the Tabernacle of the Pact. 54 The Israelites did accordingly: just as the LORD had commanded Moses, so they did.

2 1 The LORD spoke to Moses and Aaron, saying: 2 The Israelites shall camp each with his standard, under the banners of their ancestral house; they shall camp around the Tent of Meeting at a distance. 3 Camped on the front, or east side: the standard of the division of Judah, troop by troop. Chieftain of the Judites: Nahshon son of Amminadab. 4 His troop, as enrolled: threescore and fourteen thousand and six hundred. 5 Camping next to it: The tribe of Issachar. Chieftain of the Issacharites: Nethanel son of Zuar. 6 His troop, as enrolled: fifty and four thousand and four hundred. 7 The tribe of Zebulun. Chieftain of the Zebulunites: Eliab son of Helon. 8 His troop, as enrolled: fifty and seven thousand and four hundred. 9 The total enrolled in the division of Judah: hundred thousand and fourscore thousand and six thousand and four hundred, for all troops. These shall march first. 10 On the south: the standard of the division of Reuben, troop by troop. Chieftain of the Reubenites: Elizur son of Shedeur. 11 His troop, as enrolled: 46,500. 12 Camping next to it: The tribe of Simeon. Chieftain of the Simeonites: Shelumiel son of Zurishaddai. 13 His troop, as enrolled: 59,300. 14 And the tribe of Gad. Chieftain of the Gadites: Eliasaph son of Reuel. 15 His troop, as enrolled: 45,650. 16 The total enrolled in the division of Reuben: 151,450, for all troops. These shall march second. 17 Then, midway between the divisions, the Tent of Meeting, the division of the Levites, shall move. As they camp, so they shall march, each in position, by their standards. 18 On the west: the standard of the division of Ephraim, troop by troop. Chieftain of the Ephraimites: Elishama son of Ammihud. 19 His troop, as enrolled: 40,500. 20 Next to it: The tribe of Manasseh. Chieftain of the Manassites: Gamaliel son of Pedahzur. 21 His troop, as enrolled: thirty and two thousand and two hundred. 22 And the tribe of Benjamin. Chieftain of the Benjaminites: Abidan son of Gideoni. 23 His troop, as enrolled: thirty and five thousand and four hundred. 24 The total

NUMBERS 3 · במדבר ג · במדבר

enrolled in the division of Ephraim: 108,100 for all troops. These shall march third. 25 On the north: the standard of the division of Dan, troop by troop. Chieftain of the Danites: Abiezer son of Ammishaddai. 26 His troop, as enrolled: 62,700. 27 Camping next to it: The tribe of Asher. Chieftain of the Asherites: Pagiel son of Ochran. 28 His troop, as enrolled: 41,500. 29 And the tribe of Naphtali. Chieftain of the Naphtalites: Ahira son of Enan. 30 His troop, as enrolled: 53,400. 31 The total enrolled in the division of Dan: 157,600. These shall march last, by their standards.

32 Those are the enrollments of the Israelites by ancestral houses. The total enrolled in the divisions, for all troops: 603,550. 33 The Levites, however, were not recorded among the Israelites, as the LORD had commanded Moses. 34 The Israelites did accordingly: just as the LORD had commanded Moses, so they camped by their standards, and so they marched, each with his clan according to his ancestral house.

3 1 This is the line of Aaron and Moses at the time that the LORD spoke with Moses on Mount Sinai. 2 These were the names of Aaron's sons: Nadab, the first-born, and Abihu, Eleazar and Ithamar; 3 those were the names of Aaron's sons, the anointed priests who were ordained for priesthood. 4 But Nadab and Abihu died by the will of the LORD, when they offered alien fire before the LORD in the wilderness of Sinai; and they left no sons. So it was Eleazar and Ithamar who served as priests in the lifetime of their father Aaron.

5 The LORD spoke to Moses, saying: 6 Advance the tribe of Levi and place them in attendance upon Aaron the priest to serve him. 7 They shall perform duties for him and for the whole community before the Tent of Meeting, doing the work of the Tabernacle. 8 They shall take charge of all the furnishings of the Tent of Meeting – a duty on behalf of the Israelites – doing the work of the Tabernacle. 9 You shall assign the Levites to Aaron and to his sons: they are formally assigned to him from among the Israelites. 10 You shall make Aaron and his sons responsible for observing their priestly duties; and any outsider who encroaches shall be put to death.

11 The LORD spoke to Moses, saying: 12 I hereby take the Levites from among the Israelites in place of all the first-born, the first issue of the womb among the Israelites: the Levites shall be Mine. 13 For every first-born is Mine: at the time that I smote every first-born in the land of Egypt, I consecrated every first-born in Israel, man and beast, to Myself, to be Mine, the LORD's.

14 The LORD spoke to Moses in the wilderness of Sinai, saying: 15 Record the Levites by ancestral house and by clan: record every male among them from the age of one month up. 16 So Moses recorded them at the command of the LORD, as he was bidden. 17 These were the sons of Levi by name: Gershon, Kohath, and Merari. 18 These were the names of the sons of Gershon by clan: Libni and Shimei. 19 The sons of Kohath by clan: Amram and Izhar, Hebron and Uzziel. 20 The sons of Merari by clan: Mahli and Mushi. These were the clans of the Levites within their ancestral houses: 21 To Gershon belonged the clan of the Libnites and the clan of the Shimeites: those were the clans of the Gershonites. 22 The recorded entries of all their males from the age of one month up, as recorded, came to 7,500. 23 The clans of the Gershonites were to camp behind the Tabernacle, to the west. 24 The chieftain of the ancestral house of the Gershonites was Eliasaph son of Lael. 25 The duties of the Gershonites in the Tent of Meeting comprised: the Tabernacle, the tent, its covering, and the screen for the entrance of the Tent of Meeting; 26 the hangings of the enclosure, the screen for the entrance of the enclosure which surrounds the Tabernacle, the cords thereof, and the altar – all the service connected with these. 27 To Kohath belonged the clan of the Amramites, the clan of the Izharites, the clan of the Hebronites, and the clan of the Uzzielites: those were the clans of the Kohathites. 28 All the listed males from the age of one month up

NUMBERS 4 — במדבר ד

came to 8,600, attending to the duties of the sanctuary. 29 The clans of the Kohathites were to camp along the south side of the Tabernacle. 30 The chieftain of the ancestral house of the Kohathite clans was Elizaphan son of Uzziel. 31 Their duties comprised: the ark, the table, the lampstand, the altars, and the sacred utensils that were used with them, and the screen — all the service connected with these. 32 The head chieftain of the Levites was Eleazar son of Aaron the priest, in charge of those attending to the duties of the sanctuary. 33 To Merari belonged the clan of the Mahlites and the clan of the Mushites: those were the clans of Merari. 34 The recorded entries of all their males from the age of one month up came to 6,200. 35 The chieftain of the ancestral house of the clans of Merari was Zuriel son of Abihail. They were to camp along the north side of the Tabernacle. 36 The assigned duties of the Merarites comprised: the planks of the Tabernacle, its bars, posts, and sockets, and all its furnishings — all the service connected with these; 37 also the posts around the enclosure and their sockets, pegs, and cords. 38 Those who were to camp before the Tabernacle, in front — before the Tent of Meeting, on the east — were Moses and Aaron and his sons, attending to the duties of the sanctuary, as a duty on behalf of the Israelites; and any outsider who encroached was to be put to death. 39 All the Levites who were recorded, whom at the LORD's command Moses and Aaron recorded by their clans, all the males from the age of one month up, came to 22,000.

40 The LORD said to Moses: Record every first-born male of the Israelite people from the age of one month up, and make a list of their names; 41 and take the Levites for Me, the LORD, in place of every first-born among the Israelite people, and the cattle of the Levites in place of every first-born among the cattle of the Israelites. 42 So Moses recorded all the first-born among the Israelites, as the LORD had commanded him. 43 All the first-born males as listed by name, recorded from the age of one month up, came to 22,273.

44 The LORD spoke to Moses, saying: 45 Take the Levites in place of all the first-born among the Israelite people, and the cattle of the Levites in place of their cattle; and the Levites shall be Mine, the LORD's. 46 And as the redemption price of the 273 Israelite first-born over and above the number of the Levites, 47 take five shekels per head — take this by the sanctuary weight, twenty gerahs to the shekel — 48 and give the money to Aaron and his sons as the redemption price for those who are in excess. 49 So Moses took the redemption money from those over and above the ones redeemed by the Levites; 50 he took the money from the first-born of the Israelites, 1,365 sanctuary shekels. 51 And Moses gave the redemption money to Aaron and his sons at the LORD's bidding, as the LORD had commanded Moses.

4 1 The LORD spoke to Moses and Aaron, saying: 2 Take a [separate] census of the Kohathites among the Levites, by the clans of their ancestral house, 3 from the age of thirty years to the age of fifty, all who are subject to service, to perform tasks for the Tent of Meeting. 4 This is the responsibility of the Kohathites in the Tent of Meeting: the most sacred objects. 5 At the breaking of camp, Aaron and his sons shall go in and take down the screening curtain and cover the Ark of the Pact with it. 6 They shall lay a covering of dolphin skin over it and spread a cloth of pure blue on top; and they shall put its poles in place. 7 Over the table of display they shall spread a blue cloth; they shall place upon it the bowls, the ladles, the jars, and the libation jugs; and the regular bread shall rest upon it. 8 They shall spread over these a crimson cloth which they shall cover with a covering of dolphin skin; and they shall put the poles in place. 9 Then they shall take a blue cloth and cover the lampstand for lighting, with its lamps, its tongs, and its fire pans, as well as all the oil vessels that are used in its service. 10 They shall put it and all its furnishings into a covering of dolphin skin, which they shall then place on a carrying frame. 11 Next they shall spread a blue cloth over the altar of gold and cover it with a covering of dolphin skin; and they shall put its poles in place. 12 They shall take all the service vessels with which the service in the sanctuary is performed, put them into a blue cloth and cover them with a covering of dolphin skin, which they shall then place on a carrying frame. 13 They shall remove the ashes from the [copper] altar and spread a purple cloth over it.

137

NUMBERS 4 נשא ד במדבר

14 Upon it they shall place all the vessels that are used in its service: the fire pans, the flesh hooks, the scrapers, and the basins - all the vessels of the altar - and over it they shall spread a covering of dolphin skin; and they shall put its poles in place. 15 When Aaron and his sons have finished covering the sacred objects and all the furnishings of the sacred objects at the breaking of camp, only then shall the Kohathites come and lift them, so that they do not come in contact with the sacred objects and die. These things in the Tent of Meeting shall be the porterage of the Kohathites. 16 Responsibility shall rest with Eleazar son of Aaron the priest for the lighting oil, the aromatic incense, the regular meal offering, and the anointing oil - responsibility for the whole Tabernacle and for everything consecrated that is in it or its vessels.

17 The LORD spoke to Moses and Aaron, saying: 18 Do not let the group of Kohathite clans be cut off from the Levites. 19 Do this with them, that they may live and not die when they approach the most sacred objects: let Aaron and his sons go in and assign each of them to his duties and to his porterage. 20 But let not [the Kohathites] go inside and witness the dismantling of the sanctuary, lest they die.

21 The LORD spoke to Moses: 22 Take a census of the Gershonites also, by their ancestral house and by their clans. 23 Record them from the age of thirty years up to the age of fifty, all who are subject to service in the performance of tasks for the Tent of Meeting. 24 These are the duties of the Gershonite clans as to labor and porterage: 25 they shall carry the cloths of the Tabernacle, the Tent of Meeting with its covering, the covering of dolphin skin that is on top of it, and the screen for the entrance of the Tent of Meeting; 26 the hangings of the enclosure, the screen at the entrance of the gate of the enclosure that surrounds the Tabernacle, the cords thereof, and the altar, and all their service equipment and all their accessories; and they shall perform the service. 27 All the duties of the Gershonites, all their porterage and all their service, shall be performed on orders from Aaron and his sons; you shall make them responsible for attending to all their porterage. 28 Those are the duties of the Gershonite clans for the Tent of Meeting; they shall attend to them under the direction of Ithamar son of Aaron the priest.

29 As for the Merarites, you shall record them by the clans of their ancestral house. 30 You shall record them from the age of thirty years up to the age of fifty, all who are subject to service in the performance of the duties for the Tent of Meeting. 31 These are their porterage tasks in connection with their various duties for the Tent of Meeting: the planks, the bars, the posts, and the sockets of the Tabernacle; 32 the posts around the enclosure and their sockets, pegs, and cords - all these furnishings and their service; you shall list by name the objects that are their porterage tasks. 33 These are the duties of the Merarite clans, pertaining to their various duties in the Tent of Meeting under the direction of Ithamar son of Aaron the priest. 34 So Moses, Aaron, and the chieftains of the community recorded the Kohathites by the clans of their ancestral house, 35 from the age of thirty years up to the age of fifty, all who were subject to service for work relating to the Tent of Meeting. 36 Those recorded by their clans came to 2,750. 37 That was the enrollment of the Kohathite clans, all those who performed duties relating to the Tent of Meeting, whom Moses and Aaron recorded at the command of the LORD through Moses. 38 The Gershonites who were recorded by the clans of their ancestral house, 39 from the age of thirty years up to the age of fifty, all who were subject to service for work relating to the Tent of Meeting - 40 those recorded by the clans of their ancestral house came to 2,630. 41 That was the enrollment of the Gershonite clans, all those performing duties relating to the Tent of Meeting whom Moses and Aaron recorded at the command of the LORD. 42 The enrollment of the Merarite clans by the clans of their ancestral house, 43 from the age of thirty years up to the age of fifty, all who were subject to service for work relating to the Tent of Meeting - 44 those recorded by their clans came to 3,200. 45 That was the enrollment of the Merarite clans which Moses and Aaron recorded at the command of the LORD through Moses. 46 All the Levites whom Moses, Aaron, and the chieftains of Israel recorded by the clans of their ancestral houses, 47 from

138

Opening page of the Book of Numbers, from the "De Castro Pentateuch", illuminated manuscript on vellum, Germany, 1344, collection of The Israel Museum, Jerusalem

NUMBERS 5

the age of thirty years up to the age of fifty, all who were subject to duties of service and porterage relating to the Tent of Meeting - 48 those recorded came to 8,580. 49 Each one was given responsibility for his service and porterage at the command of the LORD through Moses, and each was recorded as the LORD had commanded Moses.

5 1 The LORD spoke to Moses, saying: 2 Instruct the Israelites to remove from camp anyone with an eruption or a discharge and anyone defiled by a corpse. 3 Remove male and female alike; put them outside the camp so that they do not defile the camp of those in whose midst I dwell. 4 The Israelites did so, putting them outside the camp; as the LORD had spoken to Moses, so the Israelites did. 5 The LORD spoke to Moses, saying: 6 Speak to the Israelites: When a man or woman commits any wrong toward a fellow man, thus breaking faith with the LORD, and that person realizes his guilt, 7 he shall confess the wrong that he has done. He shall make restitution in the principal amount and add one-fifth to it, giving it to him whom he has wronged. 8 If the man has no kinsman to whom restitution can be made, the amount repaid shall go to the LORD for the priest - in addition to the ram of expiation with which expiation is made on his behalf. 9 So, too, any gift among the sacred donations that the Israelites offer shall be the priest's. 10 And each shall retain his sacred donations: each priest shall keep what is given to him.

11 The LORD spoke to Moses, saying: 12 Speak to the Israelite people and say to them: If any man's wife has gone astray and broken faith with him 13 in that a man has had carnal relations with her unbeknown to her husband, and she keeps secret the fact that she has defiled herself without being forced, and there is no witness against her - 14 but a fit of jealousy comes over him and he is wrought up about the wife who has defiled herself; or if a fit of jealousy comes over one and he is wrought up about his wife although she has not defiled herself - 15 the man shall bring his wife to the priest. And he shall bring as an offering for her one-tenth of an ephah of barley flour. No oil shall be poured upon it and no frankincense shall be laid on it, for it is a meal offering of jealousy, a meal offering of remembrance which recalls wrongdoing. 16 The priest shall bring her forward and have her stand before the LORD. 17 The priest shall take sacral water in an earthen vessel and, taking some of the earth that is on the floor of the Tabernacle, the priest shall put it into the water. 18 After he has made the woman stand before the LORD, the priest shall bare the woman's head and place upon her hands the meal offering of remembrance, which is a meal offering of jealousy. And in the priest's hands shall be the water of bitterness that induces the spell. 19 The priest shall adjure the woman, saying to her, "If no man has lain with you, if you have not gone astray in defilement while married to your husband, be immune to harm from this water of bitterness that induces the spell. 20 But if you have gone astray while married to your husband and have defiled yourself, if a man other than your husband has had carnal relations with you" - 21 here the priest shall administer the curse of adjuration to the woman, as the priest goes on to say to the woman - "may the LORD make you a curse and an imprecation among your people, as the LORD causes your thigh to sag and your belly to distend; 22 may this water that induces the spell enter your body, causing the belly to distend and the thigh to sag." And the woman shall say, "Amen, amen!" 23 The priest shall put these curses down in writing and rub it off into the water of bitterness. 24 He is to make the woman drink the water of bitterness that induces the spell, so that the spell-inducing water may enter into her to bring on bitterness. 25 Then the priest shall take from the woman's hand the meal offering of jealousy, elevate the meal offering before the LORD, and present it on the altar. 26 The priest shall scoop out of the meal offering a token part of it and turn it into smoke on the altar. Last, he shall make the woman drink the water. 27 Once he has made her drink the water - if she has defiled herself by breaking faith with her husband, the spell-inducing water shall enter into her to bring on bitterness, so that her belly shall distend and her thigh sag; and the woman shall become a curse among her people. 28 But if the woman has not defiled herself and is pure, she shall be unharmed and able to retain seed. 29 This is the ritual in cases of jealousy, when a woman goes astray while married to her husband and defiles herself, 30 or when a fit of jealousy comes over a man

140

NUMBERS 6 נשא במדבר ו

and he is wrought up over his wife: the woman shall be made to stand before the LORD and the priest shall carry out all this ritual with her. 31 The man shall be clear of guilt; but that woman shall suffer for her guilt.

6 1 The LORD spoke to Moses, saying: 2 Speak to the Israelites and say to them: If anyone, man or woman, explicitly utters a nazirite's vow, to set himself apart for the LORD, 3 he shall abstain from wine and any other intoxicant; he shall not drink vinegar of wine or of any other intoxicant, neither shall be drink anything in which grapes have been steeped, nor eat grapes fresh or dried. 4 Throughout his term as nazirite, he may not eat anything that is obtained from the grapevine, even seeds or skin. 5 Throughout the term of his vow as nazirite, no razor shall touch his head: it shall remain consecrated until the completion of his term as nazirite of the LORD, the hair of his head being left to grow untrimmed. 6 Throughout the term that he has set apart for the LORD, he shall not go in where there is a dead person. 7 Even if his father or mother, or his brother or sister should die, he must not defile himself for them, since hair set apart for his God is upon his head; 8 throughout his term as nazirite he is consecrated to the LORD. 9 If a person dies suddenly near him, defiling his consecrated hair, he shall shave his head on the day he becomes clean; he shall shave it on the seventh day. 10 On the eighth day he shall bring two turtledoves or two pigeons to the priest, at the entrance of the Tent of Meeting. 11 The priest shall offer one as a sin offering and the other as a burnt offering, and make expiation on his behalf for the guilt that he incurred through the corpse. That same day he shall reconsecrate his head 12 and rededicate to the LORD his term as nazirite; and he shall bring a lamb in its first year as a penalty offering. The previous period shall be void, since his consecrated hair was defiled. 13 This is the ritual for the nazirite: On the day that his term is completed, he shall be brought to the entrance of the Tent of Meeting. 14 As his offering to the LORD he shall present: one male lamb in its first year, without blemish, for a burnt offering; one ewe lamb in its first year, without blemish, for a sin offering; one ram without blemish for an offering of well-being; 15 a basket of unleavened cakes of choice flour with oil mixed in, and unleavened wafers spread with oil; and the proper meal offerings and libations. 16 The priest shall present them before the LORD and offer the sin offering and the burnt offering. 17 He shall offer the ram as a sacrifice of well-being to the LORD, together with the basket of unleavened cakes; the priest shall also offer the meal offerings and the libations. 18 The nazirite shall then shave his consecrated hair, at the entrance of the Tent of Meeting, and take the locks of his consecrated hair and put them on the fire that is under the sacrifice of well-being. 19 The priest shall take the shoulder of the ram when it has been boiled, one unleavened cake from the basket, and one unleavened wafer, and place them on the hands of the nazirite after he has shaved his consecrated hair. 20 The priest shall elevate them as an elevation offering before the LORD; and this shall be a sacred donation for the priest, in addition to the breast of the elevation offering and the thigh of gift offering. After that the nazirite may drink wine. 21 Such is the obligation of a nazirite; except that he who vows an offering to the LORD of what he can afford, beyond his nazirite requirements, must so exactly according to the vow that he has made beyond his obligation as a nazirite.

22 The LORD spoke to Moses, saying: 23 Speak to Aaron and his sons: Thus shall you bless the people of Israel. Say to them:

24 The LORD bless you and protect you!
25 The LORD deal kindly and graciously with you!
26 The LORD bestow His favor upon you and grant you peace!

27 Thus they shall link My name with the people of Israel, and I will bless them.

7 1 On the day that Moses finished setting up the Tabernacle, he anointed and consecrated it and all its furnishings, as well as the altar and its utensils. When he had anointed and consecrated them, 2 the chieftains of Israel, the heads of ancestral houses, namely, the chieftains of the tribes, those who were in charge of enrollment, drew near 3 and brought their offering before the LORD: six draught carts and twelve oxen, a cart for every two chieftains and an ox for each one. When they had brought them before the Tabernacle, 4 the LORD said to Moses: 5 Accept these from them for use in the service of the Tent of Meeting, and give them to the Levites according to their respective services. 6 Moses took the carts and the oxen and gave them to the Levites. 7 Two carts and four oxen he gave to the Gershonites, as required for their service, 8 and four carts and eight oxen he gave to the Merarites, as required for their service - under the

NUMBERS 7   נשא   במדבר ז

direction of Ithamar son of Aaron the priest. 9 But to the Kohathites he did not give any; since theirs was the service of the [most] sacred objects, their porterage was by shoulder. 10 The chieftains also brought the dedication offering for the altar upon its being anointed. As the chieftains were presenting their offerings before the altar, 11 the LORD said to Moses: Let them present their offerings for the dedication of the altar, one chieftain each day.
12 The one who presented his offering on the first day was Nahshon son of Amminadab of the tribe of Judah. 13 His offering: one silver bowl weighing 130 shekels and one silver basin of 70 shekels by the sanctuary weight, both filled with choice flour with oil mixed in, for a meal offering: 14 one gold ladle of 10 shekels, filled with incense; 15 one bull of the herd, one ram, and one lamb in its first year, for a burnt offering; 16 one goat for a sin offering; 17 and for his sacrifice of well-being: two oxen, five rams, five he-goats, and five yearling lambs. That was the offering of Nahshon son of Amminadab.
18 On the second day, Nethanel son of Zuar, chieftain of Issachar, made his offering. 19 He presented as his offering: one silver bowl weighing 130 shekels and one silver basin of 70 shekels by the sanctuary weight, both filled with choice flour with oil mixed in, for a meal offering: 20 one gold ladle of 10 shekels, filled with incense; 21 one bull of the herd, one ram, and one lamb in its first year, for a burnt offering; 22 one goat for a sin offering; 23 and for his sacrifice of well-being: two oxen, five rams, five he-goats, and five yearling lambs. That was the offering of Nethanel son of Zuar.
24 On the third day, it was the chieftain of the Zebulunites, Eliab son of Helon. 25 His offering: one silver bowl weighing 130 shekels and one silver basin of 70 shekels by the sanctuary weight, both filled with choice flour with oil mixed in, for a meal offering; 26 one gold ladle of 10 shekels, filled with incense; 27 one bull of the herd, one ram, and one lamb in its first year, for a burnt offering; 28 one goat for a sin offering; 29 and for his sacrifice of well-being: two oxen, five rams, five he-goats, and five yearling lambs. That was the offering of Eliab son of Helon.
30 On the fourth day, it was the chieftain of the Reubenites, Elizur son of Shedeur. 31 His offering: one silver bowl weighing 130 shekels and one silver basin of 70 shekels by the sanctuary weight, both filled with choice flour with oil mixed in, for a meal offering; 32 one gold ladle of 10 shekels, filled with incense; 33 one bull of the herd, one ram, and one lamb in its first year, for a burnt offering; 34 one goat for a sin offering; 35 and for his sacrifice of well-being: two oxen, five rams, five he-goats, and five yearling lambs. That was the offering of Elizur son of Shedeur.
36 On the fifth day, it was the chieftain of the Simeonites, Shelumiel son of Zurishaddai. 37 His offering: one silver bowl weighing 130 shekels and one silver basin of 70 shekels by the sanctuary weight, both filled with choice flour with oil mixed in, for a meal offering: 38 one gold ladle of 10 shekels, filled with incense; 39 one bull of the herd, one ram, and one lamb in its first year, for a burnt offering; 40 one goat for a sin offering; 41 and for his sacrifice of well-being: two oxen, five rams, five he-goats, and five yearling lambs. That was the offering of Shelumiel son of Zurishaddai.
42 On the sixth day, it was the chieftain of the Gadites, Eliasaph son of Deuel. 43 His offering: one silver bowl weighing 130 shekels and one silver basin of 70 shekels by the sanctuary weight, both filled with choice flour with oil mixed in, for a meal offering; 44 one gold ladle of 10 shekels, filled with incense; 45 one bull of the herd, one ram, and one lamb in its first year, for a burnt offering; 46 one goat for a sin offering; 47 and for his sacrifice of well-being: two oxen, five rams, five he-goats, and five yearling lambs. That was

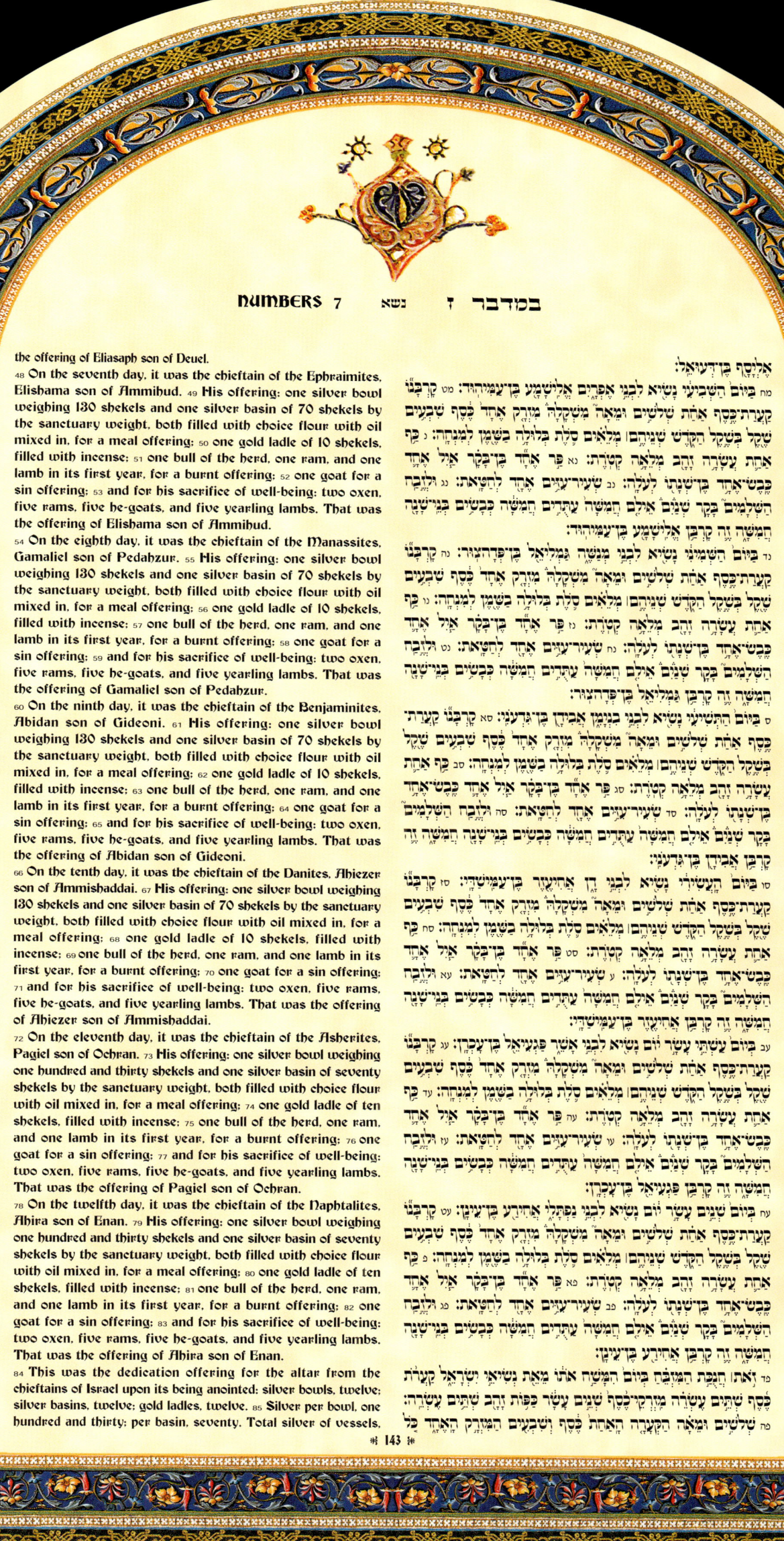

the offering of Eliasaph son of Deuel.

48 On the seventh day, it was the chieftain of the Ephraimites, Elishama son of Ammihud. 49 His offering: one silver bowl weighing 130 shekels and one silver basin of 70 shekels by the sanctuary weight, both filled with choice flour with oil mixed in, for a meal offering: 50 one gold ladle of 10 shekels, filled with incense: 51 one bull of the herd, one ram, and one lamb in its first year, for a burnt offering; 52 one goat for a sin offering; 53 and for his sacrifice of well-being: two oxen, five rams, five he-goats, and five yearling lambs. That was the offering of Elishama son of Ammihud.

54 On the eighth day, it was the chieftain of the Manassites, Gamaliel son of Pedahzur. 55 His offering: one silver bowl weighing 130 shekels and one silver basin of 70 shekels by the sanctuary weight, both filled with choice flour with oil mixed in, for a meal offering: 56 one gold ladle of 10 shekels, filled with incense: 57 one bull of the herd, one ram, and one lamb in its first year, for a burnt offering; 58 one goat for a sin offering; 59 and for his sacrifice of well-being: two oxen, five rams, five he-goats, and five yearling lambs. That was the offering of Gamaliel son of Pedahzur.

60 On the ninth day, it was the chieftain of the Benjaminites, Abidan son of Gideoni. 61 His offering: one silver bowl weighing 130 shekels and one silver basin of 70 shekels by the sanctuary weight, both filled with choice flour with oil mixed in, for a meal offering: 62 one gold ladle of 10 shekels, filled with incense: 63 one bull of the herd, one ram, and one lamb in its first year, for a burnt offering; 64 one goat for a sin offering; 65 and for his sacrifice of well-being: two oxen, five rams, five he-goats, and five yearling lambs. That was the offering of Abidan son of Gideoni.

66 On the tenth day, it was the chieftain of the Danites, Abiezer son of Ammishaddai. 67 His offering: one silver bowl weighing 130 shekels and one silver basin of 70 shekels by the sanctuary weight, both filled with choice flour with oil mixed in, for a meal offering: 68 one gold ladle of 10 shekels, filled with incense: 69 one bull of the herd, one ram, and one lamb in its first year, for a burnt offering; 70 one goat for a sin offering; 71 and for his sacrifice of well-being: two oxen, five rams, five he-goats, and five yearling lambs. That was the offering of Abiezer son of Ammishaddai.

72 On the eleventh day, it was the chieftain of the Asherites, Pagiel son of Ochran. 73 His offering: one silver bowl weighing one hundred and thirty shekels and one silver basin of seventy shekels by the sanctuary weight, both filled with choice flour with oil mixed in, for a meal offering: 74 one gold ladle of ten shekels, filled with incense: 75 one bull of the herd, one ram, and one lamb in its first year, for a burnt offering; 76 one goat for a sin offering; 77 and for his sacrifice of well-being: two oxen, five rams, five he-goats, and five yearling lambs. That was the offering of Pagiel son of Ochran.

78 On the twelfth day, it was the chieftain of the Naphtalites, Ahira son of Enan. 79 His offering: one silver bowl weighing one hundred and thirty shekels and one silver basin of seventy shekels by the sanctuary weight, both filled with choice flour with oil mixed in, for a meal offering: 80 one gold ladle of ten shekels, filled with incense: 81 one bull of the herd, one ram, and one lamb in its first year, for a burnt offering; 82 one goat for a sin offering; 83 and for his sacrifice of well-being: two oxen, five rams, five he-goats, and five yearling lambs. That was the offering of Ahira son of Enan.

84 This was the dedication offering for the altar from the chieftains of Israel upon its being anointed: silver bowls, twelve; silver basins, twelve; gold ladles, twelve. 85 Silver per bowl, one hundred and thirty; per basin, seventy. Total silver of vessels,

NUMBERS 8   במדבר ח   בהעלתך

two thousand and four hundred sanctuary shekels. 86 The twelve gold ladles filled with incense - ten sanctuary shekels per ladle - total gold of the ladles, hundred and twenty. 87 Total of herd animals for burnt offerings, twelve bulls; of rams, twelve; of yearling lambs, twelve - with their proper meal offerings; of goats for sin offerings, twelve. 88 Total of herd animals for sacrifices of well-being, twenty four bulls; of rams, sixty; of he-goats, sixty; of yearling lambs, sixty. That was the dedication offering for the altar after its anointing. 89 When Moses went into the Tent of Meeting to speak with Him, he would hear the Voice addressing him from above the cover that was on top of the Ark of the Pact between the two cherubim; thus He spoke to him.

8 1 The LORD spoke to Moses, saying: 2 Speak to Aaron and say to him, "When you mount the lamps, let the seven lamps give light at the front of the lampstand." 3 Aaron did so; he mounted the lamps at the front of the lampstand, as the LORD had commanded Moses. - 4 Now this is how the lampstand was made: it was hammered work of gold, hammered from base to petal. According to the pattern that the LORD had shown Moses, so was the lampstand made.

5 The LORD spoke to Moses, saying: 6 Take the Levites from among the Israelites and cleanse them. 7 This is what you shall do to them to cleanse them: sprinkle on them water of purification, and let them go over their whole body with a razor, and wash their clothes; thus they shall be cleansed. 8 Let them take a bull of the herd, and with it a meal offering of choice flour with oil mixed in, and you take a second bull of the herd for a sin offering. 9 You shall bring the Levites forward before the Tent of Meeting. Assemble the whole Israelite community, 10 and bring the Levites forward before the LORD. Let the Israelites lay their hands upon the Levites, 11 and let Aaron designate the Levites before the LORD as an elevation offering from the Israelites, that they may perform the service of the LORD. 12 The Levites shall now lay their hands upon the heads of the bulls; one shall be offered to the LORD as a sin offering and the other as a burnt offering, to make expiation for the Levites. 13 You shall place the Levites in attendance upon Aaron and his sons, and designate them as an elevation offering to the LORD. 14 Thus you shall set the Levites apart from the Israelites, and the Levites shall be Mine. 15 Thereafter the Levites shall be qualified for the service of the Tent of Meeting, once you have cleansed them and designated them as an elevation offering. 16 For they are formally assigned to Me from among the Israelites: I have taken them for Myself in place of all the first issue of the womb, of all the first-born of the Israelites. 17 For every first-born among the Israelites, man as well as beast, is Mine; I consecrated them to Myself at the time that I smote every first-born in the land of Egypt. 18 Now I take the Levites instead of every first-born of the Israelites, 19 and from among the Israelites I formally assign the Levites to Aaron and his sons, to perform the service for the Israelites in the Tent of Meeting and to make expiation for the Israelites, so that no plague may afflict the Israelites for coming too near the sanctuary. 20 Moses, Aaron, and the whole Israelite community did with the Levites accordingly; just as the LORD had commanded Moses in regard to the Levites, so the Israelites did with them. 21 The Levites purified themselves and washed their clothes; and Aaron designated them as an elevation offering before the LORD, and Aaron made expiation for them to cleanse them. 22 Thereafter the Levites were qualified to perform their service in the Tent of Meeting, under Aaron and his sons. As the LORD had commanded Moses in regard to the Levites, so they did with them. 23 The LORD spoke to Moses, saying: 24 This is the rule for the Levites. From twenty-five years of age up they shall participate in the work force in the service of the Tent of Meeting; 25 but at the age of fifty they shall retire from the work force and shall serve no more. 26 They may assist their brother Levites at the Tent of Meeting by standing guard, but they shall perform no labor. Thus you shall deal with the Levites in regard to their duties.

9 1 The LORD spoke to Moses in the wilderness of Sinai, on the first

A page of the Book of Numbers, from the Bible illustrated by Gustave Doré, 1832-33

NUMBERS 16

32 and the earth opened its mouth and swallowed them up with their households, all Korah's people and all their possessions. 33 They went down alive into Sheol.

NUMBERS 10

new moon of the second year following the exodus from the land of Egypt, saying: 2 Let the Israelite people offer the passover sacrifice at its set time; 3 you shall offer it on the fourteenth day of this month, at twilight, at its set time; you shall offer it in accordance with all its rules and rites. 4 Moses instructed the Israelites to offer the passover sacrifice; 5 and they offered the passover sacrifice in the first month, on the fourteenth day of the month, at twilight, in the wilderness of Sinai. Just as the LORD had commanded Moses, so the Israelites did. 6 But there were some men who were unclean by reason of a corpse and could not offer the passover sacrifice on that day. Appearing that same day before Moses and Aaron, 7 those men said to them, "Unclean though we are by reason of a corpse, why must we be debarred from presenting the LORD's offering at its set time with the rest of the Israelites?" 8 Moses said to them, "Stand by, and let me hear what instructions the LORD gives about you."

9 And the LORD spoke to Moses, saying: 10 Speak to the Israelite people, saying: When any of you or of your posterity who are defiled by a corpse or are on a long journey would offer a passover sacrifice to the LORD, 11 they shall offer it in the second month, on the fourteenth day of the month, at twilight. They shall eat it with unleavened bread and bitter herbs, 12 and they shall not leave any of it over until morning. They shall not break a bone of it. They shall offer it in strict accord with the law of the passover sacrifice. 13 But if a man who is clean and not on a journey refrains from offering the passover sacrifice, that person shall be cut off from his kin, for he did not present the LORD's offering at its set time; that man shall bear his guilt. 14 And when a stranger who resides with you would offer a passover sacrifice to the LORD, he must offer it in accordance with the rules and rites of the passover sacrifice. There shall be one law for you, whether stranger or citizen of the country. 15 On the day that the Tabernacle was set up, the cloud covered the Tabernacle, the Tent of the Pact; and in the evening it rested over the Tabernacle in the likeness of fire until morning. 16 It was always so: the cloud covered it, appearing as fire by night. 17 And whenever the cloud lifted from the Tent, the Israelites would set out accordingly; and at the spot where the cloud settled, there the Israelites would make camp. 18 At a command of the LORD the Israelites broke camp, and at a command of the LORD they made camp: they remained encamped as long as the cloud stayed over the Tabernacle. 19 When the cloud lingered over the Tabernacle many days, the Israelites observed the LORD's mandate and did not journey on. 20 At such times as the cloud rested over the Tabernacle for but a few days, they remained encamped at a command of the LORD, and broke camp at a command of the LORD. 21 And at such times as the cloud stayed from evening until morning, they broke camp as soon as the cloud lifted in the morning. Day or night, whenever the cloud lifted, they would break camp. 22 Whether it was two days or a month or a year - however long the cloud lingered over the Tabernacle - the Israelites remained encamped and did not set out; only when it lifted did they break camp. 23 On a sign from the LORD they made camp and on a sign from the LORD they broke camp; they observed the LORD's mandate at the LORD's bidding through Moses.

10 1 The LORD spoke to Moses, saying: 2 Have two silver trumpets made; make them of hammered work. They shall serve you to summon the community and to set the divisions in motion. 3 When both are blown in long blasts, the whole community shall assemble before you at the entrance of the Tent of Meeting; 4 and if only one is blown, the chieftains, heads of Israel's contingents, shall assemble before you. 5 But when you sound short blasts, the divisions encamped on the east shall move forward; 6 and when you sound short blasts a second time, those encamped on the south shall move forward. Thus short blasts shall be blown for setting them in motion, 7 while to convoke the congregation you shall blow long blasts, not short ones. 8 The trumpets shall be blown by Aaron's sons, the priests; they shall be for you an institution for all time throughout the ages. 9 When you are at war in your land against an aggressor who attacks you, you shall sound short blasts on the trumpets, that you may be remembered before the LORD your God and be delivered from your enemies. 10 And on your joyous occasions - your fixed festivals and new moon days - you shall sound the trumpets over your burnt offerings and your sacrifices of well-being. They shall be a reminder of you before your God: I, the LORD, am your God.

11 In the second year, on the twentieth day of the second month, the cloud

NUMBERS 11

lifted from the Tabernacle of the Pact ¹²and the Israelites set out on their journeys from the wilderness of Sinai. The cloud came to rest in the wilderness of Paran. ¹³When the march was to begin, at the LORD's command through Moses, ¹⁴the first standard to set out, troop by troop, was the division of Judah. In command of its troops was Nahshon son of Amminadab; ¹⁵in command of the tribal troop of Issachar, Nethanel son of Zuar; ¹⁶and in command of the tribal troop of Zebulun, Eliab son of Helon. ¹⁷Then the Tabernacle would be taken apart; and the Gershonites and the Merarites, who carried the Tabernacle, would set out. ¹⁸The next standard to set out, troop by troop, was the division of Reuben. In command of its troops was Elizur son of Shedeur; ¹⁹in command of the tribal troop of Simeon, Shelumiel son of Zurishaddai; ²⁰and in command of the tribal troop of Gad, Eliasaph son of Deuel. ²¹Then the Kohathites, who carried the sacred objects, would set out; and by the time they arrived, the Tabernacle would be set up again. ²²The next standard to set out, troop by troop, was the division of Ephraim. In command of its troop was Elishama son of Ammihud; ²³in command of the tribal troop of Manasseh, Gamaliel son of Pedahzur; ²⁴and in command of the tribal troop of Benjamin, Abidan son of Gideoni. ²⁵Then, as the rear guard of all the divisions, the standard of the division of Dan would set out, troop by troop. In command of its troop was Ahiezer son of Ammishaddai; ²⁶in command of the tribal troop of Asher, Pagiel son of Ochran; ²⁷and in command of the tribal troop of Naphtali, Ahira son of Enan. ²⁸Such was the order of march of the Israelites, as they marched troop by troop.

²⁹Moses said to Hobab son of Reuel the Midianite, Moses' father-in-law, "We are setting out for the place of which the LORD has said, 'I will give it to you.' Come with us and we will be generous with you; for the LORD has promised to be generous to Israel." ³⁰"I will not go," he replied to him, "but will return to my native land." ³¹He said, "Please do not leave us, inasmuch as you know where we should camp in the wilderness and can be our guide. ³²So if you come with us, we will extend to you the same bounty that the LORD grants us."

³³They marched from the mountain of the LORD a distance of three days. The Ark of the Covenant of the LORD traveled in front of them on that three days' journey to seek out a resting place for them; ³⁴and the LORD's cloud kept above them by day, as they moved on from camp.

³⁵When the Ark was to set out, Moses would say: Advance, O LORD! May Your enemies be scattered, And may Your foes flee before You! ³⁶And when it halted, he would say: Return, O LORD, You who are Israel's myriads of thousands!

11 ¹The people took to complaining bitterly before the LORD. The LORD heard and was incensed: a fire of the LORD broke out against them, ravaging the outskirts of the camp. ²The people cried out to Moses. Moses prayed to the LORD, and the fire died down. ³That place was named Taberah, because a fire of the LORD had broken out against them.

⁴The riffraff in their midst felt a gluttonous craving; and then the Israelites wept and said, "If only we had meat to eat! ⁵We remember the fish that we used to eat free in Egypt, the cucumbers, the melons, the leeks, the onions, and the garlic. ⁶Now our gullets are shriveled. There is nothing at all! Nothing but this manna to look to!" ⁷Now the manna was like coriander seed, and in color it was like bdellium. ⁸The people would go about and gather it, grind it between millstones or pound it in a mortar, boil it in a pot, and make it into cakes. It tasted like rich cream. ⁹When the dew fell on the camp at night, the manna would fall upon it. ¹⁰Moses heard the people weeping, every clan apart, each person at the entrance of his tent. The LORD was very angry, and Moses was distressed. ¹¹And Moses said to the LORD, "Why have You dealt ill with Your servant, and why have I not enjoyed Your favor, that You have laid the burden of all this people upon me? ¹²Did I conceive all this people, did I bear them, that You should say to me, 'Carry them in your bosom as a nurse carries an infant,' to the land that You have promised on oath to their fathers? ¹³Where am I to get meat to give to all this people, when they whine before me and say, 'Give us meat to eat!' ¹⁴I cannot carry all this people by myself, for it is too much for me. ¹⁵If You would deal thus with me, kill me rather, I beg You, and let me see no more of

NUMBERS 12   במדבר יב בהעלתך

my wretchedness!" 16 Then the LORD said to Moses, "Gather for Me seventy of Israel's elders of whom you have experience as elders and officers of the people, and bring them to the Tent of Meeting and let them take their place there with you. 17 I will come down and speak with you there, and I will draw upon the spirit that is on you and put it upon them: they shall share the burden of the people with you, and you shall not bear it alone. 18 And say to the people: Purify yourselves for tomorrow and you shall eat meat, for you have kept whining before the LORD and saying, 'If only we had meat to eat! Indeed, we were better off in Egypt!' The LORD will give you meat and you shall eat. 19 You shall eat not one day, not two, not even five days or ten or twenty, 20 but a whole month, until it comes out of your nostrils and becomes loathsome to you. For you have rejected the LORD who is among you, by whining before Him and saying, 'Oh, why did we ever leave Egypt!'" 21 But Moses said, "The people who are with me number six hundred thousand men; yet You say, 'I will give them enough meat to eat for a whole month.' 22 Could enough flocks and herds be slaughtered to suffice them? Or could all the fish of the sea be gathered for them to suffice them?" 23 And the LORD answered Moses, "Is there a limit to the LORD's power? You shall soon see whether what I have said happens to you or not!" 24 Moses went out and reported the words of the LORD to the people. He gathered seventy of the people's elders and stationed them around the Tent. 25 Then the LORD came down in a cloud and spoke to him: He drew upon the spirit that was on him and put it upon the seventy elders. And when the spirit rested upon them, they spoke in ecstasy, but did not continue. 26 Two men, one named Eldad and the other Medad, had remained in camp; yet the spirit rested upon them - they were among those recorded, but they had not gone out to the Tent - and they spoke in ecstasy in the camp. 27 A youth ran out and told Moses, saying, "Eldad and Medad are acting the prophet in the camp!" 28 And Joshua son of Nun, Moses' attendant from his youth, spoke up and said, "My lord Moses, restrain them!" 29 But Moses said to him, "Are you wrought up on my account? Would that all the LORD's people were prophets, that the LORD put His spirit upon them!" 30 Moses then reentered the camp together with the elders of Israel. 31 A wind from the LORD started up, swept quail from the sea and strewed them over the camp, about a day's journey on this side and about a day's journey on that side, all around the camp, and some two cubits deep on the ground. 32 The people set to gathering quail all that day and night and all the next day - even he who gathered least had ten homers - and they spread them out all around the camp. 33 The meat was still between their teeth, nor yet chewed, when the anger of the LORD blazed forth against the people and the LORD struck the people with a very severe plague. 34 That place was named Kibroth-hattaavah, because the people who had the craving were buried there. 35 Then the people set out from Kibroth-hattaavah for Hazeroth.

12 1 When they were in Hazeroth, Miriam and Aaron spoke against Moses because of the Cushite woman he had married: "He married a Cushite woman!" 2 They said, "Has the LORD spoken only through Moses? Has He not spoken through us as well?" The LORD heard it. 3 Now Moses was a very humble man, more so than any other man on earth. 4 Suddenly the LORD called to Moses, Aaron, and Miriam, "Come out, you three, to the Tent of Meeting." So the three of them went out. 5 The LORD came down in a pillar of cloud, stopped at the entrance of the Tent, and called out, "Aaron and Miriam!" The two of them came forward; 6 and He said, "Hear these My words: When a prophet of the LORD arises among you, I make Myself known to him in a vision, I speak with him in a dream. 7 Not so with My servant Moses; he is trusted throughout My household. 8 With him I speak mouth to mouth, plainly and not in riddles, and he beholds the likeness of the LORD. How then did you not shrink from speaking against My servant Moses!" 9 Still incensed with them, the LORD departed. 10 As the cloud withdrew from the Tent, there was Miriam stricken with snow-white scales! When Aaron turned toward Miriam, he saw that she was stricken with scales. 11 And Aaron said to Moses, "O my lord, account not to us the sin which we committed in our folly. 12 Let her not be

148

NUMBERS 13

as one dead, who emerges from his mother's womb with half his flesh eaten away." 13 So Moses cried out to the LORD, saying, "O God, pray heal her!"

14 But the LORD said to Moses, "If her father spat in her face, would she not bear her shame for seven days? Let her be shut out of camp for seven days, and then let her be readmitted." 15 So Miriam was shut out of camp seven days; and the people did not march on until Miriam was readmitted. 16 After that the people set out from Hazeroth and encamped in the wilderness of Paran.

13 The LORD spoke to Moses, saying, 2 "Send men to scout the land of Canaan, which I am giving to the Israelite people; send one man from each of their ancestral tribes, each one a chieftain among them." 3 So Moses, by the LORD's command, sent them out from the wilderness of Paran, all the men being leaders of the Israelites. 4 And these were their names: From the tribe of Reuben, Shammua son of Zaccur. 5 From the tribe of Simeon, Shaphat son of Hori. 6 From the tribe of Judah, Caleb son of Jephunneh. 7 From the tribe of Issachar, Igal son of Joseph. 8 From the tribe of Ephraim, Hosea son of Nun. 9 From the tribe of Benjamin, Palti son of Raphu. 10 From the tribe of Zebulun, Gaddiel son of Sodi. 11 From the tribe of Joseph, namely, the tribe of Manasseh, Gaddi son of Susi. 12 From the tribe of Dan, Ammiel son of Gemalli. 13 From the tribe of Asher, Sethur son of Michael. 14 From the tribe of Naphtali, Nahbi son of Vophsi. 15 From the tribe of Gad, Geuel son of Machi. 16 These were the names of the men whom Moses sent to scout the land; but Moses changed the name of Hosea son of Nun to Joshua. 17 When Moses sent them to scout the land of Canaan, he said to them, "Go up there into the Negeb and on into the hill country, 18 and see what kind of country it is. Are the people who dwell in it strong or weak, few or many? 19 Is the country in which they dwell good or bad? Are the towns they live in open or fortified? 20 Is the soil rich or poor? Is it wooded or not? And take pains to bring back some of the fruit of the land." — Now it happened to be the season of the first ripe grapes. 21 They went up and scouted the land, from the wilderness of Zin to Rehob, at Lebo-hamath. 22 They went up into the Negeb and came to Hebron, where lived Ahiman, Sheshai, and Talmai, the Anakites. – Now Hebron was founded seven years before Zoan of Egypt. – 23 They reached the wadi Eshcol, and there they cut down a branch with a single cluster of grapes – it had to be borne on a carrying frame by two of them – and some pomegranates and figs. 24 That place was named the wadi Eshcol because of the cluster that the Israelites cut down there. 25 At the end of forty days they returned from scouting the land. 26 They went straight to Moses and Aaron and the whole Israelite community at Kadesh in the wilderness of Paran, and they made their report to them and to the whole community, and they showed them the fruit of the land. 27 This is what they told him: "We came to the land you sent us to; it does indeed flow with milk and honey, and this is its fruit. 28 However, the people who inhabit the country are powerful, and the cities are fortified and very large; moreover, we saw the Anakites there. 29 Amalekites dwell in the Negeb region; Hittites, Jebusites, and Amorites inhabit the hill country; and Canaanites dwell by the Sea and along the Jordan." 30 Caleb hushed the people before Moses and said, "Let us by all means go up, and we shall gain possession of it, for we shall surely overcome it." 31 But the men who had gone up with him said, "We cannot attack that people, for it is stronger than we." 32 Thus they spread calumnies among the Israelites about the land they had scouted, saying, "The country that we traversed and scouted is one that devours its settlers. All the people that we saw in it are men of great size; 33 we saw the Nephilim there – the Anakites are part of the Nephilim – and we looked like grasshoppers to ourselves, and so we must have looked to them." **14** 1 The whole community broke into loud cries, and the people wept that night. 2 All the Israelites railed against Moses and Aaron. "If only we had died in the land of Egypt," the whole community shouted at them, "or if only we might die in this wilderness! 3 Why is the LORD taking us to that land to fall by the sword?

149

NUMBERS 14   שלח   במדבר יד

Our wives and children will be carried off! It would be better for us to go back to Egypt!" 4 And they said to one another, "Let us head back for Egypt." 5 Then Moses and Aaron fell on their faces before all the assembled congregation of the Israelites. 6 And Joshua son of Nun and Caleb son of Jephunneh, of those who had scouted the land, rent their clothes 7 and exhorted the whole Israelite community: "The land that we traversed and scouted is an exceedingly good land. 8 If the LORD is pleased with us, He will bring us into that land, a land that flows with milk and honey, and give it to us; 9 only you must not rebel against the LORD. Have no fear then of the people of the country, for they are our prey; their protection has departed from them, but the LORD is with us. Have no fear of them!" 10 As the whole community threatened to pelt them with stones, the Presence of the LORD appeared in the Tent of Meeting to all the Israelites.

11 And the LORD said to Moses, "How long will this people spurn Me, and how long will they have no faith in Me despite all the signs that I have performed in their midst? 12 I will strike them with pestilence and disown them, and I will make of you a nation far more numerous than they!" 13 But Moses said to the LORD. "When the Egyptians, from whose midst You brought up this people in Your might, hear the news, 14 they will tell it to the inhabitants of that land. Now they have heard that You, O LORD, are in the midst of this people; that You, O LORD, appear in plain sight when Your cloud rests over them and when You go before them in a pillar of cloud by day and in a pillar of fire by night. 15 If then You slay this people to a man, the nations who have heard Your fame will say, 16 'It must be because the LORD was powerless to bring that people into the land He had promised them on oath that He slaughtered them in the wilderness.' 17 Therefore, I pray, let my Lord's forbearance be great, as You have declared, saying, 18 'The LORD! slow to anger and abounding in kindness; forgiving iniquity and transgression; yet not remitting all punishment, but visiting the iniquity of fathers upon children, upon the third and fourth generations.' 19 Pardon, I pray, the iniquity of this people according to Your great kindness, as You have forgiven this people ever since Egypt." 20 And the LORD said, "I pardon, as you have asked. 21 Nevertheless, as I live and as the LORD's Presence fills the whole world, 22 none of the men who have seen My Presence and the signs that I have performed in Egypt and in the wilderness, and who have tried Me these many times and have disobeyed Me, 23 shall see the land that I promised on oath to their fathers; none of those who spurn Me shall see it. 24 But My servant Caleb, because he was imbued with a different spirit and remained loyal to Me - him will I bring into the land that he entered, and his offspring shall hold it as a possession. 25 Now the Amalekites and the Canaanites occupy the valleys. Start out, then, tomorrow and march into the wilderness by way of the Sea of Reeds."

26 The LORD spoke further to Moses and Aaron, 27 "How much longer shall that wicked community keep muttering against Me? Very well, I have heeded the incessant muttering of the Israelites against Me. 28 Say to them: 'As I live,' says the LORD, 'I will do to you just as you have urged Me. 29 In this very wilderness shall your carcasses drop. Of all of you who were recorded in your various lists from the age of twenty years up, you who have muttered against Me, 30 not one shall enter the land in which I swore to settle you - save Caleb son of Jephunneh and Joshua son of Nun. 31 Your children, who, you said, would be carried off - these will I allow to enter; they shall know the land that you have rejected. 32 But your carcasses shall drop in this wilderness, 33 while your children roam the wilderness for forty years, suffering for your faithlessness, until the last of your carcasses is down in the wilderness. 34 You shall bear your punishment for forty years, corresponding to the number of days - forty days - that you scouted the land: a year for each day. Thus you shall know what it means to thwart Me. 35 I the LORD have spoken: Thus will I do to all that wicked band that has banded together against Me: in this very wilderness they shall die to the last man." 36 As for the men whom Moses sent to scout the land, those who came back and caused the whole community to mutter against him by spreading calumnies about the land - 37 those who spread such calumnies about the land died of plague, by the will of the LORD.

מנורת שבעת הקנים, איור ל"תנ״ך סרוורה" מעשה ידי יוסף צרפתי, ספרד, 1299, אוסף הספרייה הלאומית הפורטוגלית, ליסבון
Seven-branched candelabrum (*menorah*), illustration to the "Cervera Bible" by Joseph Assarfati, Spain, 1299, collection of Biblioteca Nacional, Lisbon

NUMBERS 15 במדבר טו שלח

38 Of those men who had gone to scout the land, only Joshua son of Nun and Caleb son of Jephunneh survived. 39 When Moses repeated these words to all the Israelites, the people were overcome by grief. 40 Early next morning they set out toward the crest of the hill country, saying, "We are prepared to go up to the place that the LORD has spoken of, for we were wrong." 41 But Moses said, "Why do you transgress the LORD's command? This will not succeed. 42 Do not go up, lest you be routed by your enemies, for the LORD is not in your midst. 43 For the Amalekites and the Canaanites will be there to face you, and you will fall by the sword, inasmuch as you have turned from following the LORD and the LORD will not be with you." 44 Yet defiantly they marched toward the crest of the hill country, though neither the LORD's Ark of the Covenant nor Moses stirred from the camp. 45 And the Amalekites and the Canaanites who dwelt in that hill country came down and dealt them a shattering blow at Hormah.

15 1 The LORD spoke to Moses, saying: 2 Speak to the Israelite people and say to them: When you enter the land that I am giving you to settle in, 3 and would present an offering by fire to the LORD from the herd or from the flock, be it burnt offering or sacrifice, in fulfillment of a vow explicitly uttered, or as a freewill offering, or at your fixed occasions, producing an odor pleasing to the LORD; 4 The person who presents the offering to the LORD shall bring as a meal offering: a tenth of a measure of choice flour with a quarter of a hin of oil mixed in. 5 You shall also offer, with the burnt offering or the sacrifice, a quarter of a hin of wine as a libation for each sheep. 6 In the case of a ram, you shall present as a meal offering: two-tenths of a measure of choice flour with a third of a hin of oil mixed in; 7 and a third of a hin of wine as a libation - as an offering of pleasing odor to the LORD. 8 And if it is an animal from the herd that you offer to the LORD as a burnt offering or as a sacrifice, in fulfillment of a vow explicitly uttered or as an offering of well-being, 9 there shall be offered a meal offering along with the animal: three-tenths of a measure of choice flour with half a hin of oil mixed in: 10 and as libation you shall offer half a hin of wine - these being offerings by fire of pleasing odor to the LORD. 11 Thus shall be done with each ox, with each ram, and with any sheep or goat. 12 as many as you offer; you shall do thus with each one, as many as there are. 13 Every citizen, when presenting an offering by fire of pleasing odor to the LORD, shall do so with them. 14 And when, throughout the ages, a stranger who has taken up residence with you, or one who lives among you, would present an offering by fire of pleasing odor to the LORD - as you do, so shall it be done by 15 the rest of the congregation. There shall be one law for you and for the resident stranger; it shall be a law for all time throughout the ages. You and the stranger shall be alike before the LORD. 16 the same ritual and the same rule shall apply to you and to the stranger who resides among you.

17 The LORD spoke to Moses, saying: 18 Speak to the Israelite people and say to them: When you enter the land to which I am taking you 19 and you eat of the bread of the land, you shall set some aside as a gift to the LORD: 20 as the first yield of your baking, you shall set aside a loaf as a gift; you shall set it aside as a gift like the gift from the threshing floor. 21 You shall make a gift to the LORD from the first yield of your baking, throughout the ages. 22 If you unwittingly fail to observe any of the commandments that the LORD has declared to Moses - 23 anything that the LORD has enjoined upon you through Moses - from the day that the LORD gave the commandment and on through the ages. 24 If this was done unwittingly, through the inadvertence of the community, the whole community shall present one bull of the herd as a burnt offering of pleasing odor to the LORD, with its proper meal offering and libation, and one he-goat as a sin offering. 25 The priest shall make expiation for the whole Israelite community and they shall be forgiven; for it was an error, and for their error they have brought their offering, an offering by fire to the LORD and their sin offering before the LORD. 26 The whole Israelite community and the stranger residing among them shall be forgiven, for it happened to the entire people through error. 27 In case it is an individual who has sinned unwittingly, he shall offer a she-goat in its first year as a sin offering. 28 The priest shall make expiation before the LORD on behalf of the person who erred, for he sinned unwittingly, making such expiation for him that he may be forgiven. 29 For the citizen among the Israelites and for the stranger who resides among them - you shall have one ritual for anyone who acts in error. 30 But the person, be he citizen or stranger, who acts defiantly reviles the LORD; that person shall be cut off from among his people. 31 Because he has spurned

NUMBERS 16 במדבר טז קרח

the word of the LORD and violated His commandment, that person shall be cut off - he bears his guilt. 32 Once, when the Israelites were in the wilderness, they came upon a man gathering wood on the sabbath day. 33 Those who found him as he was gathering wood brought him before Moses, Aaron, and the whole community. 34 He was placed in custody, for it had not been specified what should be done to him. 35 Then the LORD said to Moses, "The man shall be put to death: the whole community shall pelt him with stones outside the camp." 36 So the whole community took him outside the camp and stoned him to death - as the LORD had commanded Moses. 37 The LORD said to Moses as follows: 38 Speak to the Israelite people and instruct them to make for themselves fringes on the corners of their garments throughout the ages; let them attach a cord of blue to the fringe at each corner. 39 That shall be your fringe; look at it and recall all the commandments of the LORD and observe them, so that you do not follow your heart and eyes in your lustful urge. 40 Thus you shall be reminded to observe all My commandments and to be holy to your God. 41 I the LORD am your God, who brought you out of the land of Egypt to be your God: I, the LORD your God.

16 Now Korah, son of Izhar son of Kohath son of Levi, betook himself, along with Dathan and Abiram sons of Eliab, and On son of Peleth - descendants of Reuben - 2 to rise up against Moses, together with two hundred and fifty Israelites, chieftains of the community, chosen in the assembly, men of repute. 3 They combined against Moses and Aaron and said to them, "You have gone too far! For all the community are holy, all of them, and the LORD is in their midst. Why then do you raise yourselves above the LORD's congregation?" 4 When Moses heard this, he fell on his face. 5 Then he spoke to Korah and all his company, saying, "Come morning, the LORD will make known who is His and who is holy, and will grant him access to Himself: He will grant access to the one He has chosen. 6 Do this: You, Korah and all your band, take fire pans, 7 and tomorrow put fire in them and lay incense on them before the LORD. Then the man whom the LORD chooses, he shall be the holy one. You have gone too far, sons of Levi!" 8 Moses said further to Korah, "Hear me, sons of Levi. 9 Is it not enough for you that the God of Israel has set you apart from the community of Israel and given you access to Him, to perform the duties of the LORD's Tabernacle and to minister to the community and serve them? 10 Now that He has advanced you and all your fellow Levites with you, do you seek the priesthood too? 11 Truly, it is against the LORD that you and all your company have banded together. For who is Aaron that you should rail against him?" 12 Moses sent for Dathan and Abiram, sons of Eliab; but they said, "We will not come! 13 Is it not enough that you brought us from a land flowing with milk and honey to have us die in the wilderness, that you would also lord it over us? 14 Even if you had brought us to a land flowing with milk and honey, and given us possession of fields and vineyards, should you gouge out those men's eyes? We will not come!" 15 Moses was much aggrieved and he said to the LORD, "Pay no regard to their oblation. I have not taken the ass of any one of them, nor have I wronged any one of them." 16 And Moses said to Korah, "Tomorrow, you and all your company appear before the LORD, you and they and Aaron. 17 Each of you take his fire pan and lay incense on it, and each of you bring his fire pan before the LORD, two hundred and fifty fire pans; you and Aaron also [bring] your fire pans." 18 Each of them took his fire pan, put fire in it, laid incense on it, and took his place at the entrance of the Tent of Meeting, as did Moses and Aaron. 19 Korah gathered the whole community against them at the entrance of the Tent of Meeting. Then the Presence of the LORD appeared to the whole community, 20 and the LORD spoke to Moses and Aaron, saying, 21 "Stand back from this community that I may annihilate them in an instant!" 22 But they fell on their faces and said, "O God, Source of the breath of all flesh! When one man sins, will You be wrathful with the whole community?" 23 The LORD spoke to Moses, saying, 24 "Speak to the community and say:

וְאֶת־מִצְוֺתוֹ הֵפַר הִכָּרֵת ׀ תִּכָּרֵת הַנֶּפֶשׁ הַהִוא עֲוֺנָה בָהּ׃
לב וַיִּהְיוּ בְנֵי־יִשְׂרָאֵל בַּמִּדְבָּר וַיִּמְצְאוּ אִישׁ מְקֹשֵׁשׁ עֵצִים בְּיוֹם הַשַּׁבָּת׃
לג וַיַּקְרִיבוּ אֹתוֹ הַמֹּצְאִים אֹתוֹ מְקֹשֵׁשׁ עֵצִים אֶל־מֹשֶׁה וְאֶל־אַהֲרֹן וְאֶל כָּל־הָעֵדָה׃
לד וַיַּנִּיחוּ אֹתוֹ בַּמִּשְׁמָר כִּי לֹא פֹרַשׁ מַה־יֵּעָשֶׂה לוֹ׃
לה וַיֹּאמֶר יְהוָה אֶל־מֹשֶׁה מוֹת יוּמַת הָאִישׁ רָגוֹם אֹתוֹ בָאֲבָנִים כָּל־הָעֵדָה מִחוּץ לַמַּחֲנֶה׃
לו וַיֹּצִיאוּ אֹתוֹ כָּל־הָעֵדָה אֶל־מִחוּץ לַמַּחֲנֶה וַיִּרְגְּמוּ אֹתוֹ בָּאֲבָנִים וַיָּמֹת כַּאֲשֶׁר צִוָּה יְהוָה אֶת־מֹשֶׁה׃
לז וַיֹּאמֶר יְהוָה אֶל־מֹשֶׁה לֵּאמֹר׃
לח דַּבֵּר אֶל־בְּנֵי יִשְׂרָאֵל וְאָמַרְתָּ אֲלֵהֶם וְעָשׂוּ לָהֶם צִיצִת עַל־כַּנְפֵי בִגְדֵיהֶם לְדֹרֹתָם וְנָתְנוּ עַל־צִיצִת הַכָּנָף פְּתִיל תְּכֵלֶת׃
לט וְהָיָה לָכֶם לְצִיצִת וּרְאִיתֶם אֹתוֹ וּזְכַרְתֶּם אֶת־כָּל־מִצְוֺת יְהוָה וַעֲשִׂיתֶם אֹתָם וְלֹא תָתוּרוּ אַחֲרֵי לְבַבְכֶם וְאַחֲרֵי עֵינֵיכֶם אֲשֶׁר־אַתֶּם זֹנִים אַחֲרֵיהֶם׃
מ לְמַעַן תִּזְכְּרוּ וַעֲשִׂיתֶם אֶת־כָּל־מִצְוֺתָי וִהְיִיתֶם קְדֹשִׁים לֵאלֹהֵיכֶם׃
מא אֲנִי יְהוָה אֱלֹהֵיכֶם אֲשֶׁר הוֹצֵאתִי אֶתְכֶם מֵאֶרֶץ מִצְרַיִם לִהְיוֹת לָכֶם לֵאלֹהִים אֲנִי יְהוָה אֱלֹהֵיכֶם׃

א וַיִּקַּח קֹרַח בֶּן־יִצְהָר בֶּן־קְהָת בֶּן־לֵוִי וְדָתָן וַאֲבִירָם בְּנֵי אֱלִיאָב וְאוֹן בֶּן־פֶּלֶת בְּנֵי רְאוּבֵן׃
ב וַיָּקֻמוּ לִפְנֵי מֹשֶׁה וַאֲנָשִׁים מִבְּנֵי־יִשְׂרָאֵל חֲמִשִּׁים וּמָאתָיִם נְשִׂיאֵי עֵדָה קְרִאֵי מוֹעֵד אַנְשֵׁי־שֵׁם׃
ג וַיִּקָּהֲלוּ עַל־מֹשֶׁה וְעַל־אַהֲרֹן וַיֹּאמְרוּ אֲלֵהֶם רַב־לָכֶם כִּי כָל־הָעֵדָה כֻּלָּם קְדֹשִׁים וּבְתוֹכָם יְהוָה וּמַדּוּעַ תִּתְנַשְּׂאוּ עַל־קְהַל יְהוָה׃
ד וַיִּשְׁמַע מֹשֶׁה וַיִּפֹּל עַל־פָּנָיו׃
ה וַיְדַבֵּר אֶל־קֹרַח וְאֶל־כָּל־עֲדָתוֹ לֵאמֹר בֹּקֶר וְיֹדַע יְהוָה אֶת־אֲשֶׁר־לוֹ וְאֶת־הַקָּדוֹשׁ וְהִקְרִיב אֵלָיו וְאֵת אֲשֶׁר יִבְחַר־בּוֹ יַקְרִיב אֵלָיו׃
ו זֹאת עֲשׂוּ קְחוּ־לָכֶם מַחְתּוֹת קֹרַח וְכָל־עֲדָתוֹ׃
ז וּתְנוּ בָהֵן ׀ אֵשׁ וְשִׂימוּ עֲלֵיהֶן קְטֹרֶת לִפְנֵי יְהוָה מָחָר וְהָיָה הָאִישׁ אֲשֶׁר־יִבְחַר יְהוָה הוּא הַקָּדוֹשׁ רַב־לָכֶם בְּנֵי לֵוִי׃
ח וַיֹּאמֶר מֹשֶׁה אֶל־קֹרַח שִׁמְעוּ־נָא בְּנֵי לֵוִי׃
ט הַמְעַט מִכֶּם כִּי־הִבְדִּיל אֱלֹהֵי יִשְׂרָאֵל אֶתְכֶם מֵעֲדַת יִשְׂרָאֵל לְהַקְרִיב אֶתְכֶם אֵלָיו לַעֲבֹד אֶת־עֲבֹדַת מִשְׁכַּן יְהוָה וְלַעֲמֹד לִפְנֵי הָעֵדָה לְשָׁרְתָם׃
י וַיַּקְרֵב אֹתְךָ וְאֶת־כָּל־אַחֶיךָ בְנֵי־לֵוִי אִתָּךְ וּבִקַּשְׁתֶּם גַּם־כְּהֻנָּה׃
יא לָכֵן אַתָּה וְכָל־עֲדָתְךָ הַנֹּעָדִים עַל־יְהוָה וְאַהֲרֹן מַה־הוּא כִּי תלונו (תַלִּינוּ) עָלָיו׃
יב וַיִּשְׁלַח מֹשֶׁה לִקְרֹא לְדָתָן וְלַאֲבִירָם בְּנֵי אֱלִיאָב וַיֹּאמְרוּ לֹא נַעֲלֶה׃
יג הַמְעַט כִּי הֶעֱלִיתָנוּ מֵאֶרֶץ זָבַת חָלָב וּדְבַשׁ לַהֲמִיתֵנוּ בַּמִּדְבָּר כִּי־תִשְׂתָּרֵר עָלֵינוּ גַּם־הִשְׂתָּרֵר׃
יד אַף לֹא אֶל־אֶרֶץ זָבַת חָלָב וּדְבַשׁ הֲבִיאֹתָנוּ וַתִּתֶּן־לָנוּ נַחֲלַת שָׂדֶה וָכָרֶם הַעֵינֵי הָאֲנָשִׁים הָהֵם תְּנַקֵּר לֹא נַעֲלֶה׃
טו וַיִּחַר לְמֹשֶׁה מְאֹד וַיֹּאמֶר אֶל־יְהוָה אַל־תֵּפֶן אֶל־מִנְחָתָם לֹא חֲמוֹר אֶחָד מֵהֶם נָשָׂאתִי וְלֹא הֲרֵעֹתִי אֶת־אַחַד מֵהֶם׃
טז וַיֹּאמֶר מֹשֶׁה אֶל־קֹרַח אַתָּה וְכָל־עֲדָתְךָ הֱיוּ לִפְנֵי יְהוָה אַתָּה וָהֵם וְאַהֲרֹן מָחָר׃
יז וּקְחוּ ׀ אִישׁ מַחְתָּתוֹ וּנְתַתֶּם עֲלֵיהֶם קְטֹרֶת וְהִקְרַבְתֶּם לִפְנֵי יְהוָה אִישׁ מַחְתָּתוֹ חֲמִשִּׁים וּמָאתַיִם מַחְתֹּת וְאַתָּה וְאַהֲרֹן אִישׁ מַחְתָּתוֹ׃
יח וַיִּקְחוּ אִישׁ מַחְתָּתוֹ וַיִּתְּנוּ עֲלֵיהֶם אֵשׁ וַיָּשִׂימוּ עֲלֵיהֶם קְטֹרֶת וַיַּעַמְדוּ פֶּתַח אֹהֶל מוֹעֵד וּמֹשֶׁה וְאַהֲרֹן׃
יט וַיַּקְהֵל עֲלֵיהֶם קֹרַח אֶת־כָּל־הָעֵדָה אֶל־פֶּתַח אֹהֶל מוֹעֵד וַיֵּרָא כְבוֹד־יְהוָה אֶל־כָּל־הָעֵדָה׃
כ וַיְדַבֵּר יְהוָה אֶל־מֹשֶׁה וְאֶל־אַהֲרֹן לֵאמֹר׃
כא הִבָּדְלוּ מִתּוֹךְ הָעֵדָה הַזֹּאת וַאֲכַלֶּה אֹתָם כְּרָגַע׃
כב וַיִּפְּלוּ עַל־פְּנֵיהֶם וַיֹּאמְרוּ אֵל אֱלֹהֵי הָרוּחֹת לְכָל־בָּשָׂר הָאִישׁ אֶחָד יֶחֱטָא וְעַל כָּל־הָעֵדָה תִּקְצֹף׃
כג וַיְדַבֵּר יְהוָה אֶל־מֹשֶׁה לֵּאמֹר׃
כד דַּבֵּר אֶל־הָעֵדָה לֵאמֹר

NUMBERS 17

Withdraw from about the abodes of Korah, Dathan, and Abiram." 25 Moses rose and went to Dathan and Abiram, the elders of Israel following him. 26 He addressed the community, saying, "Move away from the tents of these wicked men and touch nothing that belongs to them, lest you be wiped out for all their sins." 27 So they withdrew from about the abodes of Korah, Dathan, and Abiram. Now Dathan and Abiram had come out and they stood at the entrance of their tents, with their wives, their children, and their little ones. 28 And Moses said, "By this you shall know that it was the LORD who sent me to do all these things; that they are not of my own devising: 29 if these men die as all men do, if their lot be the common fate of all mankind, it was not the LORD who sent me. 30 But if the LORD brings about something unheard-of, so that the ground opens its mouth and swallows them up with all that belongs to them, and they go down alive into Sheol, you shall know that these men have spurned the LORD." 31 Scarcely had he finished speaking all these words when the ground under them burst asunder, 32 and the earth opened its mouth and swallowed them up with their households, all Korah's people and all their possessions. 33 They went down alive into Sheol, with all that belonged to them; the earth closed over them and they vanished from the midst of the congregation. 34 All Israel around them fled at their shrieks, for they said, "The earth might swallow us!" 35 And a fire went forth from the LORD and consumed the two hundred and fifty men offering the incense.

17 1 The LORD spoke to Moses, saying: 2 Order Eleazar son of Aaron the priest to remove the fire pans - for they have become sacred - from among the charred remains; and scatter the coals abroad. 3 [Remove] the fire pans of those who have sinned at the cost of their lives, and let them be made into hammered sheets as plating for the altar - for once they have been used for offering to the LORD, they have become sacred - and let them serve as a warning to the people of Israel. 4 Eleazar the priest took the copper fire pans which had been used for offering by those who died in the fire; and they were hammered into plating for the altar, 5 as the LORD had ordered him through Moses. It was to be a reminder to the Israelites, so that no outsider - one not of Aaron's offspring - should presume to offer incense before the LORD and suffer the fate of Korah and his band.

6 Next day the whole Israelite community railed against Moses and Aaron, saying, "You two have brought death upon the LORD's people!" 7 But as the community gathered against them, Moses and Aaron turned toward the Tent of Meeting: the cloud had covered it and the Presence of the LORD appeared. 8 When Moses and Aaron reached the Tent of Meeting, 9 the LORD spoke to Moses, saying, 10 "Remove yourselves from this community, that I may annihilate them in an instant." They fell on their faces. 11 Then Moses said to Aaron, "Take the fire pan, and put on it fire from the altar. Add incense and take it quickly to the community and make expiation for them. For wrath has gone forth from the LORD: the plague has begun!" 12 Aaron took it, as Moses had ordered, and ran to the midst of the congregation, where the plague had begun among the people. He put on the incense and made expiation for the people. 13 He stood between the dead and the living until the plague was checked. 14 Those who died of the plague came to fourteen thousand and seven hundred, aside from those who died on account of Korah. 15 Aaron then returned to Moses at the entrance of the Tent of Meeting, since the plague was checked. 16 The LORD spoke to Moses, saying: 17 Speak to the Israelite people and take from them - from the chieftains of their ancestral houses - one staff for each chieftain of an ancestral house: twelve staffs in all. Inscribe each man's name on his staff, 18 there being one staff for each head of an ancestral house; also inscribe Aaron's name on the staff of Levi. 19 Deposit them in the Tent of Meeting before the Pact, where I meet with you. 20 The staff of the man whom I choose shall sprout, and I will rid Myself of the incessant mutterings of the Israelites against you. 21 Moses spoke thus to the Israelites. Their chieftains gave him a staff for each chieftain of an ancestral house, twelve staffs in all; among these staffs was that of Aaron. 22 Moses deposited the staffs before the LORD, in the Tent of the Pact. 23 The next day Moses entered the Tent of the Pact, and there the staff

NUMBERS 18

of Aaron of the house of Levi had sprouted: it had brought forth sprouts, produced blossoms, and borne almonds. 24 Moses then brought out all the staffs from before the LORD to all the Israelites: each identified and recovered his staff.

25 The LORD said to Moses, "Put Aaron's staff back before the Pact, to be kept as a lesson to rebels, so that their mutterings against Me may cease, lest they die." 26 This Moses did; just as the LORD had commanded him, so he did. 27 But the Israelites said to Moses, "Lo, we perish! We are lost, all of us lost! 28 Everyone who so much as ventures near the LORD's Tabernacle must die. Alas, we are doomed to perish!"

18 1 The LORD said to Aaron: You and your sons and the ancestral house under your charge shall bear any guilt connected with the sanctuary; you and your sons alone shall bear any guilt connected with your priesthood. 2 You shall also associate with yourself your kinsmen the tribe of Levi, your ancestral tribe, to be attached to you and to minister to you, while you and your sons under your charge are before the Tent of the Pact. 3 They shall discharge their duties to you and to the Tent as a whole, but they must not have any contact with the furnishings of the Shrine or with the altar, lest both they and you die. 4 They shall be attached to you and discharge the duties of the Tent of Meeting, all the service of the Tent; but no outsider shall intrude upon you 5 as you discharge the duties connected with the Shrine and the altar, that wrath may not again strike the Israelites. 6 I hereby take your fellow Levites from among the Israelites; they are assigned to you in dedication to the LORD, to do the work of the Tent of Meeting. 7 while you and your sons shall be careful to perform your priestly duties in everything pertaining to the altar and to what is behind the curtain. I make your priesthood a service of dedication; any outsider who encroaches shall be put to death.

8 The LORD spoke further to Aaron: I hereby give you charge of My gifts, all the sacred donations of the Israelites; I grant them to you and to your sons as a perquisite, a due for all time. 9 This shall be yours from the most holy sacrifices, the offerings by fire: every such offering that they render to Me as most holy sacrifices, namely, every meal offering, sin offering, and guilt offering of theirs, shall belong to you and your sons. 10 You shall partake of them as most sacred donations: only males may eat them; you shall treat them as consecrated. 11 This, too, shall be yours: the gift offerings of their contributions, all the elevation offerings of the Israelites; I give to you, to your sons, and to the daughters that are with you, as a due for all time; everyone of your household who is clean may eat it. 12 All the best of the new oil, wine, and grain - the choice parts that they present to the LORD - I give to you. 13 The first fruits of everything in their land, that they bring to the LORD, shall be yours; everyone of your household who is clean may eat them. 14 Everything that has been proscribed in Israel shall be yours. 15 The first issue of the womb of every being, man or beast, that is offered to the LORD, shall be yours; but you shall have the first-born of man redeemed, and you shall also redeem the firstling of unclean animals redeemed. 16 Take as their redemption price, from the age of one month up, the money equivalent of five shekels by the sanctuary weight, which is twenty gerahs. 17 But the firstlings of cattle, sheep, or goats may not be redeemed: they are consecrated. You shall dash their blood against the altar, and turn their fat into smoke as an offering by fire for a pleasing odor to the LORD. 18 But their meat shall be yours; it shall be yours like the breast of elevation offering and like the right thigh. 19 All the sacred gifts that the Israelites set aside for the LORD I give to you, to your sons, and to the daughters that are with you, as a due for all time. It shall be an everlasting covenant of salt before the LORD for you and for your offspring as well. 20 And the LORD said to Aaron: You shall, however, have no territorial share among them or own any portion in their midst: I am your portion and your share among the Israelites.

21 And to the Levites I hereby give all the tithes in Israel as their share in return for the services that they perform, the services of the Tent of Meeting. 22 Henceforth, Israelites shall not trespass on the Tent of Meeting and thus incur guilt and die: 23 only Levites shall perform the services of the Tent of Meeting; others would incur guilt. It is the law for all time throughout the ages. But they shall have no territorial share among the Israelites; 24 for it is the tithes set aside by the Israelites as a gift to the LORD that I give to the Levites as their share. Therefore I have said concerning them: They shall have no

155

NUMBERS 19

territorial share among the Israelites. 25 The LORD spoke to Moses, saying: 26 Speak to the Levites and say to them: When you receive from the Israelites their tithes, which I have assigned to you as your share, you shall set aside from them one-tenth of the tithe as a gift to the LORD. 27 This shall be accounted to you as your gift. As with the new grain from the threshing floor or the flow from the vat, 28 so shall you on your part set aside a gift for the LORD from all the tithes that you receive from the Israelites; and from them you shall bring the gift for the LORD to Aaron the priest. 29 You shall set aside all gifts due to the LORD from everything that is donated to you, from each thing its best portion, the part thereof that is to be consecrated. 30 Say to them further: When you have removed the best part from it, you Levites may consider it the same as the yield of threshing floor or vat. 31 You and your households may eat it anywhere, for it is your recompense for your services in the Tent of Meeting. 32 You will incur no guilt through it, once you have removed the best part from it: but you must not profane the sacred donations of the Israelites, lest you die.

19 1 The LORD spoke to Moses and Aaron, saying: 2 This is the ritual law that the LORD has commanded: Instruct the Israelite people to bring you a red cow without blemish, in which there is no defect and on which no yoke has been laid. 3 You shall give it to Eleazar the priest. It shall be taken outside the camp and slaughtered in his presence. 4 Eleazar the priest shall take some of its blood with his finger and sprinkle it seven times toward the front of the Tent of Meeting. 5 The cow shall be burned in his sight - its hide, flesh, and blood shall be burned, its dung included - 6 and the priest shall take cedar wood, hyssop, and crimson stuff, and throw them into the fire consuming the cow. 7 The priest shall wash his garments and bathe his body in water; after that the priest may reenter the camp, but he shall be unclean until evening. 8 He who performed the burning shall also wash his garments in water, bathe his body in water, and be unclean until evening. 9 A man who is clean shall gather up the ashes of the cow and deposit them outside the camp in a clean place, to be kept for water of lustration for the Israelite community. It is for cleansing. 10 He who gathers up the ashes of the cow shall also wash his clothes and be unclean until evening. This shall be a permanent law for the Israelites and for the strangers who reside among you. 11 He who touches the corpse of any human being shall be unclean for seven days. 12 He shall cleanse himself with it on the third day and on the seventh day, and then be clean; if he fails to cleanse himself on the third and seventh days, he shall not be clean. 13 Whoever touches a corpse, the body of a person who has died, and does not cleanse himself, defiles the LORD's Tabernacle; that person shall be cut off from Israel. Since the water of lustration was not dashed on him, he remains unclean; his uncleanness is still upon him. 14 This is the ritual: When a person dies in a tent, whoever enters the tent and whoever is in the tent shall be unclean seven days; 15 and every open vessel, with no lid fastened down, shall be unclean. 16 And in the open, anyone who touches a person who was killed or who died naturally, or human bone, or a grave, shall be unclean seven days. 17 Some of the ashes from the fire of cleansing shall be taken for the unclean person, and fresh water shall be added to them in a vessel. 18 A person who is clean shall take hyssop, dip it in the water, and sprinkle on the tent and on all the vessels and people who were there, or on him who touched the bones or the person who was killed or died naturally, or the grave. 19 The clean person shall sprinkle it upon the unclean person on the third day and on the seventh day, thus cleansing him by the seventh day. He shall then wash his clothes and bathe in water, and at nightfall he shall be clean. 20 If anyone who has become unclean fails to cleanse himself, that person shall be cut off from the congregation, for he has defiled the LORD's sanctuary. The water of lustration was not dashed on him: he is unclean. 21 That shall be for them a law for all time. Further, he who sprinkled the water of lustration shall wash his clothes; and whoever touches the water of lustration shall be unclean until evening. 22 Whatever that unclean person touches shall be unclean; and the person who touches him shall be unclean until evening.

20 1 The Israelites arrived in a body at the wilderness of Zin on the first

A page of the Book of Numbers, from the Bible illustrated by Gustave Doré, 1832-33, עמוד מספר במדבר, מתוך התנ״ך באיורו של גוסטב דורה

NUMBERS 13

Hebron was founded seven years before Zoan of Egypt. · 23 They reached the wadi Eshcol, and there they cut down a branch with a single cluster of grapes - it had to be borne on a carrying frame by two of them - and some pomegranates and figs. 24 That place was named the wadi Eshcol

במדבר יג

וַיָּבֹאוּ עַד נַחַל אֶשְׁכֹּל וַיִּכְרְתוּ מִשָּׁם זְמוֹרָה וְאֶשְׁכּוֹל עֲנָבִים אֶחָד וַיִּשָּׂאֻהוּ בַמּוֹט בִּשְׁנָיִם וּמִן הָרִמֹּנִים וּמִן הַתְּאֵנִים: כד לַמָּקוֹם הַהוּא קָרָא נַחַל אֶשְׁכּוֹל

NUMBERS 21 · במדבר כא · חקת

new moon, and the people stayed at Kadesh. Miriam died there and was buried there. 2 The community was without water, and they joined against Moses and Aaron. 3 The people quarrelled with Moses, saying, "If only we had perished when our brothers perished at the instance of the LORD! 4 Why have you brought the LORD's congregation into this wilderness for us and our beasts to die there? 5 Why did you make us leave Egypt to bring us to this wretched place, a place with no grain or figs or vines or pomegranates? There is not even water to drink!" 6 Moses and Aaron came away from the congregation to the entrance of the Tent of Meeting, and fell on their faces. The Presence of the LORD appeared to them,

7 and the LORD spoke to Moses, saying, 8 "You and your brother Aaron take the rod and assemble the community, and before their very eyes order the rock to yield its water. Thus you shall produce water for them from the rock and provide drink for the congregation and their beasts." 9 Moses took the rod from before the LORD, as He had commanded him. 10 Moses and Aaron assembled the congregation in front of the rock; and he said to them, "Listen, you rebels, shall we get water for you out of this rock?" 11 And Moses raised his hand and struck the rock twice with his rod. Out came copious water, and the community and their beasts drank.

12 But the LORD said to Moses and Aaron, "Because you did not trust Me enough to affirm My sanctity in the sight of the Israelite people, therefore you shall not lead this congregation into the land that I have given them." 13 Those are the Waters of Meribah - meaning that the Israelites quarrelled with the LORD - through which He affirmed His sanctity.

14 From Kadesh, Moses sent messengers to the king of Edom: "Thus says your brother Israel: You know all the hardships that have befallen us: 15 that our ancestors went down to Egypt, that we dwelt in Egypt a long time, and the Egyptians dealt harshly with us and our ancestors. 16 We cried to the LORD and He heard our plea, and He sent a messenger who freed us from Egypt. Now we are in Kadesh, the town on the border of your territory. 17 Allow us, then, to cross your country. We will not pass through fields or vineyards, and we will not drink water from wells. We will follow the king's highway, turning off neither to the right nor to the left until we have crossed your territory." 18 But Edom answered him, "You shall not pass through us, else we will go out against you with the sword." 19 "We will keep to the beaten track," the Israelites said to them, "and if we or our cattle drink your water, we will pay for it. We ask only for passage on foot - it is but a small matter." 20 But they replied, "You shall not pass through!" And Edom went out against them in heavy force, strongly armed. 21 So Edom would not let Israel cross their territory, and Israel turned away from them.

22 Setting out from Kadesh, the Israelites arrived in a body at Mount Hor. 23 At Mount Hor, on the boundary of the land of Edom, the LORD said to Moses and Aaron. 24 "Let Aaron be gathered to his kin: he is not to enter the land that I have assigned to the Israelite people, because you disobeyed my command about the waters of Meribah. 25 Take Aaron and his son Eleazar and bring them up on Mount Hor. 26 Strip Aaron of his vestments and put them on his son Eleazar. There Aaron shall be gathered unto the dead." 27 Moses did as the LORD had commanded. They ascended Mount Hor in the sight of the whole community. 28 Moses stripped Aaron of his vestments and put them on his son Eleazar, and Aaron died there on the summit of the mountain. When Moses and Eleazar came down from the mountain, 29 the whole community knew that Aaron had breathed his last. All the house of Israel bewailed Aaron thirty days.

21 1 When the Canaanite, king of Arad, who dwelt in the Negeb, learned that Israel was coming by the way of Atharim, he engaged Israel in battle and took some of them captive. 2 Then Israel made a vow to the LORD and said, "If You deliver this people into our hand, we will proscribe their towns." 3 The LORD heeded Israel's plea and delivered up the Canaanites; and they and their cities were proscribed. So that place was named Hormah. 4 They set out from Mount Hor by way of the Sea of Reeds to skirt the land of Edom. But the people grew restive on the journey, 5 and the people spoke against God and against Moses, "Why did you

※ 158 ※

NUMBERS 22

make us leave Egypt to die in the wilderness? There is no bread and no water, and we have come to loathe this miserable food." 6 The LORD sent seraph serpents against the people. They bit the people and many of the Israelites died. 7 The people came to Moses and said, "We sinned by speaking against the LORD and against you. Intercede with the LORD to take away the serpents from us!" And Moses interceded for the people. 8 Then the LORD said to Moses, "Make a seraph figure and mount it on a standard. And if anyone who is bitten looks at it, he shall recover." 9 Moses made a copper serpent and mounted it on a standard; and when anyone was bitten by a serpent, he would look at the copper serpent and recover. 10 The Israelites marched on and encamped at Oboth. 11 They set out from Oboth and encamped at Iye-abarim, in the wilderness bordering on Moab to the east. 12 From there they set out and encamped at the wadi Zered. 13 From there they set out and encamped beyond the Arnon, that is, in the wilderness that extends from the territory of the Amorites. For the Arnon is the boundary of Moab, between Moab and the Amorites. 14 Therefore the Book of the Wars of the LORD speaks of "...Waheb in Suphah, and the wadis: the Arnon 15 with its tributary wadis, stretched along the settled country of Ar, hugging the territory of Moab..." 16 And from there to Beer, which is the well where the LORD said to Moses, "Assemble the people that I may give them water." 17 Then Israel sang this song: Spring up, O well - sing to it - 18 The well which the chieftains dug, Which the nobles of the people started With maces, with their own staffs. And from Midbar to Mattanah, 19 and from Mattanah to Nahaliel, and from Nahaliel to Bamoth, 20 and from Bamoth to the valley that is in the country of Moab, at the peak of Pisgah, overlooking the wasteland.

21 Israel now sent messengers to Sihon king of the Amorites, saying, 22 "Let me pass through your country. We will not turn off into fields or vineyards, and we will not drink water from wells. We will follow the king's highway until we have crossed your territory." 23 But Sihon would not let Israel pass through his territory. Sihon gathered all his people and went out against Israel in the wilderness. He came to Jahaz and engaged Israel in battle. 24 But Israel put them to the sword, and took possession of their land, from the Arnon to the Jabbok, as far as [Az] of the Ammonites, for Az marked the boundary of the Ammonites. 25 Israel took all those towns. And Israel settled in all the towns of the Amorites, in Heshbon and all its dependencies. 26 Now Heshbon was the city of Sihon king of the Amorites, who had fought against a former king of Moab and taken all his land from him as far as the Arnon. 27 Therefore the bards would recite: "Come to Heshbon: firmly built And well founded is Sihon's city. 28 For fire went forth from Heshbon, flame from Sihon's city, consuming Ar of Moab. The lords of Bamoth by the Arnon. 29 Woe to you, O Moab! You are undone, O people of Chemosh! His sons are rendered fugitive And his daughters captive by an Amorite king, Sihon. 30 Yet we have cast them down utterly, Heshbon along with Dibon; we have wrought desolation at Nophah, which is hard by Medeba. 31 So Israel occupied the land of the Amorites. 32 Then Moses sent to spy out Jazer, and they captured its dependencies and dispossessed the Amorites who were there. 33 They marched on and went up the road to Bashan, and King Og of Bashan, with all his people, came out to Edrei to engage them in battle. 34 But the LORD said to Moses, "Do not fear him, for I give him and all his people and his land into your hand. You shall do to him as you did to Sihon king of the Amorites who dwelt in Heshbon." 35 They defeated him and his sons and all his people, until no remnant was left him; and they took possession of his country. 22 1 The Israelites then marched on and encamped in the steppes of Moab, across the Jordan from Jericho.

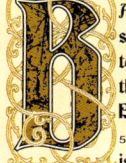

2 **B**alak son of Zippor saw all that Israel had done to the Amorites. 3 Moab was alarmed because the people was so numerous. Moab dreaded the Israelites, 4 and Moab said to the elders of Midian. "Now this horde will lick clean all that is about us as an ox licks up the grass of the field." Balak son of Zippor, who was king of Moab at that time, 5 sent messengers to Balaam son of Beor in Pethor, which is by the Euphrates, in the land of his kinsfolk, to invite

NUMBERS 22   בלק   במדבר בב

him, saying, "There is a people that came out of Egypt; it hides the earth from view, and it is settled next to me. 6 Come then, put a curse upon this people for me, since they are too numerous for me; perhaps I can thus defeat them and drive them out of the land. For I know that he whom you bless is blessed indeed, and he whom you curse is cursed." 7 The elders of Moab and the elders of Midian, versed in divination, set out. They came to Balaam and gave him Balak's message. 8 He said to them, "Spend the night here, and I shall reply to you as the LORD may instruct me." So the Moabite dignitaries stayed with Balaam. 9 God came to Balaam and said, "What do these people want of you?" 10 Balaam said to God, "Balak son of Zippor, king of Moab, sent me this message: 11 Here is a people that came out from Egypt and hides the earth from view. Come now and curse them for me; perhaps I can engage them in battle and drive them off." 12 But God said to Balaam, "Do not go with them. You must not curse that people, for they are blessed." 13 Balaam arose in the morning and said to Balak's dignitaries, "Go back to your own country, for the LORD will not let me go with you." 14 The Moabite dignitaries left, and they came to Balak and said, "Balaam refused to come with us." 15 Then Balak sent other dignitaries, more numerous and distinguished than the first. 16 They came to Balaam and said to him, "Thus says Balak son of Zippor: Please do not refuse to come to me. 17 I will reward you richly and I will do anything you ask of me. Only come and damn this people for me." 18 Balaam replied to Balak's officials, "Though Balak were to give me his house full of silver and gold, I could not do anything, big or little, contrary to the command of the LORD my God. 19 So you, too, stay here overnight, and let me find out what else the LORD may say to me." 20 That night God came to Balaam and said to him, "If these men have come to invite you, you may go with them. But whatever I command you, that you shall do."

21 When he arose in the morning, Balaam saddled his ass and departed with the Moabite dignitaries. 22 But God was incensed at his going; so an angel of the LORD placed himself in his way as an adversary. He was riding on his she-ass, with his two servants alongside, 23 when the ass caught sight of the angel of the LORD standing in the way, with his drawn sword in his hand. The ass swerved from the road and went into the fields; and Balaam beat the ass to turn her back onto the road. 24 The angel of the LORD then stationed himself in a lane between the vineyards, with a fence on either side. 25 The ass, seeing the angel of the LORD, pressed herself against the wall and squeezed Balaam's foot against the wall; so he beat her again. 26 Once more the angel of the LORD moved forward and stationed himself on a spot so narrow that there was no room to swerve right or left. 27 When the ass now saw the angel of the LORD, she lay down under Balaam; and Balaam was furious and beat the ass with his stick. 28 Then the LORD opened the ass's mouth, and she said to Balaam, "What have I done to you that you have beaten me these three times?" 29 Balaam said to the ass, "You have made a mockery of me! If I had a sword with me, I'd kill you." 30 The ass said to Balaam, "Look, I am the ass that you have been riding all along until this day! Have I been in the habit of doing thus to you?" And he answered, "No." 31 Then the LORD uncovered Balaam's eyes, and he saw the angel of the LORD standing in the way, his drawn sword in his hand; thereupon he bowed right down to the ground. 32 The angel of the LORD said to him, "Why have you beaten your ass these three times? It is I who came out as an adversary, for the errand is obnoxious to me. 33 And when the ass saw me, she shied away because of me those three times. If she had not shied away from me, you are the one I should have killed, while sparing her." 34 Balaam said to the angel of the LORD, "I erred because I did not know that you were standing in my way. If you still disapprove, I will turn back." 35 But the angel of the LORD said to Balaam, "Go with the men. But you must say nothing except what I tell you." So Balaam went on with Balak's dignitaries. 36 When Balak heard that Balaam was coming, he went out to meet him at Ir-moab, which is on the Arnon border, at its farthest point. 37 Balak said

NUMBERS 23 בלק במדבר כג

to Balaam, "When I first sent to invite you, why didn't you come to me? Am I really unable to reward you?" 38 But Balaam said to Balak, "And now that I have come to you, have I the power to speak freely? I can utter only the word that God puts into my mouth." 39 Balaam went with Balak and they came to Kiriath-huzoth. 40 Balak sacrificed oxen and sheep, and had them served to Balaam and the dignitaries with him. 41 In the morning Balak took Balaam up to Bamoth-baal. From there he could see a portion of the people. **23** 1 Balaam said to Balak, "Build me seven altars here and have seven bulls and seven rams ready here for me." 2 Balak did as Balaam directed; and Balak and Balaam offered up a bull and a ram on each altar. 3 Then Balaam said to Balak, "Stay here beside your offerings while I am gone. Perhaps the LORD will grant me a manifestation, and whatever He reveals to me I will tell you." And he went off alone. 4 God manifested Himself to Balaam, who said to Him, "I have set up the seven altars and offered up a bull and a ram on each altar." 5 And the LORD put a word in Balaam's mouth and said, "Return to Balak and speak thus." 6 So he returned to him and found him standing beside his offerings, and all the Moabite dignitaries with him. 7 He took up his theme, and said: From Aram has Balak brought me, Moab's king from the hills of the East: come, curse me Jacob, come, tell Israel's doom! 8 How can I damn whom God has not damned, how doom when the LORD has not doomed? 9 As I see them from the mountain tops, gaze on them from the heights, there is a people that dwells apart, not reckoned among the nations, 10 Who can count the dust of Jacob, number the dust-cloud of Israel? May I die the death of the upright, may my fate be like theirs! 11 Then Balak said to Balaam, "What have you done to me? Here I brought you to damn my enemies, and instead you have blessed them!" 12 He replied, "I can only repeat faithfully what the LORD puts in my mouth." 13 Then Balak said to him, "Come with me to another place from which you can see them – you will see only a portion of them; you will not see all of them – and damn them for me from there." 14 With that, he took him to Sedehzophim, on the summit of Pisgah, built seven altars and offered a bull and a ram on each altar. 15 And [Balaam] said to Balak, "Stay here beside your offerings, while I seek a manifestation yonder." 16 The LORD manifested Himself to Balaam and put a word in his mouth, saying, "Return to Balak and speak thus." 17 He went to him and found him standing beside his offerings, and the Moabite dignitaries with him. Balak asked him, "What did the LORD say?" 18 And he took up his theme, and said: Up, Balak, attend, give ear unto me, son of Zippor! 19 God is not man to be capricious, or mortal to change His mind. Would He speak and not act, promise and not fulfill? 20 My message was to bless: When He blesses, I cannot reverse it. 21 No harm is in sight for Jacob, no woe in view for Israel. the LORD their God is with them, and their King's acclaim is in their midst. 22 God who freed them from Egypt is for them like the horns of the wild ox. 23 Lo, there is no augury in Jacob, no divining in Israel: Jacob is told at once, Yea Israel, what God has planned. 24 Lo, a people that rises like a lion, leaps up like the king of beasts, rests not till it has feasted on prey and drunk the blood of the slain. 25 Thereupon Balak said to Balaam, "Don't curse them and don't bless them!" 26 In reply, Balaam said to Balak, "But I told you: Whatever the LORD says, that I must do." 27 Then Balak said to Balaam, "Come now, I will take you to another place. Perhaps God will deem it right that you damn them for me there." 28 Balak took Balaam to the peak of Peor, which overlooks the wasteland. 29 Balaam said to Balak, "Build me here seven altars, and have seven bulls and seven rams ready for me here." 30 Balak did as Balaam said: be offered up a bull and a ram on each altar. **24** 1 Now Balaam, seeing that it pleased the LORD to bless Israel, did not, as on previous occasions, go in search of omens, but turned his face toward the wilderness. 2 As Balaam looked up and saw Israel encamped tribe by tribe, the spirit of God came upon him. 3 Taking up his theme, he said: Word of Balaam son of Beor. Word of the man whose eye is true. 4 Word of him who hears God's speech, Who beholds visions from the Almighty, Prostrate, but with eyes unveiled: 5 How fair are your tents, O Jacob, Your dwellings, O Israel! 6 Like palm-groves

NUMBERS 25 | במדבר כה | בלק

that stretch out. Like gardens beside a river. Like aloes planted by the LORD. Like cedars beside the water. 7 Their boughs drip with moisture. Their roots have abundant water. Their king shall rise above Agag. Their kingdom shall be exalted. 8 God who freed them from Egypt is for them like the horns of the wild ox. They shall devour enemy nations, crush their bones, and smash their arrows. 9 They crouch, they lie down like a lion, like the king of beasts; who dare rouse them? blessed are they who bless you, accursed they who curse you! 10 Enraged at Balaam, Balak struck his hands together, "I called you," Balak said to Balaam, "to damn my enemies, and instead you have blessed them these three times! 11 Back with you at once to your own place! I was going to reward you richly, but the LORD has denied you the reward." 12 Balaam replied to Balak, "But I even told the messengers you sent to me, 13 'Though Balak were to give me his house full of silver and gold, I could not of my own accord do anything good or bad contrary to the LORD's command. What the LORD says, that I must say.' 14 And now, as I go back to my people, let me inform you of what this people will do to your people in days to come." 15 He took up his theme, and said: Word of Balaam son of Beor, Word of the man whose eye is true, 16 Word of him who hears God's speech, who obtains knowledge from the Most High, and beholds visions from the Almighty, prostrate, but with eyes unveiled: 17 What I see for them is not yet, what I behold will not be soon: a star rises from Jacob, a scepter comes forth from Israel; it smashes the brow of Moab, the foundation of all children of Seth. 18 Edom becomes a possession, Yea, Seir a possession of its enemies: but Israel is triumphant. 19 A victor issues from Jacob to wipe out what is left of Ir. 20 He saw Amalek and, taking up his theme, he said: a leading nation is Amalek: But its fate is to perish forever. 21 He saw the Kenites and, taking up his theme, he said: though your abode be secure, and your nest be set among cliffs, 22 Yet shall Kain be consumed, when Asshur takes you captive. 23 He took up his theme and said: Alas, who can survive except God has willed it! 24 Ships come from the quarter of Kittim: They subject Asshur, subject Eber. They, too, shall perish forever. 25 Then Balaam set out on his journey back home; and Balak also went his way.

25 1 While Israel was staying at Shittim, the people profaned themselves by whoring with the Moabite women, 2 who invited the people to the sacrifices for their god. The people partook of them and worshiped that god. 3 Thus Israel attached itself to Baal-peor, and the LORD was incensed with Israel. 4 The LORD said to Moses, "Take all the ringleaders and have them publicly impaled before the LORD, so that the LORD's wrath may turn away from Israel." 5 So Moses said to Israel's officials, "Each of you slay those of his men who attached themselves to Baal-peor." 6 Just then one of the Israelites came and brought a Midianite woman over to his companions, in the sight of Moses and of the whole Israelite community who were weeping at the entrance of the Tent of Meeting. 7 When Phinehas, son of Eleazar son of Aaron the priest, saw this, he left the assembly and, taking a spear in his hand, 8 he followed the Israelite into the chamber and stabbed both of them, the Israelite and the woman, through the belly. Then the plague against the Israelites was checked. 9 Those who died of the plague numbered twenty-four thousand.

10 The LORD spoke to Moses, saying, 11 "Phinehas, son of Eleazar son of Aaron the priest, has turned back My wrath from the Israelites by displaying among them his passion for Me, so that I did not wipe out the Israelite people in My passion. 12 Say, therefore, 'I grant him My pact of friendship. 13 It shall be for him and his descendants after him a pact of priesthood for all time, because he took impassioned action for his God, thus making expiation for the Israelites.'" 14 The name of the Israelite who was killed, the one who was killed with the Midianite woman, was Zimri son of Salu, chieftain of a Simeonite ancestral house. 15 The name of the Midianite woman who was killed was Cozbi daughter of Zur: he was the tribal head of an ancestral house in Midian. 16 The LORD spoke to Moses, saying, 17 "Assail the Midianites and defeat them – 18 for they assailed you by the trickery they practiced against you – because of the affair of Peor

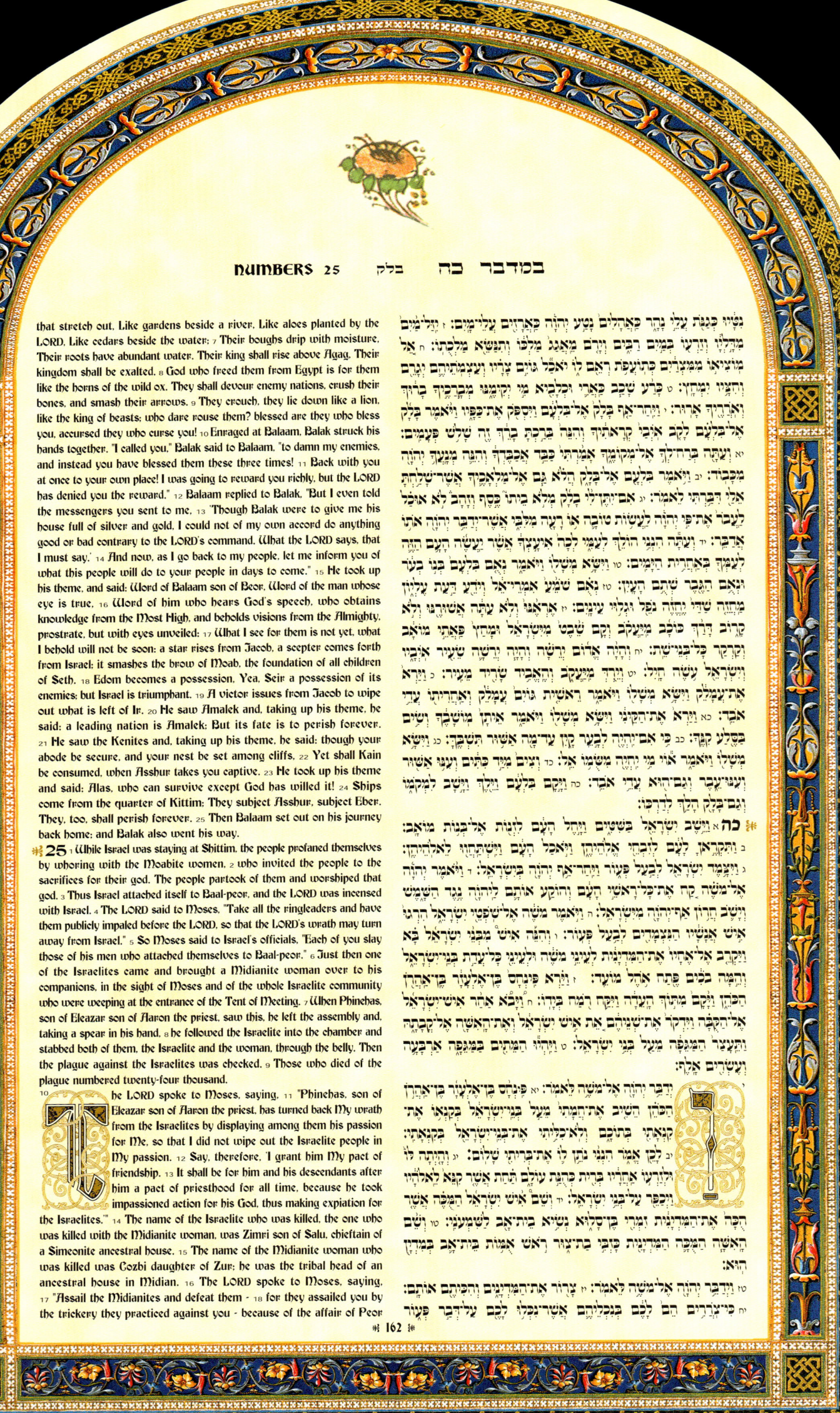

※ 162 ※

כריכה פנימית בעיטור מיקרוגרפי, מתוך "תנ"ך ליסבון", הועתק בידי שמואל הסופר, ליסבון, 1483, אוסף המוזיאון הבריטי, לונדון
Carpet page illuminated with micrography, from the "Lisbon Bible", copied by Samuel Ha-Sofer, Lisbon, 1483, collection of The British Museum, London

NUMBERS 26   פינחס   במדבר כו

and because of the affair of their kinswoman Cozbi, daughter of the Midianite chieftain, who was killed at the time of the plague on account of Peor." **26** ₁ When the plague was over, ₂ the LORD said to Moses and to Eleazar son of Aaron the priest, ₂ "Take a census of the whole Israelite community from the age of twenty years up, by their ancestral houses, all Israelites able to bear arms." ₃ So Moses and Eleazar the priest, on the steppes of Moab, at the Jordan near Jericho, gave instructions about them, namely, ₄ those from twenty years up, as the LORD had commanded Moses. Those descendants of the Israelites who came out of the land of Egypt were: ₅ Reuben, Israel's first-born. Descendants of Reuben: [Of] Enoch, the clan of the Enochites; of Pallu, the clan of the Palluites; ₆ of Hezron, the clan of the Hezronites; of Carmi, the clan of the Carmites. ₇ Those are the clans of the Reubenites. The persons enrolled came to 43,730. ₈ Born to Pallu: Eliab. ₉ The sons of Eliab were Nemuel, and Dathan and Abiram. These are the same Dathan and Abiram, chosen in the assembly, who agitated against Moses and Aaron as part of Korah's band when they agitated against the LORD. ₁₀ Whereupon the earth opened its mouth and swallowed them up with Korah - when that band died, when the fire consumed the two hundred and fifty men - and they became an example. ₁₁ The sons of Korah, however, did not die. ₁₂ Descendants of Simeon by their clans: Of Nemuel, the clan of the Nemuelites; of Jamin, the clan of the Jaminites; of Jachin, the clan of the Jachinites; ₁₃ of Zerah, the clan of the Zerahites; of Saul, the clan of the Saulites. ₁₄ Those are the clans of the Simeonites: [persons enrolled:] 22,200. ₁₅ Descendants of Gad by their clans: Of Zephon, the clan of the Zephonites; of Haggi, the clan of the Haggites; of Shuni, the clan of the Shunites; ₁₆ of Ozni, the clan of the Oznites; of Eri, the clan of the Erites; ₁₇ of Arod, the clan of the Arodites; of Areli, the clan of the Arelites. ₁₈ Those are the clans of Gad's descendants; persons enrolled: 40,500.

₁₉ Born to Judah: Er and Onan. Er and Onan died in the land of Canaan. ₂₀ Descendants of Judah by their clans: Of Shelah, the clan of the Shelanites; of Perez, the clan of the Perezites; of Zerah, the clan of the Zerahites. ₂₁ Descendants of Perez: of Hezron, the clan of the Hezronites; of Hamul, the clan of the Hamulites. ₂₂ Those are the clans of Judah; persons enrolled: 76,500.

₂₃ Descendants of Issachar by their clans: [Of] Tola, the clan of the Tolaites; of Puvah, the clan of the Punites; ₂₄ of Jashub, the clan of the Jashubites; of Shimron, the clan of the Shimronites. ₂₅ Those are the clans of Issachar; persons enrolled: 64,300.

₂₆ Descendants of Zebulun by their clans: Of Sered, the clan of the Seredites; of Elon, the clan of the Elonites; of Jahleel, the clan of the Jahleelites. ₂₇ Those are the clans of the Zebulunites; persons enrolled: 60,500. ₂₈ The sons of Joseph were Manasseh and Ephraim - by their clans. ₂₉ Descendants of Manasseh: Of Machir, the clan of the Machirites; Machir begot Gilead. - Of Gilead, the clan of the Gileadites. ₃₀ These were the descendants of Gilead: [Of] Iezer, the clan of the Iezerites; of Helek, the clan of the Helekites; ₃₁ [of] Asriel, the clan of the Asrielites; [of] Shechem, the clan of the Shechemites; ₃₂ [of] Shemida, the clan of the Shemidaites; [of] Hepher, the clan of the Hepherites. - ₃₃ Now Zelophehad son of Hepher had no sons, only daughters. The names of Zelophehad's daughters were Mahlah, Noah, Hoglah, Milcah, and Tirzah. - ₃₄ Those are the clans of Manasseh; persons enrolled: 52,700. ₃₅ These are the descendants of Ephraim by their clans: Of Shuthelah, the clan of the Shuthelahites; of Becher, the clan of the Becherites; of Tahan, the clan of the Tahanites. ₃₆ These are the descendants of Shuthelah: Of Eran, the clan of the Eranites. ₃₇ Those are the clans of Ephraim's descendants; persons enrolled: 32,500. These are the descendants of Joseph by their clans.

₃₈ The descendants of Benjamin by their clans: Of Bela, the clan of the Belaites; of Ashbel, the clan of the Ashbelites; of Ahiram, the clan of the Ahiramites; ₃₉ of Shephupham,

NUMBERS 27

of the Shuphamites; of Hupham, the clan of the Huphamites. 40 The sons of Bela were Ard and Naaman: [Of Ard,] the clan of the Ardites; of Naaman, the clan of the Naamanites. 41 Those are the descendants of Benjamin by their clans; persons enrolled: 45,600.

42 These are the descendants of Dan by their clans: Of Shuham, the clan of the Shuhamites. Those are the clans of Dan, by their clans. 43 All the clans of the Shuhamites; persons enrolled: 64,400.

44 Descendants of Asher by their clans: Of Imnah, the clan of the Imnites; of Ishvi, the clan of the Ishvites; of Beriah, the clan of the Beriites. 45 Of the descendants of Beriah: Of Heber, the clan of the Heberites; of Malchiel, the clan of the Malchielites. — 46 The name of Asher's daughter was Serah. — 47 These are the clans of Asher's descendants; persons enrolled: 53,400. 48 Descendants of Naphtali by their clans: Of Jahzeel, the clan of the Jahzeelites; of Guni, the clan of the Gunites; 49 Of Jezer, the clan of the Jezerites; of Shillem, the clan of the Shillemites. 50 Those are the clans of the Naphtalites, clan by clan; persons enrolled: 45,400. 51 This is the enrollment of the Israelites: 601,730. 52 The LORD spoke to Moses, saying, 53 "Among these shall the land be apportioned as shares, according to the listed names: 54 with larger groups increase the share, with smaller groups reduce the share. Each is to be assigned its share according to its enrollment. 55 The land, moreover, is to be apportioned by lot; and the allotment shall be made according to the listings of their ancestral tribes. 56 Each portion shall be assigned by lot, whether for larger or smaller groups."

57 This is the enrollment of the Levites by their clans: Of Gershon, the clan of the Gershonites; of Kohath, the clan of the Kohathites; of Merari, the clan of the Merarites. 58 These are the clans of Levi: The clan of the Libnites, the clan of the Hebronites, the clan of the Mahlites, the clan of the Mushites, the clan of the Korahites. - Kohath begot Amram. 59 The name of Amram's wife was Jochebed daughter of Levi, who was born to Levi in Egypt; she bore to Amram Aaron and Moses and their sister Miriam. 60 To Aaron were born Nadab and Abihu, Eleazar and Ithamar. 61 Nadab and Abihu died when they offered alien fire before the LORD. — 62 Their enrollment of 23,000 comprised all males from a month up. They were not part of the regular enrollment of the Israelites, since no share was assigned to them among the Israelites. 63 These are the persons enrolled by Moses and Eleazar the priest who registered the Israelites on the steppes of Moab, at the Jordan near Jericho. 64 Among these there was not one of those enrolled by Moses and Aaron the priest when they recorded the Israelites in the wilderness of Sinai. 65 For the LORD had said of them, "They shall die in the wilderness." Not one of them survived, except Caleb son of Jephunneh and Joshua son of Nun. 27 1 The daughters of Zelophehad, of Manassite family — son of Hepher son of Gilead son of Machir son of Manasseh son of Joseph — came forward. The names of the daughters were Mahlah, Noah, Hoglah, Milcah, and Tirzah. 2 They stood before Moses, Eleazar the priest, the chieftains, and the whole assembly, at the entrance of the Tent of Meeting, and they said, 3 "Our father died in the wilderness. He was not one of the faction, Korah's faction, which banded together against the LORD, but died for his own sin; and he has left no sons. 4 Let not our father's name be lost to his clan just because he had no son! Give us a holding among our father's kinsmen!" 5 Moses brought their case before the LORD.

6 And the LORD said to Moses, 7 "The plea of Zelophehad's daughters is just: you should give them a hereditary holding among their father's kinsmen; transfer their father's share to them. 8 Further, speak to the Israelite people as follows: 'If a man dies without leaving a son, you shall transfer his property to his daughter. 9 If he has no daughter, you shall assign his property to his brothers. 10 If he has no brothers, you shall assign his property to his father's brothers. 11 If his father had no brothers, you shall assign his property to his nearest relative in his own clan, and he shall inherit it.' This shall be the law of procedure

NUMBERS 28 פינחס במדבר כח

for the Israelites, in accordance with the LORD's command to Moses." 12 The LORD said to Moses, "Ascend these heights of Abarim and view the land that I have given to the Israelite people. 13 When you have seen it, you too shall be gathered to your kin, just as your brother Aaron was. 14 For, in the wilderness of Zin, when the community was contentious, you disobeyed My command to uphold My sanctity in their sight by means of the water." Those are the Waters of Meribath-kadesh, in the wilderness of Zin. 15 Moses spoke to the LORD, saying, 16 "Let the LORD, Source of the breath of all flesh, appoint someone over the community 17 who shall go out before them and come in before them, and who shall take them out and bring them in, so that the LORD's community may not be like sheep that have no shepherd." 18 And the LORD answered Moses, "Single out Joshua son of Nun, an inspired man, and lay your hand upon him. 19 Have him stand before Eleazar the priest and before the whole community, and commission him in their sight. 20 Invest him with some of your authority, so that the whole Israelite community may obey. 21 But he shall present himself to Eleazar the priest, who shall on his behalf seek the decision of the Urim before the LORD. By such instruction they shall go out and by such instruction they shall come in, he and all the Israelites, the whole community." 22 Moses did as the LORD commanded him. He took Joshua and had him stand before Eleazar the priest and before the whole community, 23 He laid his hands upon him and commissioned him - as the LORD had spoken through Moses.

28 1 The LORD spoke to Moses, saying, 2 Command the Israelite people and say to them: Be punctilious in presenting to Me at stated times the offerings of food due Me, as offerings by fire of pleasing odor to Me. 3 Say to them: These are the offerings by fire that you are to present to the LORD: As a regular burnt offering every day, two yearling lambs without blemish. 4 You shall offer one lamb in the morning, and the other lamb you shall offer at twilight. 5 And as a meal offering, there shall be a tenth of an ephah of choice flour with a quarter of a hin of beaten oil mixed in - 6 the regular burnt offering instituted at Mount Sinai - an offering by fire of pleasing odor to the LORD. 7 The libation with it shall be a quarter of a hin for each lamb, to be poured in the sacred precinct as an offering of fermented drink to the LORD. 8 The other lamb you shall offer at twilight, preparing the same meal offering and libation as in the morning - an offering by fire of pleasing odor to the LORD.

9 On the sabbath day: two yearling lambs without blemish, together with two-tenths of a measure of choice flour with oil mixed in as a meal offering, and with the proper libation - 10 burnt offering for every sabbath, in addition to the regular burnt offering and its libation.

11 On your new moons you shall present a burnt offering to the LORD: two bulls of the herd, one ram, and seven yearling lambs, without blemish. 12 As meal offering for each bull: three-tenths of a measure of choice flour with oil mixed in. As meal offering for each ram: two-tenths of a measure of choice flour with oil mixed in. 13 As meal offering for each lamb: a tenth of a measure of fine flour with oil mixed in. Such shall be the burnt offering of pleasing odor, an offering by fire to the LORD. 14 Their libations shall be: half a hin of wine for a bull, a third of a hin for a ram, and a quarter of a hin for a lamb. That shall be the monthly burnt offering for each new moon of the year. 15 And there shall be one goat as a sin offering to the LORD, to be offered in addition to the regular burnt offering and its libation.

16 In the first month, on the fourteenth day of the month, there shall be a passover sacrifice to the LORD. 17 and on the fifteenth day of that month a festival. Unleavened bread shall be eaten for seven days. 18 The first day shall be a sacred occasion; you shall not work at your occupations. 19 You shall present an offering by fire, a burnt offering, to the LORD: two bulls of the herd, one ram, and seven yearling lambs - see that they are without blemish. 20 The meal offering with them shall be of choice flour with oil mixed in: prepare three-tenths of a measure for a bull, two-tenths for a ram: 21 and for each of the seven lambs prepare one-tenth of a measure. 22 And there shall be one goat for a sin offering, to make expiation in your behalf. 23 You shall prepare these in addition to the morning portion of the regular burnt offering. 24 You shall offer the like daily for seven days as food, an offering by fire of pleasing odor to the LORD; they shall be offered, with their libations, in addition to the regular burnt offering. 25 And the seventh day shall be a sacred occasion for you; you shall not work at your occupations.

NUMBERS 29 · פינחס · במדבר כט

26 On the day of the first fruits, your Feast of Weeks, when you bring an offering of new grain to the LORD, you shall observe a sacred occasion: you shall not work at your occupations. 27 You shall present a burnt offering of pleasing odor to the LORD: two bulls of the herd, one ram, seven yearling lambs. 28 The meal offering with them shall be of choice flour with oil mixed in, three-tenths of a measure for a bull, two-tenths for a ram, 29 and one-tenth for each of the seven lambs. 30 And there shall be one goat for expiation in your behalf. 31 You shall present them - see that they are without blemish - with their libations, in addition to the regular burnt offering and its meal offering.

29 1 In the seventh month, on the first day of the month, you shall observe a sacred occasion: you shall not work at your occupations. You shall observe it as a day when the horn is sounded. 2 You shall present a burnt offering of pleasing odor to the LORD: one bull of the herd, one ram, and seven yearling lambs, without blemish. 3 The meal offering with them - choice flour with oil mixed in - shall be: three-tenths of a measure for a bull, two-tenths for a ram, 4 and one-tenth for each of the seven lambs. 5 And there shall be one goat for a sin offering, to make expiation in your behalf - 6 in addition to the burnt offering of the new moon with its meal offering and the regular burnt offering with its meal offering, each with its libation as prescribed, offerings by fire of pleasing odor to the LORD.

7 On the tenth day of the same seventh month you shall observe a sacred occasion when you shall practice self-denial. You shall do no work. 8 You shall present to the LORD a burnt offering of pleasing odor: one bull of the herd, one ram, seven yearling lambs; see that they are without blemish. 9 The meal offering with them - of choice flour with oil mixed in - shall be: three-tenths of a measure for a bull, two-tenths for the one ram, 10 one-tenth for each of the seven lambs. 11 And there shall be one goat for a sin offering, in addition to the sin offering of expiation and the regular burnt offering with its meal offering, each with its libation.

12 On the fifteenth day of the seventh month, you shall observe a sacred occasion: you shall not work at your occupations. - Seven days you shall observe a festival of the LORD. - 13 You shall present a burnt offering, an offering by fire of pleasing odor to the LORD: Thirteen bulls of the herd, two rams, fourteen yearling lambs; they shall be without blemish. 14 The meal offering with them - of choice flour with oil mixed in - shall be: three-tenths of a measure for each of the thirteen bulls, two-tenths for each of the two rams, 15 and one-tenth for each of the fourteen lambs. 16 And there shall be one goat for a sin offering - in addition to the regular burnt offering, its meal offering and libation.

17 Second day: Twelve bulls of the herd, two rams, fourteen yearling lambs, without blemish; 18 the meal offerings and libations for the bulls, rams, and lambs, in the quantities prescribed; 19 and one goat for a sin offering - in addition to the regular burnt offering, its meal offering and libations. 20 Third day: Eleven bulls, two rams, fourteen yearling lambs, without blemish; 21 the meal offerings and libations for the bulls, rams, and lambs, in the quantities prescribed; 22 and one goat for a sin offering - in addition to the regular burnt offering, its meal offering and libation.

23 Fourth day: Ten bulls, two rams, fourteen yearling lambs, without blemish; 24 the meal offerings and libations for the bulls, rams, and lambs, in the quantities prescribed; 25 and one goat for a sin offering - in addition to the regular burnt offering, its meal offering and libation. 26 Fifth day: Nine bulls, two rams, fourteen yearling lambs, without blemish; 27 the meal offerings and libations for the bulls, rams, and lambs, in the quantities prescribed; 28 and one goat for a sin offering - in addition to the regular burnt offering, its meal offering and libation.

29 Sixth day: Eight bulls, two rams, fourteen yearling lambs, without blemish; 30 the meal offerings and libations for the bulls, rams, and lambs, in the quantities prescribed; 31 and one goat for a sin offering - in addition to the regular burnt offering, its meal offering and libations.

כו וּבְיוֹם הַבִּכּוּרִים בְּהַקְרִיבְכֶם מִנְחָה חֲדָשָׁה לַיהוָה בְּשָׁבֻעֹתֵיכֶם מִקְרָא־קֹדֶשׁ יִהְיֶה לָכֶם כָּל־מְלֶאכֶת עֲבֹדָה לֹא תַעֲשׂוּ: כז וְהִקְרַבְתֶּם עוֹלָה לְרֵיחַ נִיחֹחַ לַיהוָה פָּרִים בְּנֵי־בָקָר שְׁנַיִם אַיִל אֶחָד שִׁבְעָה כְבָשִׂים בְּנֵי שָׁנָה: כח וּמִנְחָתָם סֹלֶת בְּלוּלָה בַשָּׁמֶן שְׁלֹשָׁה עֶשְׂרֹנִים לַפָּר הָאֶחָד שְׁנֵי עֶשְׂרֹנִים לָאַיִל הָאֶחָד: כט עִשָּׂרוֹן עִשָּׂרוֹן לַכֶּבֶשׂ הָאֶחָד לְשִׁבְעַת הַכְּבָשִׂים: ל שְׂעִיר עִזִּים אֶחָד לְכַפֵּר עֲלֵיכֶם: לא מִלְּבַד עֹלַת הַתָּמִיד וּמִנְחָתוֹ תַּעֲשׂוּ תְּמִימִם יִהְיוּ־לָכֶם וְנִסְכֵּיהֶם:

כט א וּבַחֹדֶשׁ הַשְּׁבִיעִי בְּאֶחָד לַחֹדֶשׁ מִקְרָא־קֹדֶשׁ יִהְיֶה לָכֶם כָּל־מְלֶאכֶת עֲבֹדָה לֹא תַעֲשׂוּ יוֹם תְּרוּעָה יִהְיֶה לָכֶם: ב וַעֲשִׂיתֶם עֹלָה לְרֵיחַ נִיחֹחַ לַיהוָה פַּר בֶּן־בָּקָר אֶחָד אַיִל אֶחָד כְּבָשִׂים בְּנֵי־שָׁנָה שִׁבְעָה תְּמִימִם: ג וּמִנְחָתָם סֹלֶת בְּלוּלָה בַשָּׁמֶן שְׁלֹשָׁה עֶשְׂרֹנִים לַפָּר שְׁנֵי עֶשְׂרֹנִים לָאָיִל: ד וְעִשָּׂרוֹן אֶחָד לַכֶּבֶשׂ הָאֶחָד לְשִׁבְעַת הַכְּבָשִׂים: ה וּשְׂעִיר־עִזִּים אֶחָד חַטָּאת לְכַפֵּר עֲלֵיכֶם: ו מִלְּבַד עֹלַת הַחֹדֶשׁ וּמִנְחָתָהּ וְעֹלַת הַתָּמִיד וּמִנְחָתָהּ וְנִסְכֵּיהֶם כְּמִשְׁפָּטָם לְרֵיחַ נִיחֹחַ אִשֶּׁה לַיהוָה:

ז וּבֶעָשׂוֹר לַחֹדֶשׁ הַשְּׁבִיעִי הַזֶּה מִקְרָא־קֹדֶשׁ יִהְיֶה לָכֶם וְעִנִּיתֶם אֶת־נַפְשֹׁתֵיכֶם כָּל־מְלָאכָה לֹא תַעֲשׂוּ: ח וְהִקְרַבְתֶּם עֹלָה לַיהוָה רֵיחַ נִיחֹחַ פַּר בֶּן־בָּקָר אֶחָד אַיִל אֶחָד כְּבָשִׂים בְּנֵי־שָׁנָה שִׁבְעָה תְּמִימִם יִהְיוּ לָכֶם: ט וּמִנְחָתָם סֹלֶת בְּלוּלָה בַשָּׁמֶן שְׁלֹשָׁה עֶשְׂרֹנִים לַפָּר שְׁנֵי עֶשְׂרֹנִים לָאַיִל הָאֶחָד: י עִשָּׂרוֹן עִשָּׂרוֹן לַכֶּבֶשׂ הָאֶחָד לְשִׁבְעַת הַכְּבָשִׂים: יא שְׂעִיר־עִזִּים אֶחָד חַטָּאת מִלְּבַד חַטַּאת הַכִּפֻּרִים וְעֹלַת הַתָּמִיד וּמִנְחָתָהּ וְנִסְכֵּיהֶם:

יב וּבַחֲמִשָּׁה עָשָׂר יוֹם לַחֹדֶשׁ הַשְּׁבִיעִי מִקְרָא־קֹדֶשׁ יִהְיֶה לָכֶם כָּל־מְלֶאכֶת עֲבֹדָה לֹא תַעֲשׂוּ וְחַגֹּתֶם חַג לַיהוָה שִׁבְעַת יָמִים: יג וְהִקְרַבְתֶּם עֹלָה אִשֵּׁה רֵיחַ נִיחֹחַ לַיהוָה פָּרִים בְּנֵי־בָקָר שְׁלֹשָׁה עָשָׂר אֵילִם שְׁנָיִם כְּבָשִׂים בְּנֵי־שָׁנָה אַרְבָּעָה עָשָׂר תְּמִימִם יִהְיוּ: יד וּמִנְחָתָם סֹלֶת בְּלוּלָה בַשָּׁמֶן שְׁלֹשָׁה עֶשְׂרֹנִים לַפָּר הָאֶחָד לִשְׁלֹשָׁה עָשָׂר פָּרִים שְׁנֵי עֶשְׂרֹנִים לָאַיִל הָאֶחָד לִשְׁנֵי הָאֵילִם: טו וְעִשָּׂרוֹן עִשָּׂרוֹן לַכֶּבֶשׂ הָאֶחָד לְאַרְבָּעָה עָשָׂר כְּבָשִׂים: טז וּשְׂעִיר־עִזִּים אֶחָד חַטָּאת מִלְּבַד עֹלַת הַתָּמִיד מִנְחָתָהּ וְנִסְכָּהּ:

יז וּבַיּוֹם הַשֵּׁנִי פָּרִים בְּנֵי־בָקָר שְׁנֵים עָשָׂר אֵילִם שְׁנָיִם כְּבָשִׂים בְּנֵי־שָׁנָה אַרְבָּעָה עָשָׂר תְּמִימִם: יח וּמִנְחָתָם וְנִסְכֵּיהֶם לַפָּרִים לָאֵילִם וְלַכְּבָשִׂים בְּמִסְפָּרָם כַּמִּשְׁפָּט: יט וּשְׂעִיר־עִזִּים אֶחָד חַטָּאת מִלְּבַד עֹלַת הַתָּמִיד וּמִנְחָתָהּ וְנִסְכֵּיהֶם:

כ וּבַיּוֹם הַשְּׁלִישִׁי פָּרִים עַשְׁתֵּי־עָשָׂר אֵילִם שְׁנָיִם כְּבָשִׂים בְּנֵי־שָׁנָה אַרְבָּעָה עָשָׂר תְּמִימִם: כא וּמִנְחָתָם וְנִסְכֵּיהֶם לַפָּרִים לָאֵילִם וְלַכְּבָשִׂים בְּמִסְפָּרָם כַּמִּשְׁפָּט: כב וּשְׂעִיר חַטָּאת אֶחָד מִלְּבַד עֹלַת הַתָּמִיד וּמִנְחָתָהּ וְנִסְכָּהּ:

כג וּבַיּוֹם הָרְבִיעִי פָּרִים עֲשָׂרָה אֵילִם שְׁנָיִם כְּבָשִׂים בְּנֵי־שָׁנָה אַרְבָּעָה עָשָׂר תְּמִימִם: כד מִנְחָתָם וְנִסְכֵּיהֶם לַפָּרִים לָאֵילִם וְלַכְּבָשִׂים בְּמִסְפָּרָם כַּמִּשְׁפָּט: כה וּשְׂעִיר־עִזִּים אֶחָד חַטָּאת מִלְּבַד עֹלַת הַתָּמִיד מִנְחָתָהּ וְנִסְכָּהּ:

כו וּבַיּוֹם הַחֲמִישִׁי פָּרִים תִּשְׁעָה אֵילִם שְׁנָיִם כְּבָשִׂים בְּנֵי־שָׁנָה אַרְבָּעָה עָשָׂר תְּמִימִם: כז וּמִנְחָתָם וְנִסְכֵּיהֶם לַפָּרִים לָאֵילִם וְלַכְּבָשִׂים בְּמִסְפָּרָם כַּמִּשְׁפָּט: כח וּשְׂעִיר חַטָּאת אֶחָד מִלְּבַד עֹלַת הַתָּמִיד וּמִנְחָתָהּ וְנִסְכָּהּ:

כט וּבַיּוֹם הַשִּׁשִּׁי פָּרִים שְׁמֹנָה אֵילִם שְׁנָיִם כְּבָשִׂים בְּנֵי־שָׁנָה אַרְבָּעָה עָשָׂר תְּמִימִם: ל וּמִנְחָתָם וְנִסְכֵּיהֶם לַפָּרִים לָאֵילִם וְלַכְּבָשִׂים בְּמִסְפָּרָם כַּמִּשְׁפָּט: לא וּשְׂעִיר חַטָּאת אֶחָד מִלְּבַד עֹלַת הַתָּמִיד מִנְחָתָהּ וּנְסָכֶיהָ:

NUMBERS 30   פינחס   במדבר ל

32 Seventh day: Seven bulls, two rams, fourteen yearling lambs, without blemish; 33 the meal offerings and libations for the bulls, rams, and lambs, in the quantities prescribed; 34 and one goat for a sin offering - in addition to the regular burnt offering, its meal offering and libation. 35 On the eighth day you shall hold a solemn gathering; you shall not work at your occupations. 36 You shall present a burnt offering, an offering by fire of pleasing odor to the LORD: one bull, one ram, seven yearling lambs, without blemish; 37 the meal offerings and libations for the bull, the ram, and the lambs, in the quantities prescribed; 38 and one goat for a sin offering - in addition to the regular burnt offering, its meal offering and libation. 39 All these you shall offer to the LORD at the stated times, in addition to your votive and freewill offerings, be they burnt offerings, meal offerings, libations, or offerings of well-being. 30 1 So Moses spoke to the Israelites just as the LORD had commanded Moses.

2 Moses spoke to the heads of the Israelite tribes, saying: This is what the LORD has commanded: 3 If a man makes a vow to the LORD or takes an oath imposing an obligation on himself, he shall not break his pledge; he must carry out all that has crossed his lips. 4 If a woman makes a vow to the LORD or assumes an obligation while still in her father's household by reason of her youth, 5 and her father learns of her vow or her self-imposed obligation and offers no objection, all her vows shall stand and every self-imposed obligation shall stand. 6 But if her father restrains her on the day he finds out, none of her vows or self-imposed obligations shall stand; and the LORD will forgive her, since her father restrained her. 7 If she should marry while her vow or the commitment to which she bound herself is still in force, 8 and her husband learns of it and offers no objection on the day he finds out, her vows shall stand and her self-imposed obligations shall stand. 9 But if her husband restrains her on the day that he learns of it, he thereby annuls her vow which was in force or the commitment to which she bound herself; and the LORD will forgive her. 10 The vow of a widow or of a divorced woman, however, whatever she has imposed on herself, shall be binding upon her. 11 So, too, if, while in her husband's household, she makes a vow or imposes an obligation on herself by oath, 12 and her husband learns of it, yet offers no objection - thus failing to restrain her - all her vows shall stand and all her self-imposed obligations shall stand. 13 But if her husband does annul them on the day he finds out, then nothing that has crossed her lips shall stand, whether vows or self-imposed obligations. Her husband has annulled them, and the LORD will forgive her. 14 Every vow and every sworn obligation of self-denial may be upheld by her husband or annulled by her husband. 15 If her husband offers no objection from that day to the next, he has upheld all the vows or obligations she has assumed; he has upheld them by offering no objection on the day he found out. 16 But if he annuls them after [the day] he finds out, he shall bear her guilt. 17 These are the laws that the LORD enjoined upon Moses between a man and his wife, and as between a father and his daughter while in her father's household by reason of her youth.

31 1 The LORD spoke to Moses, saying, 2 "Avenge the Israelite people on the Midianites; then you shall be gathered to your kin." 3 Moses spoke to the people, saying, "Let men be picked out from among you for a campaign, and let them fall upon Midian to wreak the LORD's vengeance on Midian. 4 You shall dispatch on the campaign a thousand from every one of the tribes of Israel. 5 So a thousand from each tribe were furnished from the divisions of Israel, twelve thousand picked for the campaign. 6 Moses dispatched them on the campaign, a thousand from each tribe, with Phinehas son of Eleazar serving as a priest on the campaign, equipped with the sacred utensils and the trumpets for sounding the blasts. 7 They took the field against Midian, as the LORD had commanded Moses, and slew every male. 8 Along with their other victims, they slew the kings of Midian: Evi, Rekem, Zur, Hur, and Reba, the five kings of Midian. They also put Balaam son of Beor to the sword. 9 The Israelites took the women and children of the Midianites captive, and seized as booty all their beasts, all their herds, and all their wealth.

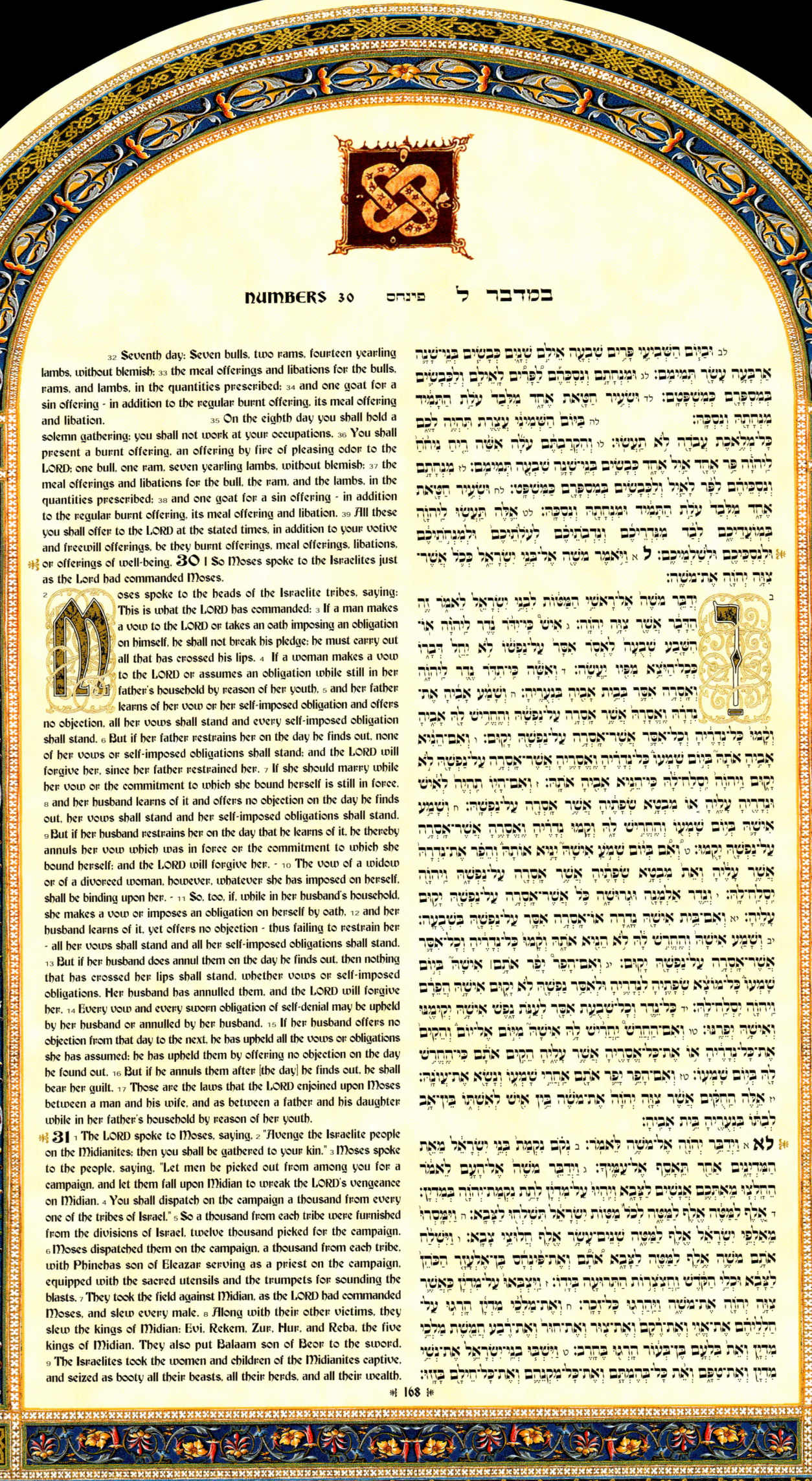

168

NUMBERS 31　　　　　　במדבר לא מטות

10 And they destroyed by fire all the towns in which they were settled, and their encampments. 11 They gathered all the spoil and all the booty, man and beast, 12 and they brought the captives, the booty, and the spoil to Moses, Eleazar the priest, and the whole Israelite community, at the camp in the steppes of Moab, at the Jordan near Jericho.

13 Moses, Eleazar the priest, and all the chieftains of the community came out to meet them outside the camp. 14 Moses became angry with the commanders of the army, the officers of thousands and the officers of hundreds, who had come back from the military campaign. 15 Moses said to them, "You have spared every female! 16 Yet they are the very ones who, at the bidding of Balaam, induced the Israelites to trespass against the LORD in the matter of Peor, so that the LORD's community was struck by the plague. 17 Now, therefore, slay every male among the children, and slay also every woman who has known a man carnally; 18 but spare every young woman who has not had carnal relations with a man. 19 "You shall then stay outside the camp seven days; every one among you or among your captives who has slain a person or touched a corpse shall cleanse himself on the third and seventh days. 20 You shall also cleanse every cloth, every article of skin, everything made of goats' hair, and every object of wood." 21 Eleazar the priest said to the troops who had taken part in the fighting, "This is the ritual law that the LORD has enjoined upon Moses: 22 Gold and silver, copper, iron, tin, and lead — 23 any article that can withstand fire — these you shall pass through fire and they shall be clean, except that they must be cleansed with water of lustration; and anything that cannot withstand fire you must pass through water. 24 On the seventh day you shall wash your clothes and be clean, and after that you may enter the camp."

25 The LORD said to Moses: 26 "You and Eleazar the priest and the family heads of the community take an inventory of the booty that was captured, man and beast, 27 and divide the booty equally between the combatants who engaged in the campaign and the rest of the community. 28 You shall exact a levy for the LORD: in the case of the warriors who engaged in the campaign, one item in five hundred, of persons, oxen, asses, and sheep, 29 shall be taken from their half-share and given to Eleazar the priest as a contribution to the LORD; 30 and from the half-share of the other Israelites you shall withhold one in every fifty human beings as well as cattle, asses, and sheep — all the animals — and give them to the Levites, who attend to the duties of the LORD's Tabernacle." 31 Moses and Eleazar the priest did as the LORD commanded Moses. 32 The amount of booty, other than the spoil that the troops had plundered, came to 675,000 sheep, 33 72,000 head of cattle, 34 61,000 asses, 35 and a total of 32,000 human beings, namely, the women who had not had carnal relations. 36 Thus, the half-share of those who had engaged in the campaign [was as follows]: The number of sheep was 337,500, 37 and the LORD's levy from the sheep was 675; 38 the cattle came to 36,000, from which the LORD's levy was 72; 39 the asses came to 30,500, from which the LORD's levy was 61. 40 And the number of human beings was 16,000, from which the LORD's levy was 32. 41 Moses gave the contributions levied for the LORD to Eleazar the priest, as the LORD had commanded Moses. 42 As for the half-share of the other Israelites, which Moses withdrew from the men who had taken the field, 43 that half-share of the community consisted of 337,500 sheep, 44 36,000 head of cattle, 45 30,500 asses, 46 and 16,000 human beings. 47 From this half-share of the Israelites, Moses withheld one in every fifty humans and animals; and he gave them to the Levites, who attended to the duties of the LORD's Tabernacle, as the LORD had commanded Moses. 48 The commanders of the troop divisions, the officers of thousands and the officers

169

NUMBERS 32 · מטות · במדבר לב

of hundreds, approached Moses. 49 They said to Moses, "Your servants have made a check of the warriors in our charge, and not one of us is missing. 50 So we have brought as an offering to the LORD such articles of gold as each of us came upon: armlets, bracelets, signet rings, earrings, and pendants, that expiation may be made for our persons before the LORD." 51 Moses and Eleazar the priest accepted the gold from them, all kinds of wrought articles. 52 All the gold that was offered by the officers of thousands and the officers of hundreds as a contribution to the LORD came to 16,750 shekels. - 53 But in the ranks, everyone kept his booty for himself. - 54 So Moses and Eleazar the priest accepted the gold from the officers of thousands and the officers of hundreds and brought it to the Tent of Meeting, as a reminder in behalf of the Israelites before the LORD.

32 1 The Reubenites and the Gadites owned cattle in very great numbers. Noting that the lands of Jazer and Gilead were a region suitable for cattle, 2 the Gadites and the Reubenites came to Moses, Eleazar the priest, and the chieftains of the community, and said, 3 "Ataroth, Dibon, Jazer, Nimrah, Heshbon, Elealeh, Sebam, Nebo, and Beon - 4 the land that the LORD has conquered for the community of Israel is cattle country, and your servants have cattle. 5 It would be a favor to us," they continued, "if this land were given to your servants as a holding; do not move us across the Jordan." 6 Moses replied to the Gadites and the Reubenites, "Are your brothers to go to war while you stay here? 7 Why will you turn the minds of the Israelites from crossing into the land that the LORD has given them? 8 That is what your fathers did when I sent them from Kadesh-barnea to survey the land. 9 After going up to the wadi Eshcol and surveying the land, they turned the minds of the Israelites from invading the land that the LORD had given them. 10 Thereupon the LORD was incensed and He swore, 11 'None of the men from twenty years up who came out of Egypt shall see the land that I promised on oath to Abraham, Isaac, and Jacob, for they did not remain loyal to Me - 12 none except Caleb son of Jephunneh the Kenizzite and Joshua son of Nun, for they remained loyal to the LORD.' 13 The LORD was incensed at Israel, and for forty years He made them wander in the wilderness, until the whole generation that had provoked the LORD's displeasure was gone. 14 And now you, a breed of sinful men, have replaced your fathers, to add still further to the LORD's wrath against Israel. 15 If you turn away from Him and He abandons them once more in the wilderness, you will bring calamity upon all this people." 16 Then they stepped up to him and said, "We will build here sheepfolds for our flocks and towns for our children. 17 And we will hasten as shock-troops in the van of the Israelites until we have established them in their home, while our children stay in the fortified towns because of the inhabitants of the land. 18 We will not return to our homes until every one of the Israelites is in possession of his portion. 19 But we will not have a share with them in the territory beyond the Jordan, for we have received our share on the east side of the Jordan." 20 Moses said to them, "If you do this, if you go to battle as shock-troops, at the instance of the LORD, 21 and every shock-fighter among you crosses the Jordan, at the instance of the LORD, until He has dispossessed His enemies before Him, 22 and the land has been subdued, at the instance of the LORD, and then you return - you shall be clear before the LORD and before Israel; and this land shall be your holding under the LORD. 23 But if you do not so, you will have sinned against the LORD; and know that your sin will overtake you. 24 Build towns for your children and sheepfolds for your flocks, but do what you have promised." 25 The Gadites and the Reubenites answered Moses, "Your servants will do as my lord commands. 26 Our children, our wives, our flocks, and all our other livestock will stay behind in the towns of Gilead; 27 while your servants, all those recruited for war, cross over, at the instance of the LORD, to engage in battle - as my lord states." 28 Then Moses gave instructions concerning them to Eleazar the priest, Joshua son of Nun, and the family heads of the Israelite tribes. 29 Moses said to them, "If every shock-fighter among the Gadites and the Reubenites crosses the Jordan with you to do battle

NUMBERS 33 במדבר לג מסעי

at the instance of the LORD, and the land is subdued before you, you shall give them the land of Gilead as a holding. 30 But if they do not cross over with you as shock-troops, they shall receive holdings among you in the land of Canaan." 31 The Gadites and the Reubenites said in reply, "Whatever the LORD has spoken concerning your servants, that we will do. 32 We ourselves will cross over as shock-troops, at the instance of the LORD, into the land of Canaan; and we shall keep our hereditary holding across the Jordan." 33 So Moses assigned to them – to the Gadites, the Reubenites, and the half-tribe of Manasseh son of Joseph – the kingdom of Sihon king of the Amorites and the kingdom of King Og of Bashan, the land with its various cities and the territories of their surrounding towns. 34 The Gadites rebuilt Dibon, Ataroth, Aroer, 35 Atroth-shophan, Jazer, Jogbehah, 36 Beth-nimrah, and Beth-haran as fortified towns or as enclosures for flocks. 37 The Reubenites rebuilt Heshbon, Elealeh, Kiriathaim, 38 Nebo, Baal-meon – some names being changed – and Sibmah; they gave [their own] names to towns that they rebuilt. 39 The descendants of Machir son of Manasseh went to Gilead and captured it, dispossessing the Amorites who were there; 40 so Moses gave Gilead to Machir son of Manasseh, and he settled there. 41 Jair son of Manasseh went and captured their villages, which he renamed Havvoth-jair. 42 And Nobah went and captured Kenath and its dependencies, renaming it Nobah after himself.

33 These were the marches of the Israelites who started out from the land of Egypt, troop by troop, in the charge of Moses and Aaron. 2 Moses recorded the starting points of their various marches as directed by the LORD. Their marches, by starting points, were as follows: 3 They set out from Rameses in the first month, on the fifteenth day of the first month. It was on the morrow of the passover offering that the Israelites started out defiantly, in plain view of all the Egyptians. 4 The Egyptians meanwhile were burying those among them whom the LORD had struck down, every first-born – whereby the LORD executed judgment on their gods. 5 The Israelites set out from Rameses and encamped at Succoth. 6 They set out from Succoth and encamped at Etham, which is on the edge of the wilderness. 7 They set out from Etham and turned about toward Pi-hahiroth, which faces Baal-zephon, and they encamped before Migdol. 8 They set out from Pene-hahiroth and passed through the sea into the wilderness; and they made a three-days' journey in the wilderness of Etham and encamped at Marah. 9 They set out from Marah and came to Elim. There were twelve springs in Elim and seventy palm trees, so they encamped there. 10 They set out from Elim and encamped by the Sea of Reeds. 11 They set out from the Sea of Reeds and encamped in the wilderness of Sin. 12 They set out from the wilderness of Sin and encamped at Dophkah. 13 They set out from Dophkah and encamped at Alush. 14 They set out from Alush and encamped at Rephidim; it was there that the people had no water to drink. 15 They set out from Rephidim and encamped in the wilderness of Sinai. 16 They set out from the wilderness of Sinai and encamped at Kibroth-hattaavah. 17 They set out from Kibroth-hattaavah and encamped at Hazeroth. 18 They set out from Hazeroth and encamped at Rithmah. 19 They set out from Rithmah and encamped at Rimmon-perez. 20 They set out from Rimmon-perez and encamped at Libnah. 21 They set out from Libnah and encamped at Rissah. 22 They set out from Rissah and encamped at Kehelath. 23 They set out from Kehelath and encamped at Mount Shepher. 24 They set out from Mount Shepher and encamped at Haradah. 25 They set out from Haradah and encamped at Makheloth. 26 They set out from Makheloth and encamped at Tahath. 27 They set out from Tahath and encamped at Terah. 28 They set out from Terah and encamped at Mithkah. 29 They set out from Mithkah and encamped at Hashmonah. 30 They set out from Hashmonah and encamped at Moseroth. 31 They set out from Moseroth and encamped at Bene-jaakan. 32 They set out from Bene-jaakan and encamped at Hor-haggidgad. 33 They set out from Hor-haggidgad and encamped at Jotbath. 34 They set out from Jotbath and encamped at Abronah. 35 They set out from Abronah and encamped at Ezion-geber. 36 They set out from Ezion-geber and encamped in the wilderness of Zin, that is, Kadesh. 37 They set out from Kadesh and encamped at Mount Hor, on the edge of the land of Edom. 38 Aaron the priest ascended Mount Hor at the command of the LORD and died there, in the fortieth year after the Israelites had left the land of Egypt, on the first day of the fifth month,

למלחמה לפני יהוה ונכבשה הארץ לפניכם ונתתם להם את־ארץ הגלעד לאחזה: ל וְאִם־לֹא יַעַבְרוּ חֲלוּצִים אִתְּכֶם וְנֹאחֲזוּ בְתֹכְכֶם בְּאֶרֶץ כְּנָעַן: לא וַיַּעֲנוּ בְנֵי־גָד וּבְנֵי רְאוּבֵן לֵאמֹר אֵת אֲשֶׁר דִּבֶּר יְהוָה אֶל־עֲבָדֶיךָ כֵּן נַעֲשֶׂה: לב נַחְנוּ נַעֲבֹר חֲלוּצִים לִפְנֵי יְהוָה אֶרֶץ כְּנָעַן וְאִתָּנוּ אֲחֻזַּת נַחֲלָתֵנוּ מֵעֵבֶר לַיַּרְדֵּן: לג וַיִּתֵּן לָהֶם מֹשֶׁה לִבְנֵי־גָד וְלִבְנֵי רְאוּבֵן וְלַחֲצִי שֵׁבֶט מְנַשֶּׁה בֶן־יוֹסֵף אֶת־מַמְלֶכֶת סִיחֹן מֶלֶךְ הָאֱמֹרִי וְאֶת־מַמְלֶכֶת עוֹג מֶלֶךְ הַבָּשָׁן הָאָרֶץ לְעָרֶיהָ בִּגְבֻלֹת עָרֵי הָאָרֶץ סָבִיב: לד וַיִּבְנוּ בְנֵי־גָד אֶת־דִּיבֹן וְאֶת־עֲטָרֹת וְאֵת עֲרֹעֵר: לה וְאֶת־עַטְרוֹת שׁוֹפָן וְאֶת־יַעְזֵר וְיָגְבֳּהָה: לו וְאֶת־בֵּית נִמְרָה וְאֶת־בֵּית הָרָן עָרֵי מִבְצָר וְגִדְרֹת צֹאן: לז וּבְנֵי רְאוּבֵן בָּנוּ אֶת־חֶשְׁבּוֹן וְאֶת־אֶלְעָלֵא וְאֵת קִרְיָתָיִם: לח וְאֶת־נְבוֹ וְאֶת־בַּעַל מְעוֹן מוּסַבֹּת שֵׁם וְאֶת־שִׂבְמָה וַיִּקְרְאוּ בְשֵׁמֹת אֶת־שְׁמוֹת הֶעָרִים אֲשֶׁר בָּנוּ: לט וַיֵּלְכוּ בְּנֵי מָכִיר בֶּן־מְנַשֶּׁה גִּלְעָדָה וַיִּלְכְּדֻהָ וַיּוֹרֶשׁ אֶת־הָאֱמֹרִי אֲשֶׁר־בָּהּ: מ וַיִּתֵּן מֹשֶׁה אֶת־הַגִּלְעָד לְמָכִיר בֶּן־מְנַשֶּׁה וַיֵּשֶׁב בָּהּ: מא וְיָאִיר בֶּן־מְנַשֶּׁה הָלַךְ וַיִּלְכֹּד אֶת־חַוֹּתֵיהֶם וַיִּקְרָא אֶתְהֶן חַוֹּת יָאִיר: מב וְנֹבַח הָלַךְ וַיִּלְכֹּד אֶת־קְנָת וְאֶת־בְּנֹתֶיהָ וַיִּקְרָא לָהּ נֹבַח בִּשְׁמוֹ:

לג אֵלֶּה מַסְעֵי בְנֵי־יִשְׂרָאֵל אֲשֶׁר יָצְאוּ מֵאֶרֶץ מִצְרַיִם לְצִבְאֹתָם בְּיַד־מֹשֶׁה וְאַהֲרֹן: ב וַיִּכְתֹּב מֹשֶׁה אֶת־מוֹצָאֵיהֶם לְמַסְעֵיהֶם עַל־פִּי יְהוָה וְאֵלֶּה מַסְעֵיהֶם לְמוֹצָאֵיהֶם: ג וַיִּסְעוּ מֵרַעְמְסֵס בַּחֹדֶשׁ הָרִאשׁוֹן בַּחֲמִשָּׁה עָשָׂר יוֹם לַחֹדֶשׁ הָרִאשׁוֹן מִמָּחֳרַת הַפֶּסַח יָצְאוּ בְנֵי־יִשְׂרָאֵל בְּיָד רָמָה לְעֵינֵי כָּל־מִצְרָיִם: ד וּמִצְרַיִם מְקַבְּרִים אֵת אֲשֶׁר הִכָּה יְהוָה בָּהֶם כָּל־בְּכוֹר וּבֵאלֹהֵיהֶם עָשָׂה יְהוָה שְׁפָטִים: ה וַיִּסְעוּ בְנֵי־יִשְׂרָאֵל מֵרַעְמְסֵס וַיַּחֲנוּ בְּסֻכֹּת: ו וַיִּסְעוּ מִסֻּכֹּת וַיַּחֲנוּ בְאֵתָם אֲשֶׁר בִּקְצֵה הַמִּדְבָּר: ז וַיִּסְעוּ מֵאֵתָם וַיָּשָׁב עַל־פִּי הַחִירֹת אֲשֶׁר עַל־פְּנֵי בַּעַל צְפוֹן וַיַּחֲנוּ לִפְנֵי מִגְדֹּל: ח וַיִּסְעוּ מִפְּנֵי הַחִירֹת וַיַּעַבְרוּ בְתוֹךְ־הַיָּם הַמִּדְבָּרָה וַיֵּלְכוּ דֶּרֶךְ שְׁלֹשֶׁת יָמִים בְּמִדְבַּר אֵתָם וַיַּחֲנוּ בְּמָרָה: ט וַיִּסְעוּ מִמָּרָה וַיָּבֹאוּ אֵילִמָה וּבְאֵילִם שְׁתֵּים עֶשְׂרֵה עֵינֹת מַיִם וְשִׁבְעִים תְּמָרִים וַיַּחֲנוּ־שָׁם: י וַיִּסְעוּ מֵאֵילִם וַיַּחֲנוּ עַל־יַם־סוּף: יא וַיִּסְעוּ מִיַּם־סוּף וַיַּחֲנוּ בְּמִדְבַּר־סִין: יב וַיִּסְעוּ מִמִּדְבַּר־סִין וַיַּחֲנוּ בְּדָפְקָה: יג וַיִּסְעוּ מִדָּפְקָה וַיַּחֲנוּ בְּאָלוּשׁ: יד וַיִּסְעוּ מֵאָלוּשׁ וַיַּחֲנוּ בִּרְפִידִם וְלֹא־הָיָה שָׁם מַיִם לָעָם לִשְׁתּוֹת: טו וַיִּסְעוּ מֵרְפִידִם וַיַּחֲנוּ בְּמִדְבַּר סִינָי: טז וַיִּסְעוּ מִמִּדְבַּר סִינָי וַיַּחֲנוּ בְּקִבְרֹת הַתַּאֲוָה: יז וַיִּסְעוּ מִקִּבְרֹת הַתַּאֲוָה וַיַּחֲנוּ בַּחֲצֵרֹת: יח וַיִּסְעוּ מֵחֲצֵרֹת וַיַּחֲנוּ בְּרִתְמָה: יט וַיִּסְעוּ מֵרִתְמָה וַיַּחֲנוּ בְּרִמֹּן פָּרֶץ: כ וַיִּסְעוּ מֵרִמֹּן פָּרֶץ וַיַּחֲנוּ בְּלִבְנָה: כא וַיִּסְעוּ מִלִּבְנָה וַיַּחֲנוּ בְּרִסָּה: כב וַיִּסְעוּ מֵרִסָּה וַיַּחֲנוּ בִּקְהֵלָתָה: כג וַיִּסְעוּ מִקְּהֵלָתָה וַיַּחֲנוּ בְּהַר־שָׁפֶר: כד וַיִּסְעוּ מֵהַר־שָׁפֶר וַיַּחֲנוּ בַּחֲרָדָה: כה וַיִּסְעוּ מֵחֲרָדָה וַיַּחֲנוּ בְּמַקְהֵלֹת: כו וַיִּסְעוּ מִמַּקְהֵלֹת וַיַּחֲנוּ בְּתָחַת: כז וַיִּסְעוּ מִתָּחַת וַיַּחֲנוּ בְּתָרַח: כח וַיִּסְעוּ מִתָּרַח וַיַּחֲנוּ בְּמִתְקָה: כט וַיִּסְעוּ מִמִּתְקָה וַיַּחֲנוּ בְּחַשְׁמֹנָה: ל וַיִּסְעוּ מֵחַשְׁמֹנָה וַיַּחֲנוּ בְּמֹסֵרוֹת: לא וַיִּסְעוּ מִמֹּסֵרוֹת וַיַּחֲנוּ בִּבְנֵי יַעֲקָן: לב וַיִּסְעוּ מִבְּנֵי יַעֲקָן וַיַּחֲנוּ בְּחֹר הַגִּדְגָּד: לג וַיִּסְעוּ מֵחֹר הַגִּדְגָּד וַיַּחֲנוּ בְּיָטְבָתָה: לד וַיִּסְעוּ מִיָּטְבָתָה וַיַּחֲנוּ בְּעַבְרֹנָה: לה וַיִּסְעוּ מֵעַבְרֹנָה וַיַּחֲנוּ בְּעֶצְיוֹן גָּבֶר: לו וַיִּסְעוּ מֵעֶצְיוֹן גָּבֶר וַיַּחֲנוּ בְמִדְבַּר־צִן הִוא קָדֵשׁ: לז וַיִּסְעוּ מִקָּדֵשׁ וַיַּחֲנוּ בְּהֹר הָהָר בִּקְצֵה אֶרֶץ אֱדוֹם: לח וַיַּעַל אַהֲרֹן הַכֹּהֵן אֶל־הֹר הָהָר עַל־פִּי יְהוָה וַיָּמָת שָׁם בִּשְׁנַת הָאַרְבָּעִים לְצֵאת בְּנֵי־יִשְׂרָאֵל מֵאֶרֶץ מִצְרַיִם בַּחֹדֶשׁ הַחֲמִישִׁי בְּאֶחָד לַחֹדֶשׁ:

NUMBERS 34   במדבר לד   מסעי

39 Aaron was a hundred and twenty-three years old when he died on Mount Hor. 40 And the Canaanite, king of Arad, who dwelt in the Negeb, in the land of Canaan, learned of the coming of the Israelites. 41 They set out from Mount Hor and encamped at Zalmonah. 42 They set out from Zalmonah and encamped at Punon. 43 They set out from Punon and encamped at Oboth. 44 They set out from Oboth and encamped at Iye-abarim, in the territory of Moab. 45 They set out from Iyim and encamped at Dibon-gad. 46 They set out from Dibon-gad and encamped at Almon-diblathaim. 47 They set out from Almon-diblathaim and encamped in the hills of Abarim, before Nebo. 48 They set out from the hills of Abarim and encamped in the steppes of Moab, at the Jordan near Jericho; 49 they encamped by the Jordan from Beth-jeshimoth as far as Abel-shittim, in the steppes of Moab.

50 In the steppes of Moab, at the Jordan near Jericho, the LORD spoke to Moses, saying: 51 Speak to the Israelite people and say to them: When you cross the Jordan into the land of Canaan, 52 you shall dispossess all the inhabitants of the land; you shall destroy all their figured objects; you shall destroy all their molten images, and you shall demolish all their cult places. 53 And you shall take possession of the land and settle in it, for I have assigned the land to you to possess. 54 You shall apportion the land among yourselves by lot, clan by clan: with larger groups increase the share, with smaller groups reduce the share. Wherever the lot falls for anyone, that shall be his. You shall have your portions according to your ancestral tribes. 55 But if you do not dispossess the inhabitants of the land, those whom you allow to remain shall be stings in your eyes and thorns in your sides, and they shall harass you in the land in which you live; 56 so that I will do to you what I planned to do to them.

34 1 The LORD spoke to Moses, saying: 2 Instruct the Israelite people and say to them: When you enter the land of Canaan, this is the land that shall fall to you as your portion, the land of Canaan with its various boundaries: 3 Your southern sector shall extend from the wilderness of Zin alongside Edom. Your southern boundary shall start on the east from the tip of the Dead Sea. 4 Your boundary shall then turn to pass south of the ascent of Akrabbim and continue to Zin, and its limits shall be south of Kadesh-barnea, reaching Hazar-addar and continuing to Azmon. 5 From Azmon the boundary shall turn toward the Wadi of Egypt and terminate at the Sea. 6 For the western boundary you shall have the coast of the Great Sea; that shall serve as your western boundary. 7 This shall be your northern boundary: Draw a line from the Great Sea to Mount Hor; 8 from Mount Hor draw a line to Lebo-hamath, and let the boundary reach Zedad. 9 The boundary shall then run to Ziphron and terminate at Hazar-enan. That shall be your northern boundary. 10 For your eastern boundary you shall draw a line from Hazar-enan to Shepham. 11 From Shepham the boundary shall descend to Riblah on the east side of Ain; from there the boundary shall continue downward and abut on the eastern slopes of the Sea of Chinnereth. 12 The boundary shall then descend along the Jordan and terminate at the Dead Sea. That shall be your land as defined by its boundaries on all sides. 13 Moses instructed the Israelites, saying: This is the land you are to receive by lot as your hereditary portion, which the LORD has commanded to be given to the nine and a half tribes. 14 For the Reubenite tribe by its ancestral houses, the Gadite tribe by its ancestral houses, and the half-tribe of Manasseh have already received their portions: 15 those two and a half tribes have received their portions across the Jordan, opposite Jericho, on the east, the orient side.

16 The LORD spoke to Moses, saying: 17 These are the names of the men through whom the land shall be apportioned for you: Eleazar the priest and Joshua son of Nun. 18 And you shall also take a chieftain from each tribe through whom the land shall be apportioned. 19 These are the names of the men: from the tribe of Judah: Caleb son of Jephunneh. 20 From the Simeonite tribe: Samuel son of Ammihud. 21 From the tribe of Benjamin: Elidad son of Chislon. 22 From the Danite tribe: a chieftain, Bukki son of Jogli. 23 From the descendants of Joseph: from the Manassite tribe: a chieftain, Hanniel son of Ephod; 24 and from the Ephraimite tribe: a chieftain, Kemuel son of Shiphtan. 25 From the Zebulunite tribe:

172

NUMBERS 35   במדבר לה מסעי

a chieftain, Elizaphan son of Parnach. 26 From the Issacharite tribe: a chieftain, Paltiel son of Azzan. 27 From the Asherite tribe: a chieftain, Ahihud son of Shelomi. 28 From the Naphtalite tribe: a chieftain, Pedahel son of Ammihud. 29 It was these whom the LORD designated to allot portions to the Israelites in the land of Canaan.

35 1 The LORD spoke to Moses in the steppes of Moab at the Jordan near Jericho, saying: 2 Instruct the Israelite people to assign, out of the holdings apportioned to them, towns for the Levites to dwell in; you shall also assign to the Levites pasture land around their towns. 3 The towns shall be theirs to dwell in, and the pasture shall be for the cattle they own and all their other beasts. 4 The town pasture that you are to assign to the Levites shall extend a thousand cubits outside the town wall all around. 5 You shall measure off two thousand cubits outside the town on the east side, two thousand on the south side, two thousand on the west side, and two thousand on the north side, with the town in the center. That shall be the pasture for their towns. 6 The towns that you assign to the Levites shall comprise the six cities of refuge that you are to designate for a manslayer to flee to; to which you shall add forty-two towns. 7 Thus the total of the towns that you assign to the Levites shall be forty-eight towns, with their pasture. 8 In assigning towns from the holdings of the Israelites, take more from the larger groups and less from the smaller, so that each assigns towns to the Levites in proportion to the share it receives.

9 The LORD spoke further to Moses: 10 Speak to the Israelite people and say to them: When you cross the Jordan into the land of Canaan, 11 you shall provide yourselves with places to serve you as cities of refuge to which a manslayer who has killed a person unintentionally may flee. 12 The cities shall serve you as a refuge from the avenger, so that the manslayer may not die unless he has stood trial before the assembly. 13 The towns that you thus assign shall be six cities of refuge in all. 14 Three cities shall be designated beyond the Jordan, and the other three shall be designated in the land of Canaan: they shall serve as cities of refuge. 15 These six cities shall serve the Israelites and the resident aliens among them for refuge, so that anyone who kills a person unintentionally may flee there. 16 Anyone, however, who strikes another with an iron object so that death results is a murderer; the murderer must be put to death. 17 If he struck him with a stone tool that could cause death, and death resulted, he is a murderer; the murderer must be put to death. 18 Similarly, if the object with which he struck him was a wooden tool that could cause death, and death resulted, he is a murderer; the murderer must be put to death. 19 The blood-avenger himself shall put the murderer to death; it is he who shall put him to death upon encounter. 20 So, too, if he pushed him in hate or hurled something at him on purpose and death resulted, 21 or if he struck him with his hand in enmity and death resulted, the assailant shall be put to death; he is a murderer. The blood-avenger shall put the murderer to death upon encounter. 22 But if he pushed him without malice aforethought or hurled any object at him unintentionally, 23 or inadvertently dropped upon him any deadly object of stone, and death resulted — though he was not an enemy of his and did not seek his harm — 24 in such cases the assembly shall decide between the slayer and the blood-avenger. 25 The assembly shall protect the manslayer from the blood-avenger, and the assembly shall restore him to the city of refuge to which he fled, and there he shall remain until the death of the high priest who was anointed with the sacred oil. 26 But if the manslayer ever goes outside the limits of the city of refuge to which he has fled, 27 and the blood-avenger comes upon him outside the limits of his city of refuge, and the blood-avenger kills the manslayer, there is no bloodguilt on his account. 28 For he must remain inside his city of refuge until the death of the high priest; after the death of the high priest, the manslayer may return to his land holding. 29 Such shall be your law of procedure through the ages in all your settlements. 30 If anyone kills a person, the manslayer may be executed only on the evidence of witnesses; the testimony of a single witness against a person shall not suffice for a sentence of death. 31 You may not accept a ransom for the life of a murderer who is guilty of a capital crime; he must be put to death. 32 Nor may you accept ransom in lieu of flight to a city of refuge, enabling one to return to live on his land before the death of the priest. 33 You shall not pollute the land in which you live; for blood pollutes the land, and the land can have no expiation for blood

NUMBERS 36   במדבר לו מסעי

that is shed on it, except by the blood of him who shed it. 34 You shall not defile the land in which you live, in which I Myself abide, for I the LORD abide among the Israelite people.

36 1 The family heads in the clan of the descendants of Gilead son of Machir son of Manasseh, one of the Josephite clans, came forward and appealed to Moses and the chieftains, family heads of the Israelites. 2 They said, "The LORD commanded my lord to assign the land to the Israelites as shares by lot, and my lord was further commanded by the LORD to assign the share of our kinsman Zelophehad to his daughters. 3 Now, if they marry persons from another Israelite tribe, their share will be cut off from our ancestral portion and be added to the portion of the tribe into which they marry; thus our allotted portion will be diminished. 4 And even when the Israelites observe the jubilee, their share will be added to that of the tribe into which they marry, and their share will be cut off from the ancestral portion of our tribe." 5 So Moses, at the LORD's bidding, instructed the Israelites, saying: "The plea of the Josephite tribe is just. 6 This is what the LORD has commanded concerning the daughters of Zelophehad: They may marry anyone they wish, provided they marry into a clan of their father's tribe. 7 No inheritance of the Israelites may pass over from one tribe to another, but the Israelites must remain bound each to the ancestral portion of his tribe. 8 Every daughter among the Israelite tribes who inherits a share must marry someone from a clan of her father's tribe, in order that every Israelite may keep his ancestral share. 9 Thus no inheritance shall pass over from one tribe to another, but the Israelite tribes shall remain bound each to its portion." 10 The daughters of Zelophehad did as the LORD had commanded Moses: 11 Mahlah, Tirzah, Hoglah, Milcah, and Noah, Zelophehad's daughters, were married to their uncles. 12 marrying into clans of descendants of Manasseh son of Joseph; and so their share remained in the tribe of their father's clan. 13 These are the commandments and regulations that the LORD enjoined upon the Israelites, through Moses, on the steppes of Moab, at the Jordan near Jericho.

חזק

Detail from a mosaic, 4th century (the Byzantine period), found at the Samaritan synagogue at Khirbat-Samara, collection of the Archeological Staff Officer, Judea and Samaria, The Israel Museum, Jerusalem

Ivory pomegranate from the top of a priest's staff, possibly from Solomon's Temple, ca. mid-8th century BCE, collection of The Israel Museum, Jerusalem

DEUTERONOMY 1 דברים א

These are the words that Moses addressed to all Israel on the other side of the Jordan. - Through the wilderness, in the Arabah near Suph, between Paran and Tophel, Laban, Hazeroth, and Di-zahab, 2 it is eleven days from Horeb to Kadesh-barnea by the Mount Seir route. - 3 It was in the fortieth year, on the first day of the eleventh month, that Moses addressed the Israelites in accordance with the instructions that the LORD had given him for them. 4 after he had defeated Sihon king of the Amorites, who dwelt in Heshbon, and King Og of Bashan, who dwelt at Ashtaroth [and] Edrei. 5 On the other side of the Jordan, in the land of Moab, Moses undertook to expound this Teaching. He said: 6 The LORD our God spoke to us at Horeb, saying: You have stayed long enough at this mountain. 7 Start out and make your way to the hill country of the Amorites and to all their neighbors in the Arabah, the hill country, the Shephelah, the Negeb, the seacoast, the land of the Canaanites, and the Lebanon, as far as the Great River, the river Euphrates. 8 See, I place the land at your disposal. Go, take possession of the land that the LORD swore to your fathers, Abraham, Isaac, and Jacob, to assign to them and to their heirs after them. 9 Thereupon I said to you, "I cannot bear the burden of you by myself. 10 The LORD your God has multiplied you until you are today as numerous as the stars in the sky. - 11 May the LORD, the God of your fathers, increase your numbers a thousandfold, and bless you as He promised you. - 12 How can I bear unaided the trouble of you, and the burden, and the bickering! 13 Pick from each of your tribes men who are wise, discerning, and experienced, and I will appoint them as your heads." 14 You answered me and said,

DEUTERONOMY 2 · דברים ב

"What you propose to do is good." 15 So I took your tribal leaders, wise and experienced men, and appointed them heads over you: chiefs of thousands, chiefs of hundreds, chiefs of fifties, and chiefs of tens, and officials for your tribes. 16 I charged your magistrates at that time as follows, "Hear out your fellow men, and decide justly between any man and a fellow Israelite or a stranger. 17 You shall not be partial in judgment: hear out low and high alike. Fear no man, for judgment is God's. And any matter that is too difficult for you, you shall bring to me and I will hear it." 18 Thus I instructed you, at that time, about the various things that you should do. 19 We set out from Horeb and traveled the great and terrible wilderness that you saw, along the road to the hill country of the Amorites, as the LORD our God had commanded us. When we reached Kadesh-barnea, 20 I said to you, "You have come to the hill country of the Amorites which the LORD our God is giving to us. 21 See, the LORD your God has placed the land at your disposal. Go up, take possession, as the LORD, the God of your fathers, promised you. Fear not and be not dismayed." 22 Then all of you came to me and said, "Let us send men ahead to reconnoiter the land for us and bring back word on the route we shall follow and the cities we shall come to." 23 I approved of the plan, and so I selected twelve of your men, one from each tribe. 24 They made for the hill country, came to the wadi Eshcol, and spied it out. 25 They took some of the fruit of the land with them and brought it down to us. And they gave us this report: "It is a good land that the LORD our God is giving to us." 26 Yet you refused to go up, and flouted the command of the LORD your God. 27 You sulked in your tents and said, "It is because the LORD hates us that He brought us out of the land of Egypt, to hand us over to the Amorites to wipe us out. 28 What kind of place are we going to? Our kinsmen have taken the heart out of us, saying, 'We saw there a people stronger and taller than we, large cities with walls sky-high, and even Anakites.'" 29 I said to you, "Have no dread or fear of them. 30 None other than the LORD your God, who goes before you, will fight for you, just as He did for you in Egypt before your very eyes, 31 and in the wilderness, where you saw how the LORD your God carried you, as a man carries his son, all the way that you traveled until you came to this place. 32 Yet for all that, you have no faith in the LORD your God, 33 who goes before you on your journeys – to scout the place where you are to encamp – in fire by night and in cloud by day, in order to guide you on the route you are to follow." 34 When the LORD heard your loud complaint, He was angry. He vowed, 35 Not one of these men, this evil generation, shall see the good land that I swore to give to your fathers – 36 none except Caleb son of Jephunneh; he shall see it, and to him and his descendants will I give the land on which he set foot, because he remained loyal to the LORD. 37 Because of you the LORD was incensed with me too, and He said: You shall not enter it either. 38 Joshua son of Nun, who attends you, he shall enter it. Imbue him with strength, for he shall allot it to Israel. 39 Moreover, your little ones who you said would be carried off, your children who do not yet know good from bad, they shall enter it: to them will I give it and they shall possess it. 40 As for you, turn about and march into the wilderness by the way of the Sea of Reeds. 41 You replied to me, saying, "We stand guilty before the LORD. We will go up now and fight, just as our God commanded us." And you all girded yourselves with war gear and recklessly started for the hill country. 42 But the LORD said to me, "Warn them: Do not go up and do not fight, since I am not in your midst: else you will be routed by your enemies." 43 I spoke to you, but you would not listen; you flouted the LORD's command and willfully marched into the hill country. 44 Then the Amorites who lived in those hills came out against you like so many bees and chased you, and they crushed you at Hormah in Seir. 45 Again you wept before the LORD; but the LORD would not heed your cry or give ear to you. 46 Thus, after you had remained at Kadesh all that long time, 2 1 we marched back into the wilderness by the way of the Sea of Reeds, as the LORD had spoken to me.

DEUTERONOMY 2 · דברים ב

and skirted the hill country of Seir a long time. 2 Then the LORD said to me: 3 You have been skirting this hill country long enough; now turn north. 4 And charge the people as follows: You will be passing through the territory of your kinsmen, the descendants of Esau, who live in Seir. Though they will be afraid of you, be very careful 5 not to provoke them. For I will not give you of their land so much as a foot can tread on; I have given the hill country of Seir as a possession to Esau. 6 What food you eat you shall obtain from them for money; even the water you drink you shall procure from them for money. 7 Indeed, the LORD your God has blessed you in all your undertakings. He has watched over your wanderings through this great wilderness; the LORD your God has been with you these past forty years: you have lacked nothing. 8 We then moved on, away from our kinsmen, the descendants of Esau, who live in Seir, away from the road of the Arabah, away from Elath and Ezion-geber; and we marched on in the direction of the wilderness of Moab. 9 And the LORD said to me: Do not harass the Moabites or provoke them to war. For I will not give you any of their land as a possession; I have assigned Ar as a possession to the descendants of Lot. - 10 It was formerly inhabited by the Emim, a people great and numerous, and as tall as the Anakites. 11 Like the Anakites, they are counted as Rephaim; but the Moabites call them Emim. 12 Similarly, Seir was formerly inhabited by the Horites; but the descendants of Esau dispossessed them, wiping them out and settling in their place, just as Israel did in the land they were to possess, which the LORD had given to them. - 13 Up now! Cross the wadi Zered! So we crossed the wadi Zered. 14 The time that we spent in travel from Kadesh-barnea until we crossed the wadi Zered was thirty-eight years, until that whole generation of warriors had perished from the camp, as the LORD had sworn concerning them. 15 Indeed, the hand of the LORD struck them, to root them out from the camp to the last man. 16 When all the warriors among the people had died off, 17 the LORD spoke to me, saying: 18 You are now passing through the territory of Moab, through Ar. 19 You will then be close to the Ammonites: do not harass them or start a fight with them. For I will not give you any part of the land of the Ammonites to you as a possession; I have assigned it as a possession to the descendants of Lot. - 20 It, too, is counted as Rephaim country. It was formerly inhabited by Rephaim, whom the Ammonites call Zamzummim. 21 a people great and numerous and as tall as the Anakites. The LORD wiped them out, so that [the Ammonites] dispossessed them and settled in their place, 22 as He did for the descendants of Esau who live in Seir, when He wiped out the Horites before them, so that they dispossessed them and settled in their place, as is still the case. 23 So, too, with the Avvim who dwelt in villages in the vicinity of Gaza: the Caphtorim, who came from Crete, wiped them out and settled in their place. - 24 Up! Set out across the wadi Arnon! See, I give into your power Sihon the Amorite, king of Heshbon, and his land. Begin the occupation; engage him in battle. 25 This day I begin to put the dread and fear of you upon the peoples everywhere under heaven, so that they shall tremble and quake because of you whenever they hear you mentioned. 26 Then I sent messengers from the wilderness of Kedemoth to King Sihon of Heshbon with an offer of peace, as follows: 27 "Let me pass through your country. I will keep strictly to the highway, turning off neither to the right nor to the left. 28 What food I eat you will supply for money, and what water I drink you will furnish for money; just let me pass through - 29 as the descendants of Esau who dwell in Seir did for me, and the Moabites who dwell in Ar - that I may cross the Jordan into the land that the LORD our God is giving us." 30 But King Sihon of Heshbon refused to let us pass through, because the LORD our God had stiffened his will and hardened his heart in order to deliver him into your power - as is now the case.

31 And the LORD said to me: See, I begin by placing Sihon and his land at your disposal. Begin the occupation: take possession of his land. 32 Sihon with all his men took the field against us at Jahaz, 33 and the LORD our God delivered him to us and we defeated him and his sons and all his men. 34 At that time we captured all his towns, and we doomed every town - men, women, and children - leaving no survivor. 35 We retained as booty only the cattle and the spoil of the cities that we captured. 36 From Aroer on the edge of the Arnon valley,

ב וַיֹּאמֶר יְהוָה אֵלַי לֵאמֹר: ג רַב־לָכֶם סֹב אֶת־הָהָר הַזֶּה פְּנוּ לָכֶם צָפֹנָה: ד וְאֶת־הָעָם צַו לֵאמֹר אַתֶּם עֹבְרִים בִּגְבוּל אֲחֵיכֶם בְּנֵי־עֵשָׂו הַיֹּשְׁבִים בְּשֵׂעִיר וְיִירְאוּ מִכֶּם וְנִשְׁמַרְתֶּם מְאֹד: ה אַל־תִּתְגָּרוּ בָם כִּי לֹא־אֶתֵּן לָכֶם מֵאַרְצָם עַד מִדְרַךְ כַּף־רָגֶל כִּי־יְרֻשָּׁה לְעֵשָׂו נָתַתִּי אֶת־הַר שֵׂעִיר: ו אֹכֶל תִּשְׁבְּרוּ מֵאִתָּם בַּכֶּסֶף וַאֲכַלְתֶּם וְגַם־מַיִם תִּכְרוּ מֵאִתָּם בַּכֶּסֶף וּשְׁתִיתֶם: ז כִּי יְהוָה אֱלֹהֶיךָ בֵּרַכְךָ בְּכֹל מַעֲשֵׂה יָדֶךָ יָדַע לֶכְתְּךָ אֶת־הַמִּדְבָּר הַגָּדֹל הַזֶּה זֶה אַרְבָּעִים שָׁנָה יְהוָה אֱלֹהֶיךָ עִמָּךְ לֹא חָסַרְתָּ דָּבָר: ח וַנַּעֲבֹר מֵאֵת אַחֵינוּ בְנֵי־עֵשָׂו הַיֹּשְׁבִים בְּשֵׂעִיר מִדֶּרֶךְ הָעֲרָבָה מֵאֵילַת וּמֵעֶצְיֹן גָּבֶר וַנֵּפֶן וַנַּעֲבֹר דֶּרֶךְ מִדְבַּר מוֹאָב: ט וַיֹּאמֶר יְהוָה אֵלַי אַל־תָּצַר אֶת־מוֹאָב וְאַל־תִּתְגָּר בָּם מִלְחָמָה כִּי לֹא־אֶתֵּן לְךָ מֵאַרְצוֹ יְרֻשָּׁה כִּי לִבְנֵי־לוֹט נָתַתִּי אֶת־עָר יְרֻשָּׁה: י הָאֵמִים לְפָנִים יָשְׁבוּ בָהּ עַם גָּדוֹל וְרַב וָרָם כָּעֲנָקִים: יא רְפָאִים יֵחָשְׁבוּ אַף־הֵם כָּעֲנָקִים וְהַמֹּאָבִים יִקְרְאוּ לָהֶם אֵמִים: יב וּבְשֵׂעִיר יָשְׁבוּ הַחֹרִים לְפָנִים וּבְנֵי עֵשָׂו יִירָשׁוּם וַיַּשְׁמִידוּם מִפְּנֵיהֶם וַיֵּשְׁבוּ תַּחְתָּם כַּאֲשֶׁר עָשָׂה יִשְׂרָאֵל לְאֶרֶץ יְרֻשָּׁתוֹ אֲשֶׁר־נָתַן יְהוָה לָהֶם: יג עַתָּה קֻמוּ וְעִבְרוּ לָכֶם אֶת־נַחַל זָרֶד וַנַּעֲבֹר אֶת־נַחַל זָרֶד: יד וְהַיָּמִים אֲשֶׁר־הָלַכְנוּ מִקָּדֵשׁ בַּרְנֵעַ עַד אֲשֶׁר־עָבַרְנוּ אֶת־נַחַל זֶרֶד שְׁלֹשִׁים וּשְׁמֹנֶה שָׁנָה עַד־תֹּם כָּל־הַדּוֹר אַנְשֵׁי הַמִּלְחָמָה מִקֶּרֶב הַמַּחֲנֶה כַּאֲשֶׁר נִשְׁבַּע יְהוָה לָהֶם: טו וְגַם יַד־יְהוָה הָיְתָה בָּם לְהֻמָּם מִקֶּרֶב הַמַּחֲנֶה עַד תֻּמָּם: טז וַיְהִי כַאֲשֶׁר־תַּמּוּ כָּל־אַנְשֵׁי הַמִּלְחָמָה לָמוּת מִקֶּרֶב הָעָם: יז וַיְדַבֵּר יְהוָה אֵלַי לֵאמֹר: יח אַתָּה עֹבֵר הַיּוֹם אֶת־גְּבוּל מוֹאָב אֶת־עָר: יט וְקָרַבְתָּ מוּל בְּנֵי עַמּוֹן אַל־תְּצֻרֵם וְאַל־תִּתְגָּר בָּם כִּי לֹא־אֶתֵּן מֵאֶרֶץ בְּנֵי־עַמּוֹן לְךָ יְרֻשָּׁה כִּי לִבְנֵי־לוֹט נְתַתִּיהָ יְרֻשָּׁה: כ אֶרֶץ־רְפָאִים תֵּחָשֵׁב אַף־הִוא רְפָאִים יָשְׁבוּ־בָהּ לְפָנִים וְהָעַמֹּנִים יִקְרְאוּ לָהֶם זַמְזֻמִּים: כא עַם גָּדוֹל וְרַב וָרָם כָּעֲנָקִים וַיַּשְׁמִידֵם יְהוָה מִפְּנֵיהֶם וַיִּירָשֻׁם וַיֵּשְׁבוּ תַחְתָּם: כב כַּאֲשֶׁר עָשָׂה לִבְנֵי עֵשָׂו הַיֹּשְׁבִים בְּשֵׂעִיר אֲשֶׁר הִשְׁמִיד אֶת־הַחֹרִי מִפְּנֵיהֶם וַיִּירָשֻׁם וַיֵּשְׁבוּ תַחְתָּם עַד הַיּוֹם הַזֶּה: כג וְהָעַוִּים הַיֹּשְׁבִים בַּחֲצֵרִים עַד־עַזָּה כַּפְתֹּרִים הַיֹּצְאִים מִכַּפְתֹּר הִשְׁמִידֻם וַיֵּשְׁבוּ תַחְתָּם: כד קוּמוּ סְּעוּ וְעִבְרוּ אֶת־נַחַל אַרְנֹן רְאֵה נָתַתִּי בְיָדְךָ אֶת־סִיחֹן מֶלֶךְ־חֶשְׁבּוֹן הָאֱמֹרִי וְאֶת־אַרְצוֹ הָחֵל רָשׁ וְהִתְגָּר בּוֹ מִלְחָמָה: כה הַיּוֹם הַזֶּה אָחֵל תֵּת פַּחְדְּךָ וְיִרְאָתְךָ עַל־פְּנֵי הָעַמִּים תַּחַת כָּל־הַשָּׁמָיִם אֲשֶׁר יִשְׁמְעוּן שִׁמְעֲךָ וְרָגְזוּ וְחָלוּ מִפָּנֶיךָ: כו וָאֶשְׁלַח מַלְאָכִים מִמִּדְבַּר קְדֵמוֹת אֶל־סִיחוֹן מֶלֶךְ חֶשְׁבּוֹן דִּבְרֵי שָׁלוֹם לֵאמֹר: כז אֶעְבְּרָה בְאַרְצֶךָ בַּדֶּרֶךְ בַּדֶּרֶךְ אֵלֵךְ לֹא אָסוּר יָמִין וּשְׂמֹאול: כח אֹכֶל בַּכֶּסֶף תַּשְׁבִּרֵנִי וְאָכַלְתִּי וּמַיִם בַּכֶּסֶף תִּתֶּן־לִי וְשָׁתִיתִי רַק אֶעְבְּרָה בְרַגְלָי: כט כַּאֲשֶׁר עָשׂוּ־לִי בְּנֵי עֵשָׂו הַיֹּשְׁבִים בְּשֵׂעִיר וְהַמּוֹאָבִים הַיֹּשְׁבִים בְּעָר עַד אֲשֶׁר־אֶעֱבֹר אֶת־הַיַּרְדֵּן אֶל־הָאָרֶץ אֲשֶׁר־יְהוָה אֱלֹהֵינוּ נֹתֵן לָנוּ: ל וְלֹא אָבָה סִיחֹן מֶלֶךְ חֶשְׁבּוֹן הַעֲבִרֵנוּ בּוֹ כִּי־הִקְשָׁה יְהוָה אֱלֹהֶיךָ אֶת־רוּחוֹ וְאִמֵּץ אֶת־לְבָבוֹ לְמַעַן תִּתּוֹ בְיָדְךָ כַּיּוֹם הַזֶּה: לא וַיֹּאמֶר יְהוָה אֵלַי רְאֵה הַחִלֹּתִי תֵּת לְפָנֶיךָ אֶת־סִיחֹן וְאֶת־אַרְצוֹ הָחֵל רָשׁ לָרֶשֶׁת אֶת־אַרְצוֹ: לב וַיֵּצֵא סִיחֹן לִקְרָאתֵנוּ הוּא וְכָל־עַמּוֹ לַמִּלְחָמָה יָהְצָה: לג וַיִּתְּנֵהוּ יְהוָה אֱלֹהֵינוּ לְפָנֵינוּ וַנַּךְ אֹתוֹ וְאֶת־בנו (בָּנָיו) וְאֶת־כָּל־עַמּוֹ: לד וַנִּלְכֹּד אֶת־כָּל־עָרָיו בָּעֵת הַהִוא וַנַּחֲרֵם אֶת־כָּל־עִיר מְתִם וְהַנָּשִׁים וְהַטָּף לֹא הִשְׁאַרְנוּ שָׂרִיד: לה רַק הַבְּהֵמָה בָּזַזְנוּ לָנוּ וּשְׁלַל הֶעָרִים אֲשֶׁר לָכָדְנוּ: לו מֵעֲרֹעֵר אֲשֶׁר עַל־שְׂפַת־נַחַל

DEUTERONOMY 3 · דברים ג

including the town in the valley itself, to Gilead, not a city was too mighty for us: the LORD our God delivered everything to us. ³⁷ But you did not encroach upon the land of the Ammonites, all along the wadi Jabbok and the towns of the hill country, just as the LORD our God had commanded. **3** ¹ We made our way up the road toward Bashan, and King Og of Bashan with all his men took the field against us at Edrei. ² But the LORD said to me: Do not fear him, for I am delivering him and all his men and his country into your power, and you will do to him as you did to Sihon king of the Amorites, who lived in Heshbon. ³ So the LORD our God also delivered into our power King Og of Bashan, with all his men, and we dealt them such a blow that no survivor was left. ⁴ At that time we captured all his towns; there was not a town that we did not take from them: sixty towns, the whole district of Argob, the kingdom of Og in Bashan – ⁵ all those towns were fortified with high walls, gates, and bars – apart from a great number of unwalled towns. ⁶ We doomed them as we had done in the case of King Sihon of Heshbon; we doomed every town – men, women, and children – ⁷ and retained as booty all the cattle and the spoil of the towns. ⁸ Thus we seized, at that time, from the two Amorite kings, the country beyond the Jordan, from the wadi Arnon to Mount Hermon – ⁹ Sidonians called Hermon Sirion, and the Amorites call it Senir – ¹⁰ all the towns of the Tableland and the whole of Gilead and Bashan as far as Salcah and Edrei, the towns of Og's kingdom in Bashan. ¹¹ Only King Og of Bashan was left of the remaining Rephaim. His bedstead, an iron bedstead, is now in Rabbah of the Ammonites; it is nine cubits long and four cubits wide, by the standard cubit! ¹² And this is the land which we apportioned at that time: The part from Aroer along the wadi Arnon, with part of the hill country of Gilead and its towns, I assigned to the Reubenites and the Gadites. ¹³ The rest of Gilead, and all of Bashan under Og's rule – the whole Argob district, all that part of Bashan which is called Rephaim country – I assigned to the half-tribe of Manasseh. ¹⁴ Jair son of Manasseh received the whole Argob district (that is, Bashan) as far as the boundary of the Geshurites and the Maacathites, and named it after himself: Havvoth-jair – as is still the case. ¹⁵ To Machir I assigned Gilead. ¹⁶ And to the Reubenites and the Gadites I assigned the part from Gilead down to the wadi Arnon, the middle of the wadi being the boundary, and up to the wadi Jabbok, the boundary of the Ammonites; ¹⁷ [we also seized] the Arabah, the foot of the slopes of Pisgah on the east, to the edge of the Jordan, and from Chinnereth down to the sea of the Arabah, the Dead Sea. ¹⁸ At that time I charged you, saying, "The LORD your God has given you this country to possess. You must go as shock-troops, warriors all, at the head of your Israelite kinsmen. ¹⁹ Only your wives, children, and livestock – I know that you have much livestock – shall be left in the towns I have assigned to you, ²⁰ until the LORD has granted your kinsmen a haven such as you have, and they too have taken possession of the land that the LORD your God is assigning them, beyond the Jordan. Then you may return each to the homestead that I have assigned to him." ²¹ I also charged Joshua at that time, saying, "You have seen with your own eyes all that the LORD your God has done to these two kings; so shall the LORD do to all the kingdoms into which you shall cross over. ²² Do not fear them, for it is the LORD your God who will battle for you."

²³ I pleaded with the LORD at that time, saying, ²⁴ "O Lord GOD, You who let Your servant see the first works of Your greatness and Your mighty hand, You whose powerful deeds no god in heaven or on earth can equal! ²⁵ Let me, I pray, cross over and see the good land on the other side of the Jordan, that good hill country, and the Lebanon." ²⁶ But the LORD was wrathful with me on your account and would not listen to me. The LORD said to me, "Enough! Never speak to Me of this matter again! ²⁷ Go up to the summit of Pisgah and gaze about, to the west, the north, the south, and the east. Look at it well, for you shall not go across yonder Jordan. ²⁸ Give Joshua his instructions, and imbue him with strength and courage, for he shall go across at the head of this people,

DEUTERONOMY 4   דברים ד ואתחנן

and he shall allot to them the land that you may only see." 29 Meanwhile we stayed on in the valley near Beth-peor.

4 1 And now, O Israel, give heed to the laws and rules that I am instructing you to observe, so that you may live to enter and occupy the land that the LORD, the God of your fathers, is giving you. 2 You shall not add anything to what I command you or take anything away from it, but keep the commandments of the LORD your God that I enjoin upon you. 3 You saw with your own eyes what the LORD did in the matter of Baal-peor, that the LORD your God wiped out from among you every person who followed Baal-peor. 4 while you, who held fast to the LORD your God, are all alive today. 5 See, I have imparted to you laws and rules, as the LORD my God has commanded me, for you to abide by in the land that you are about to enter and occupy. 6 Observe them faithfully, for that will be proof of your wisdom and discernment to other peoples, who on hearing of all these laws will say, "Surely, that great nation is a wise and discerning people." 7 For what great nation is there that has a god so close at hand as is the LORD our God whenever we call upon Him? 8 Or what great nation has laws and rules as perfect as all this Teaching that I set before you this day? 9 But take utmost care and watch yourselves scrupulously, so that you do not forget the things that you saw with your own eyes and so that they do not fade from your mind as long as you live. And make them known to your children and to your children's children: 10 The day you stood before the LORD your God at Horeb, when the LORD said to Me, "Gather the people to Me that I may let them hear My words, in order that they may learn to revere Me as long as they live on earth, and may so teach their children." 11 You came forward and stood at the foot of the mountain. The mountain was ablaze with flames to the very skies, dark with densest clouds. 12 The LORD spoke to you out of the fire; you heard the sound of words but perceived no shape - nothing but a voice. 13 He declared to you the covenant that He commanded you to observe, the Ten Commandments; and He inscribed them on two tablets of stone.

14 At the same time the LORD commanded me to impart to you laws and rules for you to observe in the land that you are about to cross into and occupy. 15 For your own sake, therefore, be most careful - since you saw no shape when the LORD your God spoke to you at Horeb out of the fire - not to act wickedly and make for yourselves a sculptured image in any likeness whatever: the form of a man or a woman, 17 the form of any beast on earth, the form of any winged bird that flies in the sky, 18 the form of anything that creeps on the ground, the form of any fish that is in the waters below the earth. 19 And when you look up to the sky and behold the sun and the moon and the stars, the whole heavenly host, you must not be lured into bowing down to or serving them. These the LORD your God allotted to other peoples everywhere under heaven; 20 but you the LORD took and brought out of Egypt, that iron blast furnace, to be His very own people, as is now the case. 21 Now the LORD was angry with me on your account and swore that I should not cross the Jordan and enter the good land that the LORD your God is assigning you as a heritage. 22 For I must die in this land; I shall not cross the Jordan. But you will cross and take possession of that good land. 23 Take care, then, not to forget the covenant that the LORD your God concluded with you, and not to make for yourselves a sculptured image in any likeness, against which the LORD your God has enjoined you. 24 For the LORD your God is a consuming fire, an impassioned God.   25 When you have begotten children and children's children and are long established in the land, should you act wickedly and make for yourselves a sculptured image in any likeness, causing the LORD your God displeasure and vexation, 26 I call heaven and earth this day to witness against you that you shall soon perish from the land that you are crossing the Jordan to possess; you shall not long endure in it, but shall be utterly wiped out. 27 The LORD will scatter you among the peoples,

180

DEUTERONOMY 5   דברים ה ואתחנן

and only a scant few of you shall be left among the nations to which the LORD will drive you. 28 There you will serve man-made gods of wood and stone, that cannot see or hear or eat or smell. 29 But if you search there for the LORD your God, you will find Him, if only you seek Him with all your heart and soul – 30 when you are in distress because all these things have befallen you and, in the end, return to the LORD your God and obey Him. 31 For the LORD your God is a compassionate God: He will not fail you nor will He let you perish; He will not forget the covenant which He made on oath with your fathers. 32 You have but to inquire about bygone ages that came before you, ever since God created man on earth, from one end of heaven to the other: has anything as grand as this ever happened, or has its like ever been known? 33 Has any people heard the voice of a god speaking out of a fire, as you have, and survived? 34 Or has any god ventured to go and take for himself one nation from the midst of another by prodigious acts, by signs and portents, by war, by a mighty and an outstretched arm and awesome power, as the LORD your God did for you in Egypt before your very eyes? 35 It has been clearly demonstrated to you that the LORD alone is God; there is none beside Him. 36 From the heavens He let you hear His voice to discipline you; on earth He let you see His great fire; and from amidst that fire you heard His words. 37 And because He loved your fathers, He chose their heirs after them: He Himself, in His great might, led you out of Egypt, 38 to drive from your path nations greater and more populous than you, to take you into their land and assign it to you as a heritage, as is still the case. 39 Know therefore this day and keep in mind that the LORD alone is God in heaven above and on earth below; there is no other. 40 Observe His laws and commandments, which I enjoin upon you this day, that it may go well with you and your children after you, and that you may long remain in the land that the LORD your God is assigning to you for all time.

41 Then Moses set aside three cities on the east side of the Jordan 42 to which a manslayer could escape, one who unwittingly slew a fellow man without having been hostile to him in the past; he could flee to one of these cities and live: 43 Bezer, in the wilderness in the Tableland, belonging to the Reubenites; Ramoth, in Gilead, belonging to the Gadites; and Golan, in Bashan, belonging to the Manassites. 44 This is the Teaching that Moses set before the Israelites: 45 these are the decrees, laws, and rules that Moses addressed to the people of Israel, after they had left Egypt, 46 beyond the Jordan, in the valley at Beth-peor, in the land of King Sihon of the Amorites, who dwelt in Heshbon, whom Moses and the Israelites defeated after they had left Egypt. 47 They had taken possession of his country and that of King Og of Bashan – the two kings of the Amorites – which were on the east side of the Jordan 48 from Aroer on the banks of the wadi Arnon, as far as Mount Sion, that is, Hermon, 49 also the whole Arabah on the east side of the Jordan, as far as the Sea of the Arabah, at the foot of the slopes of Pisgah.

5 1 Moses summoned all the Israelites and said to them: Hear, O Israel, the laws and rules that I proclaim to you this day! Study them and observe them faithfully! 2 The LORD our God made a covenant with us at Horeb. 3 It was not with our fathers that the LORD made this covenant, but with us, the living, every one of us who is here today. 4 Face to face the LORD spoke to you on the mountain out of the fire – 5 I stood between the LORD and you at that time to convey the LORD's words to you, for you were afraid of the fire and did not go up the mountain – saying:

6 I the LORD am your God who brought you out of the land of Egypt, the house of bondage; 7 You shall have no other gods beside Me. 8 You shall not make for yourself a sculptured image, any likeness of what is in the heavens above, or on the earth below, or in the waters below the earth. 9 You shall not bow down to them or serve them. For I the LORD your God am an impassioned God, visiting the guilt of the parents upon the children, upon the third and upon the fourth generations of those

181

DEUTERONOMY 6

who reject Me. 10 but showing kindness to the thousandth generation of those who love Me and keep My commandments.

11 You shall not swear falsely by the name of the LORD your God; for the LORD will not clear one who swears falsely by His name.

12 Observe the sabbath day and keep it holy, as the LORD your God has commanded you. 13 Six days you shall labor and do all your work, 14 but the seventh day is a sabbath of the LORD your God; you shall not do any work - you, your son or your daughter, your male or female slave, your ox or your ass, or any of your cattle, or the stranger in your settlements, so that your male and female slave may rest as you do. 15 Remember that you were a slave in the land of Egypt and the LORD your God freed you from there with a mighty hand and an outstretched arm; therefore the LORD your God has commanded you to observe the sabbath day.

16 Honor your father and your mother, as the LORD your God has commanded you, that you may long endure, and that you may fare well, in the land that the LORD your God is assigning to you.

17 You shall not murder.

You shall not commit adultery.   You shall not steal.

You shall not bear false witness against your neighbor.

18 You shall not covet your neighbor's wife. You shall not crave your neighbor's house, or his field, or his male or female slave, or his ox, or his ass, or anything that is your neighbor's. 19 The LORD spoke those words - those and no more—to your whole congregation at the mountain, with a mighty voice out of the fire and the dense clouds. He inscribed them on two tablets of stone, which He gave to me. 20 When you heard the voice out of the darkness, while the mountain was ablaze with fire, you came up to me, all your tribal heads and elders, 21 and said, "The LORD our God has just shown us His majestic Presence, and we have heard His voice out of the fire; we have seen this day that man may live though God has spoken to him. 22 Let us not die, then, for this fearsome fire will consume us; if we hear the voice of the LORD our God any longer, we shall die. 23 For what mortal ever heard the voice of the living God speak out of the fire, as we did, and lived? 24 You go closer and hear all that the LORD our God says, and then you tell us everything that the LORD our God tells you, and we will willingly do it." 25 The LORD heard the plea that you made to me, and the LORD said to me, "I have heard the plea that this people made to you; they did well to speak thus. 26 May they always be of such mind, to revere Me and follow all My commandments, that it may go well with them and with their children forever! 27 Go, say to them, 'Return to your tents.' 28 But you remain here with Me, and I will give you the whole Instruction - the laws and the rules - that you shall impart to them, for them to observe in the land that I am giving them to possess." 29 Be careful, then, to do as the LORD your God has commanded you. Do not turn aside to the right or to the left; 30 follow only the path that the LORD your God has enjoined upon you, so that you may thrive and that it may go well with you, and that you may long endure in the land you are to possess. 6 And this is the Instruction - the laws and the rules - that the LORD your God has commanded [me] to impart to you, to be observed in the land that you are about to cross into and occupy, 2 so that you, your children, and your children's children may revere the LORD your God and follow, as long as you live, all His laws and commandments that I enjoin upon you, to the end that you may long endure. 3 Obey, O Israel, willingly and faithfully, that it may go well with you and that you may increase greatly [in] a land flowing with milk and honey, as the LORD, the God of your fathers, spoke to you.

4 Hear, O Israel! The LORD is our God, the LORD Alone. 5 You shall love the LORD your God with all your heart and with all your soul and with all your might. 6 Take to heart these instructions with which I charge you this day. 7 Impress them upon your children. Recite them when you stay at home and when you are away, when you lie down and when you get up. 8 Bind them as a sign

182

DEUTERONOMY 7   דברים ז ואתחנן

on your hand and let them serve as a symbol on your forehead; 9 inscribe them on the doorposts of your house and on your gates. 10 When the LORD your God brings you into the land that He swore to your fathers, Abraham, Isaac, and Jacob, to assign to you – great and flourishing cities that you did not build, 11 houses full of all good things that you did not fill, hewn cisterns that you did not hew, vineyards and olive groves that you did not plant – and you eat your fill, 12 take heed that you do not forget the LORD who freed you from the land of Egypt, the house of bondage. 13 Revere only the LORD your God and worship Him alone, and swear only by His name. 14 Do not follow other gods, any gods of the peoples about you – 15 for the LORD your God in your midst is an impassioned God – lest the anger of the LORD your God blaze forth against you and He wipe you off the face of the earth.

16 Do not try the LORD your God, as you did at Massah. 17 Be sure to keep the commandments, decrees, and laws that the LORD your God has enjoined upon you. 18 Do what is right and good in the sight of the LORD, that it may go well with you and you may be able to possess the good land that the LORD your God promised on oath to your fathers, 19 and that all your enemies may be driven out before you, as the LORD has spoken. 20 When, in time to come, your children ask you, "What mean the decrees, laws, and rules that the LORD our God has enjoined upon you?" 21 you shall say to your children, "We were slaves to Pharaoh in Egypt and the LORD freed us from Egypt with a mighty hand. 22 The LORD wrought before our eyes marvelous and destructive signs and portents in Egypt, against Pharaoh and all his household; 23 and us He freed from there, that He might take us and give us the land that He had promised on oath to our fathers. 24 Then the LORD commanded us to observe all these laws, to revere the LORD our God, for our lasting good and for our survival, as is now the case. 25 It will be therefore to our merit before the LORD our God to observe faithfully this whole Instruction, as He has commanded us."

7 1 When the LORD your God brings you to the land that you are about to enter and possess, and He dislodges many nations before you – the Hittites, Girgashites, Amorites, Canaanites, Perizzites, Hivites, and Jebusites, seven nations much larger than you – 2 and the LORD your God delivers them to you and you defeat them, you must doom them to destruction: grant them no terms and give them no quarter. 3 You shall not intermarry with them: do not give your daughters to their sons or take their daughters for your sons. 4 For they will turn your children away from Me to worship other gods, and the LORD's anger will blaze forth against you and He will promptly wipe you out. 5 Instead, this is what you shall do to them: you shall tear down their altars, smash their pillars, cut down their sacred posts, and consign their images to the fire. 6 For you are a people consecrated to the LORD your God: of all the peoples on earth the LORD your God chose you to be His treasured people. 7 It is not because you are the most numerous of peoples that the LORD set His heart on you and chose you – indeed, you are the smallest of peoples; 8 but it was because the LORD favored you and kept the oath He made to your fathers that the LORD freed you with a mighty hand and rescued you from the house of bondage, from the power of Pharaoh king of Egypt. 9 Know, therefore, that only the LORD your God is God, the steadfast God who keeps His covenant faithfully to the thousandth generation of those who love Him and keep His commandments, 10 but who instantly requites with destruction those who reject Him – never slow with those who reject Him, but requiting them instantly. 11 Therefore, observe faithfully the Instruction – the laws and the rules – with which I charge you today.

12 **A**nd if you do obey these rules and observe them carefully, the LORD your God will maintain faithfully for you the covenant that He made on oath with your fathers; 13 He will favor you and bless you and multiply you: He will bless the issue of your womb and the produce of your soil, your new grain and wine and oil, the calving of your herd and the lambing of your flock, in the land that He swore to your fathers to assign to you. 14 You shall be blessed above all other peoples: there shall be no

183

DEUTERONOMY 8 דברים ח

sterile male or female among you or among your livestock. 15 The LORD will ward off from you all sickness: He will not bring upon you any of the dreadful diseases of Egypt, about which you know, but will inflict them upon all your enemies. 16 You shall destroy all the peoples that the LORD your God delivers to you, showing them no pity. And you shall not worship their gods, for that would be a snare to you.

17 Should you say to yourselves, "These nations are more numerous than we; how can we dispossess them?" 18 You need have no fear of them. You have but to bear in mind what the LORD your God did to Pharaoh and all the Egyptians: 19 the wondrous acts that you saw with your own eyes, the signs and the portents, the mighty hand, and the outstretched arm by which the LORD your God liberated you. Thus will the LORD your God do to all the peoples you now fear. 20 The LORD your God will also send a plague against them, until those who are left in hiding perish before you. 21 Do not stand in dread of them, for the LORD your God is in your midst, a great and awesome God. 22 The LORD your God will dislodge those peoples before you little by little; you will not be able to put an end to them at once, else the wild beasts would multiply to your hurt. 23 The LORD your God will deliver them up to you, throwing them into utter panic until they are wiped out. 24 He will deliver their kings into your hand, and you shall obliterate their name from under the heavens; no man shall stand up to you, until you have wiped them out. 25 You shall consign the images of their gods to the fire; you shall not covet the silver and gold on them and keep it for yourselves, lest you be ensnared thereby; for that is abhorrent to the LORD your God. 26 You must not bring an abhorrent thing into your house, or you will be proscribed like it; you must reject it as abominable and abhorrent, for it is proscribed.

8 1 You shall faithfully observe all the Instruction that I enjoin upon you today, that you may thrive and increase and be able to possess the land that the LORD promised on oath to your fathers. 2 Remember the long way that the LORD your God has made you travel in the wilderness these past forty years, that He might test you by hardships to learn what was in your hearts: whether you would keep His commandments or not. 3 He subjected you to the hardship of hunger and then gave you manna to eat, which neither you nor your fathers had ever known, in order to teach you that man does not live on bread alone, but that man may live on anything that the LORD decrees. 4 The clothes upon you did not wear out, nor did your feet swell these forty years. 5 Bear in mind that the LORD your God disciplines you just as a man disciplines his son. 6 Therefore keep the commandments of the LORD your God: walk in His ways and revere Him. 7 For the LORD your God is bringing you into a good land, a land with streams and springs and fountains issuing from plain and hill, 8 a land of wheat and barley, of vines, figs, and pomegranates, a land of olive trees and honey; 9 a land where you may eat food without stint, where you will lack nothing; a land whose rocks are iron and from whose hills you can mine copper. 10 When you have eaten your fill, give thanks to the LORD your God for the good land which He has given you. 11 Take care lest you forget the LORD your God and fail to keep His commandments, His rules, and His laws, which I enjoin upon you today, 12 When you have eaten your fill, and have built fine houses to live in, 13 and your herds and flocks have multiplied, and your silver and gold have increased, and everything you own has prospered, 14 beware lest your heart grow haughty and you forget the LORD your God — who freed you from the land of Egypt, the house of bondage; 15 who led you through the great and terrible wilderness with its seraph serpents and scorpions, a parched land with no water in it, who brought forth water for you from the flinty rock; 16 who fed you in the wilderness with manna, which your fathers had never known, in order to test you by hardships only to benefit you in the end – 17 and you say to yourselves, "My own power and the might of my own hand have won this wealth for me." 18 Remember that it is the LORD your God who gives you the power to get wealth, in fulfillment of the covenant that He made on oath with your fathers, as is still the case. 19 If you do forget the LORD your God and follow other gods to serve them or bow down to them, I warn you this day that you shall certainly

DEUTERONOMY 9 דברים ט

perish; 20 like the nations that the LORD will cause to perish before you, so shall you perish - because you did not heed the LORD your God.

9 1 Hear, O Israel! You are about to cross the Jordan to go in and dispossess nations greater and more populous than you: great cities with walls sky-high; 2 a people great and tall, the Anakites, of whom you have knowledge; for you have heard it said, "Who can stand up to the children of Anak?" 3 Know then this day that none other than the LORD your God is crossing at your head, a devouring fire; it is He who will wipe them out. He will subdue them before you, that you may quickly dispossess and destroy them, as the LORD promised you. 4 And when the LORD your God has thrust them from your path, say not to yourselves, "The LORD has enabled us to possess this land because of our virtues"; it is rather because of the wickedness of those nations that the LORD is dispossessing them before you. 5 It is not because of your virtues and your rectitude that you will be able to possess their country; but it is because of their wickedness that the LORD your God is dispossessing those nations before you, and in order to fulfill the oath that the LORD made to your fathers, Abraham, Isaac, and Jacob. 6 Know, then, that it is not for any virtue of yours that the LORD your God is giving you this good land to possess; for you are a stiffnecked people. 7 Remember, never forget, how you provoked the LORD your God to anger in the wilderness: from the day that you left the land of Egypt until you reached this place, you have continued defiant toward the LORD. 8 At Horeb you so provoked the LORD that the LORD was angry enough with you to have destroyed you. 9 I had ascended the mountain to receive the tablets of stone, the Tablets of the Covenant that the LORD had made with you, and I stayed on the mountain forty days and forty nights, eating no bread and drinking no water. 10 And the LORD gave me the two tablets of stone inscribed by the finger of God, with the exact words that the LORD had addressed to you on the mountain out of the fire on the day of the Assembly. 11 At the end of those forty days and forty nights, the LORD gave me the two tablets of stone, the Tablets of the Covenant. 12 And the LORD said to me, "Hurry, go down from here at once, for the people whom you brought out of Egypt have acted wickedly; they have been quick to stray from the path that I enjoined upon them: they have made themselves a molten image." 13 The LORD further said to me, "I see that this is a stiffnecked people. 14 Let Me alone and I will destroy them and blot out their name from under heaven, and I will make you a nation far more numerous than they." 15 I started down the mountain, a mountain ablaze with fire, the two Tablets of the Covenant in my two hands. 16 I saw how you had sinned against the LORD your God; you had made yourselves a molten calf; you had been quick to stray from the path that the LORD had enjoined upon you. 17 Thereupon I gripped the two tablets and flung them away with both my hands, smashing them before your eyes. 18 I threw myself down before the LORD - eating no bread and drinking no water forty days and forty nights, as before - because of the great wrong you had committed, doing what displeased the LORD and vexing Him. 19 For I was in dread of the LORD's fierce anger against you, which moved Him to wipe you out. And that time, too, the LORD gave heed to me. - 20 Moreover, the LORD was angry enough with Aaron to have destroyed him; so I also interceded for Aaron at that time. - 21 As for that sinful thing you had made, the calf, I took it and put it to the fire; I broke it to bits and ground it thoroughly until it was fine as dust, and I threw its dust into the brook that comes down from the mountain. 22 Again you provoked the LORD at Taberah, and at Massah, and at Kibroth-hattaavah. 23 And when the LORD sent you on from Kadesh-barnea, saying, "Go up and take possession of the land that I am giving you," you flouted the command of the LORD your God: you did not put your trust in Him and did not obey Him. 24 As long as I have known you, you have been defiant toward the LORD. 25 When I lay prostrate before the LORD those forty days and forty nights, because the LORD was determined to destroy you, 26 I prayed to the LORD and said, "O Lord God, do not annihilate Your very own people, whom You redeemed in Your majesty and whom You freed from Egypt with a mighty hand. 27 Give thought to Your servants, Abraham,

185

DEUTERONOMY 10   דברים י עקב

Isaac, and Jacob, and pay no heed to the stubbornness of this people, its wickedness, and its sinfulness. 28 Else the country from which You freed us will say, 'It was because the LORD was powerless to bring them into the land that He had promised them, and because He rejected them, that He brought them out to have them die in the wilderness.' 29 Yet they are Your very own people, whom You freed with Your great might and Your outstretched arm.

10 1 Thereupon the LORD said to me, "Carve out two tablets of stone like the first, and come up to Me on the mountain; and make an ark of wood. 2 I will inscribe on the tablets the commandments that were on the first tablets that you smashed, and you shall deposit them in the ark." 3 I made an ark of acacia wood and carved out two tablets of stone like the first; I took the two tablets with me and went up the mountain. 4 The LORD inscribed on the tablets the same text as on the first, the Ten Commandments that He addressed to you on the mountain out of the fire on the day of the Assembly; and the LORD gave them to me. 5 Then I left and went down from the mountain, and I deposited the tablets in the ark that I had made, where they still are, as the LORD had commanded me. 6 From Beeroth-bene-jaakan the Israelites marched to Moserah. Aaron died there and was buried there; and his son Eleazar became priest in his stead. 7 From there they marched to Gudgod, and from Gudgod to Jotbath, a region of running brooks. 8 At that time the LORD set apart the tribe of Levi to carry the Ark of the LORD's Covenant, to stand in attendance upon the LORD, and to bless in His name, as is still the case. 9 That is why the Levites have received no hereditary portion along with their kinsmen: the LORD is their portion, as the LORD your God spoke concerning them. 10 I had stayed on the mountain, as I did the first time, forty days and forty nights; and the LORD heeded me once again: the LORD agreed not to destroy you. 11 And the LORD said to me, "Up, resume the march at the head of the people, that they may go in and possess the land that I swore to their fathers to give them."

12 And now, O Israel, what does the LORD your God demand of you? Only this: to revere the LORD your God, to walk only in His paths, to love Him, and to serve the LORD your God with all your heart and soul, 13 keeping the LORD's commandments and laws, which I enjoin upon you today, for your good. 14 Mark, the heavens to their uttermost reaches belong to the LORD your God, the earth and all that is on it! 15 Yet it was to your fathers that the LORD was drawn in His love for them, so that He chose you, their lineal descendants, from among all peoples - as is now the case. 16 Cut away, therefore, the thickening about your hearts and stiffen your necks no more. 17 For the LORD your God is God supreme and Lord supreme, the great, the mighty, and the awesome God, who shows no favor and takes no bribe, 18 but upholds the cause of the fatherless and the widow, and befriends the stranger, providing him with food and clothing. - 19 You too must befriend the stranger, for you were strangers in the land of Egypt. 20 You must revere the LORD your God: only Him shall you worship, to Him shall you hold fast, and by His name shall you swear. 21 He is your glory and He is your God, who wrought for you those marvelous, awesome deeds that you saw with your own eyes. 22 Your ancestors went down to Egypt seventy persons in all; and now the LORD your God has made you as numerous as the stars of heaven. 11 1 Love, therefore, the LORD your God, and always keep His charge, His laws, His rules, and His commandments. 2 Take thought this day that it was not your children, who neither experienced nor witnessed the lesson of the LORD your God - His majesty, His mighty hand, His outstretched arm; 3 the signs and the deeds that He performed in Egypt against Pharaoh king of Egypt and all his land; 4 what He did to Egypt's army, its horses and chariots; how the LORD rolled back upon them the waters of the Sea of Reeds when they were pursuing you, thus destroying them once and for all; 5 what He did for you in the wilderness before you arrived in this place; 6 and what He did to Dathan and Abiram, sons of Eliab son of Reuben, when the earth opened her mouth and swallowed them, along with their households, their tents, and every living thing in their train, from amidst all Israel - 7 but

עמוד שער לספר דברים, מתוך "חומש דה-קסטרו", כתב-יד מעוטר על קלף, גרמניה, 1344, אוסף מוזיאון ישראל, ירושלים
Opening page of the Book of Deuteronomy, from the "De Castro Pentateuch", illuminated manuscript on vellum, Germany, 1344, collection of The Israel Museum, Jerusalem

DEUTERONOMY 12

that it was you who saw with your own eyes all the marvelous deeds that the LORD performed. 8 Keep, therefore, all the Instruction that I enjoin upon you today, so that you may have the strength to enter and take possession of the land that you are about to cross into and possess, 9 and that you may long endure upon the soil that the LORD swore to your fathers to assign to them and to their heirs, a land flowing with milk and honey. 10 For the land that you are about to enter and possess is not like the land of Egypt from which you have come. There the grain you sowed had to be watered by your own labors, like a vegetable garden; 11 but the land you are about to cross into and possess, a land of hills and valleys, soaks up its water from the rains of heaven. 12 It is a land which the LORD your God looks after, on which the LORD your God always keeps His eye, from year's beginning to year's end. 13 If, then, you obey the commandments that I enjoin upon you this day, loving the LORD your God and serving Him with all your heart and soul, 14 I will grant the rain for your land in season, the early rain and the late. You shall gather in your new grain and wine and oil - 15 I will also provide grass in the fields for your cattle - and thus you shall eat your fill. 16 Take care not to be lured away to serve other gods and bow to them. 17 For the LORD's anger will flare up against you, and He will shut up the skies so that there will be no rain and the ground will not yield its produce; and you will soon perish from the good land that the LORD is assigning to you. 18 Therefore impress these My words upon your very heart: bind them as a sign on your hand and let them serve as a symbol on your forehead. 19 Teach them to your children - reciting them when you stay at home and when you are away, when you lie down and when you get up; 20 and inscribe them on the doorposts of your house and on your gates - 21 to the end that you and your children may endure, in the land that the LORD swore to your fathers to assign to them, as long as there is a heaven over the earth.

22 If, then, you faithfully keep all this Instruction that I command you, loving the LORD your God, walking in all His ways, and holding fast to Him, 23 the LORD will dislodge before you all these nations: you will dispossess nations greater and more numerous than you. 24 Every spot on which your foot treads shall be yours: your territory shall extend from the wilderness to the Lebanon and from the River - the Euphrates - to the Western Sea. 25 No man shall stand up to you: the LORD your God will put the dread and the fear of you over the whole land in which you set foot, as He promised you.

26 See, this day I set before you blessing and curse: 27 blessing, if you obey the commandments of the LORD your God that I enjoin upon you this day; 28 and curse, if you do not obey the commandments of the LORD your God, but turn away from the path that I enjoin upon you this day and follow other gods, whom you have not experienced. 29 When the LORD your God brings you into the land that you are about to enter and possess, you shall pronounce the blessing at Mount Gerizim and the curse at Mount Ebal. - 30 Both are on the other side of the Jordan, beyond the west road that is in the land of the Canaanites who dwell in the Arabah - near Gilgal, by the terebinths of Moreh. 31 For you are about to cross the Jordan to enter and possess the land that the LORD your God is assigning to you. When you have occupied it and are settled in it. 32 take care to observe all the laws and rules that I have set before you this day. 12 1 These are the laws and rules that you must carefully observe in the land that the LORD, God of your fathers, is giving you to possess, as long as you live on earth. 2 You must destroy all the sites at which the nations you are to dispossess worshiped their gods,

DEUTERONOMY 12

whether on lofty mountains and on hills or under any luxuriant tree. 3 Tear down their altars, smash their pillars, put their sacred posts to the fire, and cut down the images of their gods, obliterating their name from that site. 4 Do not worship the LORD your God in like manner, 5 but look only to the site that the LORD your God will choose amidst all your tribes as His habitation, to establish His name there. There you are to go, 6 and there you are to bring your burnt offerings and other sacrifices, your tithes and contributions, your votive and freewill offerings, and the firstlings of your herds and flocks. 7 Together with your households, you shall feast there before the LORD your God, happy in all the undertakings in which the LORD your God has blessed you. 8 You shall not act at all as we now act here, every man as he pleases, 9 because you have not yet come to the allotted haven that the LORD your God is giving you. 10 When you cross the Jordan and settle in the land that the LORD your God is allotting to you, and He grants you safety from all your enemies around you and you live in security, 11 then you must bring everything that I command you to the site where the LORD your God will choose to establish His name: your burnt offerings and other sacrifices, your tithes and contributions, and all the choice votive offerings that you vow to the LORD. 12 And you shall rejoice before the LORD your God with your sons and daughters and with your male and female slaves, along with the Levite in your settlements, for he has no territorial allotment among you. 13 Take care not to sacrifice your burnt offerings in any place you like, 14 but only in the place that the LORD will choose in one of your tribal territories. There you shall sacrifice your burnt offerings and there you shall observe all that I enjoin upon you. 15 But whenever you desire, you may slaughter and eat meat in any of your settlements, according to the blessing that the LORD your God has granted you. The unclean and the clean alike may partake of it, as of the gazelle and the deer. 16 But you must not partake of the blood; you shall pour it out on the ground like water. 17 You may not partake in your settlements of the tithes of your new grain or wine or oil, or of the firstlings of your herds and flocks, or of any of the votive offerings that you vow, or of your freewill offerings, or of your contributions. 18 These you must consume before the LORD your God in the place that the LORD your God will choose - you and your sons and your daughters, your male and female slaves, and the Levite in your settlements - happy before the LORD your God in all your undertakings. 19 Be sure not to neglect the Levite as long as you live in your land. 20 When the LORD enlarges your territory, as He has promised you, and you say, "I shall eat some meat," for you have the urge to eat meat, you may eat meat whenever you wish. 21 If the place where the LORD has chosen to establish His name is too far from you, you may slaughter any of the cattle or sheep that the LORD gives you, as I have instructed you; and you may eat to your heart's content in your settlements. 22 Eat it, however, as the gazelle and the deer are eaten; the unclean may eat it together with the clean. 23 But make sure that you do not partake of the blood; for the blood is the life, and you must not consume the life with the flesh. 24 You must not partake of it; you must pour it out on the ground like water. 25 You must not partake of it, in order that it may go well with you and with your descendants to come, for you will be doing what is right in the sight of the LORD. 26 But such sacred and votive donations as you may have shall be taken by you to the site that the LORD will choose. 27 You shall offer your burnt offerings, both the flesh and the blood, on the altar of the LORD your God; and of your other sacrifices, the blood shall be poured out on the altar of the LORD your God, and you shall eat the flesh. 28 Be careful to heed all these commandments that I enjoin upon you; thus it will go well with you and with your descendants after you forever, for you will be doing what is good and right in the sight of the LORD your God.

29 When the LORD your God has cut down before you the nations that you are about to enter and dispossess, and you have dispossessed them and settled in their land, 30 beware of being lured into their ways after they have been wiped out before you! Do not inquire about their gods, saying, "How did those nations worship their gods? I too will follow those practices." 31 You shall not act thus toward the LORD your God.

DEUTERONOMY 13

for they perform for their gods every abhorrent act that the LORD detests; they even offer up their sons and daughters in fire to their gods. **13** ¹ Be careful to observe only that which I enjoin upon you: neither add to it nor take away from it.

² If there appears among you a prophet or a dream-diviner and he gives you a sign or a portent, ³ saying, "Let us follow and worship another god" - whom you have not experienced - even if the sign or portent that he named to you comes true, ⁴ do not heed the words of that prophet or of that dream-diviner. For the LORD your God is testing you to see whether you really love the LORD your God with all your heart and soul. ⁵ Follow none but the LORD your God, and revere none but Him; observe His commandments alone, and heed only His orders: worship none but Him, and hold fast to Him. ⁶ As for that prophet or dream-diviner, he shall be put to death; for he urged disloyalty to the LORD your God - who freed you from the land of Egypt and who redeemed you from the house of bondage - to make you stray from the path that the LORD your God commanded you to follow. Thus you will sweep out evil from your midst. ⁷ If your brother, your own mother's son, or your son or daughter, or the wife of your bosom, or your closest friend entices you in secret, saying, "Come let us worship other gods" - whom neither you nor your fathers have experienced - ⁸ from among the gods of the peoples around you, either near to you or distant, anywhere from one end of the earth to the other: ⁹ do not assent or give heed to him. Show him no pity or compassion, and do not shield him; ¹⁰ but take his life. Let your hand be the first against him to put him to death, and the hand of the rest of the people thereafter. ¹¹ Stone him to death, for he sought to make you stray from the LORD your God, who brought you out of the land of Egypt, out of the house of bondage. ¹² Thus all Israel will hear and be afraid, and such evil things will not be done again in your midst.

¹³ If you hear it said, of one of the towns that the LORD your God is giving you to dwell in, ¹⁴ that some scoundrels from among you have gone and subverted the inhabitants of their town, saying, "Come let us worship other gods" - whom you have not experienced - ¹⁵ you shall investigate and inquire and interrogate thoroughly. If it is true, the fact is established - that abhorrent thing was perpetrated in your midst - ¹⁶ put the inhabitants of that town to the sword and put its cattle to the sword. Doom it and all that is in it to destruction: ¹⁷ gather all its spoil into the open square, and burn the town and all its spoil as a holocaust to the LORD your God. And it shall remain an everlasting ruin, never to be rebuilt. ¹⁸ Let nothing that has been doomed stick to your hand, in order that the LORD may turn from His blazing anger and show you compassion, and in His compassion increase you as He promised your fathers on oath - ¹⁹ for you will be heeding the LORD your God, obeying all His commandments that I enjoin upon you this day, doing what is right in the sight of the LORD your God. **14** ¹ You are children of the LORD your God. You shall not gash yourselves or shave the front of your heads because of the dead. ² For you are a people consecrated to the LORD your God: the LORD your God chose you from among all other peoples on earth to be His treasured people. ³ You shall not eat anything abhorrent. ⁴ These are the animals that you may eat: the ox, the sheep, and the goat; ⁵ the deer, the gazelle, the roebuck, the wild goat, the ibex, the antelope, the mountain sheep, ⁶ and any other animal that has true hoofs which are cleft in two and brings up the cud - such you may eat. ⁷ But the following, which do bring up the cud or have true hoofs which are cleft through, you may not eat: the camel, the hare, and the daman - for although they bring up the cud, they have no true hoofs - they are unclean for you; ⁸ also the swine - for although it has true hoofs, it does not bring up the cud - is unclean for you. You shall not eat of their flesh or touch their carcasses. ⁹ These you may eat of all that live in water: you may eat anything that has fins and scales. ¹⁰ But you may not eat anything that has no fins and scales: it is unclean

DEUTERONOMY 15   דברים טו   ראה

for you. 11 You may eat any clean bird. 12 The following you may not eat: athe eagle, the vulture, and the black vulture; 13 the kite, the falcon, and the buzzard of any variety; 14 every variety of raven; 15 the ostrich, the nighthawk, the sea gull, and the hawk of any variety; 16 the little owl, the great owl, and the white owl; 17 the pelican, the bustard, and the cormorant; 18 the stork, any variety of heron, the hoopoe, and the bat. 19 All winged swarming things are unclean for you; they may not be eaten. 20 You may eat only clean winged creatures. 21 You shall not eat anything that has died a natural death; give it to the stranger in your community to eat, or you may sell it to a foreigner. For you are a people consecrated to the LORD your God. You shall not boil a kid in its mother's milk.

22 You shall set aside every year a tenth part of all the yield of your sowing that is brought from the field. 23 You shall consume the tithes of your new grain and wine and oil, and the firstlings of your herds and flocks, in the presence of the LORD your God, in the place where He will choose to establish His name, so that you may learn to revere the LORD your God forever. 24 Should the distance be too great for you, should you be unable to transport them, because the place where the LORD your God has chosen to establish His name is far from you and because the LORD your God has blessed you, 25 you may convert them into money. Wrap up the money and take it with you to the place that the LORD your God has chosen, 26 and spend the money on anything you want - cattle, sheep, wine, or other intoxicant, or anything you may desire. And you shall feast there, in the presence of the LORD your God, and rejoice with your household. 27 But do not neglect the Levite in your community, for he has no hereditary portion as you have.

28 Every third year you shall bring out the full tithe of your yield of that year, but leave it within your settlements. 29 Then the Levite, who has no hereditary portion as you have, and the stranger, the fatherless, and the widow in your settlements shall come and eat their fill, so that the LORD your God may bless you in all the enterprises you undertake. **15** 1 Every seventh year you shall practice remission of debts. 2 This shall be the nature of the remission: every creditor shall remit the due that he claims from his fellow; he shall not dun his fellow or kinsman, for the remission proclaimed is of the LORD. 3 You may dun the foreigner; but you must remit whatever is due you from your kinsmen. 4 There shall be no needy among you - since the LORD your God will bless you in the land that the LORD your God is giving you as a hereditary portion - 5 if only you heed the LORD your God and take care to keep all this Instruction that I enjoin upon you this day. 6 For the LORD your God will bless you as He has promised you; you will extend loans to many nations, but require none yourself; you will dominate many nations, but they will not dominate you. 7 If, however, there is a needy person among you, one of your kinsmen in any of your settlements in the land that the LORD your God is giving you, do not harden your heart and shut your hand against your needy kinsman. 8 Rather, you must open your hand and lend him sufficient for whatever he needs. 9 Beware lest you harbor the base thought, "The seventh year, the year of remission, is approaching," so that you are mean to your needy kinsman and give him nothing. He will cry out to the LORD against you, and you will incur guilt. 10 Give to him readily and have no regrets when you do so, for in return the LORD your God will bless you in all your efforts and in all your undertakings. 11 For there will never cease to be needy ones in your land, which is why I command you: open your hand to the poor and needy kinsman in your land. 12 If a fellow Hebrew, man or woman, is sold to you, he shall serve you six years, and in the seventh year you shall set him free. 13 When you set him free, do not let him go empty-handed; 14 Furnish him out of the flock, threshing floor, and vat, with which the LORD your God has blessed you. 15 Bear in mind that you were slaves in the land of Egypt and the LORD your God redeemed you; therefore I enjoin this commandment upon you today. 16 But should he say to you, 'I do not want to leave you' - for he loves you

DEUTERONOMY 16 · דברים טז ראה

and your household and is happy with you · 17 you shall take an awl and put it through his ear into the door, and he shall become your slave in perpetuity. Do the same with your female slave. 18 When you do set him free, do not feel aggrieved: for in the six years he has given you double the service of a hired man. Moreover, the LORD your God will bless you in all you do.

19 You shall consecrate to the LORD your God all male firstlings that are born in your herd and in your flock: you must not work your firstling ox or shear your firstling sheep. 20 You and your household shall eat it annually before the LORD your God in the place that the LORD will choose. 21 But if it has a defect, lameness or blindness, any serious defect, you shall not sacrifice it to the LORD your God. 22 Eat it in your settlements, the unclean among you no less than the clean, just like the gazelle and the deer. 23 Only you must not partake of its blood: you shall pour it out on the ground like water.

16 1 Observe the month of Abib and offer a passover sacrifice to the LORD your God, for it was in the month of Abib, at night, that the LORD your God freed you from Egypt. 2 You shall slaughter the passover sacrifice for the LORD your God, from the flock and the herd, in the place where the LORD will choose to establish His name. 3 You shall not eat anything leavened with it; for seven days thereafter you shall eat unleavened bread, bread of distress - for you departed from the land of Egypt hurriedly - so that you may remember the day of your departure from the land of Egypt as long as you live. 4 For seven days no leaven shall be found with you in all your territory, and none of the flesh of what you slaughter on the evening of the first day shall be left until morning. 5 You are not permitted to slaughter the passover sacrifice in any of the settlements that the LORD your God is giving you; 6 but at the place where the LORD your God will choose to establish His name, there alone shall you slaughter the passover sacrifice, in the evening, at sundown, the time of day when you departed from Egypt. 7 You shall cook and eat it at the place that the LORD your God will choose; and in the morning you may start back on your journey home. 8 After eating unleavened bread six days, you shall hold a solemn gathering for the LORD your God on the seventh day: you shall do no work.

9 You shall count off seven weeks: start to count the seven weeks when the sickle is first put to the standing grain. 10 Then you shall observe the Feast of Weeks for the LORD your God, offering your freewill contribution according as the LORD your God has blessed you. 11 You shall rejoice before the LORD your God with your son and daughter, your male and female slave, the Levite in your communities, and the stranger, the fatherless, and the widow in your midst, at the place where the LORD your God will choose to establish His name. 12 Bear in mind that you were slaves in Egypt, and take care to obey these laws. 13 After the ingathering from your threshing floor and your vat, you shall hold the Feast of Booths for seven days. 14 You shall rejoice in your festival, with your son and daughter, your male and female slave, the Levite, the stranger, the fatherless, and the widow in your communities. 15 You shall hold a festival for the LORD your God seven days, in the place that the LORD will choose; for the LORD your God will bless all your crops and all your undertakings, and you shall have nothing but joy. 16 Three times a year - on the Feast of Unleavened Bread, on the Feast of Weeks, and on the Feast of Booths - all your males shall appear before the LORD your God in the place that He will choose. They shall not appear before the LORD empty-handed, 17 but each with his own gift, according to the blessing that the LORD your God has bestowed upon you.

18 You shall appoint magistrates and officials for your tribes, in all the settlements that the LORD your God is giving you, and they shall govern the people with due justice. 19 You shall not judge unfairly: you shall show no partiality; you shall not take bribes, for bribes blind the eyes of the discerning and upset the plea of the just. 20 Justice, justice shall you pursue, that you may thrive and occupy the land that the LORD your God is giving you. 21 You shall not set up a sacred post - any kind of pole beside the altar of the LORD your God that you may make - 22 or erect a stone pillar; for such the LORD your God detests.

17 1 You shall not sacrifice to the LORD your God an ox or a sheep that has any defect of a serious kind, for that is abhorrent to the LORD

DEUTERONOMY 18 · דברים יח · שפטים

your God. 2 If there is found among you, in one of the settlements that the LORD your God is giving you, a man or woman who has affronted the LORD your God and transgressed His covenant - 3 turning to the worship of other gods and bowing down to them, to the sun or the moon or any of the heavenly host, something I never commanded - 4 and you have been informed or have learned of it, then you shall make a thorough inquiry. If it is true, the fact is established, that abhorrent thing was perpetrated in Israel, 5 you shall take the man and the woman who did that wicked thing out to the public place, and you shall stone them, man or woman, to death. 6 A person shall be put to death only on the testimony of two or more witnesses; he must not be put to death on the testimony of a single witness. 7 Let the hands of the witnesses be the first against him to put him to death, and the hands of the rest of the people thereafter. Thus you will sweep out evil from your midst. 8 If a case is too baffling for you to decide, be it a controversy over homicide, civil law, or assault - matters of dispute in your courts - you shall promptly repair to the place that the LORD your God will have chosen, 9 and appear before the levitical priests, or the magistrate in charge at the time, and present your problem. When they have announced to you the verdict in the case, 10 you shall carry out the verdict that is announced to you from that place that the LORD chose, observing scrupulously all their instructions to you. 11 You shall act in accordance with the instructions given you and the ruling handed down to you; you must not deviate from the verdict that they announce to you either to the right or to the left. 12 Should a man act presumptuously and disregard the priest charged with serving there the LORD your God, or the magistrate, that man shall die. Thus you will sweep out evil from Israel; 13 all the people will hear and be afraid and will not act presumptuously again. 14 If, after you have entered the land that the LORD your God has assigned to you, and taken possession of it and settled in it, you decide, "I will set a king over me, as do all the nations about me," 15 you shall be free to set a king over yourself, one chosen by the LORD your God. Be sure to set as king over yourself one of your own people; you must not set a foreigner over you, one who is not your kinsman. 16 Moreover, he shall not keep many horses or send people back to Egypt to add to his horses, since the LORD has warned you, "You must not go back that way again." 17 And he shall not have many wives, lest his heart go astray; nor shall he amass silver and gold to excess. 18 When he is seated on his royal throne, he shall have a copy of this Teaching written for him on a scroll by the levitical priests. 19 Let it remain with him and let him read in it all his life, so that he may learn to revere the LORD his God, to observe faithfully every word of this Teaching as well as these laws. 20 Thus he will not act haughtily toward his fellows or deviate from the Instruction to the right or to the left, to the end that he and his descendants may reign long in the midst of Israel.

18 The levitical priests, the whole tribe of Levi, shall have no territorial portion with Israel. They shall live only off the LORD's offerings by fire as their portion. 2 and shall have no portion among their brother tribes: the LORD is their portion, as He promised them. 3 This then shall be the priests' due from the people: Everyone who offers a sacrifice, whether an ox or a sheep, must give the shoulder, the cheeks, and the stomach to the priest. 4 You shall also give him the first fruits of your new grain and wine and oil, and the first shearing of your sheep. 5 For the LORD your God has chosen him and his descendants, out of all your tribes, to be in attendance for service in the name of the LORD for all time. 6 If a Levite would go, from any of the settlements throughout Israel where he has been residing, to the place that the LORD has chosen, he may do so whenever he pleases. 7 He may serve in the name of the LORD his God like all his fellow Levites who are there in attendance before the LORD. 8 They shall receive equal shares of the dues, without regard to personal gifts or patrimonies. 9 When you enter the land that the LORD your God is giving you, you shall not learn to imitate the abhorrent practices of those nations. 10 Let no one be found among you who consigns his son or daughter to the fire, or who is an augur, a soothsayer, a diviner, a sorcerer, 11 one who casts spells, or one who consults ghosts or familiar spirits, or one who inquires of the dead. 12 For anyone

DEUTERONOMY 19 דברים יט שפטים

who does such things is abhorrent to the LORD, and it is because of these abhorrent things that the LORD your God is dispossessing them before you. 13 You must be wholehearted with the LORD your God. 14 Those nations that you are about to dispossess do indeed resort to soothsayers and augurs; to you, however, the LORD your God has not assigned the like. 15 The LORD your God will raise up for you a prophet from among your own people, like myself; him you shall heed. 16 This is just what you asked of the LORD your God at Horeb, on the day of the Assembly, saying, "Let me not hear the voice of the LORD my God any longer or see this wondrous fire any more, lest I die." 17 Whereupon the LORD said to me, "They have done well in speaking thus. 18 I will raise up a prophet for them from among their own people, like yourself; I will put My words in his mouth and he will speak to them all that I command him; 19 and if anybody fails to heed the words he speaks in My name, I Myself will call him to account. 20 But any prophet who presumes to speak in My name an oracle that I did not command him to utter, or who speaks in the name of other gods - that prophet shall die." 21 And should you ask yourselves, "How can we know that the oracle was not spoken by the LORD?" - 22 if the prophet speaks in the name of the LORD and the oracle does not come true, that oracle was not spoken by the LORD; the prophet has uttered it presumptuously: do not stand in dread of him.   19 1 When the LORD your God has cut down the nations whose land the LORD your God is assigning to you, and you have dispossessed them and settled in their towns and homes, 2 you shall set aside three cities in the land that the LORD your God is giving you to possess. 3 You shall survey the distances, and divide into three parts the territory of the country that the LORD your God has allotted to you, so that any manslayer may have a place to flee to. - 4 Now this is the case of the manslayer who may flee there and live: one who has killed another unwittingly, without having been his enemy in the past. 5 For instance, a man goes with his neighbor into a grove to cut wood; as his hand swings the ax to cut down a tree, the ax-head flies off the handle and strikes the other so that he dies. That man shall flee to one of these cities and live. - 6 Otherwise, when the distance is great, the blood-avenger, pursuing the manslayer in hot anger, may overtake him and kill him; yet he did not incur the death penalty, since he had never been the other's enemy. 7 That is why I command you: set aside three cities. 8 And when the LORD your God enlarges your territory, as He swore to your fathers, and gives you all the land that He promised to give your fathers - 9 if you faithfully observe all this Instruction that I enjoin upon you this day, to love the LORD your God and to walk in His ways at all times - then you shall add three more towns to those three. 10 Thus blood of the innocent will not be shed, bringing bloodguilt upon you in the land that the LORD your God is allotting to you.   11 If, however, a person who is the enemy of another lies in wait for him and sets upon him and strikes him a fatal blow and then flees to one of these towns, 12 the elders of his town shall have him brought back from there and shall hand him over to the blood-avenger to be put to death; 13 you must show him no pity. Thus you will purge Israel of the blood of the innocent, and it will go well with you.   14 You shall not move your countryman's landmarks, set up by previous generations, in the property that will be allotted to you in the land that the LORD your God is giving you to possess.

15 A single witness may not validate against a person any guilt or blame for any offense that may be committed; a case can be valid only on the testimony of two witnesses or more. 16 If a man appears against another to testify maliciously and gives false testimony against him, 17 the two parties to the dispute shall appear before the LORD, before the priests or magistrates in authority at the time, 18 and the magistrates shall make a thorough investigation. If the man who testified is a false witness, if he has testified falsely against his fellow, 19 you shall do to him as he schemed to do to his fellow. Thus you will sweep out evil from your midst; 20 others will hear and be afraid, and such evil things will not again be done in your midst. 21 Nor must you show pity: life for life, eye for eye, tooth for tooth, hand for hand, foot for foot.

20 1 When you take the field against your enemies, and see horses and chariots - forces larger than yours - have no fear of them, for the LORD

194

DEUTERONOMY 21 שפטים דברים כא

your God, who brought you from the land of Egypt, is with you. 2 Before you join battle, the priest shall come forward and address the troops. 3 He shall say to them, "Hear, O Israel! You are about to join battle with your enemy. Let not your courage falter. Do not be in fear, or in panic, or in dread of them. 4 For it is the LORD your God who marches with you to do battle for you against your enemy, to bring you victory." 5 Then the officials shall address the troops, as follows: "Is there anyone who has built a new house but has not dedicated it? Let him go back to his home, lest he die in battle and another dedicate it. 6 Is there anyone who has planted a vineyard but has never harvested it? Let him go back to his home, lest he die in battle and another harvest it. 7 Is there anyone who has paid the bride-price for a wife, but who has not yet married her? Let him go back to his home, lest he die in battle and another marry her." 8 The officials shall go on addressing the troops and say, "Is there anyone afraid and disheartened? Let him go back to his home, lest the courage of his comrades flag like his." 9 When the officials have finished addressing the troops, army commanders shall assume command of the troops. 10 When you approach a town to attack it, you shall offer it terms of peace. 11 If it responds peaceably and lets you in, all the people present there shall serve you at forced labor. 12 If it does not surrender to you, but would join battle with you, you shall lay siege to it; 13 and when the LORD your God delivers it into your hand, you shall put all its males to the sword. 14 You may, however, take as your booty the women, the children, the livestock, and everything in the town — all its spoil — and enjoy the use of the spoil of your enemy, which the LORD your God gives you. 15 Thus you shall deal with all towns that lie very far from you, towns that do not belong to nations hereabout. 16 In the towns of the latter peoples, however, which the LORD your God is giving you as a heritage, you shall not let a soul remain alive. 17 No, you must proscribe them — the Hittites and the Amorites, the Canaanites and the Perizzites, the Hivites and the Jebusites — as the LORD your God has commanded you, 18 lest they lead you into doing all the abhorrent things that they have done for their gods and you stand guilty before the LORD your God. 19 When in your war against a city you have to besiege it a long time in order to capture it, you must not destroy its trees, wielding the ax against them. You may eat of them, but you must not cut them down. Are trees of the field human to withdraw before you into the besieged city? 20 Only trees that you know do not yield food may be destroyed; you may cut them down for constructing siegeworks against the city that is waging war on you, until it has been reduced.

21 1 If, in the land that the LORD your God is assigning you to possess, someone slain is found lying in the open, the identity of the slayer not being known, 2 your elders and magistrates shall go out and measure the distances from the corpse to the nearby towns. 3 The elders of the town nearest to the corpse shall then take a heifer which has never been worked, which has never pulled in a yoke; 4 and the elders of that town shall bring the heifer down to an everflowing wadi, which is not tilled or sown. There, in the wadi, they shall break the heifer's neck. 5 The priests, sons of Levi, shall come forward; for the LORD your God has chosen them to minister to Him and to pronounce blessing in the name of the LORD, and every lawsuit and case of assault is subject to their ruling. 6 Then all the elders of the town nearest to the corpse shall wash their hands over the heifer whose neck was broken in the wadi. 7 And they shall make this declaration: "Our hands did not shed this blood, nor did our eyes see it done. 8 Absolve, O LORD, Your people Israel whom You redeemed, and do not let guilt for the blood of the innocent remain among Your people Israel." And they will be absolved of bloodguilt. 9 Thus you will remove from your midst guilt for the blood of the innocent, for you will be doing what is right in the sight of the LORD.

10 When you take the field against your enemies, and the LORD your God delivers them into your power and you take some of them captive, 11 and you see among the captives a beautiful woman and you desire her and would take her to wife, 12 you shall bring her into your house, and she shall trim her hair, pare her nails, 13 and discard her captive's garb. She shall spend a month's time in your house lamenting her father and mother; after that you may come to her and possess her, and she shall be

DEUTERONOMY 22 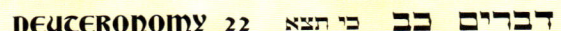 דברים כב כי תצא

your wife. 14 Then, should you no longer want her, you must release her outright. You must not sell her for money; since you had your will of her, you must not enslave her.

15 If a man has two wives, one loved and the other unloved, and both the loved and the unloved have borne him sons, but the first-born is the son of the unloved one — 16 when he wills his property to his sons, he may not treat as first-born the son of the loved one in disregard of the son of the unloved one who is older. 17 Instead, he must accept the first-born, the son of the unloved one, and allot to him a double portion of all he possesses; since he is the first fruit of his vigor, the birthright is his due. 18 If a man has a wayward and defiant son, who does not heed his father or mother and does not obey them even after they discipline him, 19 his father and mother shall take hold of him and bring him out to the elders of his town at the public place of his community. 20 They shall say to the elders of his town, "This son of ours is disloyal and defiant; he does not heed us. He is a glutton and a drunkard." 21 Thereupon the men of his town shall stone him to death. Thus you will sweep out evil from your midst: all Israel will hear and be afraid. 22 If a man is guilty of a capital offense and is put to death, and you impale him on a stake, 23 you must not let his corpse remain on the stake overnight, but must bury him the same day. For an impaled body is an affront to God: you shall not defile the land that the LORD your God is giving you to possess.

22 1 If you see your fellow's ox or sheep gone astray, do not ignore it; you must take it back to your fellow. 2 If your fellow does not live near you or you do not know who he is, you shall bring it home and it shall remain with you until your fellow claims it; then you shall give it back to him. 3 You shall do the same with his ass; you shall do the same with his garment; and so too shall you do with anything that your fellow loses and you find: you must not remain indifferent.   4 If you see your fellow's ass or ox fallen on the road, do not ignore it; you must help him raise it.   5 A woman must not put on man's apparel, nor shall a man wear woman's clothing; for whoever does these things is abhorrent to the LORD your God.

6 If, along the road, you chance upon a bird's nest, in any tree or on the ground, with fledglings or eggs and the mother sitting over the fledglings or on the eggs, do not take the mother together with her young. 7 Let the mother go, and take only the young, in order that you may fare well and have a long life. 8 When you build a new house, you shall make a parapet for your roof, so that you do not bring bloodguilt on your house if anyone should fall from it. 9 You shall not sow your vineyard with a second kind of seed, else the crop — from the seed you have sown — and the yield of the vineyard may not be used.   10 You shall not plow with an ox and an ass together. 11 You shall not wear cloth combining wool and linen. 12 You shall make tassels on the four corners of the garment with which you cover yourself.

13 A man marries a woman and cohabits with her. Then he takes an aversion to her 14 and makes up charges against her and defames her, saying, "I married this woman; but when I approached her, I found that she was not a virgin." 15 In such a case, the girl's father and mother shall produce the evidence of the girl's virginity before the elders of the town at the gate. 16 And the girl's father shall say to the elders, "I gave this man my daughter to wife, but he has taken an aversion to her; 17 so he has made up charges, saying, 'I did not find your daughter a virgin.' But here is the evidence of my daughter's virginity!" And they shall spread out the cloth before the elders of the town. 18 The elders of that town shall then take the man and flog him, 19 and they shall fine him a hundred [shekels] of silver and give it to the girl's father; for the man has defamed a virgin in Israel. Moreover, she shall remain his wife; he shall never have the right to divorce her.   20 But if the charge proves true, the girl was found not to have been a virgin, 21 then the girl shall be brought out to the entrance of her father's house, and the men of her town shall stone her to death; for she did a shameful thing in Israel, committing fornication while under her father's authority. Thus you will sweep away

196

DEUCERONOMY 23 — דברים כג כי תצא

evil from your midst. ²² If a man is found lying with another man's wife, both of them - the man and the woman with whom he lay - shall die. Thus you will sweep away evil from Israel. ²³ In the case of a virgin who is engaged to a man - if a man comes upon her in town and lies with her, ²⁴ you shall take the two of them out to the gate of that town and stone them to death: the girl because she did not cry for help in the town, and the man because he violated another man's wife. Thus you will sweep away evil from your midst. ²⁵ But if the man comes upon the engaged girl in the open country, and the man lies with her by force, only the man who lay with her shall die, ²⁶ but you shall do nothing to the girl. The girl did not incur the death penalty, for this case is like that of a man attacking another and murdering him. ²⁷ He came upon her in the open; though the engaged girl cried for help, there was no one to save her. ²⁸ If a man comes upon a virgin who is not engaged and he seizes her and lies with her, and they are discovered, ²⁹ the man who lay with her shall pay the girl's father fifty [shekels of] silver, and she shall be his wife. Because he has violated her, he can never have the right to divorce her.

23 ¹ No man shall marry his father's former wife, so as to remove his father's garment. ² No one whose testes are crushed or whose member is cut off shall be admitted into the congregation of the LORD. ³ No one misbegotten shall be admitted into the congregation of the LORD; none of his descendants, even in the tenth generation, shall be admitted into the congregation of the LORD. ⁴ No Ammonite or Moabite shall be admitted into the congregation of the LORD; none of their descendants, even in the tenth generation, shall ever be admitted into the congregation of the LORD, ⁵ because they did not meet you with food and water on your journey after you left Egypt, and because they hired Balaam son of Beor, from Pethor of Aram-naharaim, to curse you. ⁶ But the LORD your God refused to heed Balaam; instead, the LORD your God turned the curse into a blessing for you, for the LORD your God loves you. ⁷ You shall never concern yourself with their welfare or benefit as long as you live. ⁸ You shall not abhor an Edomite, for he is your kinsman. You shall not abhor an Egyptian, for you were a stranger in his land. ⁹ Children born to them may be admitted into the congregation of the LORD in the third generation.

¹⁰ When you go out as a troop against your enemies, be on your guard against anything untoward. ¹¹ If anyone among you has been rendered unclean by a nocturnal emission, he must leave the camp, and he must not reenter the camp. ¹² Toward evening he shall bathe in water, and at sundown he may reenter the camp. ¹³ Further, there shall be an area for you outside the camp, where you may relieve yourself. ¹⁴ With your gear you shall have a spike, and when you have squatted you shall dig a hole with it and cover up your excrement. ¹⁵ Since the LORD your God moves about in your camp to protect you and to deliver your enemies to you, let your camp be holy; let Him not find anything unseemly among you and turn away from you. ¹⁶ You shall not turn over to his master a slave who seeks refuge with you from his master. ¹⁷ He shall live with you in any place he may choose among the settlements in your midst, wherever he pleases; you must not ill-treat him.

¹⁸ No Israelite woman shall be a cult prostitute, nor shall any Israelite man be a cult prostitute. ¹⁹ You shall not bring the fee of a whore or the pay of a dog into the house of the LORD your God in fulfillment of any vow, for both are abhorrent to the LORD your God. ²⁰ You shall not deduct interest from loans to your countrymen, whether in money or food or anything else that can be deducted as interest; ²¹ but you may deduct interest from loans to foreigners. Do not deduct interest from loans to your countrymen, so that the LORD your God may bless you in all your undertakings in the land that you are about to enter and possess. ²² When you make a vow to the LORD your God, do not put off fulfilling it, for the LORD your God will require it of you, and you will have incurred guilt; ²³ whereas you incur no guilt if you refrain from vowing. ²⁴ You must fulfill what has crossed your lips and perform what you have voluntarily vowed to the LORD your God, having made the promise with your own mouth. ²⁵ When you enter another man's vineyard, you may eat as many grapes as you want,

197

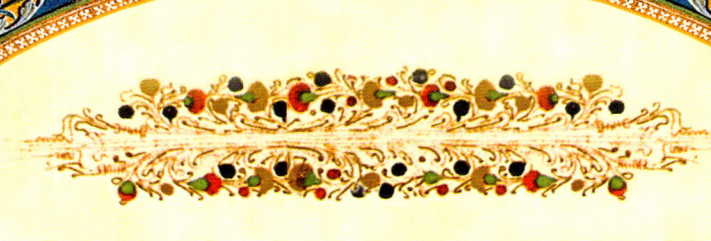

DEUTERONOMY 24 — דברים כד כי תצא

until you are full, but you must not put any in your vessel. 26 When you enter another man's field of standing grain, you may pluck ears with your hand; but you must not put a sickle to your neighbor's grain. **24** 1 A man takes a wife and possesses her. She fails to please him because he finds something obnoxious about her, and he writes her a bill of divorcement, hands it to her, and sends her away from his house; 2 she leaves his household and becomes the wife of another man; 3 then this latter man rejects her, writes her a bill of divorcement, hands it to her, and sends her away from his house; or the man who married her last dies. 4 Then the first husband who divorced her shall not take her to wife again, since she has been defiled - for that would be abhorrent to the LORD. You must not bring sin upon the land that the LORD your God is giving you as a heritage. 5 When a man has taken a bride, he shall not go out with the army or be assigned to it for any purpose; he shall be exempt one year for the sake of his household, to give happiness to the woman he has married. 6 A handmill or an upper millstone shall not be taken in pawn, for that would be taking someone's life in pawn. 7 If a man is found to have kidnapped a fellow Israelite, enslaving him or selling him, that kidnapper shall die; thus you will sweep out evil from your midst. 8 In cases of a skin affection be most careful to do exactly as the levitical priests instruct you. Take care to do as I have commanded them. 9 Remember what the LORD your God did to Miriam on the journey after you left Egypt. 10 When you make a loan of any sort to your countryman, you must not enter his house to seize his pledge. 11 You must remain outside, while the man to whom you made the loan brings the pledge out to you. 12 If he is a needy man, you shall not go to sleep in his pledge; 13 you must return the pledge to him at sundown, that he may sleep in his cloth and bless you; and it will be to your merit before the LORD your God. 14 You shall not abuse a needy and destitute laborer, whether a fellow countryman or a stranger in one of the communities of your land. 15 You must pay him his wages on the same day, before the sun sets, for he is needy and urgently depends on it; else he will cry to the LORD against you and you will incur guilt. 16 Parents shall not be put to death for children, nor children be put to death for parents: a person shall be put to death only for his own crime. 17 You shall not subvert the rights of the stranger or the fatherless; you shall not take a widow's garment in pawn. 18 Remember that you were a slave in Egypt and that the LORD your God redeemed you from there; therefore do I enjoin you to observe this commandment. 19 When you reap the harvest in your field and overlook a sheaf in the field, do not turn back to get it; it shall go to the stranger, the fatherless, and the widow - in order that the LORD your God may bless you in all your undertakings. 20 When you beat down the fruit of your olive trees, do not go over them again; that shall go to the stranger, the fatherless, and the widow. 21 When you gather the grapes of your vineyard, do not pick it over again; that shall go to the stranger, the fatherless, and the widow. 22 Always remember that you were a slave in the land of Egypt; therefore do I enjoin you to observe this commandment. **25** 1 When there is a dispute between men and they go to law, and a decision is rendered declaring the one in the right and the other in the wrong - 2 if the guilty one is to be flogged, the magistrate shall have him lie down and be given lashes in his presence, by count, as his guilt warrants. 3 He may be given up to forty lashes, but not more, lest being flogged further, to excess, your brother be degraded before your eyes. 4 You shall not muzzle an ox while it is threshing. 5 When brothers dwell together and one of them dies and leaves no son, the wife of the deceased shall not be married to a stranger, outside the family. Her husband's brother shall unite with her: he shall take her as his wife and perform the levir's duty. 6 The first son that she bears shall be accounted to the dead brother, that his name may not be blotted out in Israel. 7 But if the man does not want to marry his brother's widow, his brother's widow shall appear before the elders in the gate and declare, "My husband's brother refuses to establish a name in Israel for his brother; he will not perform the duty of a levir." 8 The elders of his town shall then summon him and talk to him. If he insists, saying, "I do not want to marry her," 9 his brother's widow shall go up to him in the presence of the elders,

— 198 —

DEUTERONOMY 26   דברים כי תבוא

pull the sandal off his foot, spit in his face, and make this declaration: Thus shall be done to the man who will not build up his brother's house! 10 And he shall go in Israel by the name of "the family of the unsandaled one." 11 If two men get into a fight with each other, and the wife of one comes up to save her husband from his antagonist and puts out her hand and seizes him by his genitals, 12 you shall cut off her hand; show no pity. 13 You shall not have in your pouch alternate weights, larger and smaller. 14 You shall not have in your house alternate measures, a larger and a smaller. 15 You must have completely honest weights and completely honest measures, if you are to endure long on the soil that the LORD your God is giving you. 16 For everyone who does those things, everyone who deals dishonestly, is abhorrent to the LORD your God.

17 Remember what Amalek did to you on your journey, after you left Egypt – 18 how, undeterred by fear of God, he surprised you on the march, when you were famished and weary, and cut down all the stragglers in your rear. 19 Therefore, when the LORD your God grants you safety from all your enemies around you, in the land that the LORD your God is giving you as a hereditary portion, you shall blot out the memory of Amalek from under heaven. Do not forget!

26 When you enter the land that the LORD your God is giving you as a heritage, and you possess it and settle in it, 2 you shall take some of every first fruit of the soil, which you harvest from the land that the LORD your God is giving you, put it in a basket and go to the place where the LORD your God will choose to establish His name. 3 You shall go to the priest in charge at that time and say to him, "I acknowledge this day before the LORD your God that I have entered the land that the LORD swore to our fathers to assign us." 4 The priest shall take the basket from your hand and set it down in front of the altar of the LORD your God. 5 You shall then recite as follows before the LORD your God: "My father was a fugitive Aramean. He went down to Egypt with meager numbers and sojourned there; but there he became a great and very populous nation. 6 The Egyptians dealt harshly with us and oppressed us; they imposed heavy labor upon us. 7 We cried to the LORD, the God of our fathers, and the LORD heard our plea and saw our plight, our misery, and our oppression. 8 The LORD freed us from Egypt by a mighty hand, by an outstretched arm and awesome power, and by signs and portents. 9 He brought us to this place and gave us this land, a land flowing with milk and honey. 10 Wherefore I now bring the first fruits of the soil which You, O LORD, have given me." You shall leave it before the LORD your God and bow low before the LORD your God. 11 And you shall enjoy, together with the Levite and the stranger in your midst, all the bounty that the LORD your God has bestowed upon you and your household.

12 When you have set aside in full the tenth part of your yield – in the third year, the year of the tithe – and have given it to the Levite, the stranger, the fatherless, and the widow, that they may eat their fill in your settlements, 13 you shall declare before the LORD your God: "I have cleared out the consecrated portion from the house; and I have given it to the Levite, the stranger, the fatherless, and the widow, just as You commanded me: I have neither transgressed nor neglected any of Your commandments: 14 I have not eaten of it while in mourning, I have not cleared out any of it while I was unclean, and I have not deposited any of it with the dead. I have obeyed the LORD my God; I have done just as You commanded me. 15 Look down from Your holy abode, from heaven, and bless Your people Israel and the soil You have given us, a land flowing with milk and honey, as You swore to our fathers."

16 The LORD your God commands you this day to observe these laws and rules; observe them faithfully with all your heart and soul. 17 You have affirmed this day that the LORD is your God, that you will walk in His ways, that you will observe His laws and commandments and rules, and that you will obey Him. 18 And the LORD has affirmed this day that you are, as He promised you, His treasured people who shall observe all His commandments, 19 and that He will set you, in fame and renown and glory, high above all the nations

DEUTERONOMY 27

that He has made; and that you shall be, as He promised, a holy people to the LORD your God.

27 1 Moses and the elders of Israel charged the people, saying: Observe all the Instruction that I enjoin upon you this day. 2 As soon as you have crossed the Jordan into the land that the LORD your God is giving you, you shall set up large stones. Coat them with plaster 3 and inscribe upon them all the words of this Teaching. When you cross over to enter the land that the LORD your God is giving you, a land flowing with milk and honey, as the LORD, the God of your fathers, promised you — 4 upon crossing the Jordan, you shall set up these stones, about which I charge you this day, on Mount Ebal, and coat them with plaster. 5 There, too, you shall build an altar to the LORD your God, an altar of stones. Do not wield an iron tool over them; 6 you must build the altar of the LORD your God of unhewn stones. You shall offer on it burnt offerings to the LORD your God, 7 and you shall sacrifice there offerings of well-being and eat them, rejoicing before the LORD your God. 8 And on those stones you shall inscribe every word of this Teaching most distinctly. 9 Moses and the levitical priests spoke to all Israel, saying: Silence! Hear, O Israel! Today you have become the people of the LORD your God: 10 Heed the LORD your God and observe His commandments and His laws, which I enjoin upon you this day. 11 Thereupon Moses charged the people, saying: 12 After you have crossed the Jordan, the following shall stand on Mount Gerizim when the blessing for the people is spoken: Simeon, Levi, Judah, Issachar, Joseph, and Benjamin. 13 And for the curse, the following shall stand on Mount Ebal: Reuben, Gad, Asher, Zebulun, Dan, and Naphtali. 14 The Levites shall then proclaim in a loud voice to all the people of Israel: 15 Cursed be anyone who makes a sculptured or molten image, abhorred by the LORD, a craftsman's handiwork, and sets it up in secret.—And all the people shall respond, Amen.

16 Cursed be who insults his father or mother.—And all the people shall say, Amen.

17 Cursed be who moves his fellow countryman's landmark.—And all the people shall say, Amen.

18 Cursed be who misdirects a blind person on his way.—And all the people shall say, Amen.

19 Cursed be who subverts the rights of the stranger, the fatherless, and the widow.—And all the people shall say, Amen.

20 Cursed be who lies with his father's wife, for he has removed his father's garment.—And all the people shall say, Amen.

21 Cursed be who lies with any beast.—And all the people shall say, Amen.

22 Cursed be who lies with his sister, whether daughter of his father or of his mother.—And all the people shall say, Amen.

23 Cursed be who lies with his mother-in-law.—And all the people shall say, Amen.

24 Cursed be who strikes down his fellow countryman in secret.—And all the people shall say, Amen.

25 Cursed be who accepts a bribe in the case of the murder of an innocent person.—And all the people shall say, Amen.

26 Cursed be who will not uphold the terms of this Teaching and observe them.—And all the people shall say, Amen.

28 1 Now, if you obey the LORD your God, to observe faithfully all His commandments which I enjoin upon you this day, the LORD your God will set you high above all the nations of the earth. 2 All these blessings shall come upon you and take effect, if you will but heed the word of the LORD your God: 3 Blessed shall you be in the city and blessed shall you be in the country. 4 Blessed shall be the issue of your womb, the produce of your soil, and the offspring of your cattle, the calving of your herd and the lambing of your flock. 5 Blessed shall be your basket and your kneading bowl. 6 Blessed shall you be in your comings and blessed shall you be in your goings. 7 The LORD will put to rout before you the enemies who attack you: they will march out against you by a single road, but flee from you by many roads. 8 The LORD will ordain blessings for you upon your barns and upon all your undertakings: He will bless you in the land that the LORD your God is giving you. 9 The LORD will establish you as His holy people, as He swore to you,

DEUTERONOMY 28 דברים כח כי תבוא

if you keep the commandments of the LORD your God and walk in His ways. 10 And all the peoples of the earth shall see that the LORD's name is proclaimed over you, and they shall stand in fear of you. 11 The LORD will give you abounding prosperity in the issue of your womb, the offspring of your cattle, and the produce of your soil in the land that the LORD swore to your fathers to assign to you. 12 The LORD will open for you His bounteous store, the heavens, to provide rain for your land in season and to bless all your undertakings. You will be creditor to many nations, but debtor to none. 13 The LORD will make you the head, not the tail; you will always be at the top and never at the bottom - if only you obey and faithfully observe the commandments of the LORD your God that I enjoin upon you this day, 14 and do not deviate to the right or to the left from any of the commandments that I enjoin upon you this day and turn to the worship of other gods.

15 But if you do not obey the LORD your God to observe faithfully all His commandments and laws which I enjoin upon you this day, all these curses shall come upon you and take effect: 16 Cursed shall you be in the city and cursed shall you be in the country. 17 Cursed shall be your basket and your kneading bowl. 18 Cursed shall be the issue of your womb and the produce of your soil, the calving of your herd and the lambing of your flock. 19 Cursed shall be your comings and cursed shall you be in your goings. 20 The LORD will let loose against you calamity, panic, and frustration in all the enterprises you undertake, so that you shall soon be utterly wiped out because of your evildoing in forsaking Me. 21 The LORD will make pestilence cling to you, until He has put an end to you in the land that you are entering to possess. 22 The LORD will strike you with consumption, fever, and inflammation, with scorching heat and drought, with blight and mildew; they shall hound you until you perish. 23 The skies above your head shall be copper and the earth under you iron. 24 The LORD will make the rain of your land dust, and sand shall drop on you from the sky, until you are wiped out. 25 The LORD will put you to rout before your enemies: you shall march out against them by a single road, but flee from them by many roads; and you shall become a horror to all the kingdoms of the earth. 26 Your carcasses shall become food for all the birds of the sky and all the beasts of the earth, with none to frighten them off. 27 The LORD will strike you with the Egyptian inflammation, with hemorrhoids, boil-scars, and itch, from which you shall never recover. 28 The LORD will strike you with madness, blindness, and dismay. 29 You shall grope at noon as a blind man gropes in the dark; you shall not prosper in your ventures, but shall be constantly abused and robbed, with none to give help. 30 If you pay the bride-price for a wife, another man shall enjoy her. If you build a house, you shall not live in it. If you plant a vineyard, you shall not harvest it. 31 Your ox shall be slaughtered before your eyes, but you shall not eat of it; your ass shall be seized in front of you, and it shall not be returned to you; your flock shall be delivered to your enemies, with none to help you. 32 Your sons and daughters shall be delivered to another people, while you look on; and your eyes shall strain after them constantly, but you shall be helpless. 33 A people you do not know shall eat up the produce of your soil and all your gains; you shall be abused and downtrodden continually, 34 until you are driven mad by what your eyes behold. 35 The LORD will afflict you at the knees and thighs with a severe inflammation, from which you shall never recover - from the sole of your foot to the crown of your head. 36 The LORD will drive you, and the king you have set over you, to a nation unknown to you or your fathers, where you shall serve other gods, of wood and stone. 37 You shall be a consternation, a proverb, and a byword among all the peoples to which the LORD will drive you. 38 Though you take much seed out to the field, you shall gather in little, for the locust shall consume it. 39 Though you plant vineyards and till them, you shall have no wine to drink or store, for the worm shall devour them. 40 Though you have olive trees throughout your territory, you shall have no oil for anointment, for your olives shall drop off. 41 Though you beget sons and daughters, they shall not remain with you, for they shall go into captivity. 42 The cricket shall take over all the trees and produce of your land. 43 The stranger in your midst shall rise above you higher and higher, while you sink lower and lower. 44 He shall be your creditor, but you shall not be his: he shall be the head and you the tail. 45 All these curses shall befall you: they shall pursue you and overtake you, until you are wiped out, because you did not heed the LORD your God and

201

DEUTERONOMY 29   דברים כט כי תבוא

keep the commandments and laws that He enjoined upon you. ⁴⁶ They shall serve as signs and proofs against you and your offspring for all time. ⁴⁷ Because you would not serve the LORD your God in joy and gladness over the abundance of everything, ⁴⁸ you shall have to serve - in hunger and thirst, naked and lacking everything - the enemies whom the LORD will let loose against you. He will put an iron yoke upon your neck until he has wiped you out. ⁴⁹ The LORD will bring a nation against you from afar, from the end of the earth, which will swoop down like the eagle - a nation whose language you do not understand, ⁵⁰ a ruthless nation, that will show the old no regard and the young no mercy. ⁵¹ It shall devour the offspring of your cattle and the produce of your soil, until you have been wiped out, leaving you nothing of new grain, wine, or oil, of the calving of your herds and the lambing of your flocks, until it has brought you to ruin. ⁵² It shall shut you up in all your towns throughout your land until every mighty, towering wall in which you trust has come down. And when you are shut up in all your towns throughout your land that the LORD your God has assigned to you, ⁵³ you shall eat your own issue, the flesh of your sons and daughters that the LORD your God has assigned to you, because of the desperate straits to which your enemy shall reduce you. ⁵⁴ He who is most tender and fastidious among you shall be too mean to his brother and the wife of his bosom and the children he has spared ⁵⁵ to share with any of them the flesh of the children that he eats, because he has nothing else left as a result of the desperate straits to which your enemy shall reduce you in all your towns. ⁵⁶ And she who is most tender and dainty among you, so tender and dainty that she would never venture to set a foot on the ground, shall begrudge the husband of her bosom, and her son and her daughter, ⁵⁷ the afterbirth that issues from between her legs and the babies she bears: she shall eat them secretly, because of utter want, in the desperate straits to which your enemy shall reduce you in your towns. ⁵⁸ If you fail to observe faithfully all the terms of this Teaching that are written in this book, to reverence this honored and awesome Name, the LORD your God, ⁵⁹ the LORD will inflict extraordinary plagues upon you and your offspring, strange and lasting plagues, malignant and chronic diseases. ⁶⁰ He will bring back upon you all the sicknesses of Egypt that you dreaded so, and they shall cling to you. ⁶¹ Moreover, the LORD will bring upon you all the other diseases and plagues that are not mentioned in this book of Teaching, until you are wiped out. ⁶² You shall be left a scant few, after having been as numerous as the stars in the skies, because you did not heed the command of the LORD your God. ⁶³ And as the LORD once delighted in making you prosperous and many, so will the LORD now delight in causing you to perish and in wiping you out; you shall be torn from the land you are about to enter and possess. ⁶⁴ The LORD will scatter you among all the peoples from one end of the earth to the other, and there you shall serve other gods, wood and stone, whom neither you nor your ancestors have experienced. ⁶⁵ Yet even among those nations you shall find no peace, nor shall your foot find a place to rest. The LORD will give you there an anguished heart and eyes that pine and a despondent spirit. ⁶⁶ The life you face shall be precarious; you shall be in terror, night and day, with no assurance of survival. ⁶⁷ In the morning you shall say, "If only it were evening!" and in the evening you shall say, "If only it were morning!" - because of what your heart shall dread and what your eyes shall see. ⁶⁸ The LORD will send you back to Egypt in galleys, by a route which I told you you should not see again. There you shall offer yourselves for sale to your enemies as male and female slaves, but none will buy. ⁶⁹ These are the terms of the covenant which the LORD commanded Moses to conclude with the Israelites in the land of Moab, in addition to the covenant which He had made with them at Horeb.

29 ¹ Moses summoned all Israel and said to them: You have seen all that the LORD did before your very eyes in the land of Egypt, to Pharaoh and to all his courtiers and to his whole country; ² the wondrous feats that you saw with your own eyes, those prodigious signs and marvels. ³ Yet to this day the LORD has not given you a mind to understand or eyes to see or ears to hear. ⁴ I led you through the wilderness forty years; the clothes on your back did not wear out, nor did the sandals on your feet; ⁵ you had no bread to eat

DEUTERONOMY 30   דברים ל נצבים

and no wine or other intoxicant to drink - that you might know that I the LORD am your God. 6 When you reached this place, King Sihon of Heshbon and King Og of Bashan came out to engage us in battle, but we defeated them. 7 We took their land and gave it to the Reubenites, the Gadites, and the half-tribe of Manasseh as their heritage. 8 Therefore observe faithfully all the terms of this covenant, that you may succeed in all that you undertake. 9 You stand this day, all of you, before the LORD your God - your tribal heads, your elders and your officials, all the men of Israel, 10 your children, your wives, even the stranger within your camp, from woodchopper to water drawer - 11 to enter into the covenant of the LORD your God, which the LORD your God is concluding with you this day, with its sanctions; 12 to the end that He may establish you this day as His people and be your God, as He promised you and as He swore to your fathers, Abraham, Isaac, and Jacob. 13 I make this covenant, with its sanctions, not with you alone, 14 but both with those who are standing here this day before the LORD our God and with those who are not with us here this day. 15 Well you know that we dwelt in the land of Egypt and that we passed through the midst of various other nations through which you passed; 16 and you have seen the detestable things and the fetishes of wood and stone, silver and gold, that they keep. 17 Perchance there is among you some man or woman, or some clan or tribe, whose heart is even now turning away from the LORD our God to go and worship the gods of those nations - perchance there is among you a stock sprouting poison weed and wormwood. 18 When such a one hears the words of these sanctions, he may fancy himself immune, thinking, "I shall be safe, though I follow my own willful heart" - to the utter ruin of moist and dry alike. 19 The LORD will never forgive him; rather will the LORD's anger and passion rage against that man, till every sanction recorded in this book comes down upon him, and the LORD blots out his name from under heaven. 20 The LORD will single them out from all the tribes of Israel for misfortune, in accordance with all the sanctions of the covenant recorded in this book of Teaching. 21 And later generations will ask - the children who succeed you, and foreigners who come from distant lands and see the plagues and diseases that the LORD has inflicted upon that land, 22 all its soil devastated by sulfur and salt, beyond sowing and producing, no grass growing in it, just like the upheaval of Sodom and Gomorrah, Admah and Zeboiim, which the LORD overthrew in His fierce anger - 23 all nations will ask, "Why did the LORD do thus to this land? Wherefore that awful wrath?" 24 They will be told, "Because they forsook the covenant that the LORD, God of their fathers, made with them when He freed them from the land of Egypt; 25 they turned to the service of other gods and worshiped them, gods whom they had not experienced and whom He had not allotted to them. 26 So the LORD was incensed at that land and brought upon it all the curses recorded in this book. 27 The LORD uprooted them from their soil in anger, fury, and great wrath, and cast them into another land, as is still the case." 28 Concealed acts concern the LORD our God; but with overt acts, it is for us and our children ever to apply all the provisions of this Teaching. 30 1 When all these things befall you - the blessing and the curse that I have set before you - and you take them to heart amidst the various nations to which the LORD your God has banished you, 2 and you return to the LORD your God, and you and your children heed His command with all your heart and soul, just as I enjoin upon you this day, 3 then the LORD your God will restore your fortunes and take you back in love. He will bring you together again from all the peoples where the LORD your God has scattered you. 4 Even if your outcasts are at the ends of the world, from there the LORD your God will gather you, from there He will fetch you. 5 And the LORD your God will bring you to the land that your fathers possessed, and you shall possess it: and He will make you more prosperous and more numerous than your fathers. 6 Then the LORD your God will open up your heart and the hearts

DEUTERONOMY 31 · דברים לא · וילך

of your offspring to love the LORD your God with all your heart and soul, in order that you may live. 7 The LORD your God will inflict all those curses upon the enemies and foes who persecuted you. 8 You, however, will again heed the LORD and obey all His commandments that I enjoin upon you this day. 9 And the LORD your God will grant you abounding prosperity in all your undertakings, in the issue of your womb, the offspring of your cattle, and the produce of your soil. For the LORD will again delight in your well-being, as He did in that of your fathers, 10 since you will be heeding the LORD your God and keeping His commandments and laws that are recorded in this book of the Teaching – once you return to the LORD your God with all your heart and soul.

11 Surely, this Instruction which I enjoin upon you this day is not too baffling for you, nor is it beyond reach. 12 It is not in the heavens, that you should say, "Who among us can go up to the heavens and get it for us and impart it to us, that we may observe it?" 13 Neither is it beyond the sea, that you should say, "Who among us can cross to the other side of the sea and get it for us and impart it to us, that we may observe it?" 14 No, the thing is very close to you, in your mouth and in your heart, to observe it.

15 See, I set before you this day life and prosperity, death and adversity. 16 For I command you this day, to love the LORD your God, to walk in His ways, and to keep His commandments, His laws, and His rules, that you may thrive and increase, and that the LORD your God may bless you in the land that you are about to enter and possess. 17 But if your heart turns away and you give no heed, and are lured into the worship and service of other gods, 18 I declare to you this day that you shall certainly perish; you shall not long endure on the soil that you are crossing the Jordan to enter and possess. 19 I call heaven and earth to witness against you this day: I have put before you life and death, blessing and curse. Choose life – if you and your offspring would live – 20 by loving the LORD your God, heeding His commands, and holding fast to Him. For thereby you shall have life and shall long endure upon the soil that the LORD swore to your ancestors, Abraham, Isaac, and Jacob, to give to them.

31 Moses went and spoke these things to all Israel. 2 He said to them: I am now one hundred and twenty years old, I can no longer be active. Moreover, the LORD has said to me, "You shall not go across yonder Jordan." 3 The LORD your God Himself will cross over before you; and He Himself will wipe out those nations from your path and you shall dispossess them. – Joshua is the one who shall cross before you, as the LORD has spoken. – 4 The LORD will do to them as He did to Sihon and Og, kings of the Amorites, and to their countries, when He wiped them out. 5 The LORD will deliver them up to you, and you shall deal with them in full accordance with the Instruction that I have enjoined upon you. 6 Be strong and resolute, be not in fear or in dread of them; for the LORD your God Himself marches with you: He will not fail you or forsake you.

7 Then Moses called Joshua and said to him in the sight of all Israel: "Be strong and resolute, for it is you who shall go with this people into the land that the LORD swore to their fathers to give them, and it is you who shall apportion it to them. 8 And the LORD Himself will go before you. He will be with you; He will not fail you or forsake you. Fear not and be not dismayed!" 9 Moses wrote down this Teaching and gave it to the priests, sons of Levi, who carried the Ark of the LORD's Covenant, and to all the elders of Israel. 10 And Moses instructed them as follows: Every seventh year, the year set for remission, at the Feast of Booths, 11 when all Israel comes to appear before the LORD your God in the place that He will choose, you shall read this Teaching aloud in the presence of all Israel. 12 Gather the people – men, women, children, and the strangers in your communities – that they may hear and so learn to revere the LORD your God and to observe faithfully every word of this Teaching. 13 Their children, too, who have not had the experience, shall hear and learn to revere the LORD your God as long as they live in

DEUTERONOMY 32 דברים לב האזינו

the land that you are about to cross the Jordan to possess. 14 The LORD said to Moses: The time is drawing near for you to die. Call Joshua and present yourselves in the Tent of Meeting, that I may instruct him. Moses and Joshua went and presented themselves in the Tent of Meeting. 15 The LORD appeared in the Tent, in a pillar of cloud, the pillar of cloud having come to rest at the entrance of the tent. 16 The LORD said to Moses: You are soon to lie with your fathers. This people will thereupon go astray after the alien gods in their midst, in the land that they are about to enter; they will forsake Me and break My covenant that I made with them. 17 Then My anger will flare up against them, and I will abandon them and hide My countenance from them. They shall be ready prey; and many evils and troubles shall befall them. And they shall say on that day, "Surely it is because our God is not in our midst that these evils have befallen us." 18 Yet I will keep My countenance hidden on that day, because of all the evil they have done in turning to other gods. 19 Therefore, write down this poem and teach it to the people of Israel; put it in their mouths, in order that this poem may be My witness against the people of Israel. 20 When I bring them into the land flowing with milk and honey that I promised on oath to their fathers, and they eat their fill and grow fat and turn to other gods and serve them, spurning Me and breaking My covenant, 21 and the many evils and troubles befall them – then this poem shall confront them as a witness, since it will never be lost from the mouth of their offspring. For I know what plans they are devising even now, before I bring them into the land that I promised on oath. 22 That day, Moses wrote down this poem and taught it to the Israelites. 23 And He charged Joshua son of Nun: Be strong and resolute: for you shall bring the Israelites into the land that I promised them on oath, and I will be with you." 24 When Moses had put down in writing the words of this Teaching to the very end, 25 Moses charged the Levites who carried the Ark of the Covenant of the LORD, saying: 26 Take this book of Teaching and place it beside the Ark of the Covenant of the LORD your God, and let it remain there as a witness against you. 27 Well I know how defiant and stiffnecked you are: even now, while I am still alive in your midst, you have been defiant toward the LORD; how much more, then, when I am dead! 28 Gather to me all the elders of your tribes and your officials, that I may speak all these words to them and that I may call heaven and earth to witness against them. 29 For I know that, when I am dead, you will act wickedly and turn away from the path that I enjoined upon you, and that in time to come misfortune will befall you for having done evil in the sight of the LORD and vexed Him by your deeds. 30 Then Moses recited the words of this poem to the very end, in the hearing of the whole congregation of Israel:

32 ¹Give ear, O heavens, let me speak; Let the earth hear the words I utter! 2 May my discourse come down as the rain, My speech distill as the dew, Like showers on young growth, Like droplets on the grass. 3 For the name of the LORD I proclaim; Give glory to our God! 4 The Rock! – His deeds are perfect, Yea, all His ways are just; A faithful God, never false, True and upright is He. 5 Children unworthy of Him – That crooked, perverse generation – Their baseness has played Him false. 6 Do you thus requite the LORD, O dull and witless people? Is not He the Father who created you, Fashioned you and made you endure? 7 Remember the days of old, Consider the years of ages past; Ask your father, he will inform you, Your elders, they will tell you: 8 When the Most High gave nations their homes And set the divisions of man, He fixed the boundaries of peoples In relation to Israel's numbers. 9 For the LORD's portion is His people, Jacob His own allotment. 10 He found him in a desert region, In an empty howling waste. He engirded him, watched over him, Guarded him as the pupil of His eye. 11 Like an eagle who rouses his nestlings, Gliding down to his young, So did He spread His wings and take him, Bear him along on His pinions; 12 The LORD alone did guide him, No alien god at His side. 13 He set him atop the highlands, To feast on the yield of the earth; He fed him honey from the crag, And oil from the flinty rock,

205

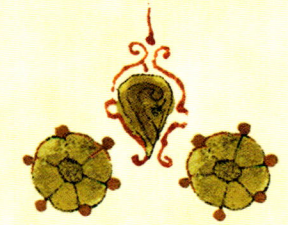

DEUTERONOMY 32 דברים לב האזינו

14 Curd of kine and milk of flocks; With the best of lambs, And rams of Bashan, and he-goats; With the very finest wheat — And foaming grape-blood was your drink. 15 So Jeshurun grew fat and kicked — You grew fat and gross and coarse — He forsook the God who made him And spurned the Rock of his support. 16 They incensed Him with alien things, Vexed Him with abominations. 17 They sacrificed to demons, no-gods, Gods they had never known, New ones, who came but lately, Who stirred not your fathers' fears. 18 You neglected the Rock that begot you, Forgot the God who brought you forth. 19 The LORD saw and was vexed And spurned His sons and His daughters. 20 He said: I will hide My countenance from them, And see how they fare in the end. For they are a treacherous breed, Children with no loyalty in them. 21 They incensed Me with no-gods, Vexed Me with their futilities; I'll incense them with a no-folk, Vex them with a nation of fools. 22 For a fire has flared in My wrath And burned to the bottom of Sheol, Has consumed the earth and its increase, Eaten down to the base of the hills. 23 I will sweep misfortunes on them, Use up My arrows on them: 24 Wasting famine, ravaging plague, Deadly pestilence, and fanged beasts Will I let loose against them, With venomous creepers in dust. 25 The sword shall deal death without, As shall the terror within, To youth and maiden alike, The suckling as well as the aged. 26 I might have reduced them to naught, Made their memory cease among men, 27 But for fear of the taunts of the foe, Their enemies who might misjudge And say, "Our own hand has prevailed; None of this was wrought by the LORD!" 28 For they are a folk void of sense, Lacking in all discernment. 29 Were they wise, they would think upon this, Gain insight into their future: 30 How could one have routed a thousand, Or two put ten thousand to flight, Unless their Rock had sold them, The LORD had given them up? 31 For their rock is not like our Rock, In our enemies' own estimation. 32 Ah! The vine for them is from Sodom, From the vineyards of Gomorrah; The grapes for them are poison, A bitter growth their clusters. 33 Their wine is the venom of vipers, The pitiless poison of asps. 34 Lo, I have it all put away, Sealed up in My storehouses, 35 To be My vengeance and recompense, At the time that their foot falters. Yea, their day of disaster is near, And destiny rushes upon them. 36 For the LORD will vindicate His people And take revenge for His servants, When He sees that their might is gone, And neither bond nor free is left. 37 He will say: Where are their gods, The rock in whom they sought refuge, 38 Who ate the fat of their offerings And drank their libation wine? Let them rise up to your help, And let them be a shield unto you! 39 See, then, that I, I am He; There is no god beside Me. I deal death and give life; I wounded and I will heal; None can deliver from My hand. 40 Lo, I raise My hand to heaven And say: As I live forever, 41 When I whet My flashing blade And My hand lays hold on judgment, Vengeance will I wreak on My foes, Will I deal to those who reject Me. 42 I will make My arrows drunk with blood — as my sword devours flesh — Blood of the slain and the captive From the long-haired enemy chiefs. 43 O nations, acclaim His people! For He'll avenge the blood of His servants, Wreak vengeance on His foes, And cleanse the land of His people. 44 Moses came, together with Hosea son of Nun, and recited all the words of this poem in the hearing of the people. 45 And when Moses finished reciting all these words to all Israel, 46 he said to them: Take to heart all the words with which I have warned you this day. Enjoin them upon your children, that they may observe faithfully all the terms of this Teaching. 47 For this is not a trifling thing for you: it is your very life; through it you shall long endure on the land that you are to possess upon crossing the Jordan.

48 That very day the LORD spoke to Moses: 49 Ascend these heights of Abarim to Mount Nebo, which is in the land of Moab facing Jericho, and view the land of Canaan, which I am giving the Israelites as their holding. 50 You shall die on the mountain that you are about to ascend, and shall be gathered to your kin, as your brother Aaron died on Mount Hor and was gathered to his kin; 51 for you both broke faith with Me among the Israelite people, at the waters of Meribath-kadesh in the wilderness of Zin, by failing to uphold my sanctity among the Israelite people. 52 You may view the land from a distance, but you shall not enter it — the land that I am giving to the Israelite people.

DEUTERONOMY 33   דברים לג וזאת הברכה

33 ¹ This is the blessing with which Moses, the man of God, bade the Israelites farewell before he died. ² He said: The LORD came from Sinai; He shone upon them from Seir; He appeared from Mount Paran, And approached from Ribeboth-kodesh, Lightning flashing at them from His right. ³ Lover, indeed, of the people, Their hallowed are all in Your hand. They followed in Your steps, Accepting Your pronouncements, ⁴ When Moses charged us with the Teaching As the heritage of the congregation of Jacob. ⁵ Then He became King in Jeshurun, When the heads of the people assembled, The tribes of Israel together. ⁶ May Reuben live and not die, Though few be his numbers. ⁷ And this he said of Judah: Hear, O LORD the voice of Judah And restore him to his people. Though his own hands strive for him, Help him against his foes.

⁸ And of Levi he said: Let Your Thummim and Urim Be with Your faithful one, Whom You tested at Massah, Challenged at the waters of Meribah; ⁹ Who said of his father and mother, "I consider them not." His brothers he disregarded, Ignored his own children. Your precepts alone they observed, And kept Your covenant. ¹⁰ They shall teach Your laws to Jacob and Your instructions to Israel. They shall offer You incense to savor and whole-offerings on Your altar. ¹¹ Bless, O LORD, his substance, And favor his undertakings. Smite the loins of his foes; Let his enemies rise no more. ¹² Of Benjamin he said: Beloved of the LORD, He rests securely beside Him; Ever does He protect him, As he rests between His shoulders. ¹³ And of Joseph he said: Blessed of the LORD be his land With the bounty of dew from heaven, And of the deep that couches below; ¹⁴ With the bounteous yield of the sun, And the bounteous crop of the moons; ¹⁵ With the best from the ancient mountains, And the bounty of hills immemorial; ¹⁶ With the bounty of earth and its fullness, And the favor of the Presence in the Bush. May these rest on the head of Joseph, On the crown of the elect of his brothers. ¹⁷ Like a firstling bull in his majesty, He has horns like the horns of the wild-ox; With them he gores the peoples, The ends of the earth one and all. These are the myriads of Ephraim, Those are the thousands of Manasseh. ¹⁸ And of Zebulun he said: Rejoice, O Zebulun, on your journeys, And Issachar, in your tents. ¹⁹ They invite their kin to the mountain, Where they offer sacrifices of success. For they draw from the riches of the sea And the hidden hoards of the sand. ²⁰ And of Gad he said: Blessed be He who enlarges Gad! Poised is he like a lion To tear off arm and scalp. ²¹ He chose for himself the best, For there is the portion of the revered chieftain, Where the heads of the people come. He executed the LORD's judgments And His decisions for Israel. ²² And of Dan he said: Dan is a lion's whelp That leaps forth from Bashan. ²³ And of Naphtali he said: O Naphtali, sated with favor And full of the LORD's blessing, Take possession on the west and south. ²⁴ And of Asher he said: Most blessed of sons be Asher; May he be the favorite of his brothers, May he dip his foot in oil. ²⁵ May your doorbolts be iron and copper, And your security last all your days. ²⁶ O Jeshurun, there is none like God, Riding through the heavens to help you, Through the skies in His majesty. ²⁷ The ancient God is a refuge, A support are the arms everlasting. He drove out the enemy before you By His command: Destroy! ²⁸ Thus Israel dwells in safety, Untroubled is Jacob's abode, In a land of grain and wine, Under heavens dripping dew. ²⁹ O happy Israel! Who is like you, A people delivered by the LORD, Your protecting Shield, your Sword triumphant! Your enemies shall come cringing before you, And you shall tread on their backs.

34 ¹ Moses went up from the steppes of Moab to Mount Nebo, to the summit of Pisgah, opposite Jericho, and the LORD showed him the whole land: Gilead as far as Dan; ² all Naphtali; the whole land of Ephraim and Manasseh; the whole land of Judah as far as the Western Sea; ³ the Negeb; and the Plain - the Valley of Jericho, the city of palm trees - as far as Zoar. ⁴ And the — said to him, "This is the land of which I swore to Abraham, Isaac, and Jacob, 'I will assign it to your offspring.' I have let you see it with your own eyes, but you shall not cross there." ⁵ So Moses the servant of the LORD died there, in the land of Moab, at the command of the LORD. ⁶ He buried him in the valley in the land of Moab, near Beth-peor; and no one knows his burial place to this day. ⁷ Moses was a hundred and twenty years old when he died; his eyes were undimmed and his vigor unabated. ⁸ And the Israelites bewailed Moses in the steppes of Moab for thirty days. The period of wailing and mourning for Moses came to an end. ⁹ Now Joshua son of Nun

Acknowledgments

The publisher wishes to thank the libraries, museums, and private collectors below for permitting the reproduction of works of art in their collection and for supplying the necessary photographs:

    The Bridgman Art Library, England

    Sassoon Collection, England

    Biblioteca Estense, Modena, Italy

    The Antiquities Authority, Jerusalem

    The Israel Museum, Jerusalem

    The National and University Library, Jerusalem

    Biblioteca Nacional, Lisbon

    The British Library, London

    The British Museum, London

    Art Resource, New York

    Pierpont Morgan Library, New York

    The Public Library, St. Petersburg

On the facing page: כורכן לתורה מקטיפה עם רקמת זהב, ירושלים, 1884, אוסף מוזיאון ישראל, ירושלים   בעמוד ממול:
Velvet Torah binder with gold embroidery, Jerusalem, 1884, collection of The Israel Museum, Jerusalem